THE MAKING OF THE MANAGER:
A World View

The United Nations Institute for Training and Research
(UNITAR)

THE MAKING OF THE MANAGER:
A World View

Edited by Sidney Mailick

The United Nations Institute for Training and Research (UNITAR)

Anchor Press/Doubleday   Garden City, New York
1974

ISBN: 0-385-05135-2
Library of Congress Catalog Card Number 73–79692
Copyright © 1974 by UNITAR
Printed in the United States of America
First edition

CONTENTS

LIST OF CONTRIBUTORS TO THE VOLUME

SIDNEY MAILICK is Professor of Public Administration and Director of the Doctoral Program in Mental Health Policy and Administration in the Graduate School of Public Administration of New York University. He is, in addition, Associate Dean of Administrative Studies of the New York School of Psychiatry. He is a consultant to the United Nations Institute for Training and Research (UNITAR), the UN Public Administration Division, the Foreign Service Institute of the U. S. Department of State, and the Institute for Child Mental Health.

SOLOMON HOBERMAN is a Management Consultant specializing in activities of urban governments and other organizations relating to work force planning, structuring, training, and development. He was formerly Personnel Director and Chairman of the Civil Service Commission for the City of New York. He is the author of a number of articles dealing with training, management development, and personnel selection.

NANCY ARNONE BORD is a Senior Associate with the international consulting firm of Cresap, McCormick and Paget, Inc., in New York City. She has held teaching positions at M.I.T., City University of New York, and the Graduate School of Public Administration at New York University and has served as a consultant to numerous corporations, nonprofit institutions and government agencies.

JOHN MORRIS is Professor of Management Development at the University of Manchester Business School in England. He has been responsible for developing new programmes of joint development activities with a number of organizations in the public and private sectors. He has written extensively in the field of management development and the psychology of learning and has participated widely in executive education and training programmes.

ANDREW LIFE is a member of the directing staff at the Administrative Staff College, Henley-on-Thames, England. He has been involved in the use of group methods of educating administrators since 1951, in England and France, with industrialists and members of government departments. He has been a consultant to the United Nations Development Programme, and a visiting fellow at the University of Aston.

R. W. REVANS is Scientific Adviser to the Inter-University College for Doctoral Studies in Management (CIM), Brussels, Belgium, and was formerly Professor of Industrial Administration at the University of Manchester and President of the European Association of Management Centers. With a group of colleagues interested in action learning and research he has formed an international group to develop new methods of management education in many different countries. He is a consultant to OECD and the ILO. His books include *The Nile Project,* OECD Development Centre, Paris, 1971, and *Developing Effective Managers,* Praeger, New York, 1971.

ROLF TH. STIEFEL is a faculty member at the Centre de Études Industrielles (CEI)/University of Geneva (Switzerland). Presently on leave, he was a "W. L. Grant-Fellow" at the Ontario Institute for Studies in Education/University of Toronto (Canada) from 1971 to 1972 and is subsequently a Visiting Scholar at the McGill University in Montreal (Canada).

ANTOINE PAPALOFZOS is Professor in Industrial Psychology at the University of Neuchâtel and is Research Associate at the Centre d'Études Industrielles with a special interest in group dynamics.

M. KUBR has been a member of the Management Development Branch of the ILO since 1966. In this capacity he has planned, controlled, and evaluated technical cooperation projects in the European, African, Asian, and other regions. His further responsibilities involve research into management education and training needs at country level, study of management education and development policies, and promotion of effective training methods.

JANUSZ GOSCISKI is Associate Professor of Management, Cybernetics, and Use of Computers at the University of Lodz. He was for many years Deputy Director of the Polish Management Development Center in Warsaw. He is the author of several books and many publications. He has often served as a short-term expert and consultant to

United Nations agencies. He has organized many top-management training programs and has engaged in extensive research work.

GAVRIIL K. POPOV is the Chief of the Management Research Centre of the Economics Faculty of Moscow State University (M. V. Lomonosov). He is the author of works on management issues and problems. Professor Popov heads a consulting agency engaged in work for planning agencies and enterprises. He is also engaged in teaching students and managers in the University and various training Institutes. He is Vice-President of the Academy of Sciences Council.

BARRY M. RICHMAN is a faculty member of the University of California at Los Angeles. He served on leave as Dean of the Faculty of Administrative Studies at York University in Ontario, Canada. He has published many books and monographs on management training and has written extensively on management practices in the Soviet Union and China.

A team of authors from the International Labour Organisation prepared Chapter Twelve "Training Managers for Development: Methods and Techniques." The leader of this group was Ibrahim A. Ibrahim, Head of Studies of the Management Development Branch. The members of the team were: Milan Kubr, Hélène Pour, Carol Gilbert and André Muller.

CHI-YUEN WU, Professor of Public Administration at the Graduate School of Public Administration, New York University, and former Professor of Economics at the National Tsinghua University (Peking, China, 1939–1947), was former Director of the United Nations Public Administration Division (1963–1972). The chapter was prepared by him when he was the Director of that Division, but the views expressed were entirely his own. He is currently a consultant in the United Nations Secretariat, writing a book on administration for development.

J. N. KHOSLA was the Director of the Indian Institute of Public Administration from 1964 to 1971. He was President of the Indian Political Science Association from 1947 to 1948 and Senior Vice-President of the Eastern Regional Organization for Public Administration (EROPE) 1968–1971. He was Chairman of the Governing Body of the Delhi University Institute for Post-Graduate Studies (1967–1971). Currently he is Adviser to the Ethiopian Government for civil service training under the United Nations Development Program.

RAGHU NATH is Associate Professor of Business and Behavioral Science and Director of the Management Training Laboratory at the University of Pittsburgh. He is also President of the Institute for the Development of Organizational and Human Potential. He has organized executive training and organization development programs for a variety of client systems in the United States, Middle East, Latin America, and Asia, using the newer participative training techniques.

R. K. READY is Professor of Management and Chairman of the Faculty of Management and MBA Program, University of West Florida, Pensacola, Florida, U.S.A. Since 1964 he has worked and traveled extensively internationally for the Ford Foundation, the United Nations, Agency for International Development, World Education, NTL Institute for Applied Behavioral Science, and other private agencies. His focus in most of this work has been training and consulting for management and organization development.

PREFACE

A considerable portion of United Nations development aid has been utilized in creating and nurturing training institutions in different parts of the world. The United Nations system has, from the very beginning, recognized the great importance of training adequately both officials and managers in developing countries. When the United Nations Institute for Training and Research was founded with the promotion of international economic and social development as one of its principal objectives, it was only logical that it should devote effort and attention to improving the quality of training.

As a number of organizations and departments within the United Nations system had already been engaged in providing technical assistance for improving the quality of training, the Institute decided to concentrate on a particular aspect to which attention had not previously been given by other institutions.

An investigation was carried out into the newer techniques of training developed in different parts of the world, especially in the highly industrialized countries, and into the different modalities by which these new techniques are applied in training the cadre of managerial staff. The plan of action required contributions from a number of developed and developing countries. This was a truly multinational and interorganizational endeavor.

These studies not only present an analysis of the application of newer techniques in the developed countries but also provide useful guidelines for their eventual application in developing countries. We hope that this study will be found useful, particularly in the developing countries, by officials and others responsible for the training of managerial personnel.

Professor Sidney Mailick of New York University, a consultant to UNITAR, has been responsible for the co-ordination of the various contributions in addition to his own substantial contribution to the volume on the experience of the United States. The Institute wishes to express its deep appreciation to all the contributors, especially Professor Mailick, for their valuable co-operation.

A number of officials at UNITAR were responsible for the original ideas for the volume and arranged both for the various contributions to be read by other experts in the subject and for the publication of the study. These officials include Mr. Oscar Schachter, the Deputy Executive Director and Director of Studies, Mr. S. P. Bapat, formerly Special Adviser on Training at UNITAR, Mr. Hamish Millar-Craig, Director of Administration, and Mr. Joseph J. Therattil, Co-ordinator for Training Programmes and the UNITAR officer responsible for this project. I am very grateful to the Board of Trustees for its continuing and vigorous interest in this study and for its encouragement and inspiration. I would particularly like to thank my predecessor, Chief Simeon Adebo, without whose wise guidance and leadership this work could not have been successfully undertaken or completed.

The views and conclusions put forward in this study are primarily the responsibility of the authors and do not necessarily reflect the opinions of the Board of Trustees or officials of UNITAR. While UNITAR takes no position on the views expressed by the authors of its studies, it does assume responsibility for determining whether a study merits publication and dissemination.

We are pleased to publish this UNITAR study on the training of managers.

Davidson Nicol
Executive Director

INTRODUCTION

The chief aim of this volume is to assemble and analyze relevant information on selected newer techniques of management training through a series of "national" or regional chapters. The book contains information about these techniques and comments about their possible applications by training officials and institutions in changing and developing countries.

A number of methods and techniques have been developed in recent years for use in the training of officials and executives in public and business administrations in the industrialized countries. Persons responsible for the training of national officials in the developing countries, as well as those concerned with the training of international staff, who are frequently urged to make use of these modern training techniques, are at times handicapped by a lack of sufficiently precise information concerning the exact nature of these techniques, the problems which arise in their application, the activities in which they are most effective, and how far they may be usefully adopted or adapted to meet the training needs of persons drawn from different cultures and varied backgrounds. Highly developed countries have been more effective in training and building up a corps of competent managers. Officials of the developing world have, in large part, recognized this and have made strenuous efforts to improve their capabilities in this area of national development. Several different formats recommended themselves for the preparation of the volume, i.e., a single author reviewing the field as a whole, a detailed comparative analysis, etc. It was decided, however, to commission independent papers from outstanding scholars and practitioners throughout the world with no effort to impose upon the authors a uniform philosophy. In this manner it is hoped that the reader will be presented with a wide variety of differing opinions, practices, and experiences from which he can construct a model best able to meet the unique conditions and needs of a particular cultural setting. Included, however, are three unifying chapters, the first two and the last. The first describes the content and approach of each of the independent chapters so that the reader may, if he desires, refer at once to those aspects of the subject that interest him most. The first two chapters, in addition, present an overview and frame of reference which should be of value for the volume as a whole. The final chapter analyzes world-wide training trends and approaches, discusses the meaning of these, provides a theoretical basis for the establishment of a training and development programme or system to meet specific organizational and national needs, and suggests means for adapting to the developing world the various methods and techniques described in the various individual chapters.

In the organization of the project, each contributor was asked to describe, analyze, and discuss the philosophy and methodology of management development, education, and training in the area, country, or institution of concern to him and to evaluate both their effectiveness and the ways in which they are changing. As a consequence of this approach, several of the chapters analyze what seem to be identical approaches—at least they are identified by the same name—and a number report diametrically opposite experiences and conclusions. Different theoretical frameworks are presented and some of the chapters question the theoretical underpinnings of certain of the others. These overlaps and differences have been purposely retained for several reasons. Where the same method is described, each contributor has brought something different to the analysis. It is rare that two use the same method in exactly the same way. It is precisely these minor points of difference which may be of major utility to a trainer from a developing country who wishes to modify a method or group of methods for use in his country. Further, in different accounts, the method tends to be integrated into the whole in an entirely unique and different way. Detailed knowledge about the different uses made of each model can be of crucial importance in building a new model. In addition, the fact that a method has been used successfully by several nations or enterprises indicates that it may possess cross-cultural values.

The clearly expressed major differences of opinion are of no less value than the minor implicit ones. The field of management development, education, and training is a field of uncertainty, with many differences of opinion. The fact that the terms "development," "education," and "training" themselves are at times used in an overlapping fashion is a clear indication of this. The chapters present the views of strong-minded individuals on all sides, for there are more than two sides in every case. These will, it is hoped, aid the reader to develop and consider alternative plans and to evaluate their possible consequences when choosing a technique or programme of action for a particular country or enterprise.

It has been the objective of this UNITAR research project to gather, analyze, and present information, research findings, and experiential data relating to the use and effectiveness of newer management development, education, and training approaches. In addition to this volume, UNITAR intends to issue a series of Occasional Papers dealing with one or another of the management training methods or approaches discussed in this volume.

The volume has been slow in appearing. Many of the chapters were written in 1968, 1969, and 1970. The first, on U.S. practice, written in 1968, adhered rigorously to the initial framework—an analysis of (then) newer techniques of training managers. It did not address itself to ideological and cultural factors in great detail. Other chapters were written in 1971 and 1972 and are far broader in the historical context and background of the area of concern. The authors in a few cases valiantly strove to write quickly in order to meet publication deadlines. If the reader is looking for an up-to-the-minute description of the "newest" technique or theory used in any given context, he should not look to this volume. If, however, he is seeking to learn about recent developments in techniques of management training (i.e., 1968–1973), he will, we hope, find it in this volume. If he has waited a long time for the publication of this volume, he will, we trust, understand and accept the fact that, by definition, any attempt to collect manuscripts through the mechanism of the UN from all parts of the world (and indeed only selected portions therein) is necessarily a slow process. Many considerations are involved and, in direct relationship to the intensity of these considerations, delay in publication necessarily results.

Deep appreciation is expressed to each of my colleagues in this project, the true authors, who, without formal meetings and discussion, co-operated fully and completely to produce manuscripts and waited patiently for their appearance. Great appreciation is expressed to Chief S. O. Adebo, who served as Executive Director of UNITAR and Under-Secretary-General during the beginning years of this project, for his most valuable encouragement and advice regarding the activity in all of its phases.

A special debt of gratitude is owed to Mr. Joseph J. Therattil, Fellow and Co-ordinator for Training Programmes of UNITAR, and Mr. Hamish Millar-Craig, Director of Administration of UNITAR, for their kindly and patient day-to-day help and guidance in the various phases of the project. I offer sincere thanks to Dr. Davidson Nicol, Executive Director of UNITAR and Under-Secretary-General of the UN, and Mr. Oscar Schachter, Director of Studies and Deputy Executive Director of UNITAR, for their enthusiastic support of the project as a whole and the field of management training in the aid of developing countries, generally. Especially appreciated is their acutely perceptive realization of complex editorial and managerial tasks involved in planning and organizing a world-wide study of this kind.

I am most grateful to the countless other officials of the United Nations, within UNITAR and in other agencies, who anonymously and conscientiously gave their advice, counsel, and wisdom. In this case, they performed their regular duties and the essential act of the international civil servant: i.e., "passionate anonymity" to help achieve international co-operation.

A special note of gratitude should go to Miss Marilyn King, for her invaluable assistance in the preparation and typing of the manuscript.

Over and above its utility for the developing countries, it is UNITAR's hope that this volume will have a "spin-off" and multiplier effect and will generate new ideas and insights into the highly important area of the training and development of the manager in national and international contexts. If this hope is realized, it will be a result of the leadership of this dynamic institution devoted to international training and research. Indeed, it is questionable whether a volume such as this could have ever been effectively planned and written without the initiative and support of an international research institution such as the United Nations Institute for Training and Research.

Sidney Mailick
New York City
December 1972

CHAPTER ONE
An Overview of the Volume as a Whole*

This volume is essentially a collection of chapters, each dealing with either a single training technique or a set of techniques or methods for training managers. Each chapter focuses on a specific country or region of the world, with the exception of a few chapters which are cross-cultural in nature. The chapters can, in general terms, be classified by region and major emphasis.

U.S. AND WESTERN EUROPE	EASTERN EUROPE AND ASIA	THE DEVELOPING WORLD
Chapter Three: Newer Techniques of Training Managers in the United States	*Chapter Eight:* Developments in Methods of Management Training in the Eastern European Socialist Countries	*Chapter Twelve:* Training Managers for Development: Methods and Techniques
Chapter Four: Experience of the Newer Management Training Techniques in Britain	*Chapter Nine:* Newer Techniques of Training for Managers in the Polish Management Development Center and Other Training Centers in Socialist Countries	*Chapter Thirteen:* The Use of Modern Training Techniques in Administration for Development: Some Lessons of International Experience

* This chapter was prepared by Sidney Mailick and Solomon Hoberman.

For the purpose of providing the reader with a frame of reference for reading and using this volume, we have analyzed and
categorized each chapter in terms of the training techniques and approaches discussed, the level of the discussion, and the author's views
of the usefulness of the techniques. This categorization is presented
in Chart 1.1.

The classifications, although based on our analysis of each chapter, represent only the judgments of the authors of this summary.
They may *not* necessarily coincide with the judgment of the author
of the chapter.

Chapter Two contains background material which we hope will be
useful as an introduction to the individual chapters which follow and
a preview of some of the dominant themes contained in the chapters.
The background material includes discussion of a broad range of
managerial and organizational development issues: the importance of
management development in large organizations; the role of career
development and training for improving management; distinctions
between executive development, executive training, and executive
education; objectives of career development training; content and
process in training; interactions between trainers and trainees; and a
comparison of older and newer training methods.

In Chapter Three, Mailick and Bord discuss management training
and development in the United States. While primarily concerned
with formal training groups, they also consider individual programmes
and organizational development. They present seven of the new techniques as representatives of the range of new approaches. These are

laboratory training, role-playing, simulation and the management game, the in-basket, and programmed instruction (all generic types), and two proprietary methods: Kepner-Tregoe and the Managerial Grid. They briefly analyze some of the more traditional training techniques before assessing the seven newer methods. Each technique is described in terms of its objectives and specific use and is assessed in terms of its strengths or weaknesses. An analytic grid for characterizing the various approaches, methods, and techniques is provided. The grid is a four-dimensional categorization of each technique in terms of (a) open—closed; (b) thinking—feeling; (c) role—person; (d) organization—individual.

In Chapter Four, Morris deals with newer management training techniques used in Great Britain. He points out that, while American influence on management programmes has been great, British culture (as expressed by managers and trainers) has simultaneously accepted and resisted imported training techniques. The programmes and approaches used are clearly British. Professor Morris notes that management training in Britain is moving from emphasis on short courses to concern with the total management of an organization and basic organizational change. The university-related business school and the use of projects and assignments are discussed in some depth.

Phases in management education and training in Great Britain are identified. The first phase was characterized by the establishment of the Administrative Staff College at Henley and the syndicate method of training; the Tavistock Institute of Human Relations which linked research, consultancy, and training; and the growth of management training programmes in the larger private enterprises. The second phase saw experimenting with "American" methods and techniques, primarily influenced by American business schools and commercial training programmes. The third and current phase is a reaction to the American "invasion."

In Chapter Five, Life recounts the history of the establishment of the Administrative Staff College at Henley-on-Thames and discusses in detail the syndicate approach which is identified with Henley-on-Thames. He brings the development and analysis into the present by discussing further development of the syndicate approach by increased knowledge of group behavior.

In Chapter Six, Revans describes and analyzes in detail the project method of training managers by having them practice management in carefully controlled settings not in their own organizations. He suggests that discussion as used in case studies, management games, discussion groups, seminars, role-playing, and all other forms of social interaction fall short by not providing operational responsibility for one's real decisions in a real world. Moving from discussions of practical experiences in training managers, Professor Revans assesses methods whereby the real problems faced by managers can be employed as a vehicle for their education and development.

The major part of the chapter is devoted to a description and discussion of the use of the project approach in the Belgian Inter-University Programme for Advanced Management. The manager's abilities to deal with practical operations are seen to increase by understanding better his own responses, emotional as well as intellectual, to action situations. Professor Revans regards as inadequate any discussion and simulation of reality. He feels that each manager must undergo and understand his reaction to the stress of managerial circumstances and that the project method is the best means by which he may be helped to do so.

In Chapter Seven, Stiefel and Papalofzos deal with the use of newer participative techniques in the countries of Western Europe, with the exception of Great Britain and Scandinavia. They present a historical summary of the development of management education in Western Europe which included first absorption and evaluation of American management development experience, then building institutions to advance management development, and now consolidating previous advances. Emphasis is placed on approaches in which participants take a more active role in the teaching-learning process. The authors describe the movement of teaching methodology from those of the American business schools to several European conceptual methodologies. They identify four conceptual schools of thought in management education: the empirical, the behavioral, the mathematical, and the synthesized or integrated, with corresponding American prototype institutes.

The use of the case method in Western Europe is discussed as the most widely used of the participative teaching methods, one which can be used independent of cultural and regional differences. Simulation, the structure of business games, the development of business games in Western Europe, and the modification of business games to meet underlying educational objectives are discussed. Sensitivity training and the difference between United States and Western European practice in sensitivity training are analyzed. A structured exercise called Personal and Managerial Feedback Groups (PMF Groups) which differs in several fundamental ways from classical T-groups is described.

In Chapter Eight, Kubr discusses the state and main trends of management training in the Eastern European countries. He examines influences on teaching and training methods, considering programme objectives, participants, teachers, trainers, and the duration and organization of training programmes. The experiences of Eastern European countries with the use of the discussion method, teamwork, case studies, management exercises and games, and the project method are described within the context of overall progress in management education and training. Emphasis is placed on the experiences of Bulgaria, Czechoslovakia, the German Democratic Republic, Hungary, Poland, Romania, U.S.S.R., and Yugoslavia. Mr. Kubr describes the early use of conferences, seminars, and technical courses for managers during the fifties, the introduction of systematic education and training of managers on a large scale at the beginning of the sixties based on clearly defined objectives and with content and methods adapted to the nature of managerial functions; the rapid advance in management development during the sixties; and the present emphasis on the establishment of educational and training institutions and off-the-job programmes. Mr. Kubr projects that more emphasis will be placed on career planning for managers, management development plans, on-the-job training, and job rotation of young managers. He describes the use of older methods—lectures, discussions, and exercises of the classical style and newer participation methods, group work, case studies, and management exercises and games and the project approach.

In Chapter Nine, Goscinski analyzes the use of new techniques of training for managers in the Polish Management Development Center and certain other training centers in socialist countries. He discusses the characteristics of an effective manager (i.e., managerial knowledge, capability to use this knowledge, managerial talent, and a proper social attitude and reaction to events) and the extent to which these can be affected by education and training. Describing the diffusion of the newer participative training techniques from Western Europe and the United States to the Polish Management Center and other Eastern European management centers, he discusses the factors which affect the effectiveness of training techniques, the objectives of training programmes for managers, and the requirements for the effective training of managers. He presents a grid relating the training techniques of field studies, the incident method, case studies, simulation, role-playing, group projects, T-group training, psychodrama, and the panel discussion to the development of management skills (motivating, communicating, deciding, solution formulation, and diagnosis capability).

The effectiveness of group dynamics, psychodrama, case studies, the incident method, role-playing, simulation, and group projects are assessed and the importance of technical equipment, experienced instructors, texts or programmes based on local intellectual, legal, cultural, and psychological conditions, and training facilities are evaluated.

In Chapter Ten, Popov presents Soviet experiences with management training methods based on the concepts of the Soviet economy as related to the concept of the "economy manager." He analyzes factors affecting management training in the Soviet Union in terms of the sociopolitical system, economy development stages, the personnel selection and placement system, the requirements for a manager, and the development of the management sciences. From this, Professor Popov moves to descriptions of the system for improving managerial skills, the history of the Soviet management training system, the present management training system, and discernible trends in the development of the Soviet managers. Professor Popov provides information about the system of knowledge about management; common features of management training programmes at higher learning establishments; the specifics of management training at higher learning establishments; and the study of management problems in postgraduation training of managers. He assesses the usefulness of self-study, on-the-job training, meetings, conferences, symposia, and congresses; describes research and educational activities; and concludes with a general examination of alternative forms of education. The crucial nature of programme content is discussed and the relationship between content and learning process is analyzed.

The role of managerial personnel policies as a component of the system of economy management and the relationship between these and social, political, economic, cultural factors are reviewed. The Soviet Union's solution to the problem of the selection and use of appropriate management training methods is presented as a consequence of a complex aggregate of interrelated issues.

In Chapter Eleven, Richman describes the view of management

held in the People's Republic of China as this affects the development, training, and utilization of managers. A point emphasized in the discussion is the performance by two distinct management groups of what are essentially the expressive and the instrumental roles, the first played by political ideologues and the latter by technical experts. The training and development efforts for these two groups tend to differ.

Two major developmental approaches are work-study and role interchange. The objective of the first is to provide a direct link between learning and practice and to permit immediate application of theory. The objectives of the second are to increase understanding and appreciation of the different roles in the enterprise, improve relationships, communications, and co-operation between workers and managers, and, possibly most important, eliminate class distinctions between workers and managers.

Three other techniques described by Richman to achieve this goal are: the mixed (worker, technician, manager) problem-solving group (three-in-one method), the requirement that all perform physical labor, and the use of the works of Chairman Mao as the theoretical base for discussion groups attempting to understand and solve management problems. There is analysis of this use of several supporting techniques to achieve, in the work location, the political goals of a common ideology and obliteration of significant permanent differences between workers and managers.

Richman also describes formal educational programmes for managers, on-the-job training, and the role of "semiprofessional" schools (at the level of technical high schools) whose graduates are considered management potential. The almost total emphasis on relating training and development with the plant or industry and the inclusion of persons from different hierarchical levels in discussion and project groups is similar in some respects to organizational development approaches.

In Chapter Twelve, Hindle discusses major issues and trends in the developing countries in management training. These include approaches and content in national training, the venue of training (i.e., whether the training is carried out inside or outside the organization), the management training cycle (which includes training courses, guided practical application, and evaluation seminars), and the multiplier effect in training, which involves training of trainers of trainers.

Recent ILO experience in the use of training and teaching methods in management development in developing countries is reviewed, including a survey of teaching methods, a discussion of the requisite conditions for the effective use of participative teaching methods, sources of teaching materials, and additional technical support desired by experts in the use of participative teaching methods in developing countries. In the course of the chapter nine participative teaching methods are analyzed: group discussions and syndicates, case studies, business games, role-playing, the in-basket exercise, programmed learning, field visits, application projects, and consultancy assignments.

The chapter concludes by discussing the need to use a mixed-techniques approach and to modify and adapt techniques and materials in the light of specific conditions of a particular country.

In Chapter Thirteen, Wu assesses the international experience gained by the United Nations Public Administration Division since its establishment in 1951. He discusses the conditions which affect success in training programmes and analyzes both traditional and newer approaches to training. After a brief description of experience-based general considerations underlying the Public Administration Division's approaches to the use of the newer training techniques, general training methods and the trainer, training methods and programme content, the nature and significance of modern training techniques, and conventional and modern training techniques, Professor Wu analyzes and evaluates the utility of participative techniques to the developing world. Included are: the management game, role-playing, the in-basket technique, simulation exercises, laboratory (sensitivity) training, study tours, programmed learning, and correspondence courses.

He discusses the importance of an overall systems concept of organizational development; a training methodology established by the Public Administration Division for handling requests for aid by developing countries focusing on the establishment of workshops designed to improve organizational performance and a series of workshops which involved the following sequence of events: discussion of the elements of this service system, diagnostic study, feedback, planning, orientation, practice, reporting and receiving feedback, and post-workshop follow-up.

Professor Wu concludes by describing the role of the United Nations Public Administration Division in training public administrators to help developing countries to assimilate, adapt, and utilize modern training techniques, to develop trainers who have insight into national conditions, and to prepare local, relevant training materials. The Public Administration Division programmes for training of trainers to help national institutions in developing their own training materials are also described.

In Chapter Fourteen, Khosla analyzes methods and techniques used for training senior administrators for the public services of developing countries in East and Southeast Asia. He considers various methods of institutional training and practice, individual-oriented training methods and techniques, study and training abroad, and various training aids. Among methods of institutional training analyzed and evaluated are the lecture method and guest speakers, conferences, seminars and group discussions, the syndicate method, the case method, and sensitivity training. Individual-oriented training methods and techniques analyzed and evaluated include field visits, practical project work, programmes of self-development, study and training abroad, and various training aids which are required for effective training.

He concludes by discussing: (a) the usefulness of training methods and techniques in relationship to the effectiveness of a training programme as a whole; (b) development of techniques for evaluating the usefulness of a training programme; (c) the relationships between training methods and objectives and the contents of the training programmes, and national and organizational conditions; (d) preparation of suitable case studies for aspects of administration.

In Chapter Fifteen, Nath and Ready discuss management training in developing countries. They describe and analyze experiences of developing countries in inventing new training techniques and in attempting to adapt training techniques invented in the developed countries. They discuss issues involved in adapting and institutionalizing new training techniques. Three innovative training techniques from Brazil, Ecuador, Ceylon and India are described. The authors use these case studies to illustrate the difficulties in getting new training techniques established in developing countries. The training techniques analyzed are the Paulo Freire method in Brazil; base level training in Ecuador; and the Aloka experience in Ceylon and India. The conditions which led to the invention of the technique and its use are described.

They amplify their analysis of experiences in adopting new training techniques and briefly review training experiences of developing countries with the case method, the syndicate method, instrumented programmes, sensitivity training, and an experimental programme based on a systems approach. The need for adapting material to local conditions is stressed and the problems involved are analyzed.

The authors conclude by pointing to three areas which demand attention: cross-cultural research; training professionals from developing countries; and establishing institutions which encourage the innovation and adaptation of newer techniques.

In Chapter Sixteen, Hoberman and Mailick present an analysis of the dominant themes explicitly stated or implicitly presented by the various contributors, discuss and evaluate the possible use of the techniques presented for developing countries and international organizations, present some guidance for trainers in integrating techniques into programmes, suggest possible hypotheses with respect to the relationships among training goals, programmes, and techniques, and indicate some areas for research related to techniques for developing managerial skills.

Chart 1.1

Note (Chapter 6* / Chapter 5 columns): *While the entire learning process focuses on the conduct & implementation of the project, there are other inputs including subject matter, lectures & tutorials, group discussions and visits to organizations.*

Technique	Ch 3	Ch 4	Ch 5	Ch 6*	Ch 7	Ch 8	Ch 9	Ch 10†	Ch 11	Ch 12	Ch 13	Ch 14
Case Study	0 N				2 N	1 P	1 P		2 P		2 V	1 P
Conferences, Seminars, Discussion Groups	0 N					1 P	0 0	1 P	2 P		1 U	
Field Studies and Observation of Organizations					2 P				1 N	0 P	1 U	
In-Basket Technique	2 N					0 N			2 P	1 V		
Incident Technique							0 P					
Individual or Self-Study Programmes								2 P		0 P	1 N	
Lecture Method	0 N					1 P		1 P			1 U	
Management Games (Simulation)	2 N				2 P	1 P	1 V		2 P	1 P		1 P
On-the-Job Training						0 N	1 P					
Organization Development	2 P									2 E		
Professional Meetings								1 P		.		1 U
Programmed Learning	2 N								1 P	0 P		
Project Method and Consultancy Assignments		2 V		3 E	2 N	1 V	1 V	1 P	2 P		1 N	
Proprietary Programmes (Kepner-Tregoe) (Managerial Grid)	2 N	1 N										1 U
Role-Playing	2 N					0 N	0 P		2 P	1 P		
Sensitivity or Laboratory Training	2 N	1 P			2 P		1 O			1 U	2 P	2 U°
Study-University or Special Institute		2 V						2 V			1 N	
Syndicate Method	0 N	2 P		3 E					2 P		2 V	1 U

Legend (numbers):

0 – While technique is mentioned, its only in passing.
1 – A brief description of the technique or its use
2 – A fairly full description of the technique and its use
3 – Discussion of the approach is a major part of the paper
† – While Popov mentions teaching approaches in general, he emphasizes content rather than teaching.

Legend (letters):

O – A very negative evaluation
U – A negative evaluation
N – A neutral description
P – A positive evaluation
V – A very positive evaluation
E – An enthusiastic evaluation
• – Ready-Math find sensitivity not usable, but describe a native developed version, GEM, which was successful.

CHAPTER TWO
General Considerations Regarding Managerial and Organizational Development*

I. INTRODUCTION

The increasing complexity of modern organizations, the rapid pace of technological change, and pressures both from within organizations and from the societies in which they exist are placing heavy demands upon administrators. These demands call for strong, flexible administrators with considerable knowledge and skill in many diverse fields. The demands are so great that development of administrators can no longer be left to the chance of appropriate on-the-job assignments and the good fortune of being able to work with, and under the direction of, skilled older administrators who want and are able to help others acquire administrative knowledge and skills. Not only is the need increasing but the nature of administrative behavior and management are changing as the result of new research findings and the development of an impressive array of management techniques and approaches by both the analytic and behavioral science schools. Most large organizations and many countries are meeting their managerial needs by training professional administrators in special educational programmes.

Besides the need to train new managers, there is an equally pressing one for the continuing education of present managers. These needs and the development of new, more effective concepts and techniques to train administrators have given rise to the increasing use of administrative training programmes throughout the world.

* This chapter was prepared by Sidney Mailick and Solomon Hoberman.

II. THE IMPORTANCE OF MANAGEMENT DEVELOPMENT IN LARGE ORGANIZATIONS

Continual shortages of skilled people in management and other fields have led to increased interest in effective manpower planning and utilization. There is wide recognition of the lack of appropriate methodologies which can evaluate and increase the effectiveness of the use of managers, determine present and future manpower needs, construct alternative programmes for solving these deficiencies, and establish standards for evaluating these alternatives and for implementing the plans adopted. The importance of considering programmes for insuring an adequate supply of effective administrators, even as only one, albeit very important, element in the overall personnel process, has hardly to be stressed.

Existing educational and employment systems in the developed countries can be depended upon to train almost all the technical and professional people required for an advanced society. This is not the case for developing nations in any discipline, and it is not the case with respect to managers in any nation. One reason is that management development calls for great co-ordination and sophisticated linkage between education and experience. Another is that many of the problems which are faced by a manager are affected—to an even greater extent than those faced by other professionals—by the continuous change that characterizes all modern social systems. The rate of change in managerial skills and knowledge required seems to be a compounding of the rates in other areas while the organizations which the manager must change are far more stable and resist change far more strongly than is the case in other professional or technical fields.

The quality of a nation's managers not only determines the efficiency and effectiveness of its goods- and services-producing systems but also determines to a large extent the career development and manpower utilization in its organizations and patterns of work satisfaction and dissatisfaction in all walks of life. It is these consequences of managerial performance which make the training of managers so important.

Modern management training and development programmes tend to use three interrelated approaches. One focuses upon the characteristics, knowledge, and experience of the individual manager and attempts to provide a special programme to meet his unique needs.

A second directs its attention to the improvement of managers as members of a class or a set of classes with overlapping membership. In this approach programmes are planned for persons in similar roles in different organizations. The third focuses upon an organization. It leads to programmes designed to improve the functioning of a specific organization, with a given staff faced with unique situations and problems.

Each of these approaches in its own way attempts to mesh the capabilities and goals of the person with the needs and goals of the organization. Some of the techniques which are used, in addition to training and education, are performance appraisal, coaching, counseling, job rotation, task force management, and job structuring. In good measure, these activities use the commonly found drive of upward-mobile managers as one of the motivational forces for self-improvement and seek to change the manager through training, education, challenging new job assignments, and temporary managerial assignments.

Personal career development is concerned with the aspirations, will, knowledge, and skill of a single person and is directed to help that person achieve his maximum potential by developing his capability to handle more difficult assignments. A balanced career development programme should be concerned not only with imparting useful technical and scientific knowledge but also with extending to the maximum the possibilities of the individual as a self-fulfilling human being.

Many who are in time expected to fill higher generalist roles in organizations enter as specialists in specific professional or technical fields. For the most part, the pre-service education and training that these specialists receive is not adequate to prepare them for these generalist roles. Management development, for these men and women, is concerned with despecialization as well as with training in specific management skills.

Management training programmes attempt to improve the manager's capabilities by increasing his knowledge and understanding of social, political, and economic forces and relationships as well as of the disciplines and technologies of management science; by providing him the opportunity to identify, analyze, and develop solutions for both technical and human problems in administration; by controlled work experience, e.g., assigning the inexperienced manager to work with competent generalists; and by special assignments in novel (for the manager) situations which provide opportunities to develop and try out new approaches, techniques, and solutions.

In technical or professional fields, we no longer can expect that a person's early formal education can satisfy the job demands during his working life. Management, along with every other professional field, must examine and solve the problem of providing effective continuing education for managers at different career and organizational levels.

III. THE ROLE OF CAREER DEVELOPMENT AND TRAINING IN OVERALL MANAGEMENT

A number of authors in this volume analyze the role of newer techniques for developing and training managers and helping them to improve their performance. They are concerned with managers in both developed and developing countries and in countries with different economic and political systems.

Programmes for developing and training managers are usually derived from the organization's manpower plan. The manpower plan, in turn, is derived from the organization's plans and programmes to reach its objectives. Thus development and training programmes and the techniques used in these programmes can be maximally effective only when perceived of as components of a co-ordinated effort to reach organizational objectives.

It is generally agreed that managers learn how to manage primarily through practical experience on the job. However, it is also generally agreed that not every experience helps to develop a good manager, that not all managers learn equally from experience, and that managerial experience is frequently insufficient to develop managers who are able to cope with the problems faced by large, complex organizations.

Despite this general consensus, formal training and development activities are not universally accepted as important components of programmes to improve managerial performance. Many executives, even in the face of failure, do not feel any need for change in their managerial styles. A frequent argument is that their organizations don't need change; they simply need everyone to work a little harder. Unless executives feel that there is absolute necessity for improved management and have some commitment to change, the organization might just as well place reliance on "simply" trying to get everyone to work a little harder.

At the other extreme, it is not realistic to expect that training and development programmes alone can produce major changes in the management of any large organization. Only after all the forces and techniques for producing an effective management team and for inducing desired change are considered and their respective roles weighed can a proper role for managerial development and training be defined.

Moving from the need for training to the process, we make the basic assumption that a cause-effect relationship exists between the technique used in the learning process and the nature of the transformation which may take place. Put in another way: not all people can use to the same degree the knowledge and skills which they possess and we believe that the manner in which they gained knowledge and skill is one reason for these differences. Further, we believe that some insights, understanding, and abilities cannot be obtained at all by passive acquisition of information. For example, while a manager can learn by reading that agreement of all participants with respect to goals makes their achievement easier, reading does not necessarily provide the deeper understanding and ability needed to obtain organizational or individual agreement.

To use training techniques meaningfully, we should be able to predict the probable consequences which can be expected to result from using one technique rather than another. Unfortunately, for reasons which we shall discuss in Chapter Sixteen, there is little reliable and valid evidence to support most predictions. However, there is equally little "hard" evidence to support predictions of specific benefits which accrue from other management improvement efforts such as planning, budgeting, and controlling. What is the case is that organizations which are well managed, in the sense of using advanced management techniques and approaches effectively, tend to be those which take management development and training seriously and also tend to be the most successful. What cannot be easily demonstrated is the direction and nature of these interrelationships. Nevertheless, while such evidence as there is tends to support the contention that changes in organizational variables which can be affected by training and development will not usually produce most of the changes desired, it would be foolhardy not to undertake a training programme to effect these. Despite our limited knowledge and understanding of cause and effect in the training process, organizations with trained managers tend to be more effective than those with untrained managers. Consequently, we must continue to develop training programmes and provide training experiences. Indeed, this conclusion is apparently so in-escapable that training efforts have been increasing geometrically dur-ing the past several decades. We turn, as a technical introduction to the rest of the volume, to a general review of training objectives and results.

IV. PRELIMINARY DEFINITIONS

Distinctions are made between executive development, executive training, and executive education. While there is overlap between these terms, it may be helpful for the analysis which follows to at-tempt to define them.

1. *Executive development* generally refers to a process of planning and programming for the growth and improvement of individuals in an organization—for the purposes of improving performance, increas-ing work satisfaction, and preparing for possible advancement. A person's executive development programme tends to be oriented to the needs of the individual. A programme may include many ap-proaches such as appraisal, coaching, counseling, internship, appren-ticeship, job rotation, study leave, training, and education, as well as the normal unplanned and unstructured processes of growth and development on the job. Executive development in this broad sense subsumes and includes the processes of training and education.

2. *Executive training* generally refers to planned learning experi-ences through formal or informal activities, classes, seminars, or con-ferences for which the focus is on a number of individuals with similar job responsibilities. Training attempts to influence performance in a defined range of jobs across the organization. It tends to be job-oriented and agency-related. Training attempts to meet "felt needs" of both a class of individuals and the organization as a whole. It is often tailored to and integrated with the agency's operations, al-though outside training resources and facilities may be employed.

3. *Executive education* is usually not directly related to a specific job or a specific organization. Its aims are not only to change the par-ticipant's job performance. Its efforts are not related to any organi-zational context. Education, as contrasted with training, may attempt not to meet felt needs but to create needs, to awaken, broaden, dis-turb, and stimulate the manager to make him want to change, to in-crease his capacity for reflection, to develop his creative capacities, and to get him to want to achieve his potential as a human being. Executive education partakes of the character of all education in that

it is more than a means to an end; it may be an end in itself. Management education is often conducted by an external educational institution rather than by the internal agency training facility. However, in recent years, some corporate enterprises have themselves been sponsoring "schools of management," which incorporate educational programmes. This volume focuses on the newer techniques which are employed in executive development, training, and educational activities.

V. OBJECTIVES OF CAREER DEVELOPMENT AND TRAINING

Effective career development for managers requires clear and well-defined objectives, standards of performance, and measures of results. The absence of clearly defined objectives makes it impossible to establish criteria to determine to what degree designed objectives are attained. Career development programmes frequently start from a definition of the skills, knowledge, capabilities, and understandings that managers should possess. However, only after these have been defined operationally with some exactness can rational consideration of specific programmes, techniques, and methods begin.

It is important that career development objectives be based on a realistic evaluation of the capabilities of training and education. It is not reasonable to expect that any administrator will emerge from any training programme with a totally new orientation, different attitudes, increased technical abilities, and changes in motivation; that these changes will be internalized to a degree to produce significant change in his behavior as a manager; that he will be able to adapt after re-entry to the work situation to the realities of this situation without reverting to his former style; and that he will be able to persuade his superiors, peers, and subordinates to accept the changes in him and make corresponding changes in their own behavior. Individual training and development can never produce these results. Most management development and training is too superficial, too diffused, too fragmented, and too general to yield even a small degree of such change. Not infrequently, there are no returns as a result of a trainer's brave attempt to accomplish too much with too few resources. Too often, unfortunately, grand objectives and meager resources seem to be accepted as necessary conditions for establishing a management training programme.

Career development is best conceived as part of a comprehensive effort to improve management. The determination of development and training needs must be made in the context of organizational goals and conditions, the expected cost return from the other elements, and the interrelationships among all elements.

An integrated approach such as this can help the manager relate and apply his knowledge to the problems of his organization, develop useful attitudes and standards for effective functioning in the organization, and develop behavioral and conceptual skills needed to carry out organizational objectives. While earlier programmes emphasized subject-matter areas, present-day programmes tend to concentrate much more on behavioral and experiential development and personal and organizational growth. Training programmes for managers may include some of the following objectives:

(a) Increasing knowledge and understanding of modern management techniques, methods, concepts, and theories.

(b) Developing greater ability to use advanced managerial techniques and methods.

(c) Increasing skills in problem identification, problem solving, and decision making.

(d) Developing more effective relationships with superiors, subordinates, and peers, and increasing ability to communicate with subordinates, peers, and supervisors.

(e) Motivating improved subordinate performance, gaining acceptance for change, and encouraging creativity and innovation.

(f) "Despecialization," i.e., developing a broader and interdisciplinary view of enterprises and of management processes.

(g) Increasing ability to collect, organize, interpret, and use data for effective reduction of chance factors.

(h) Learning to act more effectively under conditions of uncertainty.

A fundamental question in determining management development and training objectives is whether management training should help the manager acquire the capability for operating more effectively within a given system, or attempt to give him the will and ability to change the system in a given direction, or attempt a combination of these. Individual development in the agency and on-the-job training under the direction of a willing and competent manager is probably the most effective way of training managers if the goal is system stability. Experienced managers are undoubtedly best for teaching a neophyte how to get along within the system. In organizations using this approach, systemic changes, if they occur, occur almost entirely because the opportunity and the need for change develop within the system or as a result of outside pressures. Change occurs as a reaction, at best a necessary evil, and almost always in a piecemeal manner. Out-of-agency training, on the other hand, not infrequently has as its goal influencing the manager to effect change in the system upon re-entry. It tends to encourage searching for elements to change and creating opportunities for change rather than waiting passively for the need or pressure to arise. Change is seen as desirable. Training for change, training change agents, calls for more than imparting knowledge or teaching how to solve technical problems. It must include practice in inducing and gaining acceptance for change.

The problem of re-entry of the trainee is common to all external training programmes. While the problem is one faced by the organization and the trainee, it must be of prime concern to the trainer. He must be concerned with developing some force to prevent the trainee from reassuming his old style and continuing as before, without making any use of knowledge, ability, or insight gained from the training. If it is not part of the pretraining planning, the trainer must determine during training what the participants see as "possible." If the range of "possible" is too limited, he can direct his efforts toward increasing the range. All bureaucratic systems contain internal forces which seek to continue the system as it is without change or, if that is not possible, to delay change. Consequently, it is imperative to prepare managers trained to change a system to go about this task without creating havoc or being destroyed themselves.

These are a few of the problems with which trainers are concerned and for which the newer techniques were developed.

VI. A PARTIAL CATEGORIZATION OF THE FORMS, APPROACHES, AND DURATION OF TRAINING

All training, of which management training is one element, can be seen as an integration of individual career development and overall organizational development. Both objectives—individual and organizational—are essential for every training programme.

It is this relationship which makes the re-entry problem important. Implicitly or explicitly, every training approach and technique attempts to deal with it. The older training methods do not ignore it. They make the assumption that it is too complicated and too personal to be dealt with in the training programme. Consequently, they try to provide the trainee with as much information as possible and leave it up to the trainee upon re-entry to determine how best to use the information to change the organization in the direction of the learning. The older approaches do not make any attempt to condition the behavior of the trainee upon re-entry.

The newer attacks on this problem fall into four categories. Those in one category focus on knowledge and ability in rational analysis and decision making, using such training techniques as practice in the use of formal problem-solving procedures, the case study, and business games. They are derived from the hypotheses that, by discussing, analyzing, experimenting, and practicing the use of rational methods for solving managerial problems, the manager gains understanding and appreciation of the methods and confidence in his skill and ability to use them and that, consequently, he will attempt to use them upon re-entry. The problem of use upon re-entry is sometimes considered and discussed as one of the managerial problems subject to rational analysis. A second category, recognizing the gap between knowledge and insight and action, tries to help the manager to become a change agent by helping him recognize his own feelings and how others are affected by him and by providing him with opportunities to try to change behavior. Some techniques which attempt to provide this type of experience, with varying degrees of success, are role-play, sensitivity training, certain types of management games, and laboratory training.

A third approach is based upon the hypothesis that one can learn how to do something as complicated and as difficult as changing an organization only by doing it in a real-life situation. The project and task force techniques are developed from this hypothesis.

The fourth category carries this concept to its logical conclusion. It takes the position that a manager can learn how to change an organization only by actually trying to change that organization. It assumes, in effect, that all organizations are unique. It is a logical development from this hypothesis to use the organization as the focus for all training. The two major approaches in this category, vertical training and organizational development, are complete training programmes which use many different techniques.

Most complete training programmes are variations and combinations of these four methods. Few focus so directly upon the re-entry and change problems that only one approach is applicable.

The determination of whether to use internal or external training is generally made on the basis of the perceived management problem. If the problem is seen as one of effecting change in a specific operation or learning a new technique, e.g., PPBS, which will be used in the same manner by all managers, an internal training programme is the usual answer. These may be conducted by staff, or hired consultants, or by an outside educational institution. If the problem is seen as a general management problem external training is likely to be the accepted answer.

No organization can meet all its management development needs by internal training. This is especially true for small and medium-sized organizations which have too few managers to conduct extensive internal management training. But even large organizations have training needs which cannot be provided for efficiently by internal programmes alone. Few internal programmes can provide all of the learning experiences which are a major advantage of external programmes. Managers do learn from each other. Not infrequently, more information and insight are gained during social and recreational hours than during formal training sessions. The value of this type of training tends to increase at the higher management levels.

Training programmes can, also, be categorized in terms of the methods and criteria for selecting participants. These can make a major difference in the intensity of the programmes and the types of techniques used. It makes a difference in programming whether participants are self-selected or selected by their organization. In some cases when selection forces acceptance of participants who are un-equally prepared for the programme content in terms of knowledge and experience, pre-course preparation may be provided.

Another way to categorize training is in terms of location.

To some extent, this analysis overlaps into those categorizations based on the re-entry problem and "internal" and "external."

Some of the location categories are:

(a) at a regular assigned work place in the employing organization;

(b) at a special training or conference facility in the employing organization;

(c) at a work place in a co-operating organization;

(d) at an outside educational institution, in residence;

(e) at a session or series of sessions in the course of attendance at a meeting or conference;

(f) at home or some other place selected by the participant involved in self-study.

Still other categorizations are in terms of time. Some of these categories are:

1. (a) after working hours;
   (b) during working hours;
2. (a) less than a full day at any one time;
   (b) one full day for each session;
   (c) a longer period—two days to two weeks;
   (d) an extended training period exceeding two weeks and extending, in some cases, to two years or more;
3. Periodicity: (a) at regular intervals; (b) occasionally, to meet specific needs.
4. Duration: (a) short programmes with 30 or fewer programmed hours; (b) medium duration with 30–120 programmed hours; and (c) long courses with more than 120 programmed hours.

Some of the considerations in making decisions with respect to time are: cost, the extent of the programme objectives, the ability to sustain interest, keeping key people away from their jobs, internal power politics, etc. The effectiveness of short courses can be increased by providing pre-course training to bring all participants up to the same knowledge level and also to reduce the amount of programmed time spent in such activities as lectures. Sometimes, pre-course assignments are used for similar purposes. There seems to be a trend away from the short course, except for specialized technique training, to courses of longer or medium duration for both entry and advanced management development programmes.

5. Continuity: Some programmes, particularly residential programmes, are full-time programmes without the intervention of regular work activity; other programmes provide for periods of training interspersed with periods of work. This is obviously the case where programmed time is less than a day at any one time. Some of the considerations here are the ability of the organization to release the manager for an extended period, travel costs, and the use of the time between formal training sessions for studies, preparation of case material, etc.

VII. THE INITIATION OF A TRAINING PROGRAMME AND THE DETERMINATION OF CONTENT AND PROCESS

As we have indicated, success of a training programme depends upon many factors, the most important of which may not be under the control of the trainers. Some of these are: the environment, the maturity of the organization, the objectives of the organization, the relationships between these and the training programme, the relationships between training and the career development and manpower plan, and the intensity of the support for the training and development programme.

Some trainers, a small number, are completely committed to a single approach, and perform or direct all of their training and development efforts in terms of using this single approach. Trainers who are in this position obviously must be selective with respect to the training objectives which they try to achieve. There are relatively few more counterproductive procedures than to approach a problem with a ready answer. However, to approach every problem with the same answer is undoubtedly even more dangerous. This is particularly the case if the training technique involves a great degree of risk for the participant.

The choice of methods and techniques is determined by such considerations as the objectives of the training, the content and process, the location, the duration of the programme, and the characteristics of the trainer and trainees. Training requirements and priorities are set by organizational goals. From these, knowledge, skills, and attitudes needed to achieve the goals are determined. Finally, techniques are selected.

Sometimes a preliminary diagnostic study is made to develop an estimate of the situation or obtain problem census. These help identify training needs to be met in the training design, possible criteria for programme evaluation, specific difficulties within the organization, useful local training material, and possible re-entry problems.

In developing the programme, both content and process are considered. Content may include behavioral skills as well as knowledge and understanding of ideas. Process is the way in which managers do things, i.e., managerial style. Programmes which focus on process emphasize attitudinal and motivational change. Process is divided by some theorists into two phases: simple process, which consists of factors which are caused by "bad habits" in individual and group problem solving; and complex process, which consists of factors against which individuals and groups have strong unconscious resistances. Case study and problem-solving techniques are directed to affect simple process; sensitivity training, for example, focuses on affecting change in complex process.

VIII. TRAINERS AND TRAINEES: AN INTERACTING SYSTEM

In the input-output model of the training activity described in Chapter Sixteen, the trainer's locus of action is placed in the training transformation process. The most important interactions in this process are between trainer and participants and among participants. The first interaction is different from that between professor and student in a university. The relationships are different, the objectives are different, and the conditions are different. The content and approach are determined in great part by what the participants bring to the programme and by the organization and the conditions to which they will return. The participant is the key element in the process. He is the only element that the trainer can plan to change to any extent. Thus, the relationship between trainer and participant is crucial to the entire transformation process. This relationship must be developed and maintained in a manner to build and support participant confidence, will, and ability. Training techniques provide help and the occasion but not the skill, insight, and confidence needed for effective use.

Apart from techniques, there is need for constant awareness, in all relationships, of the participant's needs upon re-entry to the organization.

How a trainee acquires the necessary skills and insights is a matter of interest, not only to trainers generally, but also to a new breed of trainers, the "trainer of trainers," i.e., the professional who is responsible for transmitting the skills and knowledge acquired by trainers in the course of experiment, experience, study, and analysis. While this is a field beyond the scope of this volume, its importance is clear. The trainer of trainers has a multiplier effect; he has the opportunity to spark managerial improvement in a large number of organizations or in an entire nation. The entire area is relatively unexplored. There is little said except for the occasional cry of anguish, mostly from the "sensitivity people": "But he was not well trained."

We have noted that the selection of participants is important for determining the nature of a programme and its effectiveness. What participant characteristics are important? Obviously, the capacity to learn and use whatever it is that the programme is intended to teach. Beyond these there are few characteristics about which there is general agreement. Some of the important ones are: management training is of greater value for persons with previous management experience; all participants should have reasonably equivalent knowledge and be at, more or less, the same organizational levels; and they should come to the programme expecting to participate and to learn for use.

Training tends to be more effective when the participants play an important role in determining the objectives and content of the programme. If this is not possible (we believe that it is important to make every effort to make it possible), it is incumbent upon the trainer to ensure that each participant understands and accepts as useful the goals and content. This may be difficult but, unless it is done, doubt of relevancy may be a continuing block against effective learning. The techniques used in the programme should be discussed openly to clarify any misconceptions and to deal with the problem of possible participant concern with manipulation from the beginning. In short, it seems to us that the methods used to conduct a programme should be similar to the management methods which are advocated in the programmes.

A training and development programme can be used as a means for evaluating managers' capacities for filling higher jobs only at the cost of possibly destroying the value of the programme for development. Managers tend not to be open and free during a selection process. They try to anticipate what the observers want and to demonstrate that behavior rather than their normal behavior. They tend to try to show how capable they are rather than to try to learn. Evaluation of individual participant performance, therefore, during the course of training is not desirable for either selection or development.

IX. TRAINING METHODS: CONVENTIONAL AND MODERN

The selection of appropriate training techniques is an integral and critical part of the planning and organization of a management development programme. Some of the considerations are:

(a) The degree to which evidence indicates that the technique will be helpful for achieving programme objectives.

(b) The estimated acceptability of the technique to the participants and their organizations. A technique should not be used which is at such variance with the value systems and cultural norms of either participant or organization as to have undesirable "spillover" effects or set up significant counterproductive forces.

(c) The expected cost return for the technique compared with those for other available techniques, particularly with respect to such limited resources as time and participants' energies.

(d) The competency of training staff in the use of the technique.

(e) The nature of the reinforcement; reinforcement is probably the major force available to the trainer to move a participant from superficial knowledge to ability to use knowledge.

(f) The possible effects of using the technique on other parts of the training programme and other management improvement programmes.

(g) Programme flexibility and the ability to change direction if feedback during the programme indicates the need for change.

(h) The degree to which the technique helps or hinders informative and effective feedback during and after the programme.

(i) The effect upon re-entry.

A technique is a means, not an end. It can only have meaning and usefulness as a means. The sight of a participant working well in a training group, whether following an effective rational process for the analysis of a case study or reacting to direct confrontation in an appropriate "healthy" manner, may make the trainee feel that progress is being accomplished but may mean little or nothing to his organization. Overemphasis on any one element in any process is usually a prelude to failure in any operation. There is nowhere that this basic management principle is more true than in management training and development programmes.

Training techniques, as are most techniques, are not "useful" or "useless" in any absolute sense any more than they are "good" or "bad" in and of themselves. They become "useful" or "useless" depending upon how they are employed, why they are employed, and with whom they are employed. It is meaningless to attempt to rank training techniques in terms of an inherent or absolute "goodness" or to consider them as more or less effective.

Most training methods are not designed to be, and should not be, used alone. The combination of several techniques is almost always more useful and effective than intensive concentration on any single technique.

Management training makes many cultural assumptions. Most of these are not explicit but implicit in the complex network of content, approach, methodology, and techniques. Among the most easily identifiable assumptions are the group which comprise "scientific management." While it is questionable whether or not the hypotheses of scientific management hold for all human organizations, these are assumed in most management development programmes. Selection of training techniques is often based upon a set of hypotheses which overlap but are not identical with the set of hypotheses which determine programme content. It is desirable to make efforts to recognize these two sets of assumptions and to determine, to some degree, their validity for the specific organizations, their internal inconsistencies, and their acceptability to the programme participants.

Most all approaches, both new and old, in general use at the present time recognize the need for using training methods suitable for adult learning and attempt to relate programme content to the practical situations which participants encounter or are apt to encounter in their day-to-day activities.

In summary, there is a wide divergence of views concerning the value of different training methods. (These will be reflected in the essays which follow.) Some believe that didactic formal training is useful as a technique for training change agents. Some believe that only special exercises or experiences, e.g., T-groups, can lead to an ability to act as a change agent. Some believe that only by working on projects and real tasks under skilled guidance and through identifying essential problems and making difficult decisions can managers improve their capabilities.

For the most part, as our focus is on the newer techniques, we do not in this volume consider the more conventional training techniques. This does not mean that we believe there is no longer any use for the older, long-used approaches such as the lecture, socratic discussion, and coaching. These have been and continue to be of critical use and importance.

Most of the newer techniques discussed demand considerable and active participation on the part of the trainee. They have as only a secondary objective the imparting of information; their primary objective is to change participant attitudes and behavior. Some seek to change aspects of the administrator's conception of himself or his role; others to motivate the administrator to concern himself with the total system rather than components. They all tend to de-emphasize the objective of imparting great amounts of information and to focus on increasing ability to use information. They attempt to use, through feedback, reinforcement and other techniques to solve the re-entry problem.

The new techniques have drawn attention to the role of the trainer in relationship to the transformation and learning processes. It is clear, in a manner as never before, that the knowledge, skill, and ability of the trainer play a crucial part in both of these.

The shift in emphasis from the act of teaching to the process of learning has created a spirit of inquiry in teachers and trainers that is often quite alien to teachers using only the older formal methods. These methods tend to focus on the performance of the student and to evaluate programme results as measures of student ability and diligence. The newer methods tend to investigate the opportunities which have been provided for learning, focus on identification and removal of barriers to learning, the effectiveness of specific techniques, and the abilities of the trainer. Thus, there has been a complete turnabout from measuring what individual students learned to measuring the educational transformation process. The student is only one element in this process.

The following chapters deal with the newer techniques not in the abstract but in terms of their use in specific nations and regions, the extent to which cross-cultural borrowing of training techniques has taken place, and the degree to which such borrowing is useful and desirable. The purpose of these accounts is to provide some information concerning possible use by developing countries and international organizations. We return to the overall subject of training techniques in Chapter Sixteen.

CHAPTER THREE
New Techniques of Training Managers in the United States*

I. INTRODUCTION

In this chapter we describe some of the newer techniques of management training which have been developed in the United States, assess their strengths and possible weaknesses, and discuss the possible use of these techniques in other societies. It is important to recognize throughout our discussion that we are only beginning to formalize these training techniques and that continued use and gathering of data must necessarily precede systematic assessment of results. Nevertheless, while the assessment is not comprehensive and only incomplete data are available, we can proceed to preliminary analyses of some of the U.S. techniques. It should be noted that, by focusing on techniques themselves, we are presenting an artificial and incomplete description of the education of managers. The usefulness of any technique is a function of the total programme of which it is only one part, the frame of reference within which it is used, the manner in which it is employed, and the readiness of the persons being trained to accept the approaches.

Training is an open and emerging activity system affected by societies, organizations, trainers, and trainees.[1] The determination of usefulness of a technique is the responsibility of the professional trainer, to be determined after taking into consideration the characteristics of the total system, the individuals involved, and the changes in behavior desired. It is only through a thorough understanding of the

* This chapter was prepared by Sidney Mailick and Nancy A. Bord.

dynamics of the interplay between bureaucratic systems and individuals that successful programmes to change bureaucratic behavior can be developed and techniques used effectively.

One more important caveat: we have not attempted to discuss fundamental learning processes and educational theory and research except as these relate directly to a particular training technique.

II. A BRIEF REVIEW OF SELECTED TECHNIQUES OF TRAINING

Seven newer types of management training techniques or programmes which are in use or have been used in a large number of U.S. organizations are analyzed in this chapter. Five of the seven are generic types; the other two have been developed by private, proprietary organizations. They are: (a) laboratory training, (b) role-playing, (c) the management game, (d) the in-basket technique, (e) programmed instruction, (f) the Kepner-Tregoe Problem Solving Technique, and (g) the Managerial Grid.

Before proceeding to analyze the above, there are certain other training techniques which deserve some mention. In order to better understand some of the newer training techniques which are assessed in this study, and because a given training programme may draw upon a combination of both "conventional" and "modern" training techniques at various phases, we briefly review a few of the older and better-known techniques of training which are not examined at length in this chapter.

(a) The Lecture

The lecture is the traditional mainstay of most academic institutions and is still the most prevalent training technique in all fields including management. The lecture is the oral presentation of organized information to a class of students. The lecturer is expected to be a subject-matter specialist at a level higher than the students and sufficiently skilled in imparting information to be able to communicate his message effectively to his audience.

The major advantages of the lecture are that it allows for an orderly planned presentation without digression, affords the opportunity for review and authoritative documentation, leads to economy of time and effort for both lecturer and students, makes for consistency of presentation, and, generally, comprises a rational effort to move the student from where he is to a higher level of knowledge. An important consideration is that the size of the group need not be limited. The lecture is most successful as a means of communicating information and data. It yields quick learning. It is generally less successful in effecting long-term changes in attitudes and behavior. It is best used for providing the factual groundwork or conceptual framework needed by the trainee if he is to change his behavior in the desired direction.

The weaknesses of the lecture technique stem, for the most part, from the fact that the audience is only passively involved in the learning process. Other training techniques which utilize the active participation of trainees are generally more likely to be successful in producing deeper change.

The success of the lecture depends not only upon the subject matter, knowledge, and insight of the lecturer but on his ability to develop an interesting scenario and to deliver it effectively. This is especially important if two-way communication is not permitted. When a group of lecturers is used in the same programme, it is important that they be briefed in terms of the specific needs and abilities of the group and its level of competence in the subject area, so that each lecture is co-ordinated into an overall plan of the curriculum, builds on what has gone before, and leads to what is to come.

The weakness of the lecture method can be overcome in part by giving participants written materials in advance to prepare for the lecture and written materials afterward to reinforce learning. In addition, a discussion or question and answer period following the formal lecture is traditionally used to provide a degree of group participation, resolve unanswered questions, and reinforce learning. The lecture, properly designed for its audience, is a valid and important teaching technique for management education, especially when combined with other methods.

(b) The Conference or Workshop Method

The conference or workshop method involves the training group in a problem-solving or knowledge-acquisition situation in which trainees contribute ideas and make suggestions. The central concept is that participants learn from each other rather than through formal instruction. The conference leader asks questions to stimulate further discussion but seldom fully answers them alone. The subject or problem should be of interest to the group as a whole and the participants, through training and experience, should be capable of contributing to the discussion. This may be a very valuable technique when an exchange of information among individuals who have specialized knowledge and experience can be directed toward a problem of mutual interest.

The success of the conference method is often dependent upon the skill of the conference leader, as well as on the nature of the subject, the size of the group, and other related factors. The leader must be capable of stating the problem clearly, keeping the discussion moving, bringing out differences of opinion, periodically summarizing tentative conclusions, and drawing final conclusions. The main strength of this method as a training technique is that the participants learn through a process of independent discovery, whereby the individual must construct his own answers to the problem at hand rather than passively receiving them. This type of learning leads to a higher level of retention and has the additional advantage of more closely simulating the actual on-the-job process of decision making for the employee, where often he alone must draw his own conclusions. Also, many employees understand well the problems themselves and can draw out solutions to these problems from their own practical experience. The conference method is more useful than the lecture when the object is to attempt to deal with attitudes or to affect behavior patterns or to ascertain levels or degrees of knowledge or attitudes.

(c) The Case Method

Although there are many types of case methods, the case method developed at the Harvard Law School, and then at the Harvard Business School, is perhaps the most widely known. A management case is a written description of a management situation that includes one or more problems requiring analysis and decision or solution. After reading a case, trainees discuss it in a conference or workshop to identify the main issues and to suggest ways to solve them. Learning is promoted by individual participation and group discussion. In one type of case method trainees are given a case to read in advance of the meeting and they formulate ideas and solutions on their own before meeting for group discussion. In another, trainees both read and evaluate the case together at the group meeting. Both methods encourage individual initiative and discrimination in observing and solving problems. The trainer may also present trainees with a list of questions aimed at guiding their thinking along certain lines. Feedback is provided in group discussions where the trainee can compare and evaluate his views with those of the group. The case method usually stresses the factual aspects of a situation over affective ones and tends to focus on intellectual participation by the trainee rather than on more subjective and emotional involvement as do some of the newer training techniques.

The great advantage of the case method is that it forces the trainee to come to grips with the realities and complexities of an actual administrative situation and can involve him in a meaningful way. It is also a flexible technique which can be utilized equally well in many educational training situations from the fields of law and social work to business and public administration. A possible defect of this or, indeed, any method is that it may lead, at times, to superficial solutions to problems. Much depends on the question-raising capacity of the case instructor. In addition, the cases selected should accurately reflect typical and relevant situations so that the trainee can formulate useful concepts, principles, or techniques.

(d) The Syndicate Method

One form of the syndicate method as used in certain training programmes in the United States is a modification of the method developed at England's Administrative Staff College at Henley-on-Thames.[2] From one point of view, the syndicate approach is actually not a distinctive method as such but is, rather, a combination of group problem-solving exercises, discussions, lectures, and consultations combined together in a particular design.

In one type of variation used in the U.S. participants are divided into subcommittee groups and are directed to study work-related problems which have been developed with the aid of subject-matter resource consultants. At the end of the research period, each subcommittee chairman makes an oral presentation to the group as a whole and a final composite document is prepared for possible implementation. With variations, the following general format can be used:

1. The nature of the training group is defined.

2. The problem areas to be explored are selected and described in sufficient detail so as to permit a rational approach to problem solving.

3. In the first session the conference leader develops the general framework within which the problems are to be solved, the group is divided into subgroups, and a problem is assigned to each; each subgroup organizes itself and begins to work on its problem.

4. Resource consultants, expert in the specific problem areas, answer technical or procedural questions put to them by the subgroups, recommend bibliographies, suggest approaches, and attend the formal sessions at which the subgroups present their reports. At these sessions they act as critical, but helpful, advisers.

5. There is a variable period of time between the first and second sessions during which the subgroups meet, define their problems, gather data, analyze the data, develop alternate solutions, and discuss selection criteria.

6. At subsequent plenary sessions the subgroups present preliminary reports on their activities, findings, and tentative conclusions. These are critically discussed by all participants and commented upon by the resource consultants.

7. There is a second period of time during which the subgroups review what has happened at the plenary session and take whatever action is necessary to develop an acceptable final report.

8. At additional plenary sessions, the subgroups present their final reports, which are discussed and commented upon by all participants, and plans are developed regarding methods of implementing the recommendations.

The syndicate approach provides one way to integrate training and experience and to bring training exercises closer to real-life situations. In some few instances, where participants work on actual organizational problems, it may be possible to write off the cost of the training effort against the development of an operationally usable solution to an existing problem.

Experience with this modified form of the syndicate method has indicated that:

1. It is desirable to give administrators practice in the art of problem solving and decision making in a simulated, less risk-laden environment than is possible on the job itself.

2. Wherever possible, participants should be selected to participate in conference programmes so that they will be able to support one another on the job in use of the material learned in the programme.

3. In general, the syndicate programme should be tailored to fit

the needs of participants rather than the participants to the conference programme.

4. Whenever possible, conference programmes should stem from, and be tied back to, the operational needs of the participants.

5. Theory tends to become most meaningful when used to assist in developing solutions to real, operating problems; problems should be worked through to proposed solutions; alternate solutions should be considered; and critical discussion of proposed solutions is essential.

6. Solutions which are proposed should, wherever possible, be forwarded to the decision-making level in the agency, which should either return them with comments or implement them or take the lead in getting them implemented.

7. The best training results are obtained in syndicate groups when, in some important respects with regard to the problems being discussed, the groups are homogeneous.

(e) Brainstorming

Brainstorming, hardly in itself a complete or formal training method, is a management activity in which a group of persons attempt to develop an atmosphere in which they can uninhibitedly throw out ideas as to how to solve a selected problem. The participants are encouraged to hold in abeyance reality testing and to "let themselves go"; the more innovative and "way out" the ideas, the better for the operation of the technique. At this stage—the expression of ideas—criticism is not encouraged. Instead, group and individual elaboration on the ideas is invited. Each idea is recorded and later evaluated. Ideas which appear to be valid are subsequently investigated more fully.

As with any training technique, brainstorming is best used under specific circumstances. Normally, the group should be relatively small, possibly between five and fifteen participants; the subject should be fairly narrow and should lend itself to discussion and the group should be somewhat familiar with the topic. Brainstorming is based on the idea that seemingly irrational elements of thought or emotional ones may, at times, be as important as rational, intellectual elements.

Brainstorming has been advocated by some as a way of arriving at novel solutions to administrative problems as well as a method for the development of new approaches to the solving of administrative problems.

These brief comments on the lecture, conference, case, syndicate, and brainstorming methods can serve as a foundation for the principal point of focus of the chapter—the newer techniques of training which have been developed or utilized extensively in the United States. Before going on to the discussion of the newer methods, however, two points should be made: (1) The newer methods have not replaced the older techniques but, rather, supplement them and, in some cases, grow out of them. (2) One method should generally not be used to the exclusion of all others. The attempt, rather, should be made to produce a varied and integrated training programme which uses the appropriate technique in the area of its strength. For example, the lecture, case, conference, and participative methods used in a planned sequence can be quite effective depending on what particular outcome or result is desired. The subject matter to be taught, the goal to be achieved, the readiness level of the participants, the time and resources available, and the interrelations among these and other factors should determine the nature and mix of the training methods used in a given programme. In fairly precise functional areas, such as financial or personnel management, for example, the trainee might initially need to learn the precise language or vocabulary or technical terms and concepts which are employed and might require understanding of basic analytic techniques. The lecture method might be a useful vehicle to use as a first step in reaching these objectives and in providing maximum information as rapidly as possible. In conjunction with lectures, however, or at a second stage in the process, participative techniques such as the case or conference methods or some of the newer methods analyzed in the following sections of this study might, in addition, be employed to provide work experience and personal involvement in problem solving.

III. NEWER TECHNIQUES OF TRAINING MANAGERS

The predominant characteristic of the newer techniques to which we now turn is that they demand considerable and active participation on the part of the trainees in the educational process itself. With the exception of programmed instruction, they go beyond the mere attempt to provide knowledge or information, though they may admirably succeed in doing so. They attempt, in addition, to deal with attitudes and values so as to motivate trainees to want to change their behavior on the job or they may attempt to provide work-related skills which may be necessary to allow the trainee to succeed in so doing. Some of the techniques aim further than the trainee as an individual;

they may attempt to effect "organizational development" by establishing an organizational climate which will facilitate and encourage individual and group behavior change.

Many of the newer participative techniques have been influenced directly or indirectly by research in the behavioral sciences. The work of the social scientist Kurt Lewin is perhaps the best example of direct impact of this kind. Building on Lewin's concepts of learning, the participative techniques encourage the unfreezing of old norms and the establishing, in their place, and "refreezing" of new norms. To achieve this, participative techniques attempt to provide experiences which aid and permit the trainee to identify personal and individual goals and behavior patterns as well as organizational goals, and their mutual interrelationships, and methods and mechanisms of reaching these goals. The participative techniques are based on the assumption that learning which will lead to action needs to occur at the emotional and behavioral and not only the intellectual level. The individual must be able to integrate required knowledge and skills into his own pattern of behavior as well as into that of his organization or environment.

The objective of the discussion of new techniques is to present the following kinds of information: a definition or explanation of the management training technique, its goals and objectives, the assumptions upon which it is based, how it can be best utilized, its typical or desired results and effects, and some of the strengths and shortcomings which are judged to be associated with the technique as a tool of training managers.

We do not examine all of the newer participative techniques of training in the brief discussion which follows. Not included in the analysis are such important newer training methods as "instrumented learning" or the "instrumented lab," the "problem census" as a training technique, the "risk technique," and the incident process.[3] Nor is any attempt made to present a historical summary of the development or emergence of each technique or the philosophical or theoretical underpinnings from which the technique has emerged.[4]

A. *Laboratory Training*

Definition

The term "laboratory training" is widely used in a general sense to describe training that takes place under laboratory conditions away from the work situation. The basic concept of such training, the attempt to control the trainee's psychological environment by removing him from familiar organizational structures and social relationships, is adaptable to many different designs, but the one most frequently used is "sensitivity training," often referred to as the "T-group" (the "T" stands for training). Although among some trainers the terms are practically synonymous, "laboratory" can in fact be used accurately to describe both highly structured or relatively unstructured group training. In the former case, written exercises and theory input may constitute the basic group activities, with analysis and discussion based directly on the evaluation of the results of such exercises. In this chapter, however, we center our discussion on sensitivity training, the form of laboratory experience in which a small group engages in an examination of its own members and their mutual interactions.[5]

Perhaps the most significant feature of sensitivity training is its orientation to process rather than content. Through small group sessions (seldom over fifteen members) conducted over a period of time ranging from several days to several weeks, participants are given an opportunity to learn about themselves and their impact on others. The data for group discussion emerge from the behavior patterns generated within the group itself rather than from a predetermined curriculum or agenda and emphasis is placed on the "feeling level" of communication rather than upon the information or conceptual level.

In the management context, as distinguished from its use in social, church, or marital groups, sensitivity training is concerned not only with learning about the dynamics of groups and interpersonal relationships but also with the way in which managerial behavior affects both individual and group effectiveness.

There is a minimum of formal leadership, no prescribed roles, and no formal agenda. The T-group permits a maximum degree of participation by the individual, while the trainer's role during the group sessions is that of a facilitator rather than a teacher in the traditional sense. He does, though, play a very active role with other members of the staff in planning and organizing the laboratory. In the T-group itself he is often as powerful an influence as the therapist in group psychotherapy.

General sessions may also be conducted which utilize concepts from behavioral science, reports from subgroup meetings, role-playing exercises, or other devices designed to give additional meaning to the small group discussions. None of these, however, are a necessary part of sensitivity training and they may or may not be included in the laboratory design.

Major Aims

Although the general aim of sensitivity training is implicit in its definition, specific aims have varied over time as the method has developed and have assumed different emphases for a variety of target groups.

In an earlier period attention was focused on the dynamics of the group; the aim was to give members insight into such questions as how individual participation styles contributed to or hindered group progress toward its goals, which leadership acts were effective and which ineffective, etc. Much of what the individual was to learn about himself consisted of understanding how others reacted to him as a group member and the extent to which the group role he habitually played was helpful or not.

In its twenty years of development the technique has de-emphasized aims relating to group understanding and increasingly turned its attention to the person, his feelings, his style of relating to others, and his ability to achieve insight into himself by being open to what others tell him about their reactions to him. Taking their cue from existentialism and from the developing field of humanistic psychology, practitioners now aim primarily at helping trainees realize that mutual trust is the foundation of real team effort and that such trust can more effectively be established when intra-group conflict is brought out and dealt with openly. The contemporary thrust, then, is to work on each individual's capacity for being open with and trusting others, in a group context.

Design and Methodology

In recent years a major issue of design has been one that is prior to the experience itself: what type of group provides the most effective training target?

In management training there are two principal ways in which sensitivity training may be applied: functionally structured (sometimes referred to as vertically structured) "family" groups, which are usually found within one organization where people who work together train together; and horizontally or diagonally structured or "stranger" groups, the more usual type, which are groups of people who come together from different organizations and agencies, and who do not relate to each other on the job.

Vertically structured groups are part of the same hierarchical structure. For example, in a small agency with 100 to 150 employees, all the employees from the top administration to the secretarial staff may be part of T-groups. If members of the same group have reporting relationships one to another the group is often described as a "family" group, whereas if the members come from a "diagonal slice" within the organization it may be referred to as a "cousins" group.

There are a number of variations of the above-described formats of sensitivity training, usually aimed at more intensive efforts to transfer interpersonal skills which are learned in the laboratory to the world of work. One form which this effort has taken has been for a firm or agency to send a group of executives to separate T-groups, so that all will have had similar but separate experiences, and thus will be able to relate to one another on the same terms on return to their jobs.

Another approach is to bring an outside consultant into the firm or agency to hold laboratory sessions for managers of equivalent rank who do not work together. This procedure remains within the laboratory-training design in that it seeks to inculcate insights and change patterns of interpersonal behavior in a small-group setting, hopefully transferring these patterns, at a later stage, to the work setting.

Laboratory training thus encompasses the possibility of many alternative models. A design which differs from the usual non-directive interpersonal concentration of sensitivity training attempts a purposive injection of conflict into the laboratory group. Another design has been to set up confrontation with opposing groups, often within the same work organization, in an attempt to resolve conflicting beliefs, practices, or attitudes which may cause friction or loss of production.

A general methodology often encountered in sensitivity training in the United States may be described as follows:

1. Ground rules are established before the selection of the T-group, and consent is obtained from the trainees to comply with them.

2. There is no established goal, predetermined objective, or fixed curriculum structure, other than interpersonal group process learning.

3. There is no group chairman or discussion leader.

4. Within the T-group, participants are without hierarchical status and are devoid of titles or other symbols of rank.

5. A trainer is assigned to the T-group but he does not "lead," in the usual sense of the term. His function is mainly to observe, to ask questions and answer questions put to him by members of the group.

6. The duration of the T-group's existence is pre-set and may range from a weekend to a month, although two or three weeks is often a typical pattern.

7. During the training experience, there is little or no communication with persons outside the T-group, except in cases of emergency or extreme need.

The initial stages of T-group learning may often be characterized by feelings of frustration on the part of the members. This atmosphere is expected, and even intended, as a person placed in this situation may tend to become more aware of himself as an individual in a new social environment and is more likely to become engrossed in the group and in its processes of interaction. T-group members are faced with their own behavior as the major "content" with which they have to deal. Participants begin to look closely at the behavior of their fellow members, determining the kind of people they are, which ones they are attracted to, which ones repel or offend them, and the reasons for these impacts. Participants are encouraged to express themselves with great candor in their assessments of each other and of the group.

Frequently, the result of this interaction is greater group cohesion and group support. As objectivity and frankness increase there may come a point wherein the trainer assigns decision-making projects in skill sessions to the entire team. One objective may be to demonstrate to the members of the group that they have been enabled to operate as a group more effectively than previously had been the case.

A point may be reached, if the sessions continue for a sufficient length of time, wherein different T-groups are placed in competition with each other in completing assigned tasks.

Assessment of Effectiveness

Much of both the defense and criticism of sensitivity training has been subjectively derived and relatively little sound empirical evaluational research of its impact and lasting results has been carried out. The quality of the research has tended to range widely from the relatively crude to the relatively sophisticated.

Proponents of the technique have attempted with some success to establish the effectiveness of the programmes on two levels:

1. Subjective change in feeling and attitude. There is very little doubt of the power of sensitivity training to achieve this level of change. The majority of participants, after the completion of their training, feel that they have undergone emotionally moving experiences. Many of them feel that their effectiveness as managers has been improved.

2. Objective change in actual behavior. Evidence for this level of change is not only more difficult to obtain but, where it has been sought, has proven to be weak or contradictory. One recent review of the research, however, after allowing for reservations about methodological validity, concludes:

> It is reasonable to conclude that there is fairly strong evidence of lasting and effective change in individuals participating in T-Group training. . . . Significantly more changes are reported for sensitivity-trained participants than either matched-pair control group subjects or participants of other training programs comparable in length and in objectives. . . . There is a high agreement among observers in the kind and direction of change reported: improved skills in diagnosing individual and group behavior, clearer communication, greater tolerance and consideration, and greater action skill and flexibility. . . . Finally, changes noted in these studies were found to last for some time after training, though there are conflicting reports of fade-out after 10–20 months. . . .[6]

This so-called "fade-out" phenomenon, the gradual disappearance of the behavioral effects of training, is important because most research studies tend to suggest that the critical factor in the persistence of training-induced behavioral change is the climate and acceptance of the organization to which the trainee returns. The impact of the training experience may fade in time or not be fully realized unless the organizational climate is accepting of the change and receptive to its incorporation into the overall job and work context. This has led many persons who are sympathetic to the aims and methods of sensitivity training to conclude that what is needed is more attention to strategies of organizational development and to adopting various training methods and designs to fit into and relate to such strategies.

Critics of sensitivity training as an instrument of management development are inclined to stress the importance of the fade-out effect, as well as to point out that the magnitude of the behavior changes, though significant, is not very considerable. They point to a number of other objections as well:

1. There is always a possibility of psychological damage to a participant who may be emotionally unstable since T-groups tend to be anxiety-producing. Participation in laboratory or T-group training may at times prove to be the "straw that breaks the camel's back," i.e., for managers already under stress due to significant emotional or personal problems. It is for this reason that course designers emphasize that managers under personal psychotherapy for emotional disorders probably should not attend such programmes. In addition, it is of great importance to ensure that trainers be highly skilled in the dynamics of group process and fully qualified to deal with incipient emotional stress.

2. Though participants may gain valuable insights into human behavior in T-group training, the laboratory experience may not always be transferable to the managerial situation. If the training is done in vertically structured groups within the agency, there is greater likelihood of a meaningful transfer of learning from the training group to the work relationship within the agency. If new ideas and feelings are discussed and accepted by the group in the training session their impact should be reflected in the daily work contacts of the trainee. However, it is pointed out that, at times, this type of "leveling" and open encounter may conceivably impair, rather than aid, interpersonal relationships back on the job.

Members of horizontally structured groups, who are from different organizations, may be related by the roles they play in their own organizations. They have an opportunity to clarify for each other exactly what it is that each one needs, wants, desires, or fears, in his managerial role. But too seldom is the participant given adequate opportunity to relate these feelings to the actual work situation, even though coached in his role of change agent within his own organization when he gets back to the job itself.

3. There is often a lack of reliable norms for performance of the trainers or a clearly defined professional peer group to whom all trainers must answer. Fears are at times expressed that the trainers may use groups for their own neurotic needs or be simply incompetent. As one observer has said: "Too many people speak as lone individuals, without the backing and control of a professional institution. Consequently, the field of sensitivity training is being

troubled more and more by trainers who (a) are unqualified, (b) seek in this field personal satisfaction at the cost of the 'innocent' participant and (c) use sensitivity training as a banner to cover other goals and values."[7]

Cross-cultural Considerations

One European commentator has noted certain interesting differences in sensitivity training as practiced by United States and Western European trainers, arguing that the American approach is more interested in practical applications and immediate utility and applicable results. He lists the following general differences in tendencies:

1. U.S. trainers, generally speaking, tend to focus somewhat less on a thorough understanding of basic group relationships than is generally the case with European trainers. In addition, European trainers tend to be more psychoanalytically oriented than their American counterparts.

2. U.S. trainers tend to focus less on occurring authority issues and on relationships of group members with the trainer than is generally the case with European trainers, who often draw attention to the transference phenomena in groups and who may see the relationship between the trainer and the group as a mirror of the relations between the members of the group themselves.

3. American trainers, influenced by the tenets of "behavioral therapy," are often more eager to "help" group members while European trainers tend to be more restrained and refrain from making hasty instrumental interventions.

4. American trainers spend less time studying the temporary system which is the conference training program while European trainers focus heavily on the conference itself as a form of organizational behavior.

5. American trainers are more willing to use non-verbal exercises while European trainers have more reservations regarding "instrumented laboratory simulations."

6. American research in T-group training reflects a higher interest in practical outcomes of "produced changes" while European research generally reflects a higher concern with sociopsychological *process*.[8]

Such differences in training perspectives probably reflect other, more general cross-cultural differences. It would seem that, especially in cultures which have strongly drawn lines of respect for authority and clearly defined social classes, there may be some difficulty in achieving a high level of free-flowing communication between members of a T-group and equal participation in group process may be hard to effect.

This does not mean to imply that a high level of honesty and trust cannot exist among members of such a group. However, it is assumed by proponents of sensitivity training that the removal of the types of barriers to which laboratory training addresses itself would generally result in a still more effective network of interpersonal relationships and communications.

Some of the factors which have been noted as carrying over from social cultures into industrial organization are:

1. Habits of loyalty to a person, a superior, rather than to the organization.

2. Difficulty in identifying with work-group objectives.

3. Great social distance between organizational levels.

4. Traditional expectations, e.g., that an employee performs within very narrowly defined job requirements.

Such matters, in so far as they are of concern to the organization, must be accommodated to, or a decision must be made to change them. Classical or traditional training methods have not been greatly successful in modifying behavior patterns of which the above factors are examples. Laboratory training, permitting probing into deeper-seated value systems under conditions which approach total environment control, may offer a lever with which to change such behavior patterns.

While complete achievement of such goals in diverse cultures could undoubtedly lie beyond the scope of laboratory training as we have defined it, focusing, as it does, on values of honesty, truth, and authenticity in interpersonal relations, it is, however, within the conceptual limits of laboratory training methods.

It is, in part, this very potential that has tended to arouse resistance from critics of laboratory training who are not completely satisfied with either the quality of the professional expertise available and capable of doing such training or completely satisfied with the nature of the intentions and values of some of the trainers.

Furthermore, how far management should be permitted to go in "restructuring" the values of an employee is a moot question, especially in cultures wherein freedom of choice and the inviolability of the individual are held to be prime national values. For the most part, until this time, these objections to laboratory training have tended to be somewhat academic, for relatively few gross examples of malpractice have been exposed to public view. Indeed, as we have said, the research which has been done generally tends to support the positive value of laboratory training.

Nevertheless, the cross-cultural implications of laboratory training are very complex and require careful evaluation before "gross export" or "gross import" of such methods is undertaken. Laboratory training, which is truly non-directive and founded on interpersonal appreciation and honesty, may yet have its own latent structure and thus may provide pitfalls and problems in different cultural milieus.

When, however, in a given developmental situation, management problems are great, the needs imperative, and reasonable calculations indicate that the risks are minimal or acceptable, the door to fuller realization of human resources has been opened wider than ever before with the advent of this method of laboratory training for management and administration.

B. *Role-playing*

Definition

Role-playing is a training technique in which participants assume an identity other than their own to act out real or hypothetical problems in human relations and other areas. "Role-fitting" and "role-taking" are other terms sometimes used to describe this process. Though it is a technique often used within the laboratory context, it is a sufficiently independent methodology to warrant separate treatment and analysis. One of the features that makes it such a useful teaching device is that it can be employed in almost any training context, even as an adjunct to a primarily didactic design.

In playing their roles, participants undertake to act out behavior patterns they believe are characteristic of those roles in specific social situations. For example, two trainees might act out an interview, one taking the role of manager, the other of a subordinate, in which the manager is responsible for evaluating the job performance of the subordinate. Major variables in a role-play are the roles and their organizational interrelations, the role behavior, that is, the specific behavior patterns the player perceives as built into the role; the specific situation presented to the persons involved; and each participant's own personality as it infuses the role during the playing.

Major Aims

Role-playing allows a player to practice reacting to conflict and other stressful situations. Simulation of reality, in this way, eliminates many of the risks and accountability inherent in real life while retaining many other aspects of the interaction. Mistakes can be made, observed, and analyzed and alternative responses tried. In other words, role-playing permits experimentation with different ways of behaving in a given situation.

Roles can be selected which are in contrast to the real-life situations of the player so as to provide vicarious experience and widen the insight of the trainee into the real meaning and possible implication of the behavior of other persons with whom he comes in contact. The social situations which are presented to the participant playing a given role can be varied so as to exploit a wide range of reactions which the trainee may believe to be appropriate to the role.

In addition to the general insight into human interactions made possible by the activity, the trainees can be helped to modify their behavior patterns by getting feedback from others who have watched the role-play. When successful, this may open up communication channels and release some of the inhibitions which might otherwise hinder the effective resolution of conflict situations.

Design and Methodology

Role-playing can take place in almost any setting since no specific physical arrangements or special equipment are required. In fact, very simple, ordinary materials can be used to simulate a real-life situation.

Problems that are used should be relevant to the participants in the group so that motivation to learn will be generated from the members themselves. Although the development of roles and situations may take many forms, either of two approaches is generally used:

Structured Role-playing: In this type the leader selects both the situation and the roles to be enacted, and specifies the goals of the activity. This type of preplanned role-playing provides, in some cases, elaborate written materials which describe the roles and situation. In simpler cases—if, for example, the goal for the group is to study different leadership patterns—the trainer might assume the role of the leader in the role-play and orally assign the other roles.

A variation of this approach consists of having the role-playing planned in advance by members of the group itself rather than by the leader. The simulated situation is presented to the group first, followed by the enactment. The leader or group planning the exercise may determine the degree of spontaneity desired and adjust how much the players should or should not be told in advance.

Spontaneous Role-playing: This approach relies on the problem situation arising from the group discussion, without advance planning by the group or leader. In this instance, the enactment itself serves as the "briefing" to the group on the problem and situation.

Both structured and spontaneous role-playing relate to learning through (a) doing, (b) imitation, (c) observation and feedback, and (d) analysis. As is the case with the T-group, role-playing represents a form of experiential learning.

In addition to these two approaches, there are also two major orientations to role-playing. They involve focusing on either a situation-centered or a human-relations-centered problem. The two orientations are not confined to either of the two conceptual approaches but work within both a structured and an unstructured framework.

In a situation-centered problem, the roles of the actors are defined, and the situation is left open to allow the group the freedom to explore a problem. The second orientation focuses on how individuals function; therefore, the roles are left more flexible and the situation is well defined. The emphasis in both orientations and approaches is to analyze, evaluate, and suggest improvement in the interaction skills of participants.

A role-playing session begins with a preparation period during which the participants and the audience are given as much information, written or oral, as necessary to create a reality situation. Players must be given time to fix their characters in their minds and the audience is usually oriented to what they are to watch for.

The simple role-playing design calls for the enactment of the role-playing, followed by discussion. The analysis and discussion center around criticizing the character's handling and reaction to the conflict situation. The audience can be divided into listening or watching sections or can act as special observers, who are chosen in advance, to form a panel to discuss the role-playing. In addition, devices such as tape recorders and closed-circuit television can be used to refer back to key incidents during evaluation sessions which follow a role-playing scene.

The advantages of "single-group" role-playing before an audience are that the audience can observe and discuss the details of a particular action, the participants can benefit from the observers' comments as they are often unaware of the effect of their actions on others, and the observers can develop a sensitivity to the feelings of the participants. Another technique, referred to as "multiple" role-playing, divides the entire participant group into role-playing subgroups and everyone role-plays simultaneously. The advantages of this method are that it maximizes opportunities for all group members to try out new attitudes and behaviors; it provides data from each subgroup so that comparisons between subgroups are possible; and it gets all group members involved in a problem and may thus more quickly dispel feelings of shyness and self-consciousness. Following multiple role-playing, there is a discussion of mutual experiences led by the trainer.

Assessment of Effectiveness

Whatever the particular variation used, much of the effectiveness of role-playing as a training technique is dependent upon the group's initial understanding and acceptance of the concept and utility of role-playing as well as effective execution of the role-playing itself. This requires a trained leader who can control group interaction. The leader must also provide constant stimulation for the group to evaluate its behavior. He must know when to interrupt or stop the role-playing, where to ask questions, who should play a particular role, how to summarize remarks and issues brought out in the role-playing, and how to maintain a proper tempo to prevent boredom and yet still allow the analysis to be thorough. Conducting a role-playing session requires a high level of discussion leadership. The trainer needs to be able to demonstrate personally as well as to tell what and how things should be done. Finally, it is the task of the trainer to choose or advise about the situations which are to be acted out and these situations generally need to be planned anew for each new role-playing group.

Because role-playing is, in a sense, a case study in action, one way of looking at effectiveness is to compare the two. A research study which compared the particular benefits of role-playing with the case study as discrete training mechanisms concluded that each technique may provide a number of meaningfully different experiences.[9] For example, the following distinctions were suggested as representative of the kinds of training experiences which exposure to one method as compared with the other might be expected to provide:

Case Study	*Role-play*
1. Presents a problem for discussion.	1. Places a problem in a life-like setting.
2. The problem is derived from previous events.	2. The problem involves ongoing processes.
3. The problem typically involves others.	3. The problem typically involves the participants themselves.
4. Emotional and attitudinal aspects are dealt with in an intellectual frame of reference.	4. Emotional and attitudinal aspects are dealt with in a similar frame of reference.
5. Emphasizes the importance of facts.	5. Emphasizes the importance of feelings.
6. Discussion is typically from a psychological position "outside" the problem situation.	6. Participants are psychologically "inside" the problem situation.
7. Facilitates intellectual involvement.	7. Makes for emotional involvement.
8. Furnishes practice in analysis of problems.	8. Provides practice in interpersonal skills.
9. Provides for development of ideas and hypotheses.	9. Provides for testing ideas and hypotheses.
10. Trains in the exercise of judgment.	10. Trains in emotional control.
11. Defines action or solution.	11. Provides for execution of action or solution.
12. Consequences of action are usually undetermined.	12. Allows continuous feedback.

The data suggested that role-playing procedures quite effectively perform functions of examining feelings and provide opportunities for skill practice in a realistic manner. Thus, while new principles and concepts can be provided to the trainees by means of such information-giving procedures as lectures, reading, etc., role-playing of a problem can then be used to bring about the "experiencing" of the feelings involved as well as furnishing opportunities for continued skill practice. In addition, in post-play discussion of the role-playing or in the feedback period, insight can be given into the process of conceptualization of the problem-solving process.

There are, however, a number of drawbacks to the method, which may or may not be serious depending on the situation:

1. Much of its effectiveness depends on the skill of the leader, the importance of whose role has been indicated earlier. In the U.S. role-playing has become such a popular device at meetings and educational sessions of a wide variety that many groups use it without much serious planning or leadership; under these circumstances it tends to become merely a way for a group to ventilate its feelings.

2. Role-playing is time-consuming and necessarily restricts the number and complexity of problems that can be dealt with at one time.

3. Some feel that it is too artificial, resulting in little transfer of behavior change to real situations, and that the very theatricality that makes it engrossing for participants may lead them to forget the problem they are supposed to be dealing with.

4. On the other hand, if the problems used lack sufficient conflict or variety, participants may find it boring.

5. Of considerable significance is the place of spontaneity in the culture of the community or group concerned; it is much more likely to be successful if the group is accustomed to the informal, gamelike atmosphere required.

There have been efforts at improving real-life transfer by having individuals who are involved in a real-life conflict situation undertake role-playing together, often playing each other's roles. In the ideal case, there can be startling improvements in the resolution of conflict between members of subgroups in organizational settings.

In general, while criticisms can be and have been made regarding the effectiveness of role-playing as a management training technique, general opinion would tend to indicate that the advantages and positive factors associated with role-playing outweigh the negative ones, provided that the technique is properly used and directed.

C. *The Management Game*

Definition

This is a training technique in which participants, grouped into teams, consider a sequence of problems and organize themselves to make decisions. It is a form of *simulation,* which may be defined as sequential decision making structured around a hypothetical model of an organization's operations, in which participants assume roles in managing the simulated operations. Its most crucial aspect is the attempt to reproduce the sociopsychological and economic dynamics of organizational behavior in an artificial and protected setting.

Using a set of relationships built into a skeletal model of an organization, decisions which are made by the participants are processed to produce a series of hypothetical actions. The decisions and reports on their results pertain to a specific time period, which may be a day, a month, a quarter, or a year.

Most games concentrate on general management principles, such as long-range planning, decision making, and effective utilization of time, men, machines, and methods. Other games aim at teaching very specific skills and techniques, particularly those games which are built around the production, marketing, and financial functions.

There are many different management games in existence; the variety of games and the many different ways they are used indicate the flexibility of this training tool. Various industrial, governmental, and professional organizations have developed their own games and also use, at times, existing games. Management games are also used in colleges and universities and in various departments of the military.

Games can be incorporated into training courses in many ways. They can be used at the beginning of training courses as an orientation device. They can be used more than once, perhaps before and after a particular management principle or technique has been discussed. Whenever introduced for maximum effectiveness, games should be used only with a clear understanding of the objectives to be attained.

Games may be differentiated according to the level of management for which decision making is simulated. By and large, most general games are also top management games, while functional games are more likely to aim at middle management and the more specialized technique-focused games are directed to middle and junior manage-

ment levels. In some games, each team may be given freedom to decide exactly what parts of the management structure of the
organization the team should include, when such discretion is in line
with the purpose of the game.

Major Aims

The purpose of management games is to increase a person's understanding of (1) specific organizational problems; (2) the interre-
latedness of the functions and parts of an organization and its relation
to its environment; (3) the problems of organization policy and decision making; (4) the problems of working in a team.

Design and Methodology

Games may be extremely simple or complex and of considerable
depth. In some cases computations are made manually, perhaps with
the aid of desk calculators; in other cases the complexity of the model
demands the power of modern electronic computer equipment. Some
games may be played in a few hours, others span several weeks. Some
games have only a few participants; other games can accommodate
several dozen participants.

Most games, notably at the functional and specialty levels, are
designed for each participant to represent an individual decision-
making unit. In other games, group decision making is the rule. Very
often the internal organization of the group may be prescribed; even
where it is not, the instruments provided to the players may assume
a particular structure.

The number of teams in a game is largely predetermined by its
purpose. Manual games are generally restricted to a dozen teams or
less, owing to the computational problems encountered with great
numbers of teams. The maximum number of members per team depends largely on the complexity of the game and the time available
for an effective organization effort and intra-team communication in
decision making. Four to seven members is the usual size of teams
though some games have teams as large as fifteen members.

The number of decision activities in a game run should be great
enough to permit the teams to establish a working organization, to
become involved in planning and decision making, and to see the
results. Presumably, the optimal number of activities tends to vary

with the characteristics of both the individual participants and the game being played.

The time available for making decisions within each period of play during a game run is normally related to the complexity of the game. In practice, one finds in use periods ranging from a few minutes to two hours or more. In order to digest voluminous data, gain an overall perspective, and acquire a sense of the interrelationships between the whole and its parts, the average participant needs time for personal and unhurried reflection. This encourages the use of a pattern of several play periods, separated in time.

At other times, the games are played to provide quite deliberately too little time for participants to analyze the situation and to assess the information available to them before reaching the next decision. This can produce a situation of strain and tension between members of the group which not only adds to the general excitement of the session but produces what may be regarded as an approximation of the actual strain which is involved in the real world in making administrative decisions.

There is less objection to continuous play in quite simple games. There are no firm criteria on how long the period should be between decision meetings. However, even in highly complex games it is probable that teams are capable of formal decision meetings once or twice a week without strain, provided that the administrators of the game can furnish output data a day or two in advance of each session.

Post-play evaluation sessions are important and continuous review of decisions is usually a component of the game. In addition, provision may be made for periodic review sessions involving comparison with other teams as a part of the game.

Although there is a wide variety of management games, certain practices appear to be part of the operation in most of the games.

First, the game managers brief the participants about the objectives and the rules of the game. Second, the participants are grouped in teams, representing an organization. Each team is provided with starting information about the status of the organization, its competitors, and the environment. Next, the teams are required to analyze the information and to reach certain decisions within a given period of time. The decisions are recorded by the teams on special forms.

This cycle of receiving current information, making decisions, and obtaining feedback about results continues for several time periods. At the end of the game an overall critique session is usually held, in which the teams and the game administrators discuss the performances.

Assessment of Effectiveness

Despite their increased utilization, there is a considerable amount of discussion and debate regarding the specific merits and shortcomings of management simulation as a training device for managers. Since most of the support for management simulation is impressionistic, consisting primarily of intuitive judgments based on personal experience, its proponents as well as its opponents are generally dissatisfied with the existing empirical evidence. Surprisingly little empirical research has been undertaken to determine the educational value of this new approach to management training. The task of testing the educational value of games is indeed difficult and there have been relatively few controlled experiments that really get to the heart of the matter.

The principal criterion used to evaluate games has been player reaction, which has been generally enthusiastic. One U.S. corporation's Business Simulator was given a rating of 4.88 out of a possible 5 by participants who used it in a training session. A game played at a large university was scored 8.66 out of a possible 10 by the participants, one third of whom called it the most valuable educational experience they had ever had. Many persons have suggested that, while the educational and research potentials of management games have as yet been only superficially explored, participant enthusiasm and preliminary observations as to the capabilities of simulation exercises are sufficiently strong to warrant further applications and analyses.

Somewhat more substantial evidence comes from experiments which devise laboratory tests to measure both cognitive and attitudinal learning in management games. Results generally are positive in terms of the increase in the participants' understanding of organizational policies and their awareness of how their actions contribute to agency efficiency.

In the absence of large-scale empirical evidence, one can only examine the theoretical claims made for gaming and the reservations suggested by some observer-critics. A number of arguments in favor of the use of management games as a training device have been advanced. The first is involvement; all trainees participate, not just the motivated or especially bright ones. A second is practice; the opportunity to make mistakes is afforded and, in doing so, also the opportunity to lose the fear of making mistakes. A third factor is the exchange of ideas; games provide an opportunity to compare one's own action with those of others, usually peers, who are faced with the same problems, at the same time and under the same circumstances. A fourth argument is that games provide "learning through exposition," i.e., the manager must defend his own point of view and explain his position. This may help stimulate careful thought processes which are vital to effective learning. A fifth factor is that of "instant experience." By tackling a series of situations that would normally be encountered over a longer period of time, the participant may gain greater awareness of cause-and-effect relationships. A sixth consideration is that games may provide executives, who may have become overly concerned with their own spheres of management, with a new perspective on overall organization operations as they observe the interaction of men, money, and materials. A final argument is "decision replay." The players can return to a previous point in the game, proceed with an entirely new set of decisions, and see how the outcome is altered.

There is little question about these potential benefits of gaming, in theory. A more modest assessment of practical outcomes appears to include the following:

1. General management games probably do not teach anything very specific about the management of a specific organization. However, they may serve to demonstrate some very broad facts of organizational life such as that all areas of an enterprise are interrelated, or that they have to be co-ordinated, or that each of them is important.

2. Experienced executives probably learn little that is absolutely new to them from gaming, although the experience may affect some of their long-held attitudes. Gaming may, for example, make a functional executive more tolerant of his coworkers in other departments and more aware of their problems.

3. The emotional impact of gaming probably does make it a suitable technique for changing attitudes, provided the game situation is sufficiently clearcut to pinpoint what attitudes to be changed are involved.

4. Although gaming can hardly be said to teach organizational decision making per se, it does provide experience in learning from experience, particularly in the application of statistical and analytical methods.

5. Games undoubtedly do provoke interest, which may lead the participant to additional reading and study. They do seem to give some sort of "feel" for organizational problems.[10]

Serious criticisms of the management game generally, aside from such questions as its higher cost in both money and personnel and the requirement, in some cases, of such special (generally not available) equipment as computers, focus on three issues. One is that some of the very things that make gaming engrossing and exciting may diminish their lasting educational effectiveness. The competitive aspects of a management game, for example, may arouse motivation and may help sustain effort. But they may also detract from long-term learning by leading participants to play "conservative" strategies instead of experimenting with new approaches, by teaching participants to emphasize short-term advantages within the game context instead of building and trying to achieve long-term strategic plans, and by introducing anxieties about relative performances which may interfere with efforts to learn.

Further, the involvement and excitement of the game raise a central problem inherent in all simulation processes: the tendency for participants to attempt to "win the game" by approaching the task as *only* a game, rather than as a realistic organizational business situation. If the model underlying the game does not include the necessary attributes of reality, the training in the simulated environment is less likely to be successfully transferred to real-life organizational behavior. Although most games are based on simplified models of reality, the degrees to which they represent the actual processes of organizations vary considerably.

Participation in management games often tends to be a pleasant experience; thus there is a tendency to devote too much time to play and not enough to a careful analysis and critique of the games' results. Many game administrators emphasize that games should be used in conjunction with more conventional teaching devices. Lectures, discussion sessions, and other techniques can alert the game player to the artificiality of the assumptions in the model and help him to discriminate wisely between what can and cannot safely be applied to real-life situations.

A second major focus of criticism is on the way in which teams are often organized. Keeping groups together simply because they have worked together before does not necessarily enhance what they get from the experience. Organizing them so that they are homogeneous in ability or prior performance may also prove to have drawbacks. On the other hand, it may be detrimental to both satisfaction and performance to have teams which reflect obvious differences in potential compete against one another.

Third, some critics point out that many management games involve only quantitative variables and ignore human elements of organization; they question how such games can truly provide a realistic training ground for management. They tend to applaud, consequently, those games in which group processes and the dynamics of one of the teams are considered by the other team or by the team itself. This represents one method by which management games can be used to study intergroup and decision-making problems on the psychological dimension.

One such refinement involves the use of videotape techniques. Discussions of teams can be recorded and then played back after the end of the game in order to analyze what has taken place in making their decisions. One obvious advantage of videotape is that human behavior can be captured live and can be presented as factual data to be observed and even measured, encouraging participants to become aware of subtleties in their interactions and to reflect upon the way in which they have worked together.[11]

In sum, management games appear to be a valuable training device in emphasizing the importance of long-range planning as well as the need to operate on the basis of established policies rather than expediency. Most games are planned so that opportunism brings only temporary advantages; the real payoffs accrue to those organizations which devise an effective long-range plan and adhere to it with only minor modifications. The players are encouraged to be concerned not with one functional problem but with the agency's overall strategy.

D. *The In-Basket Technique*

Definition

The in-basket is a simulation of a manager's work load on a typical day, developed originally as a possible measure of aptitude for the administrative components of the managerial role. The name is derived from the baskets (originally wire) for mail and memoranda that formerly were seen on almost every manager's desk, marked "in" and "out." It is a form of individual rather than group simulation, each player working by himself in the exercise itself.

Major Aims

As a diagnostic tool, the exercise provides information on how a participant, under some pressure, handles a sequence of problems in a given situation, and thus provides some measure of his potential or his competency. As a training device, it can be used to help the trainee identify areas in planning, organizing, and administrative behavior in which his skills need to be improved, as well as an opportunity to practice those skills in a situation in which he can obtain feedback on his performance.

Design and Methodology

The underlying idea of the in-basket technique is that a person is required to assume the role of a fictitious executive or supervisor in a hypothetical situation. In the actual exercise, the participant is presented with background materials so that he may become familiar with the organizational situation. These may include such items as organizational charts, job descriptions, formal position papers, and informal items such as descriptions of the personalities and performance of other characters in the test situation. Though they may vary in nature and content, they share the common purpose of increasing the reality of the hypothetical situation for the participant by placing the tasks which he is to perform in context.

Once a player is familiar with the situation, the exercise itself is begun. Each player is presented with a group of letters, reports, notes, and related items which have presumably accumulated in the in-basket of the hypothetical manager. He is then asked to take any actions he deems appropriate with the in-basket items within a limited time period.

Unlike some other types of exercises in which a participant merely tells what he would do, the in-basket player must actually do it. This means that he must write all his notes and memoranda, write out his conversations with others, and put down the contents of his simulated telephone calls on paper. Thus, at the end of the exercise there is a written record of every action which each participant has taken.

An important dimension of the in-basket experience is time pressure. The situation in which each participant is placed contains a time period during which all available work must be accomplished. At the end of that time period, for example, the participant may be scheduled as part of the exercise to attend a crucial meeting or conference at which at least some of the items in his in-basket will be discussed. In order to be prepared for this conference, the participant is literally forced to scan many different items calling for different actions and to deal with them by (1) setting priorities and (2) delegating certain items to his subordinates for handling.

The in-basket game also includes a procedure which allows players to explain and justify their actions. The player's actions are either (1) scored in some manner or (2) reviewed with him by an instructor or by a group of his fellow players, or both.

Assessment of Effectiveness

The key to the in-basket's effectiveness as a training device is the fact that it is rooted in real-life situations. If the selected situation is similar to one in which the participant actually has functioned or expects to function, and if in addition it is constructed so as to call adequately for use of the participant's decision-making and problem-solving abilities, his behavior in the game may be more natural than in some other types of training techniques.

One of the advantages of the in-basket game is that it can be designed either to focus on the activities that are part of all executive positions or to emphasize certain specific aspects of performance. For instance, if the objective is to develop or improve human relations skills, the in-basket material can be weighted heavily with interpersonal conflicts, other responsibilities being held to a minimum. The in-basket can also be adapted to the level of the position for which training is required. If first-line supervisors are participating, the problems can be constructed to emphasize such factors as providing staff services, supervising work, and technical aspects of production. If it is desired to train higher-level executives, the problems may be related to activities such as long-range planning, diversification, and decentralization.

Like any other training technique, the in-basket method has certain shortcomings. It is handicapped by the fact that it is difficult to score or measure its effects. Further, since the in-basket is a form of role-playing, it may become unrealistic, no matter how "realistic" the situational setting is made. This may stem from the fact that the in-basket is essentially an individual and non-interactive device. Although each participant plays the "game," he plays it by himself, with his own materials. Except for the post-game review period, there is little opportunity for interaction between participants. The trainee who participates in the in-basket exercise is not constrained by other people's behavior in a dynamic fashion. Decisions are made during the in-basket exercise without the advantage of consultation. The in-basket exercise thus provides little training for "team management" responsibilities.

The effectiveness of the technique, in summary, clearly depends on the adequacy of the materials developed for the particular in-basket exercise. They should demand a realistic and representative sample of managerial performance across a broad variety of relevant tasks. To avoid superficiality, the in-basket must be carefully planned and carefully guided by the training director. In contrast with the more complete simulation games, however, the in-basket should not be used as the sole training method in any given programme, but only in concert with other management training techniques.

E. *Programmed Instruction*

Definition

Programmed instruction has enjoyed a great growth in popularity over the past decade in the United States, and many of the largest corporations and agencies now employ it in their training programmes. Although there are numerous types, the technique may be defined generally as any learning design that has the following characteristics:

1. Each participant works individually on the programmed instruction materials at his own pace.

2. A relatively small unit of information is presented to the participant at a time. A statement to be completed, or a question to be answered, about this information is also included. This is known technically as the stimulus.

3. The participant is required to complete the statement or answer the question about that specific bit of information. He is said to be making a response to the stimulus.

4. The participant is then immediately informed whether or not his response is correct. If it is wrong, he may also be told why. By this kind of feedback, he is rewarded if he gives the correct answer; his response is reinforced.

5. The participant is next presented with the second unit of information, and the cycle of presentation-answer-feedback, or more tech-

nically, stimulus-response, reinforcement of the correct answer is repeated. The same cycle is repeated again and again as all of the necessary information is presented in a logical sequence.

Major Aims

Programmed instruction is designed to increase the precision, effectiveness, and economy of the learning process, where learning involves the acquisition of a definable and organizable body of knowledge or cognitive skills by individualizing learning to the point where participants can proceed at their own pace.

Design and Methodology

In general, while other training techniques such as sensitivity training can be regarded as "open systems" in the sense of allowing for a large variety of possible outcomes, programmed instruction can be viewed as a "closed system" in which the possible outcomes are finite and largely predetermined.

The programme may be of several physical forms. It may be a textbook; it may be in the form of tapes or strips of paper; it may be auditory material to be used with a tape recorder. It usually consists of a series of items, referred to as frames. A frame is a unit of the programme that requires a response from the participant; the material in the frame builds cumulatively into the final programme.

A typical programmed textbook is composed of two types of pages: the information-question page and, immediately following, the answer and discussion page. Typically, the information page contains: (a) some of the data, information, concepts, etc., to be taught; (b) a problem or question, usually in the form of a sentence, with one or more blanks or deleted items; and (c) space for the participant to record his response. After he does this, he turns to the answer page to read the correct response; as soon as he has compared it with what he has written, he proceeds to the next information-question page, and so on throughout the book.

Assessment of Effectiveness

Programmed instruction is flexible and simple to use. It can provide a relatively rapid mastery of subject matter. Proponents of this technique assert that programmed instruction provides a mastery of subject matter which compares favorably with the results of other methods of instruction and increases the speed of learning. Though still in an imperfect stage of development, it has been estimated that programmed instruction can reduce learning time significantly from that consumed in traditional methods of instruction. Some evaluation of the results of this learning, in addition, has tended to reveal major improvements in skill mastery and comprehension.

By using programmed instruction over a long-range period, training costs for certain specific purposes can be reduced and its results more accurately measured than if no programmed instruction is used. To evaluate effectiveness, a programme can be subjected to rigorous tests on a variety of sample populations. The cost of a programme is explicit and can be averaged or amortized like any other cost. This is so because conventional techniques can train only a limited number of persons at any given time. The operating cost and overhead of instruction are consequently very high per worker, especially if many different specialists need to be used. Programmed instruction can dramatically reduce these per-trainee costs, but the initial capital costs can be very high, especially for programmes intended to serve only a small group of trainees, or if very specialized equipment is used in the programme.

Programmed instruction is uniquely self-controlled, requiring a minimum of trained teachers and classrooms or any special considerations regarding time or place. Indeed, it can be especially effective if there is a shortage of effective instructors and trainers.

The technique also overcomes the geographical separation of trainees. Managers who are spread out in separate divisions of an agency do not have to be transported and maintained at organization expense in a central training center. Programmes can be mailed to the trainees and they may proceed at their own rate. Programmed instruction adjusts to individual differences in ability, formal education, and job categories.

These are very considerable advantages, and especially in the field of technical subject matter, where many programme materials already exist, the costs can be minimized for the benefits obtained. Programmes designed for higher managerial levels, however, are not as numerous. One reason for this is that programmed instruction tends to be most efficient for teaching technical subject matter, such as facts and procedures. It is far less useful for shaping attitudes or value systems, and since many higher-level managerial activities do not rely primarily upon knowledge of specific technical information, programmed instruction may be of somewhat more limited use in formal training programmes at these levels.

A possible source of weakness is the absence of a live teacher, with the trainee left largely to his own resourcefulness and motivation level. Programmed instruction depends on intrinsic motivation of one kind or another. The vast majority of the programmes appear to rely upon the satisfaction which trainees tend to feel in having "correctly" answered the questions presented to them. Failing that type of motivation, however, or some other at least equally powerful, the man-machine interaction will not occur, and learning will not proceed. American schools are increasingly providing for a teacher to be present while a group of students are at work at programmes.

The quality of learning which is obtained through programmed instruction is still a matter of controversy. Certain critics maintain that the acquired learning may be "shallow" or merely "mechanical" memorization. Proponents deny this and insist that a properly programmed course can achieve results as good as or better than can a lecture course given by a live instructor. There are those who view programmed instruction as being "one-dimensional" and lacking in the roundedness and insight which many believe can only result from face-to-face interaction with living people. There are others for whom the potential uses of programmed instruction are virtually unlimited.

The research which has been attempted is not very helpful in resolving these differences of opinion. Although a significant amount of empirical study of programmed instruction has been undertaken, most of it leaves much to be desired for several reasons. The methodology and controls of most studies are often of inferior quality and their results must be assessed accordingly. Very little of the research, moreover, has attempted to measure the specific utility of programmed instruction in management development.

Studies in groups of engineers attempting to compare the effectiveness of programmed instruction with conventional classroom techniques have shown that programmed instruction reduces the time needed for presenting subject matter, and on comprehensive tests of material covered, a programmed instruction group might demonstrate a learning gain of up to 10 per cent.

Other research findings have indicated that the use of programmed instruction may have the effect of increasing the motivation of trainees to apply the results of their learnings.

We conclude that, while programmed instruction is a relatively new

technique for training managers and while construction of new programmes is necessarily a slow and difficult process, the prospects and
horizons of effective management training by the use of this method
are widening rapidly and exhibit many positive potentialities.

F. *The Kepner-Tregoe Problem Solving Program*

Definition

A widely used proprietary management development training programme is the system developed by two U.S. social scientists, Charles
H. Kepner and Benjamin B. Tregoe. They became interested in how
people use information in a highly automatic data-processing system
while they were doing advanced systems research at the RAND Corporation. This interest led them to study the effects of automation and
the steps in decision making. Their studies convinced them that there
were principles underlying decision making and that techniques could
be developed to apply these principles to the improvement of the
process.

Kepner-Tregoe programmes view managerial situations as problems which are subject, in part at least, to rational, objective solution.
They offer basic courses oriented toward the problems of different
groups in typical large enterprises. Their firm does not insist that their
own programme leaders conduct the training sessions but will make
provisions for training course leaders who can then conduct K-T
training inside their own organizations. The managerial courses are
conducted over a period of five consecutive days, at a centralized facility. The general outline of the K-T programmes involves a tripartite
training method which is developed in class seminars:

1. Preliminary study of concepts basic to problem solving. The
specific training techniques used in this are lectures, discussions,
audio-visual, and case-study methods.

2. Intensive practice of the concepts and procedures in a simulated
business situation. Here the training techniques are similar to the
management game, the in-basket, and role-playing.

3. Feedback sessions in which the participants and the course
leader discuss the actions and decisions made in dealing with the
problem material in a free interchange, with the assistance of tape
recordings of the actual conversations of the members during their
conferences.

In one of the simulations designed by this firm, fifteen or more managers are assigned to a simulated organization, which is made up of two divisions of a medium-sized company. Its plan of organization incorporates both line and staff functions. The manager-trainees receive background information on the simulated company and ground rules covering each session. They also receive study materials which provide the concepts and procedures which will be used during the experience of problem analysis and decision making. Managers meet both as a whole group and in separate subgroups of four or five participants throughout the five days of the training.

Major Aims

The aim of the one-week training session is the re-education of the problem-analysis and decision-making activities of managers so that they will perform more efficiently when they return to their jobs. Since major tangible and visible changes in the behavior of managers are unlikely to be accomplished in one week, Kepner-Tregoe offers a six-month management development programme as a follow-up.

The programme is very much anchored to a systematic approach to problem solving, decision making, and the identification and analysis of potential problems. It is not designed to develop leadership skills or to change leadership styles, nor does it attempt to improve interpersonal skills or understanding. A deliberate attempt is made to avoid the subjectivity inherent in the introspective analyses of interpersonal relations employed in sensitivity training and its ideological descendants. The focus is on the problem, not on the problem solver, and even less on superior, subordinate, or peer groups.

Specific Design and Methodology

Training sessions are usually held in a residential facility where managers live, eat, and work together from Sunday evening through the following Friday afternoon. Daily sessions start at 8:30 A.M. and run through 5:00 P.M. or so, with an hour for lunch. Evenings are devoted to the study of the materials on the concepts and procedures, and to work on those problem assignments that are to be done individually and reported on the next day.

Before each session, managers and the course leader discuss the concepts and techniques involved and the managers receive exercise materials setting out what has happened in the simulated company recently in connection with some problem. The materials include memoranda from within their own department, from other departments, and from outside the company, as well as policy directives, requests for information, financial statements, production and sales records, and other such information. The material varies for each of the management positions assumed by the participants during the week. Each of the members of the four- or five-man team is assigned to a different functional position each day. These positions include general manager, production manager, sales manager, distribution manager, financial manager, and industrial relations manager.

The managers read through the material, organize the information, take notes, or perform as they normally do in a real-life situation. Using the rooms of the residential facility as "offices," the managers begin the task of managing the company by communicating, coordinating activities, and making decisions. Since they have only about an hour and a half to analyze the problem and make a decision, managers work under great time pressure. This means they must coordinate their activities and communicate as effectively as they can. In the controlled situation, the major causes of the problem can be determined, provided that the information has been used accurately and objectively. Direct feedback as to how the managers have worked on the problem together is provided by a tape recording which registers the actual conversation of the managers during their conferences.

Feedback takes place in group sessions following each assignment. At this time the course leader explores with each team the procedures and reasoning they have used in dealing with the problem, and managers examine their own performance and that of the whole management team.

Almost half of the course time is spent in using the concepts taught on real-life problems and concerns of the participants. Managers in the group attack their unsolved problems and decision situations and resolve them in so far as possible, given the information available. They are thus using the ideas on the job before they leave the course.

Assessment of Effectiveness

Certain critics of the rational approach suggest that the problems which are dealt with tend to have a particular character, i.e., they are problems which most often have an accepted solution or are "puzzles" which tend to have unexpected or surprising answers. Less emphasized are other types of decision-making issues which often bedevil management especially at higher levels, wherein (1) there may be no correct "answers," (2) data are partial or largely unavailable, or (3) complex values must be reconciled.

Kepner-Tregoe's rational approach to problem solving is not designed to take into account an organization's largely unconscious, intuitive, emotional, and unplanned elements which, as experience shows, can usually withstand most assaults by strict logic. These nonrational and irrational elements are found, of course, not only in organizations but also in the individuals who manage the organizations. There is more involved in decision making than the manager's ability to think through problems logically and systematically. The manager needs judgment to make effective decisions. This capacity is itself a mixture of experience and values which may, on occasion, dictate courses of action that should not derive solely from strictly logical reasoning. A decision made by a manager, especially one made by a high-level executive, depends both on the relative weight that is given to factual and value objectives and on judgment as to the extent to which any given course of action will attain each objective.

Whatever the merit of the above reservation, there would tend to be general agreement that Kepner-Tregoe's exclusion of the improvement of interpersonal relationships or change in the manager's values as objectives of the programme provides at least two advantages over some other training programmes. The first is that their programmes avoid some of the risks that other training programmes, e.g., laboratory training, assume when dealing with such highly charged subjects as individual and group behavior in an anxiety-producing climate. The second advantage, which is closely related to the first, is that, in an evaluation of the Kepner-Tregoe programme, results may be more visible than the results in evaluations of other programmes, because it works at more tangible aspects of the managerial role.

G. *The Managerial Grid*

Definition

Managerial Grid[12] training represents an approach to management development that goes beyond the training of individual executives and concentrates, as well, on the organizational context of which they are a part. Developed by two American behavorial scientists, Robert R. Blake and Jane S. Mouton, this comprehensive programme was one of the first in the field now referred to as organization development. This approach incorporates the training of managers into the larger goal of increasing the operational effectiveness of a total organization. The Managerial Grid Seminar is Phase 1 of a six-phase programme and is one of a number of seminars developed and conducted by this firm on a proprietary basis. It has been used by large numbers of corporations both in the United States and abroad for the training of their managers.

The Grid organization development approach is based on the assumption that a manager's purpose is to provide a climate which develops and maintains high degrees of performance, stimulates creativity, and fosters innovation. Within an organizational climate which is conducive to effectiveness, the manager and his subordinates operate on a basis of high concerns both for production and for people. The manner in which the two dimensions—concern for *production* and concern for *people*—are linked together by a manager determines his managerial style.

Diagrammatically, in Figure 1, concern for production is represented along the horizontal axis, and concern for people up the vertical axis. Grid styles are combinations of particular degrees of these two concerns. The five styles, whose underlying assumptions are summarized in Figure 1, are briefly described in a subsequent section (p. 72).

Grid Seminars are conducted either for groups of "strangers" from different organizations or for "family groups," e.g., administrators at various levels within one organization. Those who attend a Grid Seminar from a single organization are normally selected from a truncated diagonal slice of the organization, so that immediate superiors and subordinates are not included.

Major Aims

The objectives of a Grid Seminar include: learning different styles of leadership; testing the problem-solving results of each style; finding out more about personal styles of the participants; pinpointing causes of communication breakdown within their organizations; considering ways of dealing effectively with conflict and disagreement; acquiring the skill of learning from experience; and developing action plans to apply back on the job immediately after the seminar.

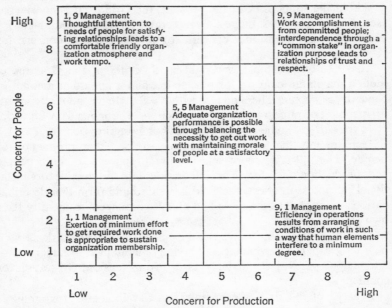

Figure 1   The Managerial Grid

From Robert R. Blake and Jane S. Mouton, *The Managerial Grid.* Houston: Gulf Publishing Company, 1964, p. 10.

Design and Methodology

Phase 1 of the Grid approach to organization development is a one-week seminar in which participants learn the concepts of the Managerial Grid. In practice, however, this phase may represent both the initial and final exposure to the Grid for those managers whose organizations do not make use of the complete six-phase development programme.

A Grid trainee is given thirty hours of pre-work self-study assignments and reading materials. The seminar week itself encompasses seventy-two hours, typically starting on a Sunday afternoon and ending at noon on the following Friday. In the seminars participants attempt to solve managerial problems, and the behavior of both individuals and the team of which they are a part is assessed and evaluated. Participants also evaluate their own behavior and try to identify and employ alternative techniques of problem solving.

Within the framework of the seminar, the Grid itself is considered (see Figure 1). This defines five theories of managerial behavior based on two dimensions: concern for production and concern for people.

The 9,1 style in the lower right-hand corner of the Grid represents a maximum concern for production and a minimum amount of concern for people. The manager with a 1,9 style has a great concern for people but almost none for production. The manager with a 5,5 style tries to get some production without upsetting people. The 1,1 style represents the least possible concern for either production or people. The 9,9 style represents maximum concern for both people and production and for their integration into productive organizational purposes. In effect, the Grid is a shorthand form that describes various management practices and enables managers to identify their own styles.

A third dimension, which can be added to the Grid, deals with how long a particular managerial style is maintained in situations of interaction, particularly under pressure from tension, frustration, or conflict.

Phase 2 of the six-phase organization development programme is concerned with teamwork development. The purpose of Phase 2 is to assist managerial personnel in applying to team operation what they have learned in Phase 1. Teamwork development begins with key executives at the top of the organization and works down. Each superior and his subordinates define factors which may be hindering their effectiveness and plan ways to overcome them. Teams agree on ground rules for operations and learn to use critique to improve communication, controls, and problem solving. They set standards and goals as the basis for management by objectives both for team participants individually and for the teams as a whole. For a programme of this kind to be fully effective, it should move on from Phases 1 and 2 (which fall within the category of "executive education") to Phases 3 through 6, which invoke interfunctional and interlevel co-operation in studying real problems of the actual organization.

Assessment of Effectiveness

Where organizations limit their Managerial Grid experience to Phase 1 only, it is doubtful whether a supportive climate can be fully established in the organization. Team and intergroup development, as represented by Phases 2 and 3 respectively, provide the opportunity for concerted effort toward a greater emphasis on the integration of task and people concerns. Yet the six-phase programme may extend over several years, and smaller organizations may find it difficult to afford the time and/or the costs of a total programme. The six-phase programme, however, has been found equally applicable to small and large organizations and has been found to be practical in countries of varying degrees of industrial development.

There are those who argue that there may be certain difficulties in Phase 1. They cite the above-mentioned fact that it may be quite time-consuming and not inexpensive. Furthermore, the advantages of including a "diagonal slice" of the organization in the seminars may be offset by a corresponding disadvantage in the fact that a substantial number of key management people may be taken away from their jobs simultaneously. However, the question of time and cost is relative and a difficult one to assess, at best. Costs for an interagency programme tend to be less than for an intra-agency seminar. Furthermore, because of the truncated diagonal slice method of selecting Grid Seminar participants, the few who are removed from the organization for off-the-job training represent a wide variety of operations and, as a consequence, the effect of their absence from the job may be minimized.

A fundamental characteristic of the Grid programme is that it is dependent upon a specific conceptual framework and the assumptions upon which it is based. The Grid programme posits that there is one most effective managerial style (9,9) toward which administrators should aim, and a second best or "backup" style, usually 9,1 or 5,5, which should be employed when for some reason one cannot make use of 9,9. This makes the Grid technique less "open-ended" than other management training techniques since in the Grid programme both the preferred outcomes and the means of achieving them are specified by the technique itself.

Supporters of the method argue that the fundamental strength of the Grid approach to organization development lies precisely in the fact that it has a specific conceptual framework as a basis. This framework, they assert, has been tested through translation into many languages, used throughout the world, and found to be useful in varying degrees despite language barriers and cultural differences.

It can be concluded that the concept of the Managerial Grid and the Grid approach, in general, have made significant contributions to managerial and organization development—a concept we will examine in a future section of this chapter.

V. ANALYSIS OF THE NEWER MANAGEMENT TRAINING TECHNIQUES: GENERAL SIMILARITIES AND DIFFERENCES

There are fundamental similarities as well as marked differences among the management training techniques which have been described. The differences among them seem to be most apparent, since they tend to be differences of focus, approach, structure, and operation. However, at a somewhat higher level of abstraction, the various management training techniques and programmes appear to have some fundamental objectives in common. There is also a strong similarity in the basic assumptions and value predispositions which underlie these techniques and programmes.

The newer management training techniques have as their objective to impart information, of course, but their particular goal (except for programmed instruction) is to change attitudes and/or behavior. More specifically, they seek to change some aspect of the administrator's conception of himself or his role. They all, to varying degrees, attempt to teach or train the administrator to broaden his focus, to concern himself with the total system rather than with single components, and to orient himself toward the future.

These techniques and programmes seem to be based on a view of human nature in which man tends to be perceived of as inherently "good" and infinitely perfectible.

Related to this view is a set of assumptions about interpersonal relationships which these management training techniques and programmes seem to hold in common. These assumptions are that man, most often, is positively motivated toward others and is predisposed to co-operate.[13] A corollary to the assumption of altruism is that interpersonal harmony is normally the preferred condition of interpersonal relations, and that disharmonies among individuals and groups can be remedied consciously. These general assumptions underlie various training techniques providing specific conditions are appropriate. Thus, sensitivity training assumes that man can be most perfectible under a given set of conditions and values. Under other conditions, he will tend to act in ways that conditions require or coerce or elicit. For this reason sensitivity training is identified with a "laboratory approach," for it creates a specific social order which elicits generally consistent behavior patterns.

These training techniques and programmes also share, at some levels, a common model of the learning process and a common model of attitude and behavior change. Those who created and developed the various training techniques and programmes appear to assume that learning capabilities, as well as motivation levels, tend to be generally similar among those in their target audiences and that exposure to the appropriate stimuli is likely to have significant and desirable results. Since it is assumed that certain personal and organizational behavior patterns are generally valued, it is also assumed that guided exposure to the "proper" modus operandi is likely to produce managers who accept and use the valued attitudes and behavior patterns. In other words, a direct cause-and-effect relationship in shaping managerial behavior seems, at times, to be posited.

Finally, the management training techniques and processes seem to share a common model of complex organizations and the social processes which occur within them. Many of these techniques focus on the formal, hierarchical role relationships within the organization and acknowledge the importance of the informal infrastructure of personal relationships and the centrality of the management function as a determinant of the organizational style.

That there are similarities in the fundamental assumptions which underlie the various management training techniques is not at all surprising since they have their origins in a common intellectual tradition. This tradition, that of modern behavioral sciences, draws upon concepts and models from anthropology, sociology, economics, and various branches of psychology. To these are added propositions and hypotheses from such hybrid fields as public administration, business administration, group dynamics, operations research, and mathematics. It is important to note that many of these disciplines which attempt to treat human behavior in a "scientific" or at least a systematic manner are still in relatively early stages of development. Many propositions and hypotheses have yet to be empirically verified. Consequently, many of these propositions about human behavior, of which management training techniques and programmes are an "applied form," are still in the realm of assumptions. Understandably, too, the assumptions reflect the cultural biases and dominant value orientations of the social scientists who were instrumental in their conception and development and of the culture in which they were developed.

Figures 2A and 2B attempt to summarize the chronological and intellectual evolution of trends in the development of the behavioral sciences from which the newer management training techniques and programmes emerged.

Figure 2A shows the coalescence of various intellectual and developmental phenomena from which a non-coercive communications concept of social control emerged. Contemporary management training techniques and programmes in turn seem to have developed from approaches to structuring human activity based upon such a concept of command and control.

The intellectual and developmental phenomena depicted in Figure 2A have roots in much earlier history and, in fact, could be traced backward almost indefinitely in the chronology of world culture. Nevertheless, one can somewhat arbitrarily fix the beginning of the dominant influences which altered the concept of managerial command and control in organized human enterprises at the point at which the industrial revolution in Western Europe was consolidated. Noting such gross categories as social, economic, and political theories of the eighteenth and nineteenth centuries does not mean that all theories in these categories contributed to a communications concept of social control.[14] There were intellectual strands within each of these categories that did not contribute to such a concept but rather reinforced authoritarian control concepts and mechanisms. The labels "liberal," "conservative," "equalitarian," and "elitist" are often applied to economic, social, and political theories. The theories labeled "liberal" and "equalitarian" are those which seem to be related to the evolution of a non-coercive concept of social control.

Philosophical propositions relating to the nature of man, thought, and knowledge also contributed to the development of a communications concept of command and control. Psychological theories about human needs and behavior based on the studies of a wide variety of psychological schools were also an important component of the intellectual base of management training techniques. In addition, technological change, the increased specialization of function, and the accompanying trends toward professionalization of managerial functions contributed to the development of a non-coercive concept of social control.

The definition of a non-coercive concept of command and control is the central point in the development of the new management train-

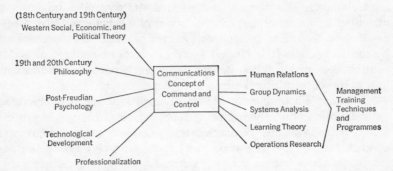

Figure 2A Intellectual evolution of management training techniques and programmes

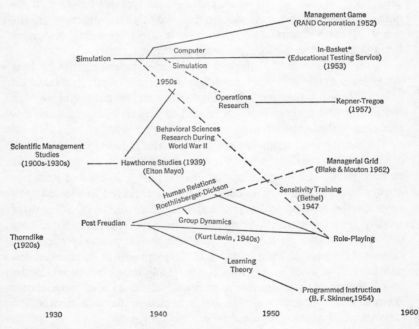

*The British Civil Service was using similar methods (e.g., "in-tray") in the 1940s.

Figure 2B Chronology of management training techniques and programmes

ing techniques. This concept of command and control is the opposite of authoritarian, externally imposed control mechanisms. It is predicated upon the use of control mechanisms generated and internalized by the individual. It is termed a communications concept of social control because it relies heavily on maximizing communications flow as one of its principal means of implementation.

The views about human behavior which have been enumerated as assumptions underlying management training techniques are directly related to this communications concept of command and control. Indeed, it is this concept of control which links similar assumptions about human behavior derived from various disciplines.

The communications concept of social control, in turn, affected various social science disciplines and approaches and resulted in the generation of others. Development of management training techniques represents the next step in the evolutionary process, the attempt of these disciplines to incorporate their operating principles into the management of complex organizations.

Figure 2B shows the chronological development of the various management training techniques in greater detail. In effect, it takes up where Figure 2A leaves off. It indicates how the management training techniques and programmes are related to various disciplines and approaches in the social sciences.

The names in parentheses are those of the individuals, groups, or organizations who are credited with development of a particular management training technique or programme. Those listed were not always the only individuals and institutions involved in the development of the various techniques but rather are those who are most usually associated with a particular technique. The dates listed also do not imply that all the techniques emerged at precisely one point or that they were at similar stages of development at their initial appearance. The dates on Figure 2B are simply the points at which the first publications relating to the various techniques and programmes seem to have become available and at which professionally accepted labels were affixed to the techniques.

Solid lines indicate direct relationships between events, orientations, and analytical tools and the development of management training techniques. Dotted lines indicate less direct or less clear relationships.

Simulation, scientific management theories, and post-Freudian psychology seem to be dominant stimulating influences. Although simulations of some form have existed for centuries, systematic simulation of social phenomena is based upon recent systematic social science models. The Hawthorne Western Electric Studies are a major event in the development of management training techniques and represent a link and a turning point in the history of management studies. They are considered to be among the most sophisticated scientific management studies and at the same time to be the first modern behavioral science studies of organizational behavior.[15]

Role-playing and sensitivity training are among the "oldest" of the newer training techniques and are closely related to a specific disciplinary base.[16] Both simulation and the in-basket techniques also are closely related to their disciplinary base, developed at approximately the same time. The management game was initiated and refined at the RAND Corporation in Santa Monica, California. One of the clearest and most direct relationships between a body of theory and a management training technique is that between the learning theories of B. F. Skinner and the development of programmed instruction.

There are numerous dimensions along which one can differentiate the training techniques and programmes. One dimension is their range of application, and another is their orientation to substance or process. Techniques and programmes such as the Managerial Grid, Kepner-Tregoe problem solving, the in-basket, and the management game are designed primarily for managerial personnel, while role-playing and sensitivity training may be used for either managerial or non-managerial personnel. Programmed instruction, simply because its greatest utility lies in imparting new factual or technical knowledge, appears at the present time to be less appropriate for behaviorally oriented management training and more likely to be useful primarily for technical training programmes.

In terms of orientation, role-playing and sensitivity training are oriented most exclusively to interpersonal relationships. Kepner-Tregoe and the in-basket are oriented primarily toward decision-making and problem-analysis processes. The Managerial Grid, the management game, sensitivity training, and role-playing, depending upon their design, may incorporate both orientations, though the main emphasis in the case of the latter technique is likely to be upon decision processes. Programmed instruction is the only one of the techniques under discussion which is primarily subject-matter-oriented (though it is indeed possible to combine managerial and teamwork effectiveness learning with specific subject-matter learning).

Management training techniques may also be differentiated according to the locus of and amount of control over their flexibility and scope of their use. Kepner-Tregoe and the Managerial Grid are the most restrictive techniques along this dimension. Both of these techniques are the specific products of specific companies and are elaborately designed. When a company or agency "buys" the Kepner-Tregoe or Managerial Grid training programme they also implicitly accept the operating assumptions of the techniques.

In general, managerial games and the in-basket games are somewhat more flexible. Since they are not specific products but are rather generic types of techniques, any agency can design its own version of either game and many companies or agencies have done so. Both games are more "open-ended" in that they are not predicated on "one best" way to do things. Also both types of simulation games can take cognizance of a wide range of variables.

Sensitivity training is almost completely "open-ended" with regard to both content and locus and degree of control. The range of applicability in an organizational setting is extremely wide. In sensitivity training, the almost complete lack of controls or structure which characterize these techniques may, at times, dilute their usefulness unless a skilled training director imposes some structure upon them.

The various management training techniques and programmes differ, too, according to whether their principal focus is on individual behavior or group dynamics. Programmed instruction is clearly an individual activity; indeed, that is one of its principal characteristics. The in-basket is essentially an individual task game, but it may be played in a group setting and a player's activities scrutinized by members of a group. Kepner-Tregoe and the Managerial Grid are usually undertaken as group training activities. The management game tends to emphasize group problem-solving activities but a focus on the role of the individual in the group is built into many games, as well. Role-playing and sensitivity training both focus on the individual as a member of a group as well as part of a specific situation.

Another dimension along which the training techniques may be differentiated and categorized is that of their cognitive or affective or "thinking" vs. "feeling" components. Role-playing, sensitivity training, and, in some respects, Phase I of the Grid approach appear to be the most highly affective. Indeed, unless there is a skillful and perceptive training director to supervise the use of these techniques, the affective aspects of these training procedures are likely to remain unstructured, and in many cases unarticulated. On the other hand, Kepner-Tregoe and programmed instruction deal almost entirely with the cognitive, since the first involves the application of problem-solving techniques and the second has as its principal objective to impart new substantive knowledge. The Managerial Grid approach attempts to integrate cognitive and affective considerations in organization development. Management games played in groups are likely to emphasize affective components to a greater extent than games in which individuals play separately since, in the former instances, emotional factors and interpersonal relationships become ingredients in playing the game.

In the management game, the in-basket, and the Managerial Grid, the managerial role rather than person is the primary focus, whereas, in the programmes based upon sensitivity training and role-playing, the attempt, at times, is made to induce changes in one's personal style apart from one's organizational role. Kepner-Tregoe's problem solving is, in this case, more like role-playing and sensitivity training than other techniques in that the kinds of learning which are supposed to occur pertain directly to the person rather than to the person in the context of his organizational role. Programmed instruction is somewhat different from the other techniques in that it is not overtly designed to change attitudes or behavior directly as are the other training techniques.

These newer management training techniques can be categorized according to the time, money, and other resources involved in their utilization. Programmed instruction can, in certain cases, be the easiest and least expensive technique to use. However, if already developed programmes are not used, initial programming costs can be extremely high. In assessing the costs of the other techniques, these vary according to whether one purchases the services of outside consultants or manages the training efforts "in house." Management games and in-basket exercises which are generated from within an agency may be relatively inexpensive as compared with the benefits that accrue. Week-long sessions, such as Kepner-Tregoe, or sending a great many participants to "public" Grid Seminars, rather than having an "in-company" programme, can tend to be somewhat more expensive. Role-playing and sensitivity training can range widely in their costs. The length of the training programme, whether it is an "in-house" activity, and the numbers of managers involved are all variables in the calculation of these types of costs.

In addition, it might be noted that each of the various techniques may (but need not) make use of a wide range of technology. For example, management games may be simple pencil-and-paper games or may utilize sophisticated computer programmes. Similarly, sensitivity training and role-playing may make use of electronic monitoring devices of various sorts. Programmed instruction may be easily computerized. Whether such technologies are used will, of course, affect the money costs of using the various techniques. Table 1 summarizes this comparison of the seven management training techniques and programmes along some of the dimensions of differentiation which have been discussed.

Techniques/Dimension or Programme	Range of Application	Locus of Control	Comprehensiveness	Flexibility
Management Game	Primarily Management	Designer or User	System	High
In-Basket	Either Management or Non-Management	Designer	Component	Moderate
Kepner-Tregoe Problem Solving	Primarily Management	Designer	Component	Low/Moderate
The Managerial Grid	Primarily Management or Non-Management	Designer	System	Low/Moderate
Sensitivity Training	Either Management or Non-Management	User	Component	High
Role Playing	Either Management or Non-Management	User	Component	High
Programmed Instruction	Primarily Non-Management	Designer	Component	Low

Learning Unit	Orientation	Learning Domain	Change Objective	Costs Equipment	Money
Individual and Group	Interpersonal Relationships & Decision Making	Cognitive & Affective	Managerial Role	Variable	Moderate to High
Individual	Decision Making	Cognitive	Managerial Role	Variable	Moderate
Individual and Group	Problem Solving Decision Making	Cognitive	Personal Style/ Managerial Role	Variable	Moderate to High
Individual and Group	Decision Making & Interpersonal Relationships	Cognitive & Affective	Managerial Role	Variable	Moderate to High
Individual and Group	Interpersonal Relationships	Affective	Personal Style	Little	Moderate to High
Individual and Group	Interpersonal Relationships & Decision Making	Affective	Personal Style/ Managerial Role	Little	Moderate
Individual	Personal Knowledge	Cognitive	Personal Knowledge	Variable	Moderate to High

Table 1   Analysis of seven newer management training techniques and programmes along selected dimensions

VI. THE UTILIZATION OF TRAINING TECHNIQUES IN ORGANIZATIONAL DEVELOPMENT

An important conceptual framework which has developed in the past decade in the U.S. has been the realization that training programmes for individual executives should be only part of a far larger strategy of organization-wide or system-wide goals and methodologies. There has been an important shift of emphasis from the individual executive as the sole or major objective of change and development to the view that the proper "client" is the total organization or, indeed, the total system of which the organization is a subsystem. It is recognized and accepted today in many quarters in U.S. private industry and government service that it does relatively little good to change the attitudes or behavior patterns of individual managers through out-of-agency training programmes if they return to organizational contexts which effectively frustrate meaningful implementation and application of the learned and acquired concepts and behavior. At times, such training, directed at individuals alone, may be dysfunctional, as the individual, having undergone a positive and useful training experience, finds little meaningful opportunity to apply what he has learned and experiences feelings of frustration as a consequence. Organizational development, therefore, directs its attention to the total organization in which the individual must function. It accepts the responsibility of attempting to induce organization-wide and system-wide change and integrates within such an overall framework the training and development of individual members of the organizations.

Organizational development projects aim at a more effective integration of employee needs and organizational goals, through change in organizational and individual behavior at a number of levels. To achieve this objective, programmes begin by investigating (1) the gap between the desired level of employee morale and its present level; (2) the gap between the desired level of organizational goal achievement and its present level.

On the basis of the data obtained about these discrepancies in a particular organization, a change-agent team (usually a combination of outside consultants and key organizational personnel) constructs change models specifying action that must be taken at all levels of the organization to reduce the gaps. In sharp contrast to another recent trend in training (toward the marketing of packaged training programmes) organizational development intervention methods are tailored to the particular complex life of the organization, a condition which is considered crucial to effective organizational renewal. Final stages of an organizational development programme aim at evaluating the results of intervention, which serves as the basis for a renewal of the cycle of organizational development activity.

Because of the movement's heavy emphasis on evaluation and feedback, organizational development projects often resemble "before-after with control group" studies and usually consist of three general stages:

1. PREPARATORY STAGE:

    a. *Needs Analysis.* During this stage the change agents study the major organizational and human problems of the organization. Data gathering typically includes interviews in a diagonal cut through the agency, observations of management meetings, focal points of decision making, conflict-resolution arrangements, etc., and content analysis of existing records such as personnel files, budgets, and the like.

b. *Morale Survey*. Data on a number of kinds of satisfaction and dissatisfaction levels can be obtained by questionnaires administered to large samples of employees, supplemented by smaller numbers of depth interviews.

c. *Analysis*. The data from both of these stages are processed and presented analytically and interpretatively to key levels of management. Where there is an emphasis on outside consultation, the presentation is generally made to a small management group. At times, data are released to all levels of management.

2. INTERVENTION STAGE: During this period the organizational development change-agent group, the internal agency executives, and whoever else these two groups may decide to include, jointly analyze the findings and they then outline future action. The purpose of these sessions is to secure the fullest possible commitment to change among key personnel and to choose intervention methods most appropriate to the particular organization and most promising for optimal results. Methods selected generally include some mix of group discussion, group decision training, confrontation meetings, training in participatory management, simulation exercises, management games, job-enrichment techniques, team analysis, etc., depending on the special problems of the agency.

3. EVALUATION AND FEEDBACK: The major techniques of the preparatory stage are usually repeated here, including the morale survey and the interviews. Using the earlier observations as benchmarks, an assessment of improvement in both employee satisfaction and organizational goal achievement is now possible. If a control group was employed, the "post" measures are, of course, administered to them as well. The findings of the evaluation are fed back to whatever core group is involved as change agents, who proceed to an analysis on which further plans for organizational change can be based.

It is important that the underlying values of the training methods used in organization development be consonant with the values of the trainees themselves, in order to effect change. In addition, these values need to be consonant with overall organization values to be able to influence and change the organization as a whole through the resulting behavior change of the trainees. Acceptance of the basic principles of organization development by top management is a vital precondition of any activity, and at all levels of the organization there must be a willingness to strive for authentic interpersonal exchange for any change programme to be effectively launched and conducted.

If specific management training programmes using any or all of the techniques which have been discussed are not directly related to overall organization development, the likelihood is that the individual training efforts, without regard to the particular technique or method employed, will yield less than optimal results.

This was clearly suggested in an original empirical research project conducted by a group of graduate students at New York University expressly for this study.[17] Training programmes conducted at the Port Authority of New York and New Jersey (a public corporation whose responsibilities include redevelopment of transportation facilities and the promotion of trade in the Port of New York) and at the Foreign Service Institute of the U. S. Department of State were evaluated under the guidance of the authors of this chapter. Both organizations generously allowed interviews to be conducted and questionnaires to be filled out by a group of their key employees who had participated in a number of training programmes making use of some of the participative techniques analyzed in this study. The objective of the study was to determine the effectiveness of these managerial training techniques in terms of perceived behavioral and attitudinal change.

A series of interviews were conducted in the Port Authority with ninety managers who had participated in three training programmes: (1) the Managerial Grid Seminar; (2) the Kepner-Tregoe Problem Solving Program; and (3) sensitivity training. The sample population included managers in administrative and technical positions from all levels of management. Each of three graduate students interviewed thirty managers. Additionally, seventy supervisors of training participants filled out questionnaires designated to correlate their perceptions with those of the trainees who were interviewed.

The three training programmes evaluated in the State Department were the Managerial Grid, Kepner-Tregoe Problem Solving, and an executive studies course especially designed for the Foreign Service Institute. The executive studies course is behavioral in its approach and emphasizes the psychology of human relations.

The findings of the study must be viewed with due caution and represent impressionistic judgments rather than hard, "scientific" facts and conclusions. Unavoidably, there were certain important procedural limitations to the research. For one thing, a significant length of time (over three years for many of the trainees) had transpired between the time the course was attended and the time the evaluation was conducted. A related problem was that in many cases the participants' supervisors had changed as a result of personnel changes, so that they could not recall behavior or attitude change in the participants. Also important was the fact that the data on participant perceptions and attitudes were gathered by a group of interviewers of varied interviewing experience. As may be the case in any research effort, it is possible that personal biases and distortions may have been unconsciously built into the interviews. In addition, it was not possible to use control groups nor was "before and after" testing employed to confirm alleged knowledge, attitude, and behavior changes. Indeed, changes may have been perceived by the participants and attributed to training when, in reality, they may have been actually caused by any number of personal or organizational factors.

Nevertheless, the findings of the study are of significance and interest. In the case of the Port Authority study, the reaction of the participants to all three of the training programmes was positive and, in some cases, high; some knowledge and attitude change was generally perceived and noted. Behavior change ranged from "some" to "almost none." Most respondents concluded that participating in the programme was a positive educational experience, fully or partially fulfilling most major programme objectives set out for it.

Many participants indicated that they felt that they better understood their managerial styles as a result of the training and a significant number of trainees reported an improvement in their interpersonal skills with both superiors and subordinates.

However, the study suggested that knowledge acquired and attitudes changed were unable to be fully transferred to on-the-job behavior. Furthermore, while the training was viewed as possibly instrumental for organizational growth by many respondents, its results were perceived as being inconsequential or even detrimental for individual career growth by many of those sampled. The chief reason for this seems to have been that participants believed that the individual training programmes were not fully woven into larger patterns of organizational development. For example, some of the respondents said that systematic procedures for trainee selection for these programmes had not been established by the Port Authority. Several participants had little idea as to why they had been selected and some thought they had been selected at random or to fill out a training quota. Further, the evidence does not indicate that the trainees were aware of the programme's objectives prior to the training experience. In certain cases, limited pre-training counseling was provided. In addition, many of those sampled suggested that little or no post-training evaluation or reinforcement was provided by the organization. Other factors discussed were perceptions of limited leadership support, obviating some of the training or making it partly dysfunctional, and some concern in the Personnel Department at the Port Authority for the mechanics of training rather than the substance of the programmes.

With regard to the study conducted in the U.S. foreign service, there were remarkable overall similarities between the data gathered on foreign service officers and the Port Authority data, with an unusual degree of congruency between the Managerial Grid and Kepner-Tregoe responses.

Empirical data for the study were gathered in a two-part survey of foreign service officers who had taken one of the above two courses or the executive studies course designed and directed by the Foreign Service Institute itself. In all, 550 foreign service officers attended one of the three courses, of whom approximately 444 took part in the survey. The first part of the research consisted of a series of fifty-nine interviews and the second part was a survey consisting of a structured, non-disguised questionnaire distributed to all foreign service officers in the group who were not interviewed.

Many of the same methodological problems which characterized the Port Authority study (such as the impact on memory and recall of a time lapse of three or more years between training and evaluation) existed in this instance also, so results must be assessed with due caution. It can be concluded, nevertheless, that, in general, the majority of the participants reacted fairly positively to the course they had attended. Over 90 per cent of the group believed that they had gained at least some knowledge from their course and the majority of respondents indicated that their attitudes had been changed to at least some degree. More than half of the respondents acknowledged some work change as a result of the training. Very few officers left the course which they took, regardless of which it was, without perceiving some benefit from the experience.

In addition, the executive studies course showed a relatively consistent degree of higher perceived success, effectiveness, and relevance than did either the Managerial Grid or Kepner-Tregoe courses. This would be in keeping with the assumption that a programme designed by an agency specifically to fulfill its needs would tend to be perceived as being more useful and would conform to the values and rewards system of the organization more closely than would an outside training programme, however useful the latter might be. It was concluded, therefore, that internally designed training courses may be more effective change mechanisms than training courses which have the same objectives but are designed outside of the organization, unless the latter give specific attention to organizational uniqueness.

The question of transfer of the results of training to on-the-job behavior showed some of the same characteristics in the foreign service as was revealed in the Port Authority study. The chief reason seems to have been the question of integration of individual training programmes into a total framework of individual and organizational development. Some of the officers believed that their course would have a negligible effect upon their career advancement or that there would be no relationship whatsoever.

Both studies suggested that some degree of misunderstanding regarding the training programmes and their specific objectives existed in each organization. This type of misconception tended to obviate and diminish the full impact and effect of the training on participants and supervisors. Of interest is the fact that both organizations were selected for this research study because they represent "enlightened employers," genuinely committed to the importance of management development and investing heavily in training activities. Since these research studies were completed, both organizations have taken significant strides forward in refining their total training efforts. The Port Authority has begun to institute a more comprehensive programme of organization development and the Foreign Service Institute, based in part on the recent Macomber Report,[18] is instituting an overall review and reform of its administrative training programmes, with the objective of building a balanced series of progressively more meaningful experiences throughout a foreign service officer's total career span.

It can be concluded that, for most meaningful change, top management should correlate management training programmes with individual and organizational objectives in order to make them as effective and functional as possible and should utilize specific management training techniques within an overall strategy of individual and organizational development.

CHAPTER THREE—FOOTNOTES

1. Cf. Arne Walle, "Beyond Teaching Methods: Educational Encounters in Need of a Theory." Unpublished manuscript, 1968.

2. Chapter Five of this volume is devoted to the syndicate method of training in Great Britain.

3. For brief descriptions of some of these techniques, see the manual developed by the UN Public Administration Division, *Guidelines for the Training of Professional and Technical Personnel in the Administration and Management of Development Functions.*

4. For some of these matters it is planned that a series of Occasional Papers will accompany this volume and will analyze specific management training techniques in detail as well as some of the basic issues involved in management education.

5. When the volume was originally planned and this chapter written, sensitivity training and the T-group were very much in vogue in management training in the U.S. In the past five years, there seems to have been a decrease in the use of strict sensitivity-training techniques and, in some cases, experimentation with non-verbal "encounter" techniques. In general, the sensitivity-training movement seems to have reached its peak in the early and mid-1960s.

6. Ian Mangham and Cary L. Cooper, "The Impact of T-Groups on Managerial Behavior," *Journal of Management Studies,* February 1969, p. 72.

7. Leopold S. Vansina, "Sensitivity Training or Laboratory Methodology in Western Europe." Unpublished manuscript (mimeographed), 1970.

8. Ibid.

9. Allen R. Solem, "Human Relations Training: A Comparison of Case Study and Role Playing," *Personnel Administration,* September 1960, pp. 29–37.

10. Lois Stewart, "A Survey of Business Games," in *Simulation and*

Gaming: A Symposium (American Management Association Report No. 55, 1961), p. 24.

11. Cf. the ERGOM (European Research Group on Management) exercises in group and organizational development problems developed by Professor B. Bass of the Management Research Center of the University of Rochester. This series contains at least one exercise dealing specifically with problems of developing countries, has been translated into a dozen or more languages and used extensively since 1967 in Latin America, India, and (though on a more limited scale) Africa as well as Europe, Japan, and North America. These exercises are also being used as the basis of a major cross-cultural research project into managerial attitudes.

12. Registered as a trade mark symbol.

13. Obviously, these views are generally stated. Some training programmes help the participant examine and compare his own position relative to others, i.e., the view that man is "inherently good" versus the view that "man tends toward evil unless he is firmly controlled."

14. We do not attempt to differentiate specifically within these gross categories. We do not distinguish, for example, Rousseau's *Emile* (a view of man as inherently good) from what was the mainstream viewpoint in eighteenth-century social, educational, and political philosophies.

15. These studies, conducted by Harvard industrial psychologists at Western Electric's Hawthorne plant, were the first substantial evidence that worker performance and satisfaction were affected less by such factors as fatigue or job rationalization than by the social relationships among the work group and their group attitudes toward work goals.

16. Role-playing, as used in the military, goes back to an earlier period and, in the civilian sphere, it goes back at least to Jacob Moreno's post-World War I work leading to socio-drama, sociometrics, and psychodrama.

17. Great appreciation is expressed to the following students who participated in the research project connected with this chapter:

Jonathan Reader, Earle Lerner, Stanley Hurst, Martin Schlissel, John E. Savage, David Schwartz, Susan Begelman, Lenore Deutcher, Edward Tomeski, Bernhard Meyer, David Lombardo, Marion Bentley, Manuel Romero, Cary Hershey, Richard Herbek.

18. A series of task force reports developed by members of the foreign service and devoted, among other things, to improving management practice in the United States Department of State.

CHAPTER FOUR
Experience of the Newer Management Training Techniques in Britain*

THE ARGUMENT

The argument of this chapter is simple. The British culture (as expressed by managers and trainers) has simultaneously accepted and resisted the newer training techniques, because these are associated with values about which many influential managers, civil servants, and educators have strong feelings. The American influence on management programmes has been great but is becoming increasingly intertwined with British ventures in training and development. Up to this point, management training has been concerned with establishing or confirming efficient routines and rituals in organizational affairs, working mainly through short courses. Now there is increasing awareness of the need for help with the dramas of management, by becoming deeply involved in organizational change.

Management training methods, unlike the techniques of technical training, rest upon important cultural assumptions. Technical training bases its authority on the effective manipulation of materials or machines. The standards by which effectiveness is judged are often quite clear-cut. Management training, on the other hand, rests upon a complicated network of beliefs and assumptions. In many cases, it will work if people have faith in it. This is because effectiveness is bound up with such matters as confidence, trust, authority, and discipline.

The study of the transfer of management training methods (a term

* This chapter was prepared by John Morris.

which I prefer to the narrower concept of 'techniques') from one country to another, therefore, gains a particular interest. In Britain, the similarities of attitude, values, and managerial skills with those of managers in the United States seem to be very close. This is a conclusion supported by recent work on cross-cultural comparisons of management attitudes. Nevertheless, economic growth in Britain has been disappointingly slow. In many ways, Britain is still a staggeringly rich country, not only in material assets, but in the quality of its life. I hope that my acceptance of this point will not be forgotten as the argument develops. The difficulties with Britain seem to arise from many sources, including anxiety about the implications of economic growth, radical change, the achievement of corporate excellence, and the systematic improvement of efficiency. Many of these values seem to have been firmly embraced by large American companies, at least at the level that expresses its views in official managerial ideologies. So has the idea of the organization committing itself to objectives that guide and support the objectives of the individual members. These ideas seem to run counter to powerful values in British culture which are concerned with the idea of community, commitment to a deep-rooted national way of life, and such character qualities as love of one's country, one's work, and acceptance of the duty to preserve the cultural heritage. All of these are characteristic of a very old society which has placed a great deal of weight on the virtues of continuity. Against these values, the emphasis upon rapid, single-minded organizational growth can seem almost shockingly opportunistic and insensitive.

But this, in turn, leads to some complexities because one of the major themes of American management training has been the importance of participation of those undergoing training in the activity, partly to foster a sense of independence, partly to gain the advantages of motivation. This creates concern among British managers, because there is still a strongly hierarchical paternalistic emphasis in British management. It is no accident that the so-called "classical theory" or organization came from extensive British and German experience in organizing effective armies. Much of the British wisdom in administration has been derived from the experience of war, and this has given very little encouragement to the development of a "permissive" attitude. There is a contrast here between two sets of values, one stressing continuity and qualities of persistence, and the other stressing the masterful handling of emergency and conflict. American values, it would seem, stress dynamism and vigorous participation, British values stress continuity and the acceptance of an established elite.

And yet I may be wrong to talk so glibly of American standards. Conflicts of values are certainly not absent from American culture. The point seems to be that the ideas embodied in American management techniques have been rather too optimistic and explicit to be readily accepted in the more traditional and disenchanted British culture. The interesting aspect of this conflict of values, from the point of view of applying the newer management training techniques in Britain, is that conflict has been worked out in a rather muffled way in a number of institutions, such as the new business schools, the training departments of many large industrial and commercial concerns, and in commercial training organizations.

I believe that by focusing on these institutional conflicts we can observe many of the problems of selecting and developing new training methods. It is just because Britain is in so many ways committed to the same values as the United States that the hazards of assuming a ready transfer of methods to different cultures can be put into a sharp and possibly disturbing perspective.

LIMITATIONS OF THIS CHAPTER

The broad title of this chapter, "Experience of the Newer Management Training Techniques in Britain," might suggest a comprehensive and judicious survey of what has been happening to the whole range of newer training approaches, methods, and techniques in Britain. Unfortunately, I have neither the temperament nor the competence to perform that particular task. I feel deeply committed to one kind of institution (the university-related business school) and to one approach (the use of projects and assignments for developing managers), and these commitments have led to strong views and a limited perspective.

I would like, then, to take full advantage of these limitations by using a theatrical device in order to focus on some of the problems, issues, and trends that seem to be important in the development of managers in Britain. Please imagine a drama in three acts, the third of which has only recently begun. The first act is concerned with the growth of management education and training in Britain before the business schools were started in the 1960s. It sees the successful establishment and development of the Administrative Staff College at Henley and the Tavistock Institute of Human Relations. The first of these is a profoundly British institution, the second attempts a unique fusion of European and American theories and methods in understanding people in organizations, without giving undue weight to the American viewpoints. Both of these institutions were profoundly influenced by the experience of rapid organizational change during the Second World War. At the same time, we see the growth of management training programmes in many of the larger companies, and a slow development of organizational self-consciousness.

The second act is concerned with the growing feeling that management education has now reached the point at which it can be tackled on a much wider front through institutions charged with responsibility for looking closely at the needs of present and future general management of the key economic institutions of Britain—in industry, commerce, and the public sector. This is the point at which, after many years of sporadic study of the secrets of American productivity, people turn to experimenting with "American" methods and techniques of management training. The influence of American business schools, on the one hand, and commercially available training programmes, devised by American educators, on the other become particularly important. The third act, recently begun, has seen the beginning of a response to this American "invasion" of ideas and practices. It is difficult to recognize the themes of this act, but a certain amount of coherence can be gained by focusing upon the experience of one major new educational institution—the Manchester Business School. In addition to this, an element of drama is gained from looking at the response to the so-called "package programmes" of management training.

The limitations of this study, therefore, stem from its being deliberately dramatic, impressionistic, and concerned with a few central problems rather than comprehensive, judicious, and rigorously empirical. Its values, I hope, are those of individuality, candor, and a certain amount of commitment.

ACT I. AFTER THE WAR: NEW INSTITUTIONS AND RISING HOPES

After the Second World War the British people set themselves to the complicated task of getting their country back on its feet again. It was evident that morale was high and the sense of possible new worlds to build, explore, and enjoy was strong. Managers were going to be among the leaders of the new society. The main contrast between "old Britain" and "new Britain" would be that new Britain would use all its possible talent, would be lively rather than boring, and would be able to harness technology to human needs and sensitivities. The difficulty with all this was that it was distinctly unrealistic. But this is a comment made in retrospect, in the light of our present sober realization of the intractability of human organization and attitudes. In 1945 almost everything seemed possible.

From the training point of view, the most obvious institutional outcomes of this upsurge of optimism were the Administrative Staff College at Henley and the Tavistock Institute of Human Relations. These were founded very shortly after the war was over and expressed a recognition that it was now becoming increasingly possible to plan management development in the context of organizational change. The Administrative Staff College was the more conservative institution. In the words of one of its staff members, Andrew Life (in Rapoport et al., 1970, p. 27) "The concept [of the college] had been discussed since the late 1930's by a small group of men with wide experience who were familiar with the staff colleges of the fighting services and felt that a similar kind of institution might be able to improve the administration of large scale civilian enterprises. . . . The aims and objects of the college included the development of the manager or administrator from a person of technical competence to one capable of bearing the highest responsibility, and the extension of the practical experience of the individual rather than the enlargement of this specific field of his knowledge in the academic sense."

The major educational method used by the college was syndicate discussion between skilled and able managers in their middle to late thirties. The topics of discussion were matters of relevance and concern in industry, commerce, and the public sector. The syndicate discussions were carefully organized, and in order to avoid wasted time, chairmen were well briefed, help was given in the control of meetings, external consultants were provided to give relevant information from time to time, and the Staff College provided very experienced tutors. These were men of ability and administrative competence, with an interest in the field of management education.

The selection of men for the courses (or sessions) of the college was carefully devised to produce a kind of microcosm of industry and commerce, together with the public sector. The managers were all of high caliber, commanding the confidence of their seniors and destined for high places within their organizations. The whole philosophy of the college was that if these people could be encouraged to make their experience freely available to one another, in terms that they could all understand, then an enormous gain in confidence and professional competence should follow. It is partly because this proposition seems so reasonable and almost self-evident that very little has been done until recently to evaluate the effectiveness of the Henley experience.

The Tavistock Institute of Human Relations was established by a group of very experienced psychologists and psychiatrists, many of them with medical training, who had worked together in the armed services during the war on problems of selection, training, therapy, and rehabilitation. They wished to devote their skills and energies to increasing the effectiveness of human activities, especially at work. From the very beginning the aim was to establish a very close link between research, consultancy, and training, along the lines of the best clinical practice. An early slogan was, "No research without therapy." The theories and practice of the members of the Tavistock Institute were sophisticated and inter-disciplinary. They quickly included doctors, psychiatrists, psychologists, sociologists, anthropologists, economists, statisticians, as well as engineers, operational researchers, and many others. Powerful links were established with American research and training institutions, particularly the research center for group dynamics at the University of Michigan. The major theoretical approaches were psychoanalysis, especially of the kind developed by the "British school," and group dynamics, as developed in the United States by Kurt Lewin and his followers. When these approaches were combined in a systematic form of human relations training (later called "sensitivity training") the results were profound and sometimes disturbing.

Alongside these programmes of training ran a great stream of management programmes of enormously varying types. All of them seemed to have in common the attempt to be all things to all men. In this respect they were in sharp contrast to the very much more clearly thought-through programmes of Henley and the Tavistock Institute. They included lectures, discussion groups, syndicate meetings, role-playing exercises, a limited amount of field work, and every other kind of approach that the training officer could find available. The contrast is not perhaps surprising. The Tavistock Institute and the Staff College were working with carefully selected managers, eager and able to learn. The training programmes arranged within companies were often part of a training policy decided on by senior management, and applicable willy-nilly to all members of a particular level of management. Since the needs of these managers were clearly diverse and often most unclear, the tendency in training courses was to provide a very wide range of activities in the hope that some would be appropriate.

If this sounds somewhat negative, it should be borne in mind on the positive side that training was now coming to be taken for granted. This was the result of many years of intensive, skilled, and often imaginative training in the forces. This had accustomed most people, long suspicious of education after school or college, to short but useful injections of ideas, information, and even material relevant to attitudes at periodic intervals.

During this act of the drama, however, training remained at a relatively modest level of self-awareness. It was overwhelmingly confined to individuals being sent on courses, and then left very much at their discretion to decide what use if any they would make of what they had learned.

Gradually, however, the constant emphasis on routine training, with some ritual overtones, began to give rise to some aspirations after something better, something more focused and dramatic.

ACT II. THE FERMENT OF MANAGEMENT EDUCATION AND DEVELOPMENT

One of the great advantages of the theatrical form of drama over real-life dramas is that the playwright can build in sharp discontinuities between the stages of his action. He can do this by the curtain rising and falling, by indications that several years have passed, or by other conventions that enable one to be sharply jolted into the realization that something quite new is now confronting us.

But when it comes to human affairs, especially those on a large scale, the discontinuities seldom appear to be so sharp. As the computer specialist would put it, we are working in "real time." Things usually happen fairly slowly in real time, and even wars and revolutions, though bloody enough, are seldom really discontinuous. All of this is meant as an introduction to the second act, which took some time to develop into a ferment. Even the word "ferment" might be better understood as a fairly brisk movement toward a changed situation rather than a great bubbling mass of exciting and diverse activities.

The business schools came into existence in the 1960s. From outside, the whole thing seemed quite sudden, but insiders knew that this was the result of long years of patient lobbying by a group of very distinguished senior managers, mostly from the oil, chemical, and engineering companies. Lord Franks, as a universally trusted and dispassionate man of affairs, wrote his admirably succinct report, and two British business schools were set up forthwith, in conditions of unprecedented affluence for British educational institutions. They were both closely associated with universities, somewhat in the American style. It was at this stage that management education and development became most closely associated with American models and American influence. In the first set of the drama, the Administrative Staff College was very much a British affair, and the Tavistock Institute was well able to sustain its part as an independent British contributor to international behavioral science, though it had close ties with powerful American institutions. Management courses might find themselves depending for much of their material on vigorous American writings, but there was no strong feeling of the whole management training movement as being part of an American invasion. I think this was because in the first act it was too scattered, too diffuse, and (perhaps more important than either of these) too dependent on technical and administrative procedures as compared with more global concerns. It was the American business schools which took the broad view, which looked at marketing, international business, and the application of systems theory to business.

All of this, and very much more, was highlighted when the British business schools came into existence. It could hardly be otherwise, because when the schools were at last set up there was bound to be a sense of occasion. In 1966 the Foundation for Management Education responded quite magnificently to this feeling by sponsoring a quite unique event in British management education—a four-week residential seminar at the London Business School which provided an opportunity for some of the most influential figures in British management education and training to meet some of the bluest of blue-chip American management educators from the top American business schools. Their declared aim was to inform the British business educators about the experiences of American business schools over the sixty or more years of their checkered history, to point to successes and failures, and to suggest ways in which the British could get off to a flying start in their own business schools.

For those at this seminar, about fifty of them, the opportunity was extraordinary. They hardly knew what to make of it. On the whole they were overwhelmed by the professionalism and confidence of the American educators. One felt that the crown jewels (if the parallel were not impious) were being packed carelessly but with extraordinary elegance into a hatbox.

When the seminar was over, decisions had to be made. What kind of courses did business schools want to run? How were they going to deal with academic subjects? Were they going to give great weight to research as compared with teaching? Was teaching going to be informal discussion and tutorial work or formal exposition and even instruction?

What kind of participants were the business schools hoping to deal with? Did they want to work with those firms that were already well established in the economy and making a great contribution? Or did they want to act as talent spotters or remedial workers? At this stage, the business education movement could be seen as an extraordinarily mixed bag. There were the two business schools, only very newly set up; there were new universities with powerful business studies departments or departments very closely similar; there were university departments of economics, accounting, marketing, and so on; there were independent colleges including Henley itself; and there were people from the training departments of major organizations wanting to get some conception of an appropriate strategy.

What did all this mean in terms of methods? It was felt that formal lectures had only a very limited place in the education of experienced adults, because these would be a little impertinent as well as presenting them with rather considerable difficulties in assimilating new material and its underlying ideas. There was great interest in case teaching, simulation exercises (and especially business games), and the use of direct experience in industrial settings in the form of project work or field work.

The American influence tended to move in somewhat different directions. There was the enormous influence of Harvard, standing foursquare on its vast accumulation of business cases drawn from different functions and different organizations all over the world, and emphasizing the necessity or reflected business policy to the integration of a varied set of analytical and judgmental skills. Then there was the more recent high distinction of Carnegie Institute of Technology Graduate School, and the Sloan School at M.I.T., with their more analytical scientific basis, using mathematical and statistical techniques freely to shape up and make decisions about complicated management problems. Those who supported the complex case method would suggest that only a very limited number of problems in management lend themselves to being treated mathematically or statistically. They claimed that managers produced by such a rigorous system would run out of steam when they got halfway up the organization and the information began to become very messy and rich with feeling. The critics of Harvard and its case method, on the other hand, would say, "If you know something, you can teach it; if you don't, you give a case!"

Standing at an angle to these two contrasting points of view were other famous American business schools such as Chicago and Stanford, employing less easily recognizable philosophies and training strategies. In some ways, they have provided more attractive models for many British management educators because they have been less controversial. The relevance of all these schools (and others such as Wharton, Case Western Reserve, and Indiana) for the development of British business schools was obviously immense. They were well established in their environment and were widely recognized as the best of several hundred business schools. They all had sound academic reputations, combined with high acceptability to business. If British business schools wanted to have experienced business school teachers, from what better place could they come than one of the leading American schools? If they wanted to establish durable links between Academia and the market place, what better model than these centers of learning—with M.B.A.s, D.B.A.s, Ph.D.s, and short mid-career programmes? And yet what would this mean to the successful development of a characteristically British kind of business school? This, as I understand it, was part of the dilemma of British business educators in the middle 1960s. On the one hand they had very powerful and prestigious models already very firmly established and successfully operating; on the other, they were exhorted by the visiting American management educators to take full advantage of the splendid opportunity to make a relatively fresh start in management education. As soon as they returned from the seminar the British educators were hard at work, in the full glare of publicity, implementing their programmes. The London Business School programme turned out to be very close indeed to one type of well-established and eminently practical American business school programme; namely, a three-part curriculum beginning with basic disciplines relevant to business, continuing with the major functional specializations of a firm, and finally attempting to integrate these in a business policy course. The Manchester Business School was greatly influenced by the precepts of Herbert Simon of the Carnegie Graduate School of Administration. He proposed that the basic disciplines relevant to business should focus on the fundamental concepts and theoretical models that seemed of long-term significance to the present and future problems of general management. Thus, economics might provide the concepts of resource allocation, rationality, utility, and marginal analysis, while sociology could concern itself with applying the ideas of social system, status, role, and structure to organizations. These concepts and models, clearly related to work in the applied sciences, could then be used by managers as powerful intellectual instruments of general problem solving. This approach raised a series of formidable problems for the Manchester Business School since it was already running a variety of courses and had to innovate as it went along, a theme to which we shall return later in more detail.

So far, we have been considering the influences acting on the business schools. This can be justified once we realize that they saw themselves as being the "carriers" of the new managerial ideology that was going to make a significant impact on the British economy. But the schools were only the most visible part of the ferment in British management education and training. By far the most obvious influence from America came through the programmes of management training associated with Blake (the Managerial Grid), Kepner and Tregoe (systematic problem solving), and the various forms of "sensitivity training" (concerned with the development of interpersonal skills). The first two of these were available in skillfully conceived and well-organized "packages" (a term which I hope I can continue to use without offense in a purely descriptive sense). Sensitivity training has been a very much more complex method, because it combines considerable variability of style with a widely used label, which implies some degree of homogeneity in the basic approach. Sensitivity training had been developed by the Tavistock Institute and in the United States by the National Training Laboratories (NTL). A number of British and European trainers were slowly developed through this period, but because of the complexities of the training procedure (mainly through intensive apprenticeship experience, leading eventually to assessment and acceptance by one's training peers), the number of trainers grew very slowly. The reader is recommended to turn to Professor Mailick's chapters on training techniques in the U.S.A. for fuller description of all these techniques.

Their impact on British management was very difficult to ascertain, and only became subject to systematic evaluation in the third act of the drama. At this point in the development of management training, only a small number of large organizations prone to experimentation with new training procedures used the newer techniques, and recommendations were largely by word of mouth, and against criteria of a rather global kind.

At this stage the idea of organization development was far from the minds of British managers and trainers. As I understand the term, it aspires to nothing less than enabling the whole human organization to become conscious of its own objectives and potential resources, so that it can continuously develop in its chosen environment. This is such a long way from the traditional British approach to management training that it is not surprising that the package approaches in particular, and even the different forms of sensitivity training, were seen as convenient methods of management training, to be used on a subcontracting basis rather than as the beginning of a major change in the whole conception of the organization.

I hope it will not slow down the action too much if I pause at this point to distinguish three aspects of management education and training that are particularly relevant in considering the "package programmes" and sensitivity training. First, there is some kind of *systematic problem-solving approach,* often formalized into a number of steps which can be learned off by heart and practiced in a variety of situations (including, as a very valuable aspect of such an approach, situations that are derived from the manager's own work place).

Second, there are two aspects of what is most simply called "process." This refers to the whole complex of factors that can strengthen or weaken (usually weaken) managerial activity. The best definition of process I have heard of is one used by the Oxford psychologist Bernard Babington-Smith, who has said, "Process is anything that you haven't taken into account in your plans." This is obviously a very broad definition, and in practice the people concerned with management training programmes have focused on two classes of factors. The first, *simple process,* consists of factors that are due to "bad habits" in individual and group problem solving. Second, and growing out of the first, but constituting a very difficult category to handle in training programmes, are the factors against which people and groups have strong unconscious resistances (*complex process*). An example of the first set of factors would be the failure of the chairman of a discussion group to indicate the broad aims of the group meeting. Another would be the failure to check on understanding of other people's points of view before criticizing them.

For examples of the second set, consider the unwillingness of an individual to commit himself to a clear point of view, or his envy of the leadership performance of another member of the group. In the manager's experience, the first kind of behavior might be condemned as moral cowardice, and the second contemptuously dismissed as jealousy. Therefore, there are strong resistances to recognizing such behavior in oneself. Other examples can be drawn from group processes, such as the desire to be dependent upon a strong leader, or a reluctance to engage in any work that requires careful thought and effort rather than the easy routines of everyday life. Dependency and inertia are not approved in the manager's value system, and so once again there are strong group resistances to recognizing such processes going on within a group of people at work. The "package programmes" pay a good deal of care and attention to the first kind of problem (simple process) but are rather more careful about their handling of the second (complex process). The reactions of a very old, rather skeptical culture like Britain to the examination of complex process in systematic training are somewhat hostile, and it is with good reason that the organizers of training programmes regard the whole "process" area with considerable concern.

So far, I have taken two extreme poles of management education and development. First I have looked at the new business schools, which I believe tell us most about the impact of British culture on the newer methods of management training, and the impacts of these methods (with their supporting ideas and values) on British culture. Second, I have contrasted these with the imported package training programmes first successfully established in the United States. In between these two poles there continued to run a considerable variety of management training programmes. For the most part, these were professionally decent, pedestrian affairs with a good deal of emphasis upon what are still called "modern management techniques" of analysis, decision, and control, together with a reasonably clear affirmation of the official values of the organization for whom the training was being provided. Looking at this from the point of view of a social anthropologist, one could say that the training programmes were still a somewhat uneasy mixture of ritual affirmations of the central values of the organization, especially as interpreted by the senior management, and training in the technical requirements of one's job. Unfortunately, in most organizations training requirements were difficult to establish for the most energetic and successful men, who could rarely be spared from their jobs for more than very short periods, and therefore most of the people who received training were those who could be spared from their employment because of impending job changes or some degree of overmanning (a condition not at all conducive to managers engaging in energetic change to their organizations on return from periods of training!).

The picture that I would like to convey, then, is of the middle ground of somewhat unreflective and eclectic training being stretched visibly between the two extremes of self-conscious business schools, anxious to show that the massive investment of national resources in them had been well worth while, and imported training programmes, run on a very demanding commercial foundation, equally anxious to show their purchasers that they were going to give a good return on the training investment (I would hasten to add here that this in no way implies that this concern was either improper or expressed itself in providing misleading information about the effectiveness of the programmes).

What was the outcome of all this? Mainly to dramatize the whole position of management training in the economy. The Industrial Training Act of 1964, one of the really striking innovations in British industrial training, was originally directed to providing new skills and (hopefully) more flexible attitudes in the traditional British work force. But it inevitably extended to include managers and supervisers, particularly when it came to be clear that they were often the major resisters of change. It is characteristic of an old culture that most of its activities go on under the surface, in the form of largely unrecognized and subtle transformations of attitudes and values in a deeply continuous way. As has often been remarked, the genius of British society (one of the oldest and most successful continuous cultures in the world) has been to put "new wine in old bottles." Without intending to appear in any way chauvinistic, I would draw attention to the possible advantages of developing in an evolutionary fashion. The first, and obvious, advantage is that man himself is an evolutionary creation, and his very limited ability to conceptualize problems at a level of consciousness makes it highly desirable that many of his activities should be under the control of reasonably benign and complex individual habits and social conventions. It is quite impossible to have a society that is carried around in full consciousness in the heads of its members, let alone in the heads of its leaders.

Having made this point, I now make a contrasting point of equal importance. This is that British society has very often mistaken complacent stagnation for sensible evolution, and ineffective hereditary control for natural leadership. So it was a very good thing that the unreflective characteristics of British management practice (and to some extent the more eclectic forms of management training) were brought to a considerable extent into consciousness by the joint action of the newly established business schools, the British institutions established earlier and now growing to maturity (for example, the Tavistock Institute and the Administrative Staff College at Henley), and the commercial package management training programmes. Some of the training managers in quite substantial organizations thought to deal with the heightened visibility of the problems by neatly dividing their responsibilities into two parts: sending the more senior people to courses at the business schools (and their equivalents) and sending the rest to the package programmes. Others, more intractable (or perhaps more responsible), attempted to find some training strategy that would enable them to make decisions with their vastly increased resources, now that they were gaining fuller awareness of the implications of their decisions. They got relatively little help from the business schools in this respect, because these were much too busy in developing and improving their own programmes. Neither, of course, did they get very much help from the "package programmes" because these were extensions of American programmes (now often grown into international big business) which had their own considerable difficulties of staffing and quality control, and were not very well placed for radical innovation to suit different cultures or subcultures.

The greatest help came from the professional associations to which training managers belonged, and from some simple devices set up by firms who wanted some rough indications of what their members thought of the training courses that they had attended, and were willing to make these devices to other organizations (one British firm, in particular, gained the gratitude of their colleagues by establishing a medium of this kind, the De la Rue index). Lastly, but by no means least, there came help from the British Institute of Management with its published reviews of the whole range of management courses and its short seminars giving further information and assessment of the objectives and achievements of these programmes.

To sum up: the ferment of management education and training brought about a heightened self-consciousness in British management training, and this focused on the established achievements of American business education, both in the major business schools and in commercially available training programmes. The rising professional standards and competence of training managers from the public and private sectors led them to raise a series of questions about the appropriate forms of management training, the institutions most appropriate for engaging in these different forms, and problems of evaluating the effectiveness of training. At this point of developing professionalism, the scene was set for the curtain to rise on Act III.

ACT III. RESPONSE TO THE NEWER TRAINING METHODS

So far we have been looking at the enormously complicated management training scene in terms of three major influences. First we have looked at the new business schools which played a large part in focusing the awareness of senior management on potentiality of organizational change. Secondly, we contrasted these with the commercially available management training programmes that used specific techniques. These were almost wholly American imports. In between, we looked at a third much more varied source of influence—the in-company management training programmes, organized within either training centers or industrial staff colleges. The suggestion so far has been that in their different ways the business schools and the "package programmes" showed clear signs of American influence. The in-company programmes represented a very much more variable mix of training techniques, because they were (and are) much closer to the influence of their own organizations. It is noteworthy that the newer training methods have usually been "cut down to size" when they enter British organizations, because of the insistence of the trainers and the managers that they should fit into the existing conventions of the organization, even to denaturing them. (Many who have taken part in training programmes will have rueful memories of half-day systematic problem-solving sessions and one-day sessions on sensitivity training!)

There are at least two other sources of influence that it might be useful to mention here. First there is the pervasive and benign influence of the Tavistock Institute, which as an independent center of research, training, and consultancy has done a great deal to translate American practices into acceptable British forms and to develop a comprehensive system of training conferences, drawing on continuing research into a large variety of organizations. In this stage of the drama, the work of the Tavistock Institute grew so complex that it found it convenient to divide into a number of clearly marked segments, concerned with organizational work on the one hand, and individual and group work on the other. (See for examples of the work, particularly in training, Rice, 1965, and Miller and Rice, 1967.)

There is no doubt whatever that work of the Tavistock Institute was distinguished by any standards (the Tavistock staff members were highly acceptable in the "international business school" league). But, as an independent institute, it was able to pursue a very much more flexible pattern of mutual influence between research, consultancy, and training than occurred in the business schools. Following the academic pattern, the schools insisted on long and arduous programmes of study, took their graduate programmes rather more seriously than their mid-career programmes, and in their insistence on rigor made an oversharp distinction between research and consultancy. I shall return later to the question of the relationship between the Tavistock Institute and the business schools, and shall meanwhile continue with the second set of influences: the independent management colleges, headed by Henley and Ashridge. As can be seen from the fascinating study of Henley as a "developmental community," referred to earlier, the Administrative Staff College has continued to focus on programmes for mid-career development with a major use of the syndicate method, but has fed into syndicate discussion rather more systematic inputs of information. It has, as part of this process, also developed a research wing.

Ashridge College is a leading example of a number of independent colleges using a large variety of methods for working with managers on residential short courses. In terms of distinctions made in a discussion of package programmes in "Act II," it has concerned itself mainly with systematic problem solving, using a variety of participative methods (business games, role-playing, discussion methods) and a concern with "simple process."

It is in this third act of the drama that it becomes apparent that one characteristic feature of British life is its way of dealing with conflict. One way is to turn one's back on it and pretend it isn't there, and the other is to ritualize it. In the field of management training methods, both tendencies are clearly evident. The first is to expound strongly contrasting or conflicting views on the needs of British management and totally to ignore what other institutions are committed to in this respect. For example, the business schools have had virtually no contact, so far as I am aware, with the Blake Managerial Grid, Reddin's 3-D, or the Kepner-Tregoe problem-solving approach. There is very little contact between the British management consultants, who run a large variety of extremely eclectic management training programmes using every conceivable training technique, and the business schools. To this may be added the observation that the business schools themselves seem to have very little to do with one another, except on a rather formal level. The more ritualized form of conflict can be found in the pronounced tendency of various groupings in the management education and training field to develop stereotypes of one another. The business schools are seen by industrial training managers as "well meaning but academic, intended only for high-fliers." The staff who are working in short intensive training programmes likewise see the business schools as being able to work over enviably long time periods, with very little demand for evidence of cost-savings and other indicators of effectiveness. In their turn, the business school faculty often regard the "package programmes" (a term often used pejoratively) as overambitious, given the short period of time in which they have to work. Or they say, as I have done, that industrial programmes are "eclectic" rather than "stimulating and varied."

I think there are signs that in this act of the drama the conflicts are less sharp, because the various institutions and agencies in the management training field are becoming more aware of what they are trying to do and what kinds of achievements are possible with the resources available. It is interesting to note that at the present time (autumn 1970) active steps are being taken to bring about an informal association of senior staff members of the major university and independent management centers. An important part has been played in this convergence by the publication of a British Institute of Management report written by a young I.B.M. management development executive, Alistair Mant. The Mant Report crystallized a good deal of rather diffuse discussion and enabled it to be considered in high places. The report raised questions rather than provided answers. But the whole tenor of the report, together with a small amount of survey information derived from the views of senior managers, was that too much management education had been focused on people who were going to be successful anyway, and not enough was being done within organizations for experienced managers who are the "backbone" of their organizations. The report suggested that in many management training centers there was still far too much use of formal methods of instruction, materials of study that were unrelated to the problems of the managers, and an unrealistic expectation of managers being able to learn a good deal in a very short time and translate it into action back in their jobs.

The questions raised by the Mant Report, and the emphasis on helping the manager to manage his own learning, in relation to the problems most important to him, are close to the line taken by the Manchester Business School (at which Mant spent time prior to writing the report, as a tutor on the school's management course). In many ways, Manchester is not only a reasonably important actor in the third act of the drama but a source of drama in itself. It represents an intersection of all the most powerful influences working on the British management training scene. It is part of a major international university, with a tradition of scholarship and research in the arts, sciences, technology, and public affairs. It has been strongly influenced by American business schools, notably Carnegie, M.I.T., and Harvard. It is deeply embedded in an industrial culture of some antiquity, devastating ugliness, and strong civic pride. Not surprisingly, the school has a complex reputation—"sound, pragmatic, interested in the behavioral problems of organization, quite academic, hard working, international but in some ways provincial." Vigorous internal disagreements are legion; when a distinguished visiting professor, Stafford Beer, came to write a report on the reorganization of the school, he noted nineteen polarities around which arguments raged (he believed them all to be false)!

What has been happening, then, at Manchester, that might throw light on the newer management training methods in Britain? First, it has been learning just how deeply entrenched the traditional methods can be in an academic institution. Academics tend to be self-selected for an academic life. They are seldom there for the money (even with the additional earnings of a business school). They have passed through a selection process that stresses verbal facility, a good memory, and marked analytical and logical thinking. The intellectual bias, coupled with strong interest in a particular subject matter, often puts emphasis on a formal, systematic, "linear" process of learning and teaching. It is noteworthy that most of the "older" techniques of teaching are of this type—lecturing, guided reading, tutorial discussion (usually only apparently informal!), and seminar work. The universities reverse McLuhan's dictum, as one would expect from the inhabitants of "print culture." In place of "The medium is the message," they assert, "If the message is important, the medium doesn't matter."

In the hands of academic teachers, discussions become "guided," with a clear objective and a set of guidelines which the teacher uses fairly single-mindedly; seminars become rigorous discussions of a draft paper for later publication; cases become a set of "teaching points" covered with some rather flabby flesh; and business games become a familiar world for the teacher to rule, through his intimate knowledge of the dynamics of student confusion. I am using dramatic license of course, but I believe the underlying point to be sound: the academic life encourages a strong commitment to intellectual control of the subject matter. Where the subject matter is of relevance to the manager, this control can be of great value, especially in fields that deal with standardized materials (money, plant, some raw materials), long time perspectives, and complex patterns of interaction. Much management activity is concerned with such fields, and in these there is often a close affinity between the successful academic and the effective manager (a view, I might add, which in Britain, not in Germany, is strongly resisted by both managers and academics, despite the successful interchange of managers and professors that quite frequently takes place).

The successful changes that have been made in this pattern at the Manchester Business School are of three kinds: developments in the organization of subjects of study, establishment of some of the newer training approaches, and an emphasis on the development of "learning consultants" in addition to the more familiar subject specialists. The second and third of these are of direct relevance for training techniques: but they depend to some extent on the first.

The school has found that there is not much point in making changes in the organization of subjects if these merely become well-meaning "umbrella" titles, beneath which the familiar academic disciplines of functional areas are all too clearly visible. I still remember the shock, some years ago, of asking a group of experienced managers taking part in a mid-career programme at the school what they thought of Human Behavior in Organizations, to be told that the sociology was very interesting. When I turned to ask about the Analysis of the Business Environment, they said they were pleased with the macroeconomics. And the fine clothes of Analysis for Decision and Control were ruthlessly stripped off, to reveal accounting and statistics. Once the changes have become real, however, it appears that intellectual rigor and control are not enough—the expectation of relevance and the possibilities of implementation become important factors in the situation. And, with these, the development of social skills and the understanding and changing of attitudes become important.

It is at this point that the newer methods of training become significant. Instead of fashionable trimmings to a new-look programme, they become essential elements in a learning experience. The changes in subject organization raise questions concerning the problems and themes that the academic disciplines claimed to be studying (social order, an internal world of meaningful symbols, effective allocation of scarce resources in a real world, for example)—central topics of great relevance to general management, but often forgotten in technical problems of measurement or in the search for theoretical elegance. How can present and future managers, pressed for time and with limited resources of energy and skill, make effective contact with these problems and relate them to the world of their practical interests and experience? How can managers be encouraged and enabled to develop an understanding of the skills of learning, becoming managers of their own learning and that of the people for whose work they are responsible?

The present inclination of the school faculty is to use different forms of project work as the main foci of learning and teaching. Cases are splendid devices for compressing a complex sequence of events into a manageable, but still realistic, form. They are slices of life. The project is a slice of living. My experience is that projects and cases have a natural affinity. A successful project often grows out of a desire to bring a case to life, in role-playing, decision-simulation, or even in life itself, in "real time." A good case is often written up from a real-life project.

The word "project" is often used in a very broad sense, to mean some kind of task in which a person participates, so that he can learn from his direct involvement in a relevant situation. The long habits of tight control of training activities by educators or trainers have frequently led to projects offering very little freedom for the person taking part in them. Often, the project brief is very precise, the time scale is demanding, and the criteria of evaluation are specified by the trainers.

In the Manchester Business School, we are coming to recognize three kinds of project: (1) management education projects; (2) management development projects; (3) organizational change projects. The first type of project is devised by educators, often with the use of various simulation procedures (as in business games, role-playing, and classroom projects). The aims are limited to the professional development of the participants, within the framework of the school. The second type moves the locus of learning into the work place, and the task around which the project is organized is part of the real life of the organization. Nevertheless, it has been chosen for its contribution to the professional development of the participating manager rather than its organizational significance. The third type of project is the process through which planned change occurs in the organization. It is real, dramatic, engrossing: a "start-up" programme for new plant, a research project in product development, or perhaps a market research project. On a more extensive scale, it may be a merger or acquisition, a move into a major new product line, or an extension of activities to a new market, possibly in another country.

In many organizations, these activities are far too urgent and important to be used for management development. For such organizations, management development is "Mickey Mouse" and organizational change is real. There are, however, signs that an increasing number of organizations in Britain are beginning to bring management development and organizational change closer together. I.C.I. with its extensive programmes of organizational development, the Reed Group with intensive studies of organizational improvements by members of the management "cadre," and the recent collaboration of the Manchester Business School with Rolls-Royce on a management development project for a team of senior managers—these are all examples of British companies bringing the professional development of managers and the key processes of organizational change into fruitful relationship.

It is at this point that the practitioners of the newer training techniques have begun to link up with one another. Members of the Industrial Management Division of Leeds University, experienced in sensitivity training, have developed extensive evaluative procedures which indicate the effectiveness of such training in different situations and national cultures. Another experienced trainer at the University of Sussex has been asked to evaluate the effectiveness of Grid training in a large industrial organization, and has shown that modest but positive gains in social awareness and skills have been transferred to the job situation. There is a distinct possibility that the London and Manchester Business Schools, the Tavistock Institute and the Engineering Industry Training Board (one of the most influential industrial training bodies) will collaborate on a programme of action-research into the effectiveness of management development activities in the engineering industry.

Another link between the Manchester Business School and the Tavistock Institute is now firmly established—a joint one-week working conference (in the development of effective authority relationships) for M.B.A. students. This type of institutional collaboration can be expected to develop. For example, a successful form of systematic problem solving, combined with process analysis, has been developed by a group of British management trainers, headed by Ralph Coverdale. This forms a kind of link between Kepner-Tregoe training and the Managerial Grid. Since evaluation studies (unpublished as yet) suggest that this form of training is particularly effective in improving meetings and the conduct of project groups, it is not surprising that it has been found useful to combine Coverdale training with longer programmes. This has occurred on many senior civil service management programmes and on some London Business School programmes.

It is becoming increasingly apparent that the newer methods, in their shift from the act of teaching to the process of learning, have created a spirit of inquiry in teachers or trainers that is quite alien to the users of formal methods. The formal methods are inclined to focus on the performance of the student and to see the results as an indication of ability or diligence. The users of the newer methods, for the most part, have been interested in the opportunities that can be provided for the person who wishes to learn, and in the identification and removal of constraints. This is true even of an apparently "formal" new training technique such as programmed instruction, which has proved very acceptable in Britain as a means of conveying information quickly and effectively. (In parentheses, it may be remarked that programmed instruction has appealed greatly to the value system of British management, since it is orderly, continuous, task-oriented, and direct.)

I do not intend to suggest that this convergence of interested parties is startlingly dramatic. The visitor to Britain would still find vast areas of managerial ignorance of the activities of the business schools, of the "package programmes," and of any methods of managerial training other than talks, demonstrations, and discussions. Recently it proved necessary for me to give an elementary talk on management training methods to a group of senior managers from one of the largest and most sophisticated business organizations in the country. But the changes in the last five years have been impressive, even to the eye of an overzealous insider like myself.

SOME REFLECTIONS ON THE BRITISH EXPERIENCE

Perhaps one could sum up the foregoing account by saying that Britain is a very old country, full of experience of attempts to change which have come to nothing. It looks at other countries and sees change in the form of breakdown, catastrophe, and social tragedy. It concludes that any change is likely to be for the worse, unless it has been very carefully thought through, discussed by all parties, and then pushed ahead by somebody who is trusted, purposive, and practical. "Hasten slowly" might have been invented by the British rather than the Romans.

This may make my choice of a dramatic format for my account somewhat ironic. And yet we might do well to remember the difference between theatrical drama and the real life to which it somewhat remotely refers. Theatrical drama is a ritual, performed before an audience and taking place according to a reasonably well understood set of conventions; this enables the audience to experience at second hand a number of things that they would probably shy away from experiencing themselves. This quite precisely catches the development of management education and training. From being a relatively mild and agreeable ceremony, a reward for work well done, management training has become more exciting, more demanding. It condenses time, it exaggerates risk, and, not least, it is beginning to take a more direct place in the manager's career. As we left the third act of our drama, it seemed to be increasingly evident that management training has now to confront reality and the ritual drama of the training center, with its business games, closed circuit television, lively lectures, and role-playing, must give place to projects and assignments in which trainers act to prepare and guide people through some very taxing experiences in real life.

But this will not happen automatically. Some trends are set in the direction of increasing the reality of management training. But the British culture is very old and very convoluted and enters deep into the hearts and minds of training managers and practitioners. It is no accident, for example, that most forms of management training within companies, until recently, have been fragmented, opportunistic, and yet conservative. Most organizations have kept their training personnel at some distance from the central concerns of the firm. There has been a great fear that competence might be undermined if changes of behavior are allowed to go on within the mainstream of the organization. As international competition grows, and the penalties for variations in performance increase, these fears seem well founded. They point to the value of training settings which can be regarded as what I would like to call "areas of licensed incompetence." The price that people will pay for being given time on full pay by their organizations to enter these areas will be that they try hard to develop competence in areas relevant to their own careers. Whether, as a result of developing new skills, acquiring new information, and possibly modifying their attitudes as a result of all this, they will wish to return to their organizations remains a fairly open question. All one can say is that large organizations, at least, are willing to take the risk.

The unfortunate thing about training centers in organizations as "areas of licensed incompetence" in the past has been that incompetence has been so widely regarded as a bad thing that trainers as well as people sent on training were seen to be incompetent. The assumption was all too readily made that a really able man will only want to spend his time working with able people, and trainers, since they are apparently willing to spend their time working with people who are, "by definition," incompetent, must themselves be incompetent. This has led to an assumption that the most prestigious forms of training are those which deal with people who do not for a moment appear to need training! Examples would be the elite business schools which take people who are outstandingly able and are clearly going to be successful whether they attend the business school or not. Charles Handy, of the London Business School, has talked very cogently of the "accolade effect," which he describes as the rather complacent state of mind of somebody who goes to a form of training with a strong conviction that there is nothing really important for him to learn. All this may sound rather depressing. We seem to be suggesting either that the trainer has low status because the people with whom he is working obviously need help, or that he gets high status for doing nothing in particular. But these are probably the extremes of the training dimension. In Britain, the problem has partly been solved by defining areas in which even the most able people can legitimately display incompetence, such as the use of sophisticated quantitative methods, or a knowledge of some of the more complex "process aspects" of individuals, groups, and organizations.

On reflection, I feel convinced that the use of project and assignment approaches is of enormous value in bringing about individual, group, and organizational change. The great attraction of projects and assignments is that they are under the control of organizations, or the senior managers acting on their behalf, and yet as part of their design they must also express some of the interests and needs of the individuals for whose career development the projects and assignments are designed. The only commitment that this requires is that senior managers be willing to concede that it is worth setting up a specific kind of organized experience within which managerial learning can take place. It does, of course, mean abandoning quite a number of training assumptions that are fairly deep-rooted in British society. For example, a man is not "sent to be trained," and he manages his own learning within a generally agreed context of learning objectives and learning strategies. But once we come to think of it, British culture, as we said at the outset, is very deeply committed to change through continuity rather than radical discontinuity.

CHAPTER FIVE
Henley and the Syndicate Approach*

To account for the approach to management education characteristic of the Administrative Staff College at Henley-on-Thames from its inception, one has first to see the institution and its choice of learning situations as the product of a particular set of circumstances existing at the time of its foundation in 1945 as an independent private non-profit-making establishment. Accordingly, we shall begin by outlining briefly the circumstances which led to the creation of Henley and which influenced its approach to the achievement of its objectives. We shall then continue by describing how that approach evolved and how recent research at the college has thrown light on the way in which the approach can be developed with the aid of our increasing knowledge of individuals and their behavior in groups.[1]

Britain in 1945 faced the reconstruction of its economy after the exhausting effects of World War II. Even before the end of that war the government had acknowledged some of the deficiencies of the existing educational system by passing the Education Act of 1944, which made provisions for all those accepted for a university place to be financially supported if in need. This represented a belated step toward greater educational opportunities, already characteristic of American society, and acknowledged one lesson of the war—that no society can afford to ignore or to underutilize the potential of its human resources and still hope to survive.

A group of British businessmen and educationists, conscious of this national need to mobilize resources for postwar recovery, had

* This chapter was prepared by Andrew Life.

met from time to time during the war to discuss the most practical way of improving the quality of administration in the country when peace returned. An Institute of Industrial Administration had been formed as long ago as 1919. This, however, contributed to the education of managers mainly by its role as an examining body linked to the requirements of the engineering institutions that their associate members should pass certain papers on industrial administration in order to qualify. For these, most students studied part time in the evenings at technical colleges, where the learning process had the primary objective of enabling students to gain the coveted professional status of an engineer as soon as possible. Although such men often became managers, the narrowness of their education could be a handicap at more senior levels. Furthermore, since the part-time education had an individual and professional emphasis, it was not always in line with the interests of the student's employer. The conclusion drawn by the British group of businessmen in 1945 was that capable and experienced but narrow managers could benefit from a period of broadening residential study paid for by their employers—if an appropriate institution could be found to provide it.

Unfortunately, British universities at that time commanded only lukewarm support from businessmen for their undergraduate courses leading to degrees in commerce or to diplomas in business administration. Some businessmen had been prepared in the 1930s to encourage and give financial support to new ventures in the universities, such as the Department of Business Administration Research and Training established within the London School of Economics with the help of a group of firms. But while London attempted to innovate, at Oxford and Cambridge even commerce failed to gain recognition as a subject worthy of study, although at Cambridge engineering students did have the opportunity to attend a few lectures on industrial administration from 1931 onward.

By contrast, in the United States "commerce" as an area of study had been replaced widely by "business administration." Business schools within universities, endowed by businessmen, had gained the confidence of industrial and commercial managements to the extent that firms were releasing executives, many of whom were nongraduates, for full-time residential study.

If the founders of Henley were looking for a parallel to the education of experienced managers, they discovered it in the long history of education for staff officers in European armies. The senior division of the Royal Military College in Britain was founded in 1799, but it did not become the "Staff College" by name until 1858, when two-year courses were introduced for serving officers who aspired to positions on the General Staff. Meanwhile, Von Scharnhorst had reorganized the Prussian Army in 1806 and created a staff college with entrance based upon competition. Similar institutions eventually appeared as a part of the organization of most of the European armies during the nineteenth century.

In the British Army Staff College at Camberley, it was the custom to divide the officers on the course into groups known as "syndicates." Each syndicate included representatives from a variety of arms, services, and advisers, who collectively worked on assignments set to them as a group by the directing staff. A feature of this system was, and currently still is, a directing-staff solution to each problem; in other words, what the staff members would have answered if confronted with the same problem. Following their attendance at the Army Staff College, members would alternate between staff and regimental duties, and in some instances return as directing staff. Historically, many of the more famous British commanders such as Slim, Templer, Montgomery, and Alexander followed this career pattern.

Among those who met to discuss the project which ultimately led to the foundation of Henley, Colonel Lyndall Urwick as a former staff officer had created one of the earliest and most widely known management consulting partnerships in Britain. He had also written extensively about administration. He envisaged a British industrial staff college as a civilian equivalent to Camberley, with a twelve-month course, but such a lengthy programme found little favor in the 1940s with industrialists who felt that three months was the longest continuous period for which they could release experienced managers of high potential.

Thus the situation confronting those who were debating the project was as follows: The managements of leading British companies and institutions conceded the desirability of trying to utilize further the potentiality of their executives by means of some educational experience. Existing part-time studies of administration for examinations in technical colleges were felt by many businessmen to put too much emphasis on absorbing knowledge uncritically and were dissociated from managerial performance. While British universities, by contrast, encouraged critical discussion, there was a suspicion, based on studies of graduates' choices of career, that many academics were prejudiced against industry and commerce. Those in departments of commerce committed to the study of business enterprises nevertheless tended to use a narrow focus considered by industry and commerce to be insufficiently managerial in its conception. In practice, the most firmly established institutions concerned with the education of managers were the service staff colleges, which had consistently worked through and built upon the knowledge and experience of participants by means of structured group discussion and problem solving.

With the foregoing perceptions in mind, the progenitors of Henley saw the solution to the form of the institution as an independent college with residential facilities, untrammeled by examinations or professional bodies, and with entrance dependent upon acknowledged managerial experience and potential rather than upon academic qualifications.

This detached view of academic qualifications did not, however, imply the rejection of university standards of excellence. Nor did it betoken disrespect for disciplines like applied economics, whose practitioners had demonstrated their administrative competence in important wartime roles. Accordingly, the governors of the newly founded college displayed no inconsistency by appointing as the first principal Mr. Noel Hall—a former professor of political economy at University College, London, the first director of the independent National Institute for Economic and Social Research, and a wartime head of the War Trade Department in the British Embassy at Washington.

The aims and objects of the college compensated for the perceived deficiency of existing arrangements for the education of managers by concentrating upon the development of the manager or administrator from a person of technical competence to one capable of bearing the highest responsibility within the enterprise. This objective, with its practical orientation toward personal development and more flexible use of the human resources of the enterprise, pointed to requirements both of knowledge and of personal skills and attributes. These in turn posed problems of what should be studied, what skills should be practiced during the course, and what personal attributes should be elicited by the tasks given to the participants.

Here, again, wartime administrative experience influenced the perceptions of the principal and the governors. During World War II it had been common practice to establish ad hoc meetings between small groups of specialists for the purpose of co-ordinating inter-departmental and inter-enterprise projects and keeping seniors in-formed of progress, and it was observed that the participants learned much about each other and about their departments in the process of pursuing a common task. It was also believed that a feature of work at the highest levels within an enterprise was involvement with representatives of other enterprises and institutions in all sectors of the economy—public and private. With these points in mind, the col-lege has therefore aimed from its inception to recruit for each course a balance of participants from a wide variety of enterprises and ad-ministrative bodies, simultaneously representative of different man-agerial functions. In this respect its aim resembles that of the service staff colleges in ensuring an adequate representation of different arms and advisers, and the college has similarly adopted the principle of dividing each course into groups called "syndicates."[2]

A syndicate at Henley normally consists of eleven members, rep-resenting different types of industrial company, a nationalized cor-poration, a government department, commercial enterprise, local government or the fighting services, and a national from a country overseas. At the same time, each syndicate includes members repre-sentative of different functions of an enterprise, such as production, sales, accounting, and finance, or of ancillary services like personnel. Since participants are men and women who have already proved a measure of their competence as practitioners, and have the experience upon which to draw and relate to the study of administration, they and the staff are regarded jointly as "members" of the college sharing in the pursuit of understanding.

For a mature approach to the critical analysis of management the-ory and practice by the members of the college, a prerequisite is a considerable degree of mutual confidence and understanding between members. For this reason, and in order to enable each individual to compare the practices of his enterprise and his own personal experi-ence with those of other members, the college keeps the number of members on a course to a limit of sixty-six, so that members can get to know one another well. This process of gaining acquaintance and promoting the wider interchange of ideas is accelerated by the practice of modifying the membership of syndicates for certain areas of study during a "session."

Because of the predetermined structure of each syndicate and hence of the total membership of a course, the college carefully describes the period in residence of members as a "session," and in fact uses the terminology of "sessions" rather than "courses" to refer to each body of members. Naturally, the assembling of the right mixture of individuals to produce a balanced session takes time, patience, and shared understanding on the part of the college and of nominators.

To each syndicate the college appoints a member of its directing staff (DS) who gives guidance on the resources available to the syndicate for the completion of the tasks assigned to it. He attends most of the discussions, which are led by members appointed as chairmen, ensures that the main issues are identified and probed, and assists the members to gain insight into the dynamics and decision-making processes of the group by working from their own immediate experience. To perform these functions, each member of staff has to be thoroughly conversant with the individual experience, capacities, and needs of the members of his syndicate, and to be well informed on the aims, content, and methods of the course of studies as a whole.

Each staff member takes responsibility for one or more subdivisions of the course, for which he prepares the documentation. This responsibility requires him to keep up to date by means of personal study and contacts with individuals outside the college, to write or commission papers for use in the course of studies, and to arrange talks and organize visits by members to other institutions during a session.

The work of the staff is co-ordinated by a colleague who holds the post of director of studies on a rotational basis, usually for one or two years at a time. He chairs regular staff meetings, prepares the timetable for the session, allocates members to syndicates, and through his secretary provides clerical services to the course. He also takes personal responsibility for some of the subjects.

To summarize, the major components of the staff role are: (a) a specialist function, relating to the knowledge and expertise which a DS might put at the disposal of a syndicate or an individual as a resource relevant to a task or to the maintenance of a syndicate as an effective working group; (b) an executive function, linked to an administrative responsibility for a subject and to the authority given by the college to a DS as its representative; (c) a consultative function, in which a DS helps an individual or a syndicate to find its own solutions to a variety of problems; and (d) a teaching function, exemplified by the occasions on which DS lead their syndicates in discussions, conduct case studies, or talk to the whole session.

In devising suitable learning situations for men likely to become senior managers, the college aims to give members practice in behavior which it believes to be appropriate to the higher levels of management, believing, for example, that at these levels managers work more by persuasion and consultation than by giving orders. It thus becomes important for a manager to be able to reach decisions and to share responsibility with others of comparable status, many of whom have vocational backgrounds different from his own. These processes expose him to a variety of professional attitudes and to the task of evaluating specialist contributions in relation to the solution of problems in their enterprise setting. The college also believes that senior managers have to work with a greater volume of more imprecise data than their subordinates, and that at the higher level the pressure of time becomes a factor of increasing importance.

In order to simulate some of the situations typical of the work of senior managers, the college designs the work of syndicates to involve the assimilation by the group of an extensive amount of information within stringent time limits. In addition, each syndicate is usually asked to evaluate the information collected in terms of its opinions and conclusions. These tasks each syndicate performs under the chairmanship of one of its members, to whom, for most subjects, the college assigns the responsibility with the aid of another member nominated as secretary.

Typically each subject of the course is introduced in a set of documents issued to each member. These "subject papers" include a brief outlining the field of study and its relationship to other subjects and specifying the task to be performed by the syndicate; a note for each chairman and secretary detailing the procedures to be adopted and some of the difficulties that may be encountered; a precise timetable; and an extensive reading list. The chairman and secretary normally receive their papers several days in advance of the opening meeting on the subject, thus enabling them to meet the member of staff assigned to their syndicate to discuss the scope of the subject and to ensure that the arrangements for its treatment are properly understood. The two members can then prepare their own scheme for organizing the work of the syndicate in that subject. Prior to the first meeting, this will also involve the examination of the books and other documentation which will have to be shared among the members of the syndicate if the task is to be completed adequately and on time.

The college arranges a series of visits to a variety of establishments at intervals through the programme. These visits enable members to supplement reading and discussion with face-to-face encounters with other managers who are handling the practicalities of a problem, care being taken to arrange that persons of adequate authority are present to answer questions effectively since the questioning members are briefed by their colleagues in syndicate beforehand. Usually about six members proceed on a visit together. Besides having to plan their questions, members also learn the art of finding means of testing the validity of the answers where these appear to be at variance with on-the-spot observations. Subsequently, members report back on the visits to their syndicates.

In addition to the inputs from reading, visits, and personal experience, members question chosen visitors to the college in their syndicate rooms. This permits questioning closer to the interests of each syndicate in relation to a particular subject than is possible with a speaker on the platform in plenary session, and exercises members in the skills of interrogation. Platform speakers may be visitors from other institutions or members of the staff, but in either instance they are normally expected to allocate half their time to answering questions from members.

These processes help members to acquire the skill of formulating penetrating questions, opportunity also arising for equally critical questions to be posed to members of other syndicates. Very often these questions relate to the reports produced by syndicates as part of the task assigned to them. The college duplicates the reports from each syndicate and circulates copies to each member; syndicates then examine each other's reports critically for a specified purpose. This may include the selection of specific issues which syndicates would like to hear discussed in more detail by all the members of the college in a plenary session.

Plenary sessions vary in form according to the subject, the syndicate task, and the timing within the session. In the more formal presentations, the members sit in syndicate groupings with the chairman and secretary at their head, while the principal or a member of the directing staff presides over the meeting. Each chairman in turn will be allotted time within which to talk about selected aspects of the subject distinctive of the work of his syndicate. The speeches are often followed by a general discussion, open to all members, on an agenda of issues raised from the study of syndicate reports. To give practice in the experience of speaking before a sizable audience, members in the early part of the session may be asked to stand on their feet when making their points to the meeting, whereas later in the session the plenary sessions may be less formal, without speeches and with chairmen merely putting points forward for discussion. Sometimes, indeed, the chairmen may themselves run the meeting from the platform. On other occasions, expert visitors may be invited to comment on the discussion. As a means of permitting more members to participate in discussion while still incorporating views from all six syndicates, there may be two parallel conferences with thirty-three members in each.

Since the caliber and experience of individuals are so important to the success of discussions in syndicate, the college has always required each nominee to attend an interview. This enables an assessment to be made of the relevance and appropriateness of the individual's qualifications and experience to the normal demands of a session. Like Harvard in its approach to the advanced management programme, Henley eschews the use of academic qualifications as conditions of entry, but because of the insistence upon successful experience, it watches age carefully, preferring men within the range thirty-three to forty-three years with a usual average age of thirty-nine for each session. In practice about half the members in any one session are university graduates.

In aiming to develop a manager from his more restricted and specialist competence to being capable of bearing the highest responsibility within the enterprise, the Administrative Staff College creates a temporary community of similarly placed men and women in their late thirties coming from a wide range of enterprises. In so doing, the college eschews any political, social, or economic bias and deliberately encourages members to search for a comparative understanding of the administrative process across the range of private and public sector enterprises.

Just as the decision to organize studies collectively on the basis of syndicates was based in part on an analysis of the work performed by senior managers and of the skills that appeared necessary to perform it well, so the content of the course of studies derives essentially from a view of the enterprise as an open system. At the time of

writing in 1971, the first part of the course views the enterprise from
the level of the members at their time of entry to the session, examining the nature of their enterprise as they see it in relation to their
own knowledge and experience. The second part concentrates upon
the resources of people and information disposed within the subsystem
of the enterprise, and the manner in which these resources can be
acquired, maintained, managed, and controlled in the interest of
achieving its overall objectives and its primary task. Following this
concern with internal administration, the third part switches attention
to the relationships of the enterprise with institutions external to
its boundaries as a system, including local and central government,
social policies, trade unions, and financial houses. The members having thus looked at the enterprise in terms of its structure, relationships,
and resources, part four of the course puts emphasis upon the dynamic aspects of enterprise management, exemplified in a study of
decision making under conditions of uncertainty, corporate policy
making, organization development, and problems in the merging of
enterprises. Members are then led to study international enterprise
operations in part five, before finally in part six undertaking a study
of the position of those who carry responsibility at the highest level
of the enterprise.

In addition to its interest in the international community as a subject of study, and in the special international comparative experience
of its overseas members, the college has strong international ties deriving from its association with similar ventures elsewhere. As early
as 1949 the setting up of the college attracted attention in India, and
in 1957 the Administrative Staff College of India came into being at
Hyderabad with the support of the central government and of businessmen. In India, and in Australia from the time of the inception
of the Australian Staff College in 1955, members of the directing
staff on secondment from Henley gave assistance in the formative
stages—assistance which was subsequently repeated with the Pakistan
Administrative Staff College and the Philippine Executive Academy,
in the latter instances in conjunction with American institutions. In
most instances the syndicate approach has been modified to allow for
cultural differences in attitudes toward authority and learning, and for
other variations in the age, maturity, status, and experience of the
participants.[3] More recently, colleges using some elements of the
Henley model have been set up in East Africa and Ghana.

This strong international interest continues to be expressed in other ways. The college now offers a programme on the direction of international operations. Members of its staff travel a great deal on international assignments and undertake a goodly number of missions for United Nations agencies. Staff members have published short reviews on management education in Belgium, the Netherlands, West Germany, and Spain; they also keep closely in touch with developments in the United States and with management training centers in Western Europe, as well as with some in Eastern Europe.

Until the 1960s the college concentrated mainly upon the development of the course of studies and upon its adaptation to suit the needs of other countries. It then embarked on a policy of prosecuting research more vigorously, being especially interested in the relationship of the Henley experience to the career patterns of its members and the policies of their enterprises. In this area, the college arranged that an action research study should be undertaken as a collaborative venture with the Human Resources Centre of the Tavistock Institute of Human Relations. As soon as initial research findings of significance became available, the college considered their implications for course content, learning situations, and staff roles.

Questionnaires focusing attention on individual and group behavior had already been tested out experimentally in some syndicates, and it was decided to extend their application to all syndicates at regular intervals, the object being to help members to find out more precisely the impact of their own behavior upon others. Staff also inaugurated a practice of periodic formal syndicate reviews during session, both of the course and of its own effectiveness. These developments were linked to behavioral science research and to the processes of feedback.

Taking the feedback principle a stage further, the college during 1968 began to collaborate with the Industrial Training Research Unit of University College, London, in a study of members' decision making in groups within an extended executive management exercise. This exercise embodied the training and use of members as group observers and the presentation of the results of their observations to their groups and to the session as a whole. In order to investigate the effect of the composition of a group upon its performance in the exercise, and hence ultimately to contribute more generally to knowledge about factors making for effectiveness in managerial groups, members were invited to take a battery of psychological tests covering various facets of intellectual ability and personality. To ensure confidentiality for the individual, the results remained confidential to the psychologist from University College and to each member who was offered, and who generally accepted, a private consultation with the psychologist. This consultation provided a further opportunity for the individual to obtain information and insights about himself, and represented one further way of trying to meet the expressed wish of many members for more personal guidance and counseling.

It is in ways such as these that the college has related the findings of its research to its own policies and organization, the roles of its staff, the design of new learning situations for its members, and its more general institutional adaptation.

In evaluating the effectiveness of this approach there are likely to be some differences as well as overlap in the criteria used by the nominating enterprise, the individual nominated, and the college staff. The college seeks to clarify any important differences during the nomination phase so that nominations go forward on a basis of shared aims and expectations. The college also sees a special need for close collaboration between the college, the nominating employers, and the members to ensure that an appropriate information system is devised which will enable the syndicate as a learning environment to be adapted constantly to the needs of the member and the pressure of the enterprise environment. However, the college also seeks to make it clear that, once an individual is nominated, it should be subject to the understanding that he must feel free to use the opportunity to test out his own thinking and behavior, and to experiment with different ideas and relationships. This it sees as central to the whole purpose of an adult learning community.

CHAPTER FIVE—FOOTNOTES

1. It is interesting to note that the analysis of the situation made by the founders of the college closely fits the conceptual framework advocated quite independently by Gavriil Popov in his analysis of the choice of management training methods in the Soviet Union (Chapter Ten), and illustrates clearly the importance of the environmental factors to which the ILO and Chi-Yuen Wu draw attention in their contributions to this volume (Chapters Twelve and Thirteen).

2. In England, a "syndic" was originally a person deputed to represent and transact the affairs of a corporation, such as a university. In the University of Cambridge the term "syndicate" came to be applied to committees appointed to perform specific duties by the Senate.

3. Dr. Khosla, in his contribution to this volume, refers to the use of the syndicate approach in Australia, India, Pakistan, and the Philippines and gives an excellent example of a situation where the immaturity and lack of experience of the participants were inappropriate to the use of the approach.

CHAPTER SIX
The Project Method: Learning by Doing*

FOREWORD

Although I have been asked by Chief Adebo to write on new methods in management education, I must hasten to point out that, in its philosophical essentials, what I wish to describe is not new.

The idea which I am to describe to you as being apparently novel in the field of management education must be, in fact, of great antiquity. It is the idea that nobody learns merely by talk or discussion—and, for my argument, talk includes case studies, management games, discussion groups, seminars, role-playings, and all other forms of social interaction *that fall short of taking operational responsibility for one's real decisions in a real world.*

I claim no originality for these reservations about argument and analogy. They have existed for thousands of years and would be better understood if only more management teachers had been self-critical enough to pay them the attention they deserve.

The skill-contending school may teach us contention; it does not teach us action. Since management is an action-oriented trade, the conscientious management professor must needs ask himself how to make good the deficiency.

A LESSON FROM AFRICA

In 1964 I was invited, through the Ford Foundation, to visit Eastern Nigeria to discuss with Professor Harold Martin, then of Rensselaer Polytechnic Institute, New York, and his colleague, Simcha

* This chapter was prepared by R. Revans.

Bahiri, a project on which they were engaged at the Institute of Productivity and Management in Enugu. The basic problem was to improve the operational performance of about a hundred small mills for extracting oil from the nuts of the wild palm tree. No process could more typify a primitive economy. The fruit was gathered by bare-footed African women and carried on their heads to these small mills, scattered sparsely across the scrublands, and usually employing but two or three managers. Their total output, however, formed a signifi-cant part—about one fifth—of Eastern Nigeria's export of palm oil. Since this oil trade was, at the time, the most important element in maintaining her balance of payments, the contribution of this primitive commerce to her national economy was more than welcome. Yet, overall, the mills were losing money and the economic adviser to the development corporation that had set them up was, at the time of Professor Martin's visit, strongly urging their closure.

The first objective of the Institute of Productivity and Management was not, however, to save the mills, nor was Professor Martin's visit to Enugu primarily to suggest how this might be done. Martin, al-though a first-class industrial engineer with some original work on operational cost analysis to his credit—and work that should be better known—was in Nigeria as a teacher. He was mainly interested in en-couraging the managers of the oil mills to understand themselves; they might then save themselves, if salvation they needed. With Bahiri, he set up a field study project, motivating a first sample of a dozen mill managers to analyze their own operations, after running with them a short discussion course upon the nature of flow proc-esses, whether of materials, the use of labor, or information about costs. It was impressed upon these comrades in adversity that, how-ever various their local problems, they had one in common: to use more effectively their resources, including in these their own knowl-edge and their own skills. I was privileged, on my visit, to learn many things, but what impressed me beyond all reach of my own corroding forgetfulness was this: that, although both Martin and Bahiri had, and could present, ideas on systems design of the most lucid simplic-ity, it was only at the mills themselves that these managers seemed to come alive and to learn. Here, sorting out each other's problems as if they were their own, reading afresh each other's records, watching and intervening in each other's physical operations, from the first bargains struck with the black goddesses balancing forty pounds of fruit on their heads to the final trickle of the precious oil from its reeking ooze; here, exchanging ideas, making suggestions and counter-suggestions, showing off ingenious gimmicks (such as a corrugated iron shaker to sort out overripe fruit that should be processed at once from that which could keep a few more days without going sour), describing economies of method (such as asking the goddess to tip her load into a gravity-feed hopper at the top of a short flight of steps rather than upon an inert heap on the bare earth), airing their favorite management ratios, and roaring together at their pet jokes; here it was evident that by identifying themselves, not with Martin and Bahiri and their ingenious ideas, but with their colleagues facing their practical problems, they were ready for constructive change. Their perceptions of who they were, of what they did, and of what they knew were thereby being not only critically examined but also fundamentally rebuilt. The managers were learning not indirectly from Martin expounding his models, or even directly from their colleagues retelling their anecdotes, but from the immediate challenges of and responses to the tangible realities before their eyes. There, in each mill, were the manifold variations of the problems they all knew well. Indeed, the sweltering reality before their eyes became for an hour reality even richer than any of theirs back home, for it was a reality reflected to them in a dozen different ways, bouncing in a dozen distinctive images off the past experiences of their dozen colleagues, like the kaleidoscopic views of a strip-tease dancer reflected in a set of tilted mirrors. Each of these uncomplicated men, on his visit to another mill, fought a dozen times the battles of managing it better, and returned to run his own with a new insight into his own professional task and into his own personal self. It was no surprise for me to hear some months later that, because of the great improvements in output that soon followed, the corporation had changed its mind and kept the mills open. It took a civil war to close them.

The Principle of Insufficient Mandate

It is difficult, in so remote a culture as that of the Biafran scrublands, for me to suggest precisely what was the educational process so vigorously at work among those eager and forthcoming men. I have trouble enough to identify the educational forces of my own programmes in Europe. But I believe that, in Eastern Nigeria, it was the sense of comradeship in adversity that provided both the motivation to learn and the media for doing so. To each of these managers the essential task was to increase the effectiveness of his own mill, and for this he needed not only Martin's new technical ideas but also the emotional involvements of questioning his own self-image, of taking real financial risks, of changing his attitudes and bearing toward his staff and his superiors, of recognizing and admitting to others his past ineffectiveness; all these are the inescapable stresses and anxieties of responsible action and they are not evoked by intellectual discussion of such action alone. Discussion about responsible action, on the one hand, and here-and-now commitment to and involvement in responsible action, on the other, are different not only in metaphysics: they differ in their impact upon the realities of responsible action. The differences may not, perhaps, equal those between discussing how to swim the English Channel, on the one hand, and actually cleaving through its tides and currents, on the other, but I believe them to be significant to management education all the same. Our technical dilemma is how to import into the educational process both the emotional stress of the responsible decision and the emotional support of others with the same educational needs and with the same determination to fulfill them. It is, in my opinion, first necessary that we should recognize the importance of group *support* in learning from any emotional experience that may threaten the self-image; it is fatally easy for the traditional classroom exercise to become a group *competition,* with all hands (including the teacher) trying to demonstrate intellectually how well they have grasped the situation already. Only a confrontation with some overriding reality can then help to convince them, both intellectually and emotionally, how much there yet may be to learn. It is thus to the search for a different methodology of management education that this essay is devoted, with the message of St. James ringing in our ears: ". . . But be ye doers of the word, and not hearers only, deceiving your own selves. . . ." What is expressed by this exhortation we may call the Principle of Insufficient Mandate.[1] However great the authority and respect we may grant to dialectic, they are alike inadequate for governing our actual world. We change what is around us when, and only when, we ourselves are changed in the process.

THE CONSORTIUM OF LONDON HOSPITALS

About this time, back in London, I had become involved in the study of communications between specialist and general service departments, between nurses and doctors and patients, between management committees and professional staff, in a number of large hospitals. A decade of operational research had suggested that, in the conditions of anxiety characteristic of the hospital, the perception that persons, whether staff or patients, have of each other and of the needs of others can be very different from the perceptions held by those others about themselves. We are none of us, alas, often allowed to see ourselves as others see us, but in some hospitals it appears that these obliquities of vision may seriously affect both the morale of the staff and the recovery of the patients. In accordance with the principle of insufficient mandate, it would be useless to imagine that such perceptual distortions can be corrected by any methods, educational or administrative, that do not involve the staff, deeply and personally, in an examination of their own specific behavior and of their impact on other individuals in the particular work situation. On this account, the management committees of ten large hospitals agreed to join together in a consortium, in which teams from one particular hospital visited another; here they were to identify problems of communication, of a kind with which they might already be generally familiar in their home hospitals, but for which, as visitors, they were not originally responsible in any way. All ten hospital teams began, therefore, to reflect upon the study of communications, not by listening to lectures, as hearers of the word only, or by trying at once to examine their own behavior, each beholding his natural face in a glass, *but by observing and analyzing the real problems of others with a view to offering responsible advice about them.* Such was then the oath of their educational baptism: to reply with a tentative "Yes" to the question "Am I my brother's keeper?" In the discussions that followed between the teams from the different hospitals, the stereotypes that were held of what each communication system was for and of what was blocking it came in for realistic reassessment. Out of each discussion there flowed, in both the home and away teams, some provisional learning at two levels: personal and individual, institutional and group. This learning was then reinforced by a series of operational projects, spread over four years, in which the home teams tried not only to identify more closely the problems suggested by the visitors but to solve them through the co-operation of those currently working in the hospital system under review. In these exchanges—about, for example, improving record flows; co-operation between ward and laboratory; the more effective use of critical resources, like beds or theaters—the hospital teams had the advice of members of staff and of students from the social science departments of a few universities and colleges of technology; they also had the support of a central team attached, on the one hand, to a large teaching hospital with a department of community medicine and, on the other, to a foundation that, for over half a century, has been actively supporting the identification and solution of hospital problems. Nevertheless, the success of this method of staff development seems to depend first and foremost upon the extent to which the senior staff of the hospital wish to become engaged in the action projects themselves; the self-perception of the supporting academic staff is also relevant, for they must abandon their traditional role of telling others what to do, or even (should they themselves know) how to do it, and see themselves as helping to provide the conditions in which the different hospital groups may learn from each other. In many cases, this demands a change of viewpoint, a reorganization of the self-image, by the senior staff of the hospital or by the teachers from the supporting college, that is to be accomplished only after deliberate effort, and only after a reluctant capitulation to the uncompromising demands of reality. The principle of insufficient mandate must be recognized in all corners of the management system under review and of those systems, such as teachers or research workers, associated with it.

A LESSON FROM AMERICA

These experiences of interaction between those facing comparable problems in comparable hospitals—based on our interpretation of the experiences of the mill managers of Nigeria sharing their expert knowledge and their professional mistakes as a process of mutual education—naturally raise the question "To what extent can we employ the problems faced by managers in the real world as a vehicle for their education and development?" Can we offset the principle of insufficient mandate by drawing upon the manager's inescapable involvement with reality? Can we contrive that three major problems of management theory and practice are brought into one operationally useful and scientifically instructive programme? The problems are:

1. How do managers learn to *apply* their knowledge in the stressful and unstructured world of reality, as distinct from learning to *talk* about it in the ordered security of the classroom?

2. How do we develop not only *individual managers* but also the *organizations as a whole* in which they work?

3. How do we bring the teachers of management into face-to-face contact with the *actual processes of responsible action?*

These three questions are to some extent answered below by Professor Carl Larson of the University of Wisconsin at Milwaukee, with whom I have had several interesting conversations. What he writes here suggests that managers who undertake the study of the problems of others gain a new insight into their own; that those who face the problems, and who are interviewed by action-oriented managers from another enterprise, are more disposed to co-operate in the solution of the problems uncovered; and that the professors who advise on points of survey design and data interpretation get close enough to the points of managerial action to acquire some insight into the conditions essential to practical achievement.

The Milwaukee Consortium was a cooperative project involving six Wisconsin companies. The project was a joint venture of the Executive Committee Group I (Mr. Robert Nourse, Chairman) and the University of Wisconsin-Milwaukee Speech Communication Center (Professor F. E. X. Dance, Director). I served as Project Coordinator. The project proper began with the selection of analysts from each of the participating companies, all of whom were top executive officers in the companies.

These analysts attended a two day orientation program in which they acquired some basic interviewing skills and developed a research plan which would guide the collection of data in the participating companies. The general focus of the research plan concerned the discovery of "communication problems" between supervisors and subordinates.

After the development of an interview schedule, a pilot study in a non-participating Milwaukee company, and the selection of representative samples from each of the participating companies, the analysts returned to the participating companies and completed their interviews. *Each analyst interviewed employees of every company other than his own.* At the completion of the interviews, the analysts gathered for extensive analysis meetings in which they compiled the results of the interviews, identified both unique and common problems, and translated their findings into standard analysis form. At the completion of the analysis meetings, each company analyst (with the combined findings from all interviews conducted in his company) conferred with the appropriate chief executive officers to outline action programs directed toward the solution of the problems that were discovered in the interviews.

My own observations on this project were:

(1) The company analysts felt intensely and consistently that they had benefited greatly from the interviewing orientation program, from the opportunity to compare their own company operations with those of other companies, and from the information which other analysts provided them concerning problems within their companies.

(2) The problems identified were markedly similar from company to company and in most cases were sufficiently grave so as to represent extremely valuable discoveries for the participating companies.

(3) Participating companies have undertaken serious action programs to correct the problems which were discovered.

(4) The program was unique in that the companies discovered for themselves their own problems and were in a good position to evaluate realistically both the extent of the problems and their abilities to resolve these problems. In other words, there was little resistance to accepting the results of the interviews and very little difficulty in understanding the implication of these results. The staff of the Speech Communication Center have engaged in many research and consulting programs for business and professional organizations, but found that the usual resistance to suggestions originating from an academic institution was missing in this project.

(5) We encountered no difficulty with any of the employees, nor were any problems created by the design or conduct of this project.

THE FIRST BELGIAN CONSORTIUM

The group of enterprises of which Professor Larson writes were all comparatively small; they were deliberately chosen for that reason. The results nevertheless suggest that, given drive enough at the top, it is possible for these methods of learning by doing to be a useful approach for the firm finding it hard to send their key men away on full-time management courses. But in Belgium the approach has also been used with particular effect in large multi-unit organizations, in which the managers and other senior staff of a dozen different factories have met together to discuss the same theme as it arises in different forms in those different factories. A fruitful theme, for example, is the better use of middle management talent, since to achieve this presents difficulties in most industrial firms throughout Western Europe. When the facts about this vexatious subject have been assembled by a joint team of field managers themselves, trained as suggested above by Professor Larson and released to interview their colleagues in other firms, they are no longer reluctant to interpret and to use the evidence they assemble; this is rarely their attitude toward identical data assembled by academic or other professional workers. Naturally enough, the use to which these interpretations are then put must be entirely local and situationally specific, and to make such use effective it must be planned, introduced, and evaluated by the managers locally in charge. As in the hospital projects, success depends upon how far the principle of insufficient mandate is recognized by those in power. If, for example, the middle managers on looking into each other's problems of human resources find that the most unfavorable opinions from subordinates are reserved for the topic of constant interruption from above, then only the top managers who are seen to generate the interruptions can usefully speculate upon their origins and, what is more difficult, upon their correction. It is, alas, easier to observe and to describe these distressing features of a management system than it is to cure them, as the principle of insufficient mandate suggests, and in any search for improvement the critical and objective advice of the academic social scientist may be of value. Indeed, if a consortium of practice and theory such as Professor Larson describes cannot throw operational light on the three questions set out above, it is hard to see how a traditional study course could begin to answer them at all.

It is not the place, in this first development of our thesis, to go into the detailed design of a consortium programme; this was, historically, no more than a pilot experiment for the exercise next described. The need for motivation on the parts of the senior managers within the co-operating enterprises has already been indicated as the key condition predisposing to success. Such motivation must embrace a willingness for personal involvement, alike in the definition of the problem to be studied, in the support of the visiting manager who is to study it, and in the setting up within his own enterprise of the necessary management-action group to anticipate and act upon the diagnosis and the recommendations of the visitor. Details of these and other needs as they developed in our first consortium are to be found elsewhere; all we stress here are the words of St. Ambrose:

"It hath not pleased God to grant his people salvation by dialectic." He asks for works as well as faith, deeds no less than promises, and action rather than talk about action—demanding, in fact, that we do not overlook the principle of insufficient mandate.

THE INTER-UNIVERSITY PROGRAMME

But operationally directed management education, based upon my experiences in Eastern Nigeria and on the principle of insufficient mandate, has so far reached its point furthest from tradition in the current Inter-University Programme for Advanced Management organized in Belgium by a consortium of her largest firms and of the management centers of the five Belgian universities. Thus the new programme assumes, in management as in medicine, that the integration of the manager's abilities into practical operation must be significantly improved by understanding better his own responses, emotional as well as intellectual, to action situations. It follows the lead developed in previous courses and regards as inadequate any mixture of dialectics about or simulations of reality, such as in-basket exercises, case studies, management games, role-playing, and workshop maneuvers, however rich, detailed, and laborious: all these are artifices prefabricated in some intellectual mold which is not the manager's own. To accept them as working material is to set aside the manager's most necessary talent: his powers of original observation. Moreover, an exercise, pursued with and against other students, all equally lacking responsible involvement in the abstracted situation, to unravel the manuscript of some unknown third party, is different from an obligation to act upon one's own impressions of some here-and-now reality for which one is inevitably responsible. It is for each particular decision maker to trace the perceptual profiles that his own personal qualities impress upon each reality; in practical affairs, the manager's task will never be assigned to him as a package of jigsaw pieces, selected and shaped in the intellectual workshop of another, and brought up for discussion among a score of others handed the same package. It will be for him first to sort each different and amorphous reality into such elements as he may conveniently manipulate, for only so will he guess which pieces may be missing and what areas of his ignorance they represent. Indeed, the medical schools have already grasped this principle of insufficient mandate, for no university has (yet) proposed to replace its hospital beds and their patients by standardized files of case notes for students to argue out, by textbook rules and scholastic models, with their professors. It remains, of course, to be seen. The explosive power of management education may yet drive the medical schools to abandon live clinical apprenticeship on the grounds that hospital reality too severely limits the imagination of the student and too severely cramps the swing of the professorial trapeze.

Any educational policy aimed at developing the capacities of identifying what action to take, of then taking that action and of subsequently living with its consequences, therefore, must at least contrive that the manager, like the clinician, will develop a skill in asking the specific questions relevant both to him and to each unique and unstructured situation in front of him. The development of this diagnostic skill is possible only if the managers seeking it are, like the apprentice doctors in the medical school, brought into direct and responsible contact with open-ended cases having no approved answers; they must attack and treat the current problems of the enterprise and meet realistically, if not always successfully, the challenge that the unknown makes to their non-intellectual qualities.

There are thus three main parties to the experiment in Belgium that attempts to shake the processes of management education free from the constraints of the principle of insufficient mandate: the participants, or fellows, who were given the opportunity to examine in detail their own managerial styles; a number of supporting enterprises (most of whom also sent fellows), who provided the strategic opportunities necessary for the participants both to observe and to practice their managerial skills; and the university staff, whose primary task was to provide the programme of study and research under which these styles might be examined and perhaps improved.

The Timetable

The fellows, after their selection approximately six months before the formal start of the programme in September 1968, were each allocated to a personal tutor at one of the five university centers. This tutor advised each participant how, either by reading or by written exercises, to reach and maintain the academic standard thought necessary for entering the formal scheme. This was composed of a two months' introductory course, a three months' diagnostic phase, a month's visit to America, and a four months' action phase. Each fellow became acquainted with certain cognitive ideas germane to management action (these are further described in the section entitled

"Basic Cognitive Ideas"). Each fellow acquired operational skill (in so far as he did not already have it) in the use of these cognitive ideas during his project work; he developed, in particular, some acquaintance with his own learning processes. For his project, he was assigned to a full-time field study, lasting eight months, of some strategic management problem in an enterprise *other than his own*. This project may have ranged from help on an existing working party established within his receiving enterprise to assess the possibility of a new process (such as to install a computer, establish a marketing department, or introduce a new major product) to an entirely original identification of some better use of a firm's critical assets or unexploited opportunities. His share in such a field study may, on the one hand, have helped to install the computer more effectively or, on the other hand, to convince the firm that they should be devoting their energies toward new goals. When the programme was designed, however, the outcome of the project as such was not a primary aim of his participation. The field exercise, not only realistic but real, was primarily to offer the participant an opportunity to examine his own field behavior and his influence upon the host enterprise. After the event, the interactions of some participants with the companies to which they were assigned were so searching that their catalyzing effect upon the enterprises in the long term will probably be significantly more powerful than their learning effect upon the participants at the time. At frequent intervals each fellow examined, with a few of his colleagues, with the teaching staff, and with representatives of the supporting enterprises the progress of his field activities, using as his tools of description and analysis the cognitive ideas with which the introductory course had made him acquainted. His first aim, during the three months of diagnosis, was to produce trial recommendations for action upon some facet of his assignment; the educational importance of this, both for the fellow and for his supporting enterprise, lay in the opportunity it gave to examine, not the technical substance of his proposals alone, but also his ostensible reasons for making them and the reception they met from the host management.

At the end of this diagnostic phase, all the fellows visited America to present their reports and recommendations for criticism by independent experts. Ten professors, some from the Sloan School of Management at M.I.T., and others from the Harvard Business School, had already been in correspondence with ten of the fellows whose projects fell in the expert fields of each professor—finance, marketing, data processing, organizational change, corporate strategy, and so forth. Each fellow was allotted half a day to introduce his report before all his colleagues, and to start a dialogue, between fellows and faculty, both particular to his own study and general to the expertise of the professors, as a learning process for all. After these ten presentations at the two schools, some of the remaining fellows presented their reports to the experts of four large firms, American Telephone and Telegraph, General Electric, Standard Oil of New Jersey, and International Business Machines; other fellows offered their projects for comment to specialists from McKinsey & Co. and from Arthur D. Little. In addition to these closely organized sessions, many fellows accepted invitations from other American universities and from other business firms, including banks and insurance companies, to discuss their projects with their faculties or managers.

The Action Phase

After this American visit, each fellow was occupied in putting some part of his proposals into effect within the supporting enterprise itself. This series of steps, lasting four months, was to ensure that effective action of some kind would flow from the trial recommendations, and it is the essence of the programme. Here is the critical attack upon the principle of insufficient mandate. Both the field studies and the recommendations based on them at all times kept clearly in view the need for action, and it is in respecting this need that the programme differs from other management courses, particularly those offered by universities. During this stage each participant was called upon deliberately to attract and realistically to assess the responses, both positive and negative, of the enterprise to his recommendations. These were sometimes radically changed in his efforts to apply them, but even in this he also learned much about both his own imperfect perceptions of reality and of the unanticipated effects that he might have been having upon that reality. Such learning might be painful, although each of the five university groups into which the fellows were integrated from the start of the programme was charged to offer him support during what could be a frustrating, if instructive, course of self-recognition. It was of great interest to observe the fellows, all with at least ten years of responsible action-oriented management experience, in their efforts to identify the essential nature of getting things done—as distinct from discussing what they should do; rarely, if ever, has so large and qualified a sample of men worked together to explore the fundamentals of managerial action. During this therapeutic stage, too, most participants also became more clearly aware of their needs for further theoretical ideas, and the university staff continued to advise them upon supplementary study programmes.

The Role of the Receiving Enterprises

The role of each receiving, or supporting, enterprise was to provide the opportunity for a participant to examine, against a suitable background, his individual managerial capacity. This could be exercised in a wide variety of ways and the projects upon which the fellows exercised them were no less varied. The choice of supporting enterprises was restricted, since the criteria of their suitability were fairly rigorous. A condition for joining the programme was that each senior management was aware of some feature of its corporate strategy demanding major improvement; the enterprise must also have been willing to offer to a fellow from another firm the chance to share in or, better, to direct an investigation of the problem, and the enterprise must already have demonstrated—such as by a resolution of the board or by the provision of money in the budget—its intention to do something about its problem. These conditions were cardinal: a clear recognition of need, a willingness to co-operate with the fellow, and a predisposing resolution to act. A fourth condition, that the enterprise establish a working party specifically to introduce, if not to implement, the recommendations for action, was asked during the action phase; the deliberations of some of these working parties, or users' committees, had already begun to produce telling effects before the programme was over, and it is now evident that, taken over all nineteen enterprises, about two hundred persons were significantly involved in the changes set in motion by the fellows. In about a third of the receiving enterprises, the changes started by their visiting fellows began to take effect only after the end of the programme. These firms have now set up a new relationship with their university management centers, to draw from them advice and assistance, and to offer opportunities for further studies, to a degree unknown in the past.

It was thus their contribution to the programme that each enterprise proposed to study and helped to design, with the university staff and with the visiting participant himself, a project, to fulfill in some degree three conditions: namely, to enable the participant to examine his own methods of work; to clarify the enterprise's own problems and suggest the means and effectiveness of their possible solutions; and to help the university staff improve their operational knowledge of management processes.

Project Characteristics

Nineteen projects were organized for twenty-one fellows, two of them engaging two fellows each. They may be briefly described as follows:

PROJECT NUMBER	RECEIVING ENTERPRISE	PROJECT THEME
1	An international fabric and paper company	To identify the main problems of innovation and of marketing policy
2	The world's largest producer of zinc	To examine critically the information network of the enterprise and to recommend accordingly
3	A major Belgian bank	To examine the changes taking place within the world of banking and the consequent need for the bank to develop a marketing strategy
4	An international producer and seller of wire and of articles based on the technology of wire forming	To examine the potential of the computer in developing and controlling the operations of this enterprise
5	A major Belgian bank	To examine the incidence of change upon the staff of this bank, and to suggest the magnitude and causes of problems facing the introduction of new methods
6	An electricity generating and distributing corporation	To suggest an information service for management adequate to the effective decentralization of the enterprise
7	An international oil company	To help in the introduction of a scheme of management information useful for anticipating change and for controlling operations
8	A large insurance company	To improve the commercial services offered by the enterprise

PROJECT NUMBER	RECEIVING ENTERPRISE	PROJECT THEME
9	An international producer of electronic apparatus	To examine the organizational problems of a complex assembly system, and to suggest a set of procedures adequate for the procurement and stocking of many component parts
10	A large insurance company	To examine the human and social problems of automatic data processing
11	An international chemical company	To match the principal information streams of the enterprise with its main decision centers
12	An international company making, installing, and maintaining commercial and marine telegraphy systems	To review the system of information now focused around the present computer and to ask in what way it should be developed
13	An international firm making and marketing wood products of all kinds	To consider the information and organization useful in the development strategy of a principal product
14	A refiner of non-ferrous metals, handling the largest annual tonnage of copper in Europe	To consider whether changes in the management structure of the enterprise (notably by increasing decentralization of decision making) is likely to improve the effectiveness with which middle management now uses its abilities
15	An old established and world-famous steel company	To study the transfer and use of information about the needs and potentials of the enterprise for innovation
16	A major producer of sheet steel	To review in detail the conditions for defining, developing, and launching (or not launching) a new product

PROJECT NUMBER	RECEIVING ENTERPRISE	PROJECT THEME
17	An international producer of photographic apparatus and materials of all kinds	To examine the relations between the departments of production, marketing, and finance with reference to the demand for and supply of light-sensitive products
18	A large Belgian bank	To examine the potential of the computer for this bank and its probable impact upon the organizational structure
19	An international producer of large-scale civil engineering materials	To examine the relations between the enterprise and its customers in the light of improved information services

Some Themes Expanded

In order to stress that the projects were not academic exercises and could by no stretch of the imagination be so regarded, six of their themes are more fully expressed forthwith:

PROJECT NUMBER	EXTENDED SUMMARY OF PROJECT
3	The main factors of change in Belgium are a challenge to the established supremacy, based on agreed credit rates, of the three large banks, alike from other national banks and from government agencies; from private savings banks; and from foreign banks. The study of the effect of this competition is made sharper, although not necessarily simpler, by the recent setting up of a marketing department within the bank; this department has representation at all levels of the bank's structure, although it is not yet clear what influence its staff will have throughout the organization, both regional and local. Thus the total problem is two-sided: to clarify relations between the bank as a whole and its customers as a whole; and to structure the organization internally so as to strengthen these bank-customer relations as much as possible. The study lends itself admirably to a monograph on the new marketing strategies being forced upon an old and traditional financial service, in whatever country it may exist.

PROJECT NUMBER	EXTENDED SUMMARY OF PROJECT

4 In the past the computer has been used for traditional data processing: wages, sales, cost analysis. Some of this has been integrated in a straightforward fashion, and the existing computer is occupied for about two thirds of its time. It is now desirable to extend the data processing to the physical operations of wire production, such as the linking of delivery and of order dates; the advising of the shipping department about completed orders; the control of finished or semifinished products; the allocation of work to machines, and so forth. If such extensions of data processing are to be made, then changes of organization and procedure and of the allocation of responsibilities may be no less required than the purchase of a large computer. The project aims to examine some of these changes—in the recruitment and training of manpower, in the design of operating systems, in the need for information-processing equipment, and so forth—and to suggest where management's critical problems are likely to arise, and on what time scale they are likely to be solved.

6 The corporation is one of the principal generators and distributors of electrical energy in Belgium, with an annual growth rate of 12 per cent; it pursues a policy of strong decentralization, working through a national headquarters and fifteen management regions. It is also organized in three management divisions, one for production and two for distribution. Managers at each level are responsible for all decentralized services: technical, commercial, financial, and personnel. There is an extensive data-processing system, generally handling accounts and costs, but inadequate for many operational or other management decisions. What is needed is an information system adequate for management effectively to allocate and control its operational decisions; on the one hand, between levels and, on the other, across functions.

8 This large insurance company conducts its business with customers partly through independent agents who may also deal with other companies. The lowest level of full-time staff employed are known as inspectors and are intended to help the independent agents on all branches of insurance. These inspectors therefore deal, on the one hand, with a variety of external agents displaying a wide range of motivations and,

on the other hand, with a range of internal technical services offering a variety of contracts. They are, on this account, key members of staff, and their relations to the existing organization, including its functions of publicity and sales, need careful examination. The project seeks to suggest what types, if any, of changes, as in structure, remuneration, or training, would best help to extend and improve relations between the company and its markets.

14   The receiving enterprise refines non-ferrous metals in three large plants; it is facing two radical changes at the present moment: innovation in the actual refining processes and a general expansion of most production activities. Thus both the managements and the physical plants show evidence of overloading that are likely to grow increasingly stressful, and a thoroughgoing analysis of the total enterprise as a system of inputs and outputs is most desirable. Basically the need is to invest, integrate, or expand at those particular points most likely to ease the total situation within the enterprise as a whole. For this reason, a start has been made at the plant levels and a survey of how the operational managers perceive the present deployment of their time and energy is now under way.

15   This is a large steel-producing concern with a strongly production-oriented tradition. Many different departments and agencies are concerned with short-term problems of adaptation and adjustment, but fresh thought needs to be given to the integration of ideas and of effort that might lead to long-term changes based on major capital investment, whether in plant or technology. The project is being developed through several stages that are already clearly defined: (1) an interview programme among key members of the management; (2) the integration of these interviews in terms of both an organization chart and a flow system of essential information; and (3) the response of this organization and of this information flow to certain known and specific attempts at innovation. The study is aimed at identifying the relations within the management critical to the progress of innovating ideas.

The leaders of Belgian industry who came forward with these project themes in 1968 have already resolved to repeat the exercise on a wider scale in 1970; they have also agreed to the inclusion of higher government officials in the programme and to its extension across the Belgian frontier. Quite evidently new problems of organization and control will be thrown up by our efforts to meet these new demands, but the 1970 programme will in consequence offer new opportunities for research into the operations of international business and into the relations between government and the world of industry and commerce. I mention these extensions of the first programme here in order to encourage the many professors of management and directors of business schools with whom I have discussed our Belgian experience. For their comment is usually that, in the locality of their particular institutions, whether in Europe or America, the businessmen would never agree to such an exchange of fellows for so intimate and revealing a mission or, indeed, could never be expected to do so. I believe this comment to be a further illustration of the principle of insufficient mandate: namely, that it is impossible for professors to understand a situation affecting their own schools merely on the authority of talking about it; their actual approaches to groups of local businessmen might produce evidence leading to very different insights.

Project Development

The chief executive of each enterprise nominated some responsible subordinate to look after their fellow, and this subordinate was chosen to see the presence of the visitor as of some advantage to him, generally because he was a potential client, already responsible within his own firm for the attack upon the perceived strategic problem. For this reason, the universities also arranged preparatory seminars for these subordinates; they were also brought into regular conferences during the field studies themselves, along with the fellows allocated to the university centers.

The participants were senior and experienced men accustomed to work on their own initiative; they were introduced within each supporting enterprise as persons expected to seek information and interviews wherever it may have seemed appropriate. Each had soon identified himself with the problem under review; none asked for a change of theme, all had completed their first proposals for action by the end of the diagnostic phase, and most had soon received a number of instructive lessons in the apparent strengths and weaknesses of their hosts. Since the solution of any operational problems can be successfully attempted only when those involved in it are reasonably clear about its nature, one early task of the participant was invariably a synthesis of how the problem was perceived by different members of his host management. All receiving enterprises cooperated adequately to enable the participants to make these reviews, although, not unnaturally, they differed markedly among themselves in willingness to accept their internal contradictions as significant. That aspect of strategic problem definition which aroused the widest general interest among the fellows was the concept of value. Again and again, the diagnoses of the problems turned upon the simple questions: "But what is this enterprise, in the final analysis, trying to do?" "Who, within it, really cares *what* it does?" "What, for example, are they striving to offer the customer?" "What is the coalition of key persons who are trying to clarify this offer?" "What does the enterprise see as the key role of innovation and research? To do present things better or to replace present things with new ones?" "And when this question has found an answer, does anybody really *want* to act upon it?" . . . It seems that the gaps in most enterprises are not in capital finance, production technology, market acumen, and so forth, but in a reluctance to define and to agree upon a clear line of business, especially if change is thereby demanded in the roles or self-images of the top management.

It was always necessary both to narrow and to deepen the specific aspect of the problem on which the visiting fellow was to make his recommendations for action. This area was, as far as possible, concerned with several main departments of the enterprise and aimed to involve them all in some degree. Generally, the action demanded setting up a task force to achieve some specific goal; sometimes several task forces were called for, to search for fresh ideas or information, to change existing methods of assessment or evaluation, or to improve co-ordination between departments. Nevertheless, the most effective as well as the most essential outcome of the deliberations of these task forces, working parties, or users' committees was always the further definition of the questions: "Where is the power in this enterprise? What is it used for?" Because of the specific nature of the first answers to these questions and of the structured recommendations made upon them, the American visit produced a wide range of responses from and contacts with successful practice. One fellow, studying for the first time in his life the problem of banking strategy, made a network of interviews from New England to California. The senior officials of American banks proved more than ready and more than academically interested to discuss their own strategic problems with an action-oriented manager from Europe who did not happen to be a banker. It has become fairly clear that, even in the most traditional industries, the recommendations of the intelligent outsider, *when framed in specific action terms,* can be a powerful solvent of established and restrictive policies.

The Support of the Universities

One feature of the programme was the integration of the fellows in small groups around their five university centers; this enabled them, against standards of professional effectiveness, individually to compare and to contrast among themselves their successes and failures in translating recommendation into action. The origins of the strategic problems facing top management were, in general, so similar from one enterprise to another that the fellows could not fail to learn from discussing each other's progress, especially in communicating among themselves about the communication problems within their hosts. Seldom in the history of management research had twenty experienced men, with the close and interested co-operation of a full-time university staff, simultaneously attacked twenty examples of this basic problem; their discussions over the eight months, when edited by the fellows themselves, should teach us something about both the problems of policy formation and those of organizational change.

The staff of these five university centers had several roles, some not traditional for management teachers. Their main responsibility was to help with the design and development of the projects, whatever they may have been, in which the fellows were engaged. In so helping, they were themselves called upon to supply practical advice upon sampling, programming, statistical analysis, and questionnaire design, and to introduce fellows to other experts upon the university staff able to discuss the many general questions—economic, cultural, technological—with which the fellows from time to time found themselves confronted. Each member of staff was expected to act in the traditional role of personal tutor to the four or five participants at his center, especially in advising them upon any supplementary reading that they found it necessary to undertake. Each was also responsible both for developing the catechism of cognitive subjects set out below and for engendering an opening balance of operational skills among the participants. Each played an active part in visiting the participants at their supporting enterprises and in the weekly seminars at which the progress of the participants was examined; each also acted as a contact between the fellows and any academic research at his own university, of which the field projects of the fellows provided practical application. The university staff also kept in touch with nominated persons at the supporting enterprises; and discussed from time to time with them, and among themselves, the main implications, for management science and other scholarly pursuits, of what was discovered, suggested, or disproved. Perhaps the strongest among the staff were those who saw their role not as teachers but as providers of an opportunity to learn; not as sources of knowledge or information but as collaborators in the framing of questions and in the sharing of doubts.

Theoretical Foundations of the Programme

For managers to perceive their influence on the situations they are trying to manage, they need the opportunities to understand their own imperfect responses to the unstructured situations into which they are necessarily thrust, and the behavior on their own part that will best help them and their colleagues to define the tasks by which they believe themselves to be faced. This will involve them in continuously specifying and amending their supposed objectives, the obstacles that stand in the way of reaching these objectives, and the resources available to remove or reduce the obstacles. This search for corporate strategy will suggest the data they may need to collect; the observations and sources most likely to provide them; their relevance, reliability, and so forth; the evaluation and treatment of these data; and, among much else, the subjective effects that these observations and suggestions produce on those from whom they have collected the data or with whom they will wish to discuss it. By observing these effects among themselves, the fellows in the programme may learn how their own behavior has affected others and thus be able to test their own self-understanding; they can compare their own impressions, conclusions, and actions with those of others; they will learn how they and others respond to different attempts to influence and to be influenced; and how differences between persons in the same situation, if intelligently contrasted and compared, can lead to learning and to improved communication.

These ideas, a mixture of scientific method, decision theory, and learning process, have been the foundation of the frequent discussions, both at the five university centers and among the fellows assembled as a whole, about goals and progress. There has at no time during the course been ex cathedra teaching of academic principles, and the aid of specialized techniques has been offered only when asked for, and even then primarily to develop the powers of observation and criticism already latent in each fellow. If we have been guided by any single aspect of educational experience, it has been to avoid, at all costs and in all conditions, the staging of professorial exhibitions, with the associated risk of reducing what is intended to be a serious educational programme to yet another transitory bill of popular entertainment.

Basic Cognitive Ideas

One of the outstanding needs in the education of managers is a frame of reference for describing, communicating, and evaluating *the subjective consciousness of personal action*. The language of the management academy is a code of depersonalized abstractions, such as economic theory, industrial law, network analysis, quantitative methods, and so forth; it is not always clear what the introduction of these topics, in all their normative purity, is intended to achieve. But the manager who personally challenges reality must first ask: "What view of the ME-HERE-AND-NOW is appropriate in using any of my knowledge?" Although it is the first assumption of this programme that only practice will enable him to treat this question satisfactorily, it is nevertheless suggested that an integrated perception of six particular subjects may help him better to structure his subjective experience. The pursuit of this perception, through practice in interviewing skills, exercises in the design of study projects, discussions to illuminate interpersonal understanding, and similar preparations for a programme of inquiry and action occupied the fellows for the first two months of the programme.

1. *The nature of values*

All management action implies a set of purposes; the manager should be trying to achieve *something*. Thus those who set out to observe their own managerial behavior should be aware of the general notion of value systems, of things seen as worth while, of goals to be striven for, of criteria for identifying them, and of sacrifices to be made in reaching them. (It has already been observed how imperative the fellows felt the need among top management for such awareness to be structured and specific, rather than broad and general.) Any discussion of value systems raises a host of ideas, from economic utility and the measurement of cash flow, to intuitive judgments made by experts against scales of purely experiential origin.

2. *The nature of information*

The working material of managers is information, and at all times the fellows concentrated upon its nature and upon the differing managerial uses to which it is put. Incidental methods of sampling; problems of transmitting data through intermediaries whose perceptions of its meaning may transform it in the process; estimates of the value of information to a manager who without it would be obliged to take greater risks: these were a few of the ideas examined. Fellows were greatly impressed both by the problems of getting information to where it should be needed and by the insensitivity of many key managers to the lack of it.

3. *The logic of systems*

All management activity occurs at a point in time: it is conjured from some previous state of affairs and creates fresh situations in the future. Ideas of flow or transfer, including purpose, delay, storage, loss, transformation, control, and so forth, whether applied to cash, funds, or working capital, on the one hand, or to materials, energy, or information, on the other, are cardinal in any analytical approach to the manager's task.

4. *The theory of decision*

Once strategic values have been provisionally identified, certain operational decisions need to be taken both to test and to fulfill the objectives specific to local conditions. Thus each fellow was informed, before he started his field observations, on the general nature of decisions. It has been possible, with the caliber of participant attracted by the programme, to discuss with most of them not only the main elements of any decision but also the basic ideas of statistical decision theory and the common models of operational research.

5. *The estimation of uncertainty*

The manager's world is full of uncertainty, not only because reality cannot be foretold, but also because it cannot be accurately known even in the present. Thus ideas of inference from limited data; of statistical significance, suggesting the measurable likelihood of such-and-such a relationship; of concordance, suggesting the amount of agreement between independent subjective judgments; of variance analysis, suggesting some order in much confusion: a minimum acquaintance with all of these was encouraged among the fellows to help them identify the structure of their managerial environment.

6. *Learning and adaptation*

Finally, managers do not change situations without themselves being changed in the process. Managers resistant to new ideas are unlikely to bring about new situations around them. Such interactions are a learning process, although, in a culture dominated by books, it is not always appreciated how effectively men learn from their own practical experience. It is fundamental to this programme that all managers touched by it should become aware of the nature of their own learning processes; indeed, there is something to be said for the opinion that the first objective of all management education is, or should be, to acquaint the subject with this awareness.

It may be useful to illustrate the use of these concepts with an example from the programme. A given firm wishes to understand more clearly its experiences both of change and of resistance to change. It is the first task of the fellow, by his practical description of a recent change within the enterprise—or of the recent abortion of some new idea—to identify the perceptions that key persons have of their goals. What do they believe to be worth doing and proper for them to do? What aspects of the change do they approve of or even actively promote? What, if anything, are they against in it, and for what reasons? (What comments on their answers does the fellow himself have to make? What is his own value system in contrast to those of his hosts?) Secondly, the fellow will need to ask what kinds of information are available to the enterprise. How does the management *know* whether what it is trying to do is, in any sense, in accord with its values and ambitions? How much of what is discussed and reported is genuine information and how much is guesswork? (What information does the fellow himself think the enterprise ought to collect and to use?) Thirdly, through what manner of system or organization does this information flow, and what are the critical points therein? How is this network perceived by those who occupy these critical points? Does the accountant, for example, say that he could measure every item of cost in the production process—and so advise the manufacturing superintendent upon his most economical production methods —if only he were asked? Or does the manufacturing superintendent say that, since he is a master of all known production methods, then, if only the accountant would give him the detailed costings of his present processes, he could very soon bring his factory expenditure to an absolute minimum without in any way sacrificing quality? (How does the fellow himself see this critical obstruction to change? What advice should he give the accountant or the manufacturing superintendent? What should be their places in any task force? How will he convey his views to the president?) Fourthly, given such gaps in the transfer of critical information, what kind of decisions are taken or can be taken? What, indeed, is the nature of the decision necessary to close these system gaps? What ought to be the key decisions necessary for launching—or intelligently opposing—some proposed innovation? What are, or should be, the criteria of its acceptance or rejection? How are the various parties brought together to agree upon their opportunities and upon their strengths? (And how does the fellow see his own part in this decision process? What has been made possible by his intervention? Does he prepare the management to take decisions that, in his absence, they would not have taken? What is his catalyzing role?) Fifthly, what are the principal areas of risk and uncertainty in the management system? Are they of two kinds: those of inherent uncertainty and those created by the management themselves? How are the second kind eliminated? What kind of information shortages create the first? How far can research overcome them? In trying to describe the total risk, what factors are most relevant? How far do different members of the management estimate differently the risks involved? Is it possible to reduce the total risk by comparing and contrasting the different estimates of it made by different experts? (What does the fellow think the risks to be? What does he feel about the attitudes of the management toward them? Are some too rash? Are others too cautious? For what reasons? What set of arguments would the fellow set out in a written judgment of the risk, should the president invite him to submit one, and what experience from outside the project would he bring to drawing up his case?) Finally, to what extent will the project, by this first involvement of the management in clarifying their values, tracing their information flows, discovering the gaps in their organization, structuring better their present decisions, and assessing more accurately their present risks, help the management to deal more effectively with some second or future major issue? The present exercise, concerned to understand innovation, will not illuminate all the troubles likely to torment the management, either now or henceforth. But if, having worked systematically through one strategic question with the help of a visiting fellow, the enterprise will be better equipped to tackle a second—such as to match better the decision system with the information system—it can be said that true learning has taken place. (How does the fellow see the project as a lesson for himself? As he reads back to his early formulations of its design and of its action stages, can he identify how immature were his first impressions of it? What were the main influences bringing about these changes in his own perception of the issues? What relevance to his own tasks does he see in this experience as a change agent in another enterprise?)

CONCLUSION

The Inter-University Programme, even in its present primitive form, is far from the scrublands of Nigeria; there is a wide gap between the search for a banking strategy in the capital city of the European Economic Community and the barefooted African girl with a baby on her back searching the trees of wild palm for their meager harvest of oil nuts. But the evolution of the central idea is continuous: that action alone teaches men how to act, whereas talking about action teaches men merely how to talk about action—and thus may conceivably postpone or even annihilate potential action. And equally continuous is the development of another idea: that a man learns how to perceive the blockages of his own perception by looking at familiar problems that belong to managerial colleagues, and by listening to how these colleagues in turn describe the problems that are his own. And yet a third: that it is the true role of teachers not to teach but to offer the conditions in which others may learn; it is advice upon the technique of observation, analysis, and use of data that the action-oriented manager may need from his teacher. The problems to which he chooses to apply these methods and the solutions by which he chooses to resolve them are for the manager to settle; in these important particulars—of what kind of outcome is to be preferred from what priority of problem—the subjective value system of the manager must take over. Our educational system must be designed primarily to help the managers overcome their real problems in the real world; it is not there merely to offer the academic profession the opportunities to exhibit their knowledge, however dazzling these exhibitions may eventually become. It is in themselves first identifying the nature of their troubles and in evaluating the outcome of their strategies for handling them that action-oriented managers will gain insight into their own behavior, not by attentively following the intellectual logic of scholastic convention. This logic and these conventions may, of course, be helpful and even necessary; they do not, however, begin to be sufficient. Our need is not for new and ingenious deals of the old educational cards; it is to recognize that management is a personal and emotional game played in the dark against unknown opponents, and that the first obligation of each manager is to understand his personal and emotional responses to the stress of managerial circumstance. Our consortia are one means by which, perhaps, he may do so. In a technical sense they may be new, but it is on the ancient wisdom of the patriarchs that they must rely.

CHAPTER SIX—FOOTNOTE

1. Efforts to express complex ideas in precise philosophical terms are often unsuccessful; the words of St. James must remain more evocative than any attempt at defining their essential message. I have chosen the word "mandate" from a number of competitors, including "concern," "responsibility," "mission," "trust," "charge," and "involvement," as it implies, to me, not only what is specifically commanded to be done but also what ought to be done over and above that for which specific commands have been issued. Thus a group of managers striving to master a particular situation, but unable either, at the start, to identify it in terms of their own experience or, subsequently, to monitor the decisions they take about it, are seen to be handicapped by an insufficient mandate. They may lack information, feedback, power, and, not seldom, motivation to act. In particular they must possess all of these in terms of changing themselves in the course of mastering the situation.

CHAPTER SEVEN

The Use of Newer Participative Teaching
Methods in Western Europe*

INTRODUCTION

This chapter deals with the use of newer participative techniques in Western Europe, Britain, and Scandinavia as well as Eastern Europe.

While there may be any number of conceivable participative teaching methods, the ones that are to be emphasized here are the case method, business game, sensitivity training, field studies, and management consulting.

HISTORICAL DEVELOPMENT

Although there are several institutional predecessors to management education in Western Europe,[1] the institutional development of management education only started after World War II.[2]

Management development in Western Europe, viewed in a historical perspective, appears to have gone through three phases: the first, that of information gathering and evaluation of the American management development experience; the second, that of institute-founding and of consolidation; and finally, the phase of consolidation.

During the first phase, which lasted until 1952, a major impetus of management education was provided by the Marshall Plan and the foreign aid programmes that arose from it. Thousands of managers from European countries went to the United States to study management and management education. The reports of most of the various

* This chapter was prepared by Rolf Th. Stiefel and Antoine Papalofzos.

national study teams which were formed to investigate these areas by and large concluded that their country of origin also needed some sort of management development institutionalization.[3]

Only a very few schools had been established up to that time in that part of Western Europe with which we are dealing. One of these was the Centre d'Etudes Industrielles (CEI), which was founded in Geneva in 1946 in order to prepare managers from the Aluminum Company of Canada for international operations. However, since the school was a company-owned institute at that time, very few Western Europeans were trained there. A major breakthrough for the Western European management development institutes was the foundation of the Administrative Staff College at Henley-on-Thames, which became the model for several continental schools like the Centre de Recherches et d'Etudes des Chefs d'Entreprises in Jouy-en-Josas, France, or the Stichting Studiecentrum Bedrijfsbeleid, Arnhem, Netherlands. Basically, this was an attempt to introduce the concept of the Harvard Business School in Europe without duplicating the weaknesses of the programme structure.[4]

Once having assessed American experience concerning management development, most of the Western European countries founded their own management schools. Interestingly enough, several smaller countries with outstanding personalities—Leon Bekaert in Belgium, Rolf Waaler in Norway, among others—were the forerunners during the phase of institute-founding. By the end of the fifties, nearly all the Western European countries had their own management development schools.

The national study teams which had been analyzing the American experiences were, however, often advising their countries without having co-ordinated their observations with those of other national teams. This led to a situation where most of the schools were nationally oriented. With the founding of the European Association of Management Training Centres (EAMTC) in Brussels, and with increased co-operation among different schools—like Eurogestion, which was formed by two German institutes, one Belgian, one French, and one Italian institute—a very fruitful period started in European management development. This was well exemplified in the mid-sixties, when the European Research Group on Management (ERGOM) was founded in order "to promote management education, to innovate new training approaches and to assemble a body of information on intercultural similarities and differences in management and organizational behavior in Europe." ERGOM, together with EAMTC, thus became institutional symbols for the consolidation phase in the history of European management development.

In reviewing these phases, it can easily be inferred that participative teaching methods were not used at all before World War II. Only with the establishing of management development institutes were new kinds of pedagogy set up, and only then did students and participants begin to take a more active role in the teaching-learning process.

In the first years after the schools were founded, concepts of teaching methodology were very much oriented toward the American business schools. However, with the increasing consolidation of their programme structure, several European schools created their own concepts.

CONCEPTS CONCERNING THE USE OF TEACHING METHODS IN WESTERN EUROPE

Although most of the Western European management development institutes are relatively young, several distinct concepts concerning the use of teaching methods can already be distinguished.

In the following section, we shall attempt to map out different "management development schools of thought," an approach first used by Hawrylyshyn.[5]

In examining the varying management schools of thought, which in turn result from the variety of approaches to management theory, it is logical to distinguish equivalent concepts. The reason for this management theory jungle, and for the simultaneous intermingling of many management development conceptions, is simply that we do not know exactly what makes a successful manager.

A confrontation of schools of thought in both management theory and management development is shown in the Appendix, Table 1.

1. Management Process School
2. Empirical School
3. Human Behavior School
4. Social System School
5. Decision Theory School
6. Mathematical School
7. Industrial Dynamics School
8. Strategy School[6]

In analyzing these different schools of thought, we clearly recognize that not all of them represent essential distinctions; several are, rather, versions of one or another of the main schools of thought. It is thus that we can distinguish among the following four concepts with their examples (Table 2): Empirical Conception, Behavioral Conception, Mathematical Conception, and Synthesized Conception.

Since most of these concepts were first realized in the United States, the corresponding American prototype institutes are also mentioned.

THE CASE METHOD IN WESTERN EUROPE

Although the case method is the oldest method in management education, first used as such in 1911 at Harvard Business School, previously developed in the law and medical schools, it is today still the most widely used device among all the participative teaching methods. At the same time, the method is regarded as being the prototype of the "American" teaching method for training managers.

It is fair to say that, being of United States origin, the case method has been approached in quite a standardized fashion without major changes due to cultural and regional differences. Thus the structure of the method follows the same rules in Western Europe.

In this section, we do not treat the case method as such extensively, since several monographs exist in the field. Our focus is rather on the varieties of the case method in management education; the constituent variables of cases (a comparative view); and the Western European experience with the method.

Varieties of the Case Method in Management Education

The case method exists in various versions, all of which are used in European management schools. Those schools which were established with United States know-how and staffed by American professors rely heavily on the Harvard type of cases. These schools are represented by examples such as Institut pour l'Etude des Méthodes de Direction de l'Entreprise (IMEDE) in Lausanne, the Instituto de Estudios Superiores de la Empresa (IESE) in Barcelona, and the Universitätsseminar der Wirtschaft in Cologne.

The case method in the Harvard fashion is a very lengthy case with an abundance of detail and figures. Not all of these are relevant to the underlying problems. "The desired result of the [Harvard] case method is the ability to reason in dealing with problems in the area of the course. Appropriate use of theory, and the acquisition of factual material and procedural skills are also important goals, but the heart of the method is the use of problems to train the student to discover and then to fix in his mind ways of thinking which are productive in the chosen field."[7]

Concerning the handling of the method in class, both students and teacher have equal access to the data. The role of the teacher is rather that of a catalyst who provides a permissive environment for a group discussion. His style is non-directive.

Another version of the case method is the "living case" where a case of events is presented to the students. These events have just happened or are still going on. "Living cases" are used by different teachers, particularly in the post-experience courses. In Europe there is usually not the rigid sequence of steps that is found at, say, the Wharton School of Finance and Commerce. While at this institution a specific procedure of using an outside expert was developed, in Europe one normally follows a more informal pattern by inviting an experienced businessman who is treating a specific topic in a case manner. The CEI, for example, has invited several guests for case discussions, particularly in the fields of "corporate strategy" and "management of international operations."

"Living cases" are more rewarding than the other type of cases because the participants can identify themselves with an ongoing operation, while the Harvard type of case is felt as being someone else's problem to which one does not have any specific kinship.

A highly structured way of handling cases is represented by the "syndicate method" developed at the Administrative Staff College in Henley-on-Thames. There were a few schools in Scandinavia, especially the "Solstrand" management school in Bergen and the Management Institute in Helsinki, which used the syndicate method after its development in 1948 at Henley. But nowadays the method is largely confined to Henley and to a few management schools outside Europe (New Zealand and India).

Another version of the case method—the incident method—was developed by the Pigors.[8] This method is also highly structured and formalized. Basically we can distinguish the following steps:

a. *Individual study of an incident:* Each individual in a class analyzes an incident which normally consists only of a few sentences. Hence there are usually a lot of unclear points which are questioned in the subsequent step.

b. *Getting additional data on the case:* After studying the incident, the students ask the instructor for further information. Necessarily, the instructor has to be well prepared.

c. *Individual decisions on how to cope with the perceived issues:* The incident normally presents many facets. Hence the pursuit of the various issues as they are perceived takes place in a different way. The students write down individually how they proceed in solving the problems.

d. *Meetings in small groups:* Small groups of like-minded students are set up according to their various approaches in formulating solutions. Each elects a spokesman who seeks to substantiate the decisions represented by his group.

e. *Role-playing:* The groups convene in plenary session where a kind of role-playing situation between the group leaders takes place. Each of them defends the chosen path, putting forward the reasons for doing so.

f. *Confronting the class with the history of the case:* The instructor finally explains how the problem was solved.

Finally, we might distinguish another kind of case, often referred to as "abbreviated case." This involves concentrating on one issue of a particular case which offers a complexity of problems or eliminating all but the essential facts of a comprehensive case in order to expose only the bare skeleton of the problems. The abbreviated case method generally represents no new type but draws upon a combination of other forms.

Constituent Variables of Different Case Methods
Certain structural elements are characteristic of each case. Table 3 in the Appendix compares these variables.

Experience in Western Europe:
It should be frankly stated that there is a shortage of European teaching material, particularly cases dealing with European business. The whole body of case material originated more or less in the United States and is used widely in Western Europe. In countries where the English language is commonly taught in the school system (Netherlands, Sweden, Germany), the cases are not even translated and are simply used in the original version.

The exclusive use of American case material has obvious disadvantages. This was early realized in the area of personnel management where the situation obtaining in the various European countries was not structured as it was in the United States. Furthermore, the case material for international business left much to be desired on the part of European managers since the cases were naturally written according to experiences with United States-based companies. Moreover, there is nowadays only a limited series of multinational cases involving European parent companies (e.g., Olivetti, Alfa Laval).

If we seek the reasons for the lack of European case material, we immediately find that one of them is due to the shortage of experienced case writers. There are only a small number of institutions known to have competence in the field of case writing. Among these are IMEDE (Lausanne) and IESE (Barcelona), which annually recruit faculty members from Harvard University to devise European cases for their international management courses. In this way at least a limited supply of superior European case material has been developed.

Another reason appears to be the lack of contact between business schools and the business world. When we consider that it is not long since management education had great difficulty in obtaining acceptance in Europe, we can then understand why the in-depth contact typical of the situation in the United States has as yet no real European counterpart.

Closing the gap in European case material means developing case-writing abilities and skills among young European professionals in the management field. A good case is not just a business story but a well-structured procedure and layout of facts and data. It is not possible to take the report of a management-consulting assignment in one class and use it as teaching material for students in other classes. The report must be completely rewritten by somebody who was involved in the information-gathering process in the field.

No recital of Western European experience in this area would be complete without mention of the pitfalls and shortcomings that have been encountered. The European teacher who has traditionally used lecture methods has felt uneasy in his new role of guiding a case where certain rules and techniques have necessarily to be observed. The functions of a teacher as a case discussion leader are rather complex and require skills which were never asked for previously in his career. It is no exaggeration to say that in European countries excellence of teaching ability is not normally considered a specific asset by which a career can be made. Skills in doing research and in mastering one's subject take priority, since the system grants a bonus only for these. By the same token, a teacher hesitates to spend his time creating case material when it may not be accepted as valid research—even assuming that he has developed the necessary case-writing skills.

If the situation is to change, teaching ability and the development of appropriate case material will have to carry more weight among the career requirements of an instructor in management education.

BUSINESS GAMES IN WESTERN EUROPE

Business games are one of the salient methods in the portfolio of management education. The simulation of management decisions in all variations—with and without computerized equipment—is a specific feature of management education in all parts of the world.

Business games appeared in management courses toward the end of the 1950s. In 1957 the American Management Association developed a business game[9] which was the first computerized version. In 1958 Andlinger described a manual business game in the *Harvard Business Review*[10] which was sold at an extremely low price. In one way or another all the business games developed in the subsequent years were modeled on these two examples.

Although business games have been on the curricula of management schools for only about ten years, games as a learning tool are much older. Certainly the Prussian war game was one of the roots of the business games existing today. Military education has used war games for ages, and it is amazing that it was only in the second half of the fifties that this experience found an equivalent in the business world.

Structure of Business Games

Since business games have been extensively described in the existing literature available in all the modern languages, we will be brief, outlining their essence only. Approaching business games from a practical point of view and looking at the basic structure of a game—regardless of whether it is a functional game as in marketing, finance, or production, or whether it is a general management game, and whether or not it is manually or electronically umpired—the basic fabric of the game remains unchanged.

A number of participants form a team and play against several

other teams. They are informed about the simulated business reality
(rules of the game). After each decision period, the participants hand
in their decisions to the umpires, who evaluate the decisions. Assessment of the decisions can be done manually but must be done on a
computer if the model is complicated. After the assessment session
the teams receive their evaluated decisions and the cycle starts again.

Business games in their structural sense normally differ in their
degree of complexity. This has some technical implications, particularly in the allotment of time to the teams per decision period and use
of electronic data processing in assessing the results of the participants. Moreover, one can establish the rule that the more complicated
a game the more people must be in a team. After the game is finished,
a review session or a so-called maneuver session follows which explains the model of the game.

Development of the Business Games in Western Europe

If we summarize a history of the development of business gaming
in Western Europe, we can distinguish the following phases:

Uncontrolled use of American business games in Europe. Immediately after what can only be called the business gaming craze started
in the United States, European institutions by and large adopted the
American games and used them in their courses. In some instances
only the most relevant variables of these games were taken and a
new model was built around them. The procedure of the CEI in
Geneva of developing a new game on the basis of the Andlinger variables was followed and applied in several institutes. Characterizing
this period was a general "acceptance on faith," as Boocock and Schild
point out.[11] As in the United States, the tendency to verify the impact
on learning of the new device was outweighed by the enthusiasm with
which it was used. Since course co-ordination believed in the magic
power of business games, the most important question in education
was not asked: how helpful is a business game in terms of learning
apart from being an enjoyable exercise for the participants?

*Development of European games and the beginnings of educa-
tional research in gaming.* During the mid-sixties more and more
games were developed in Europe, all but displacing the American
business games. A similar trend occurred in other areas where, after
a period of strong dominance of American educational software,
European methods took over. Boocock and Schild describe this pe-

riod as the honeymoon phase and write of the sobering conclusions which arose after some research ventures in business gaming were undertaken. It was realized that the expectations that had been held in business games were too high, particularly that they could not be used as a panacea in management education. During the first period personal satisfaction on the part of the participant was identified with learning output. Research carried out with more objective measurement yardsticks showed clearly that this assumption was unrealistic.

Recognition that business games are a teaching tool among others. The disillusionizing outgrowth of this research led to a concept among teachers of management in Europe that games should be used more carefully and in accordance with desired objectives. Thus, business games are presently used in addition to, and not at the expense of, the existing range of devices.

It must be pointed out, however, that the underlying learning objectives differ now from school to school. We have presently a situation where different management schools use games for different purposes. In the following section we present some of the ways in which various institutions follow different concepts in integrating business games into their methods mix.

Modified Use of Business Games

We can identify a number of the underlying learning objectives under which the use of business games can be categorized as follows:

Familiarization with computers. Several computer manufacturers have developed their own games, the objective of which is to provide increased familiarity with computers.

By using a computer as an evaluator of the decisions, the participants become accustomed to using both the hardware and the computer output. They obtain a better understanding of computer application. On the attitudinal level, business gaming of this kind has helped to create a positive feeling for the emerging man-machine system which is so widely representative of the mid-management level of all organizations.

Business games as part of a learning package. Another feature of the use of business games is its strong emphasis on behavioral phenomena. The game as such becomes part of a larger exercise, which represents both a laboratory in human relations and a laboratory in decision making.

By pinpointing the procedure of CEI, we can show the general practice of using a business game in this fashion.

The actual decision sessions of the teams are preceded by two or three lecture-based sessions on leadership patterns and determinants of managerial styles. Concepts like Blake and Mouton's Managerial Grid,[12] McGregor's "Theory X and Y,"[13] and Tannenbaum and Schmidt's continuum[14] are presented to the whole class. After familiarizing themselves with the basic concepts, the participants meet in teams and map out their basic strategy for the game. It should be mentioned that the teams are composed so as to be as multinational as possible.

During the game, which is of a rather simple Andlinger type, the teams are observed by a trained psychologist who uses a structured observational plan. The categories that have been used by observers over the past few years are: information seeking, information giving, analyzing, proposing action, deciding action, seeking decision, opinion giving, support giving, opposing, joking, laughing, and talking together.[15]

After collecting these data, it is possible to make a profile of each team with respect to seven elements. These are: group climate, data flow, communications, goal formation, goal seeking, control, discipline. The information thus assembled is fed back to the teams in the review session. In addition both the observer and the group members have to rate the group leader independently on the Managerial Grid. Finally, after discussing this behavioral input in small groups, the teams convene in plenary to compare their performance in terms of "Wall Street Criteria" with the managerial style they have used.

One recent development in business games seem to be the tendency to emphasize the behavioral aspects. On the occasion of a seminar on business games in management education in December 1969 organized by the International University Contact for Management Education (IUC) and the EAMTC, this new direction was discussed at some length. Hoekstra points out that business games, which have served in the past mainly as decision laboratories, can greatly benefit from experiments in psychological or social laboratories.[16] This new approach would make it possible to promote both economic and social learning.

In addition to Hoekstra, who is at the Institute for Social and Industrial Psychology at the University of Groningen, another Dutch school of thought will be mentioned here. The Nederlands Paedagogische Instittuut (NPI) uses the pedagogical principles which Rudolf Steiner developed in the early 1920s for the teaching process at the Waldorf schools.

Considering the stated objective of the NPI, "to give assistance in the development of people and organizations," it is again the social learning which is pinpointed here. There are several institutions in Europe, among them the Institut für Führungslehre an de Technischen Akademie in Wuppertal, which are combining their business games sessions with group dynamics sessions carried out by NPI representatives.

While the observers in the CEI pattern of business gaming were almost by definition completely passive, the new designs for using business games as laboratories in social learning impose a more active role on the behavioral scientist. Hulshof and Verburg propose that the observer should take over the role of trainer and ask questions during the game, which enables the group to reflect immediately on its own behavior.[17] This new design assumes that by giving feedback afterward the learning situation will be placed outside the game situation since reflecting on games ex post facto does not permit of application or experience with respect to certain principles leading to a positive result.

The newly emerging combination of a laboratory in decision making and a laboratory in social learning is bound to have certain consequences for the design and administration of new games. Especially the time-pressure issue has to be rethought, since it does not stimulate social learning. While this issue makes a lot of sense for bringing the decision-making exercises close to reality, social learning will suffer, because in stress situations people tend to close their eyes.

It is a rewarding undertaking to marry the advantages of two disciplines, both business games and group dynamics, and enhance the learning process, thus making the method more effective. There are some pitfalls, however, because sometimes a compromise in the game design has to be made which would have negative impact both on economic and on social learning.

Integrated use of business games. If a business game is used integratedly, the game is more or less a skeleton of the total course. The structure and problem areas of the simulation model are the cornerstones for building up a complete course.

The game is played with intermissions. A decision period might be preceded by a lecture on international marketing strategy and by a lecture-discussion type of session on controlling subsidiaries abroad. The decision sessions provide the opportunity for applying the more theoretical contents of a lecture.

It goes without saying that this kind of game must be highly realistic. The game designer has to face this issue directly by reconciling it with another requirement—that a game must be playable. While this may be a built-in conflict, nevertheless in this category of usage it has to be overcome.

There are few games which can truly be used as skeletons for a course, hence few schools have used or are using this approach.

Business games are used for a range of educational objectives, but not every business game can be used for each purpose. It is the major role of a method expert with an institution in management education to select games according to the underlying objectives. In addition to this, a key role is played by the game administrator, who can make the game a success or a failure.

SENSITIVITY TRAINING IN WESTERN EUROPE[18]

Originally, sensitivity training was introduced in various management conferences as a new method to teach human relations group dynamics and even leadership skills.[19] The T-group was the basic element in the programme around which lectures, role-playing, and other exercises were woven. Later, intergroup relations[20] were introduced and the learning experience was widened to include the study of the total seminar as a community or mini-society (the administration of the conference included G. Hjelholt's[21] conferences in Scandinavia and the study of the organizing processes within the conference (T. Lindner, 1968).[22]

Although the place of sensitivity training in management courses is still debated by a number of social scientists, its role is becoming more and more important.

Since 1963, efforts have been made to use the laboratory methodology to gain understanding and to develop better international or intercultural relations. Although much has been learned about which designs and group composition may facilitate or hinder understanding or intercultural work, these types of programmes are not very successful on the market. On the one hand, the human individual seems to be extremely sensitive and reluctant to expose his cultural or national feelings and to learn from them; on the other hand, the temporary system—*in casu,* conferences—fosters the development of an "international" spirit, which in turn facilitates the temporary denial of cultural values and sense of belonging. Furthermore, cultural or national stereotypes are often masked by interpersonal and inter-group animosities which seem to be much easier to focus on.

The training-group programmes for managers (mostly aimed at industrial organizations) have, with a few exceptions, been organized as "stranger conferences" attended by individuals from different companies and countries. The participant body is generally composed of higher-middle management and senior managers.

We know of only a few industrial organizations in Europe that have sensitivity training within their companies: a Danish shipping company, a food distribution firm, and I.B.M. World Trade Corporation in its Educational Center. But many more organizations have sent their key people to foreign conferences as a matter of training policy.

Sensitivity training has, however, received its warmest response from social organizations. Social workers, social nurses, parents, and youth leaders were among the first to include training groups in their educational or follow-up programme. Then churches and various religious organizations and orders gained interest in this approach as a means of renewing or deepening their convictions or to initiate a programme of organizational change.[23] More recently, the laboratory methodology has appeared in the curriculum of university departments of social sciences and by now it is considered to be part of the training in psychotherapy.

In most cases, faculty members and outside trainers share in taking on the trainer's role in T-groups for students. This is believed to facilitate comparison and understanding of attitudes toward the outside trainer and the faculty-member-trainer.

The latest development of the laboratory methodology in Western Europe is its application to organizational development. In this field, the training group—or some variation of it—is introduced as preparation for solving problems existing within the organization. Its role can then be used in building sufficient openness and thrust to allow free discussion of organizational issues to learn about group work and hidden agendas or to strengthen one's motivation toward improving the organization.

Sensitivity training is thus moving in varied directions in industrial, social, and professional organizations. Although various objectives are being pursued, more work could be done on improving international relations and on conflict resolution. Furthermore, it appears that, besides the mini-society labs, most programmes are designed for participants belonging to a higher or middle social class.

Some Observable Differences

Although greatly inspired and influenced by NTL and its members, sensitivity training in Europe has some notable features of its own.

The basic philosophy behind the European work is different from that in the United States, and so is the culture which the participants bring to the conference. Unfortunately, not much research is being done on this subject, and one must rely only on observations, incidents, and comparisons of scientific literature.

First, European trainers focus more on the understanding of the group processes and the basic anxieties and needs in immediate relationships than is generally the case in the U.S.A.

The works of Bion, Lewin, and philosophers such as Scheler, Heidegger, and P. Sartre have deeply influenced the European behavioral scientists, in particular the work of Max Pages.[24] The life of the group, according to this author, is nothing but a continuing dialogue to clarify the experience of the immediate affective relationships which the members develop through being together. Participants in such groups learn about basic aspects of their human existence: anxieties, love, and separation; and their relation with others.

Emphasis is placed on basic existential experiences and less on the more obvious, manifest forms of these experiences. Members tend to try to overcome the inability to communicate one's inner self to others and to explore other ways of improving one's communication habits.

Second, European trainers focus more on the actual authority issues and on the relationship of the members with the trainers than is presently the case in the U.S.A. There may be several explanations for this focus.

One of these is the psychoanalytic background of many trainers. Psychoanalytic theory, especially the works of Bion, draw attention to the transference phenomena in groups and, in particular, emphasize the importance of the relationship between the trainer and the group. This latter relationship is conceived, by Max Pages, as a mirror of the relationships between the members themselves.

Another is the role of authority issues. Such issues still play a more important role in a group in Europe than in the United States. Many American trainers reported that the observed dependency needs of the participants were particularly strong in their European groups. Consequently, if the objective of the T-group is to learn about and to develop group work, a high learning priority should be given to clearing the authority issues.

A third observable difference in sensitivity work on the two continents is that European trainers tend to refrain from making *instrumental interventions,* whereas American trainers are much more eager to "help" the group members. Behavioral therapy, which has stimulated many American trainers to intervene more often in an instrumental way, does not seem to fit the dominant European values. The latter stress understanding, reflection, and authenticity. Consequently, we feel that instant intimacy and exercises in expressing affection or resentment are unnatural and interfere with the basic emotions and anxieties of the group.

The "too good mother" approach of the trainer, who is haunted by the need to be helpful, to be liked by the group, and to avoid aggression, is strongly rejected in Europe. Life, we believe, is not a chain of *immediate* satisfactions, and though one may strive to understand and to improve real life, one should not make it out to be a Nirvana. Besides, instrumental interventions would make it increasingly difficult to clear the dependency or the authority issues.

Fourth, European trainers reserve much time for the study of *community phenomena* or *organizational behavior* in the temporary system, which is the conference. Furthermore, the community or the organization of the conference is not conceived of as being one large training group but as a pattern of interrelated groups, developed during the course of the programme.

Fifth, in general, the European trainer has greater reservations about *non-verbal exercises* and *sensory development.* The key to this reservation is the observation that both approaches are rather egocentric, the individual developing or expressing himself for the sake of development or self-expression. The other-directedness and the relationship with others, which is so important in Europe, is often lost or ignored in such programmes.

And sixth, the European research or studies made on training groups and sensitivity work reflect a higher interest in the sociopsychological *processes* than in the practical outcomes or produced changes.[25] On the process side, one has to mention the various studies of the Tavistock Institute,[26] the outstanding analysis of Max Pages (1969),[27] the work of R. Meigniez (1963),[28] the doctoral dissertations of R. Hoogengraad (1966)[29] and L. Vansina (1967).[30]

These differences, however, should not obscure the many similarities in this work on both continents. Our intention is merely to point out that major differences do exist. Only a few European scientists have done some serious research on the outcomes of sensitivity training, namely, D. Moscow (1969, 1970)[31] and P. Smith (1963 and 1965).[32]

We have repeatedly and purposely used the word "differences" because it does not imply any evaluation. Indeed, an evaluation assumes a value position. If one should look at sensitivity work on both continents, from the standpoint of practical and immediate usefulness, one rightfully would conclude that the European approach scores generally lower than the American one. If, on the other hand, one values existential depth, then the European approach ranks generally higher than the American one. Much still remains to be learned before the two approaches can find a new, more optimal integration, assuming this appears to be desirable.

Present Concerns and Plans for the Future

One cannot leave a historical review of the sensitivity movement in Europe without explicitly discussing certain concerns and hopes for the future with respect to recent developments within this field.

One immediate area of concern is that too many people are operating as lone individuals, without the backing and control of a professional institution. Consequently, the field of sensitivity training is being troubled more and more by unqualified trainers who seek in this field personal satisfaction at the expense of "innocent" participants, and who use sensitivity training as a banner to cover other goals and values.

As to unqualified trainers, a number of psychologists, sociologists, and social workers still believe that with or even without experience as participants in a training group they may freely experiment with this methodology on other human beings. In such instances, the poor, not to say painful, results should not come as a surprise.

One example will illustrate what can be expected with unqualified trainers. A general manager broke into tears in a T-group and received warm support for this from an "inexperienced" trainer. Obviously, the latter saw in this a demonstrative example that the stereotyped tough manager was a human being after all. Fortunately, the same manager participated in another training group and there it became clear that he was using "softness" to repress his deep-rooted anxieties about being firm and aggressive. A company study revealed later that his previous lack of firmness and aggressiveness was the key issue in the organization, and in the personal life of the manager as well. Although many social scientists complain about this type of irresponsible behavior,[33] only EIT has a firm set of built-in appraisals in its programme for the development of sensitivity trainers.

Turning to the question of improper need satisfaction, we strongly believe that most, if not all, human beings try to satisfy some personal needs in their professional work. The question, therefore, is not whether one satisfies personal needs but *what* the needs are and *how* they are being satisfied. We cannot but agree with Drs. Kuehn and Crinella when they observe: "It seems that such approaches of the leader (trainer) may serve as an outlet for himself—for behaviors that are not accessible to the leader (trainer) outside the laboratory." But, this observation is not too helpful. One ought to have a set of criteria to evaluate and to decide whether this or that need-satisfaction behavior is inappropriate to the trainer's role. It is not good enough to say that all behavior is permitted as long as one can learn from it. One can always attach a learning value to the trainer's behavior and then anything goes!

Other trainers will wave the banner of (misconceived) "authenticity," thus allowing themselves to do anything they like. "I must be true to myself" is the statement that legitimizes trainers who have fallen in love with, or feel sexually attracted to, one of the T-group members, to have sexual intercourse with them,[34] or that allows trainers to break staff decisions and agreements freely. Persons like this are opposed to supervision and countertransference analysis, which they regard as paternalistic.

Whether the participant can learn from such satisfaction behavior from the trainer is only one among the many criteria but it is not an easy one to apply. Indeed, the group does not always have the maturity to pursue the learning goal when the one who represents it—*in casu* the trainer—is emotionally overinvolved himself. It still remains to be seen whether learning about this particular area of behavior can be considered to be the most important.

A second criterion is human dignity—the extent to which the participants have the possibility of using options, of studying them, and of making decisions in the existing situation.[35]

A third criterion we like to use is individual growth—the degree to which the participants' possibilities for personal growth are maintained or increased. There is some real danger that the trainers—carried away by their feelings of omnipotence—may venture into psychotherapeutic interventions, bringing about deep emotional problems on the part of those whose awareness is being sought. The resulting cognitive awareness rarely produces the desired result. On the contrary, it tends to undermine one's belief in, and willingness to go into, psychotherapy where needed.

Regarding sensitivity training as a means of introducing hidden values, we do not want to argue here to what extent this behavior is related to improper need-satisfaction on behalf of the trainer, discussed above. The fact is that one often cannot escape the feelings of *revolt* against institutions and society—under the name of training for *social change*. The point I would like to make is that the trainer should be open to the sociopolitical (and ethical) values he or she *intends* to *introduce* in the course. The programme brochure should clearly inform the public about its objectives. The participants have the right to have this information in advance so that they can question actual deviations from these stated objectives in the course of the programme.

Even apart from these hazards, many trainers operate from institutions that are not designed for, or capable of, taking the responsibility of sensitivity programmes. The director's knowledge about sensitivity training may be limited, or his actions may be predominantly guided by financial considerations with respect to hiring and keeping qualified professional talent, and to providing a secure base from which the professionals can work, learn, and handle possibly disturbed participants. Some centers put so much pressure upon their staff that they have to pretend to be qualified and must cover up unfavorable incidents. In such circumstances, it becomes very hard to learn from one's experience—one's countertransference behavior—and to maintain professional standards.

More and more people, however, are becoming aware of these almost inevitable weaknesses and dangerous developments within sensitivity training. Concrete plans are being made to improve or build institutions which have the competence and the organizational capabilities to investigate, develop, and apply the laboratory methodology.

First one has to develop professional and institutional competence before claiming the right to train and supervise other professional talent while maintaining high standards.

We know of such projects, one of international and the other of national scope. EIT is investing considerable effort in designing a genuine international training-of-trainers programme and in providing the institutional means for adequate supervision and continental learning. Hopefully, it will also be able to make more use of the research and conceptual competence within its membership body, thus providing a theoretical and empirical spine for the sensitivity movement in Europe.

In the Netherlands, the universities, the public administration, and the professional associations are jointly planning to build an Institute of Applied Group Dynamics (Stichting in Toegepaste Groepsdynamica). They will become responsible for training of sensitivity trainers, the co-ordination of training programmes, and research projects in applied group dynamics.

Such an institution may not provide *maximum* opportunity for free experimentation in this field, but it can guarantee continuity in research and application, leading to goal-oriented innovations.

Having shown the streams and tendencies of the classical unstructured format of sensitivity training in Europe, we should mention a new kind of T-group training which was developed for the international management education activities in Western Europe.

PERSONAL AND MANAGERIAL FEEDBACK GROUPS

In 1967–68 Professor Howard V. Perlmutter[36] had been experimenting with a more structured exercise in order to cope with the multinational composition of the IMEDE participants in Lausanne. The exercise, called Personal and Managerial Feedback Groups (PMF Groups), differs in several fundamental ways from classical T-groups. For example, the exercise takes place over a three-day period (while T-groups last from one to three weeks). In addition, PMF Groups are made up of participants who have known each other for several months and have seen each other in various managerial roles, as opposed to the typical T-group, which is composed of strangers.

On the following pages, Alden G. Lank, PMF Group trainer,[37] describes the exercise.

Some Assumptions

Like all other forms of sensitivity training, PMF Groups make certain important assumptions about people and their behavior.

One major assumption concerns the feelings and attitudes about the participant which are held by his bosses, colleagues, and subordinates in his "back home" work situation. These feelings and attitudes have been created at least partially by the participant's behavior in various job-related contexts. If these reactions were known to the participant, they could provide extremely useful inputs concerning his managerial behavior and its effects upon others. Likewise, these inputs could provide an important basis for improving certain managerial skills. Unfortunately, all too often the typical organization does not provide the appropriate climate or channels for the "feedback" of this kind of information.

PMF Groups are designed to provide just such an opportunity in a carefully controlled setting for the participant to receive feedback concerning the impact of his behavior upon others. In this case, the source of information is his CEI colleagues. To the extent that they represent a range of reactions similar to those he might encounter on the job "back home," the feedback could have high utility in improving certain of his managerial skills. As this feedback takes place within a group setting (eight to twelve persons), PMF Groups also provide each participant with the opportunity to learn more about his colleagues as he watches and listens while each gives, receives, and reacts to feedback.

PMF Goals

The PMF Group experience has five stated goals: to increase self-awareness; to increase awareness of others; to change attitudes about self; to change attitudes about others; and to increase certain communication skills, such as listening, giving constructive feedback, and breaking down communication barriers.

PMF Structure—Day 1

The first day starts with a review of the goals of the experience. These goals have already been stated during an introductory hour-and-a-half session given some weeks before. After that introductory session, led by the monitor, participants chose whether or not to participate in the

PMF Group experience. It is the CEI's policy that PMF Groups are an optional activity and that each participant is completely free in making his choice.

This is followed by an open discussion on why participants had decided to take part in PMF Groups. Once the different expectations about the experience have been clearly stated, the monitor then asks the group to share any feelings either positive or negative that participants have at the start. Should any anxieties exist, they can be considered by the group. Normally, such discussion reduces the level of anxiety to a point where the participant concerned is in a proper frame of mind for starting to learn more about himself.

The next item on the agenda is of critical importance. Each participant is asked to write a two- to three-page "self-description." Without initially identifying the authors, the monitor reads the self-descriptions to the group which then attempts to identify each author. An accuracy index ("How many did I get right?") and a transparency index ("How many got me right?") are then calculated. Results are often surprising to the participants. The subsequent discussion provides some important insights into the problems of accurately "sizing up" others and of adequately communicating to others the image that one has of oneself.

In the afternoon of the first day, the first of four sociometric questionnaires is given to the group. The group is asked to decide who are the three persons in that particular PMF Group with whom they find it relatively easy to communicate and the three persons with whom they find it relatively easy or relatively difficult to communicate.

The data collected from this source are then presented in a graphic, sociometric form. Each of the two-way reactions is discussed in depth and provides the basis for feedback. The monitor carefully ensures that feedback is provided in such a way as to be constructive and helpful.

Day 2

The second day is spent discussing the result of three similar questionnaires which are completed late in the evening of the first day.

However, on this occasion, the subject matter is how individuals in the group see each other as bosses, colleagues, and subordinates. Discussion is always lively since the group has learned quickly how to give constructive feedback and participants are eager to maximize the amount of feedback. The morning is spent on the boss question-naire results, the afternoon on the subordinate ones, and the evening on the colleague ones. Once again, each of the two-way reactions is analyzed.

Late evening of the second day is reserved for an important ac-tivity: each participant is asked to think of one to three questions about his own managerial behavior that he would like to ask his col-leagues. These queries are read out to the group and each member is asked to think carefully about his response to the questions posed before the following morning.

Day 3

The third day is devoted to responding to each participant's ques-tions. Respecting very strict time limits, each person receives from three quarters of an hour to one hour during which his colleagues and the monitor attempt to provide helpful suggestions and advice related to the issues raised the previous night.

The questions tend to reflect concern for a perceived need to change certain behavior in line with the feedback received during the previous two days. Typical examples are the following:

"How can I open the door to closer relations with colleagues, superiors, and subordinates?"

"I am too hesitant in making decisions. What shall I do to improve my ability to make timely decisions?"

"What managerial approach should I use with my subordinates, given the fact that they expect and desire me to operate in an au-thoritarian fashion while I myself strongly believe in a participative style of management?"

A Japanese participant asked: "In what ways do I have to change my behavior to be effective in a multinational firm outside of Japan?"

Another participant wondered: "What can I do to reduce over-sensitivity to other people's feelings? On occasion, I avoid making a necessary decision simply because I am afraid of hurting others." Another participant was concerned about what he should do to "ef-fectively manage a department, given the fact that I am significantly older than all my subordinates." Yet another participant was inter-ested in knowing whether or not changing certain behavior so as to be more effective in a boss role would automatically mean a deteriora-tion of his effectiveness as a colleague.

Not surprisingly, most participants have found that the real "pay-off" of the PMF Group experience comes during this third day.

The Future

Reactions of IMDP[38] participants over the last three academic years indicate that PMF Groups (which are only offered at the CEI and the Wharton School of Finance and Commerce) are an extremely useful learning device. One of the most impressive new insights, they feel, concerns the destruction of certain national stereotypes. It becomes extremely difficult after a PMF Group experience to characterize people in terms such as "the inscrutable Japanese," "the cold-blooded Englishman," "the sex-crazy Swede," and so on. During PMF, participants are able to break through the wall of national stereotyping and see the individual standing behind. This very fact could have major repercussions upon the effectiveness of multinational teams to which many IMDP participants will belong upon their return to business life. While stereotypes may be handy generalizations on occasion, in international business they may cause great harm to interpersonal relations.

FIELD STUDIES

Two methods remain which are closely related with the business world yet have not received professional consideration by writers in management education. It is remarkable that almost no literature on their use exists. These are field studies and management consultancy assignments, and basically we can confine our review of the method to how it is used at CEI. No other school—at least to our knowledge—is using field studies in such a structured way and no other school has the experience that CEI has with this method.

The section deals with two versions—industry study trip and management systems study—both of them field studies in the way they are structured.

Industry Study Trip

If we were seeking a less sophisticated definition we could apply this term whenever students of management courses go into the field. Yet this broad definition is useless since it does not distinguish management consultancy assignments from industry study trips. We understand by an industry study trip a teaching method that fulfills the following set of criteria:

(a) the visit to a well-chosen company;
(b) a careful examination of the company's annual reports and of the environment in which the company operates, and some preparation as to the expected problems should precede the trip;
(c) the participants must meet the policy-making level of the company;
(d) the participants have to report on their studies in the field; this report should not only protocol the situation in the company but should show the author's opinions about the problems and the means of tackling them practically.

Let us explain the various criteria in more detail:

Regarding (b) above, the company must be an "interesting case." At the same time, it must be assessed according to its openness and willingness to respond to questions. By "interesting case" we mean the company should have a striking strategy event in the recent corporate records. This can either be a take-over of a competitor, a development of a diversified product range, or even simply an outstanding rate of growth which makes it interesting to know more about it.

The participants want to know more about the company when meeting the management. Hence they have to study the company's situation before they visit it. Assessing a company's situation means studying and analyzing the last annual reports, the competitive situation, and the whole environmental sector in which it operates. Only then can the right questions be brought up which may lead to a deeper understanding of the present situation.

At CEI a series of sessions on the environment sectors given by a guest lecturer, if necessary, precede the actual trip. At the same time, small study groups analyze different aspects of the company and present them in class so that enough background material on the company is available. Let us exemplify this statement. At one stage a Swiss aluminum company was selected, which then had the highest rate of growth among the competition. The participants were analyzing the strength and weakness of the company beforehand, by analyzing the annual reports, the competitors' balance sheets and annual reports, etc. Moreover, guest lecturers gave a series of sessions on the situation of the industry as well as on the environmental sectors of the companies. This preparation enabled the students to talk very competently with the managers they met.

Turning to (c), it is absolutely necessary that the participants meet the top management people in the field. The most interesting issues normally have a strategic character. However, strategy is not formulated at middle management but at the top. If the participants meet only functional department managers, the discussion necessarily focuses on administrative and operational matters and just deals with strategic issues to a minor extent, owing to the position of the managers in the company.

And as regards (d), at the end of an industry study trip, the participants come up with a report which reflects the visit in a strength-and-weakness balance after discussions with the responsible people. This report is discussed in class and is also sent to the company, which, incidentally, often gets some remarks out of it worthy of consideration.

Management Systems Study

The second version of field study is a trip of several weeks to selected companies in different cultural, political, and economical settings. The main features that distinguish the management systems study from the industry study trip are in the limited range of topics (mostly one theme), the number of companies (preferably in different environments), and the duration.

The preselection of a topic known to both the students and the company people well in advance guarantees a certain depth in the discussion between them. If one does not specify the topic when visiting a company, the discussion will stay normally very much on the surface owing to the number of areas which are of general interest.

The following list represents the topics chosen in the last few years which comprise the current areas of interest.

—Factors contributing to company growth

—Control of international operations

—The effect of internationalization, including foreign trade, on the organization of the enterprise

—Technical innovation

—Motivation of man

—Training of managers and other personnel within the enterprise

—Practices and techniques in market research, sales promotion, and distribution

The management systems study as a teaching method is especially useful in international business education. It can be intriguing to see, for example, how diversification strategies are pursued in different countries or how innovation is organizationally structured in different economic systems. This method is particularly rewarding for a student who has to deal with international issues. It gives him a broader outlook and a feeling that there is not just one panacea available to tackle and handle business matters. It prevents him from getting locked into a certain type of thinking by being repeatedly confronted with various approaches that are often equally successful. It stimulates readiness to become more creative and innovative—characteristics which are required in a business world that is constantly changing.

The time spent in using this method must necessarily be longer than in the industry study trip, since it will have a minor impact if only two or three companies are seen. In our opinion, there is a certain threshold of exposure which leads to learning the management systems study as a training method in the way we described that is only used by CEI.

Its one drawback is that it is a fairly expensive learning device.

Although there are no effectiveness studies on the method, it is well accepted in industry. Especially the Japanese participants in our courses have been enthusiastic about the method, a fact often recognized when referring to it as the Japanese learning method.

MANAGEMENT CONSULTANCY ASSIGNMENTS

The management consultancy assignment is a teaching method whereby the participants are faced with real problems in the business world. There are, of course, a number of ways in which students can be exposed to the method, but in general it is a business problem in a company that has to be tackled by a group of students. Let us exemplify the method by referring to CEI experience.

Before the method in its present structure was introduced, the school was using so-called "industrial projects." A group of participants dealt with a fictitious major industrial investment venture and simulated all the necessary information and decision steps in order to execute the given task. The teams were normally made up of four to five participants.

In 1968 the fictitious character of the investment projects was replaced by assigning real projects to the students, since several European companies had been asking the school every year if a group of students could not make a field analysis of a certain problem or range of problems. Otherwise these companies would have set up a kind of task force team to view the problem or problems in question from different angles.

Before the students go into the field, several sessions are given by experienced management consultants not only on the process of problem solving but also on report writing. The students then go in small groups into companies. After three or four weeks they return to the school and come up with a proposal which is often implemented afterward by the companies.

Participants who attend a longer course are normally faced with certain re-entry difficulties when they go back to their companies. Hence, among other reasons, the management consultancy assignment is scheduled at the very end of a course. It also serves, then, as a kind of re-entry tool and avoids the situation in which the students are immediately plunged into the business world after a long off-the-job exposure to a management course.

At the same time, when CEI introduced management consultancy assignments as a teaching method, Revans used a similar approach in Belgium's Inter-University Programme for Advanced Management (AMP). Since management consulting is a major part of the ten months' course in Belgium, the objectives aimed at are a bit different from those at CEI.[39]

It is quite evident that management consultancy assignments can only be used in post-experience courses where people often have considerable management expertise. Moreover, the method as such can only be practiced in a longer course since it is relatively time-consuming, although the (not yet) measured effectiveness might justify the time. Use of the method is restricted to only the longer courses also because both preparatory and follow-up work are necessary, a fact that should not be neglected.

These requirements make the method, as originally designed, a rarely used instrument in management education, simply due to the fact that the number of long post-experience courses in Western Europe is very limited.

FUTURE DEVELOPMENT IN THE DESIGN AND USE OF PARTICIPATIVE TEACHING METHODS

Basically, there are two areas of impact which will shape concepts of teaching methods in the future. One is that each teaching method has strengths and weaknesses (effectiveness-orientation). The other is that the rapidly emerging field of educational technology will generate new methods.

The past use of participative teaching methods was often dogmatically determined. The extensive use of the Harvard-type case method in the early stages of European management education reflected a belief that this classical method of preparing American managers for business careers must have a superior role in the schedules of business schools. It was a question of status to teach management via cases.

The panacea character of any one method in the past will be replaced by a different view in the future, as has been mentioned several times throughout this chapter. We believe that each teaching method has a comparative advantage over all other methods within certain areas of teaching objectives. This implies, in other words, that we have to develop an operationally defined enumerative taxonomy of teaching objectives in management education. Subsequently, we have to pinpoint the potential of the various methods to obtain these objectives.

This search should lead to very effective ways of teaching. At least two ways of operating with the strengths of methods can be foreseen. One either adds method to method according to empirically validated potential or one designs a new method which is a combination of the strengths of already existing methods. We may refer to a forerunner of this latter way of design by mentioning the Kepner-Tregoe method. Analyzing this method, we may state that it is actually an amalgam of elements of the case, the incident method, and the in-basket technique, in combination with a highly formalized and structured procedure applied to the small-group work.

Another example for designing new methods by adding strengths to the strengths of existing methods is the emerging pattern of combining business games or, more generally, simulation exercises with group dynamics. Hitherto, the users of business games have seen gaming primarily as a laboratory in decision making. By attaching a group-dynamic dimension to it, a lab for social learning is simultaneously achieved. While the participants in the classical business game received only feedback on the economic effects of their decisions, they are now also exposed to feedback on their behavior in the groups.

Major impulses for the design of newer participative teaching methods probably will spring from the rapidly developing field of educational technology. Teaching methods will be closely connected with the "educational hardware" and the design of learning environments. The latter term, especially, is not very familiar to programme designers in management education nowadays, yet it is an area which has enormous impact on the development of methods.

By simplifying this new direction, we could coin the phrase "holistic" design of methods. This means, in other words, a departure from the view identifying various pedagogical elements in the teaching-learning process and operating only with these points to achieve objectives. The new concept is based on the "whole," where integration of the elements occurs not *during* the teaching-learning process but *beforehand,* by a preconceived design of method, subject, teacher, learning environment, and student.

Table 1

Management Theory/Management Development

1. School of Thought: *Management Process School*

    a. CHARACTERISTICS: Management is a process of getting things done through and with people. The approach aims at establishing a conceptual framework for it, at identifying principles underlying it, and at building up a theory of management from it.

    b. DIDACTICS: Subjects related to the managerial functions.

    c. METHODS: No distinct method pattern. Since the choice of methods is made on the assumption that understanding of the managerial functions is principally a "knowledge" question, the traditional methods (lecture, guided and free discussion, and other information conveying techniques) are used.

2. School of Thought: *Empirical School*

    a. CHARACTERISTICS: Management is a permanent decision-making exercise which is based on a historical analysis of business events.

    b. DIDACTICS: The didactics reflect the premise that if we study the experience of successful managers, or the mistakes made in management, we will somehow understand and learn to apply the most effective kinds of management techniques.

    c. METHODS: Study of cases, especially the "classical Harvard" cases, which are very rich in data.

3. School of Thought: *Human Behavior School*

    a. CHARACTERISTICS: Management is seen as a process in which people work together as groups in order to accomplish objectives.

b. DIDACTICS: The programmes are built on the basis that people should understand other people. Psychology and social psychology are the dominant areas in the structure of the courses.

c. METHODS: Group dynamics. Role-playing. Psychodrama and other versions of methods having an impact on human behavior.

4. School of Thought: *Social System School*

a. CHARACTERISTICS: Management is understood as a social system, that is, a system of cultural interrelationships.

b. DIDACTICS: Programmes are loaded with themes that study group behavior in the framework of social systems. Heavy sociology orientation concerning didactics.

c. METHODS: Emphasis on different kinds of group exercises (both structured and less structured).

5. School of Thought: *Decision Theory School*

a. CHARACTERISTICS: Management is a rational approach to decision making.

b. DIDACTICS: Subjects are built around the decision-making process. Emphasis is on model construction and rationalization of the steps, especially the generation and the assessment of alternatives in the process.

c. METHODS: "Computer exercises" in various versions.

6. School of Thought: *Mathematical School*

a. CHARACTERISTICS: Management is understood as a system of mathematical models and processes.

b. DIDACTICS: The schedule is highly oriented toward management science and applied mathematics.

c. METHODS: Model-building exercises, such as simulation techniques, with co-operation of highly advanced computers (business games with an immense number of parameters).

7. School of Thought: *Industrial Dynamics School*

a. CHARACTERISTICS: Management is seen as a network of systems and subsystems. The functional areas of management are reduced to a common base by recognizing that any economic or corporate activity consists of flows of money, orders, materials, personnel, and capital equipment.

b. DIDACTICS: Didactics of management is systems-oriented. Tendency to include a larger and larger universe in the schedule.

c. METHODS: "Equation" exercises and study of simulation models with the computer.

8. School of Thought: *Strategy School*

a. CHARACTERISTICS: Management is understood as a very structured approach toward configuring and directing the resource-conversion process in such a way as to optimize the attainment of the objectives.

b. DIDACTICS: Distinct feature is the combination of mathematical model-building subjects with the environmental orientation.

c. METHODS: "Packaged" learning modules of subject matters, methods, and teaching technology, as well as a variety of teaching methods according to their effectiveness in obtaining teaching objectives.

Table 2

Management Development School of Thought 1. Empirical Conception

a. MANAGEMENT SCHOOL OF THOUGHT: Part of the Management Process School, Empirical School.

b. METHOD PATTERN: Case method and discussion of the abbreviated case.

c. WESTERN EUROPEAN INSTITUTES: IMEDE (Institut pour l'Etude des Méthodes de Direction de l'Entreprise), Lausanne, Switzerland; IESE (Instituto de Estudios Superiores de la Empresa), Barcelona, Spain.

d. CORRESPONDING U. S. INSTITUTES: Harvard University, Cambridge, Massachusetts.

Management Development School of Thought 2. Behavioral Conception

a. MANAGEMENT SCHOOL OF THOUGHT: Human Behavior School, Social System School, Part of the Management Process School.

b. METHOD PATTERN: Role-playing, Sensitivity training, Psychodrama.

c. WESTERN EUROPEAN INSTITUTES: EIT (European Institute for Transnational Studies), Louvain, Belgium

Institut d'Administration des Enterprises, Université de Bordeaux, France.

d. CORRESPONDING U. S. INSTITUTES: Yale University, New Haven, Connecticut.

Management Development School of Thought 3. Mathematical Conception

a. MANAGEMENT SCHOOL OF THOUGHT: Decision Theory School, Mathematical School, Industrial Dynamics School.

b. METHOD PATTERN: Simulation and model-building exercises with much use of a computer that has great potential.

c. WESTERN EUROPEAN INSTITUTES: No European school is similarly using this concept. Relatively similar is, e.g., Vervolmakings Centrum voor Bedrijfsleiding, Katholieke Universiteit te Leuven, Belgium.

d. CORRESPONDING U. S. INSTITUTES: M.I.T. (Massachusetts Institute of Technology), Cambridge, Massachusetts
Carnegie-Mellon University, Pittsburgh, Pennsylvania.

Management Development School of Thought 4. Synthesized Conception

a. MANAGEMENT SCHOOL OF THOUGHT: Strategy School.

b. METHOD PATTERN: Basic feature: teaching effectiveness—conscious choice of methods.

c. WESTERN EUROPEAN INSTITUTES: Very explicitly CEI (Centre d'Etudes Industrielles), Geneva, Switzerland.

d. CORRESPONDING U. S. INSTITUTES: Vanderbilt University, Nashville, Tennessee.

Table 3

Variables of the Different Case Methods

1. Harvard Case Method

a. CASE REPORT: Very lengthy report with abundance of data often having nothing to do with solution of outstanding problems.

b. CASE ANALYSIS: Students prepare case individually, major portion of time being devoted to extracting most relevant data from the bulk of data.

c. CASE DISCUSSION: Discussion is non-directively led by the teacher.

He has no more information on the case than the students. His role will be that of a catalyst seeking to bring out differences of opinions among the participants.

2. Living Case Method

   a. CASE REPORT: Orally presented report of main events of a problem.

   b. CASE ANALYSIS: Students meet in small groups and analyze situation. Each student then writes report containing his analysis and solution of problem.

   c. CASE DISCUSSION: Class divides into small groups and discusses reports with instructor. One student is elected as discussion leader. In final meeting, an executive familiar with case discusses final solution with whole class.

3. Incident Method

   a. CASE REPORT: Presentation of bare incident comprising only a few sentences.

   b. CASE ANALYSIS: For analyzing situation the whole class has to ask for more information. After selecting relevant data, they decide individually on solution.

   c. CASE DISCUSSION: Separated according to differences in written decisions, small groups of like-minded members are set up and elect a spokesman. Then spokesmen of the different groups discuss their solution.

4. Abbreviated Case Method

   a. CASE REPORT: Presentation of most relevant data of a problem or list of problems essential to a report.

   b. CASE ANALYSIS: Individual analysis of facts in case.

   c. CASE DISCUSSION: Discussion led by teacher in a non-specified fashion.

CHAPTER SEVEN—FOOTNOTES

1. E.g., the Prussian military academies and the institutions for training the elite of the Roman Catholic Church and for diplomacy. For a more detailed description, see Stiefel, Rolf Th., *"Entwicklung und gegenwärtige Situation der externen Unternehmerschulung in Europa,"* in *Betriebswirtschaftliche Forschung und Praxis,* Vol. 21, No. t18, pp. 430–41.

2. The 1960 EPA *Guide to General Courses in Business Management* lists 171 general courses. Of these, 6 were founded before 1937 and 108 after 1947. European Productivity Agency: *European Guide to General Courses in Business Management* (Paris: OEEC, 1960).

3. See, for example, Vaubel, Ludwig, *Unternehmer gehen zur Schule* (Düsseldorf, 1952).

4. For a more detailed discussion, see Taylor, H. J. B., "Report on the Methods used for advanced management training by the Harvard Business School (USA) and the Administrative Staff College, Henley-on-Thames (England)," Project T.A., Henley-on-Thames, 1952, pp. 57–118.

5. Hawrylyshyn, Bohdan, "Le Perfectionnement des dirigeants—un investissement pour l'avenir," *Revue économique franco-suisse,* No. 1/1969, pp. 24–26.

6. Koontz, Harold, "The Management Theory Jungle," *Journal of the Academy of Management,* Vol. 4, No. 3/1961, pp. 174–88.

7. Hunt, Pearson, "The Case Method of Instruction," *Harvard Educational Review,* Summer 1951, p. 175.

8. Pigors, Paul and Faith, *Case Method in Human Relations: The Incident Process* (McGraw-Hill, 1961).

9. Ricciardi, F. M., Craft, et al., *Top Management Decision Simulation* (American Management Association, 1956).

10. Andlinger, G. R., "Business Games—Play One," *Harvard Business Review,* March/April 1958.

11. Boocock, Sarane S., and Schild, E. O., *Simulation Games in Teaching* (Sage Publications, Inc., Beverly Hills, 1968), p. 15.

12. Blake, R. B., and Mouton, J. S., *The Managerial Grid. Key Orientation for Achieving Production through People* (Gulf, 1964).

13. McGregor, D., *The Human Side of Enterprise,* (McGraw-Hill, 1960).

14. Tannenbaum, Robert H., and Schmidt, Warren H. "How to Choose a Leadership Pattern," *Harvard Business Review,* March/April 1955.

15. These categories were developed by Hawrylyshyn, B., and Papalofzos, A., "Group Effectiveness in a Management Exercise Setting" (Geneva, 1964). Unpublished research paper.

16. Hoekstra, Martin H. R., "Experimental Learning in Simulation Laboratories," paper written for the first seminar on "Business Games in Management Education—Application and Administration" at Wuppertal, December 14–19, 1969, organized by the International University Contact for Management Education (IUC) and the European Association of Management Training Centres (EAMTC).

17. Hulshof, A. H., and Verburg, P. *Enige ervaringen met bedrijpspelen Maandblad voor Accountancy en Bedrijhuishondkunde,* 39, 2/3 1965, p. 65.

18. This section is an abbreviated version of a paper by Dr. Leopold Vansina, Leuven, Belgium.

19. Bridger, H., "An Intergroup Project" in *T-Group Training: Group Dynamics in Management Education,* edited by G. Whitaker. Association of Teachers of Management, Occasional Papers, No. 2 (Oxford: Basil Blackwell, 1965).

20. Higgin, G., and Bridger, H., "The Psychodynamics of an Intergroup Experience," *Tavistock Pamphlet No. 10, 1965.*

21. Hjelholt, G., "Training for Reality," *NTL Human Relations Training News,* 1963, Vol. 7, No. 4.

22. Hofstedde, G. H., and Lindner, T., "Measuring Social Distance: Computer Analysis of Sociometric Data as a Means to Identify Informal Sub-groupings in Social Systems." Mimeographed paper, 1968.

23. Decock, G., "Werken met kommissies tijdens het kapittel gebeuren," *De Kloosterling, Tijdschrift voor Religieuzen,* 1968.

24. Pages, M., "Note sur le T-groupe ou groupe de diagnostic," *Bulletin de Psychologie Sociale,* 1959.

Pages, M., *La Vie affective des groupes: Esquise d'une théorie de la relation humaine* (Paris: Dunod, 1969).

25. Trist, E. L., and Sofer, C., *Explorations in Group Relations* (Leicester: Leicester University Press, 1959).

Jacques, E., "Social systems as a defense against persecutory and depressive anxieties," in Klein, M., Keinmann, P., Money-Kyrle, R. (eds.), *New Directions in Psychoanalysis* (New York: Basic Books, 1957), pp. 478–88.

26. Sofer, C., *The Organization from Within* (London: Tavistock Publications, 1961).

Bion, W. R., *Experiences in Groups* (London: Tavistock Publications, 1959).

27. Pages, M., op. cit.

28. Meigniez, R., *Cinq études sur le groupe-centré-sur-le-groupe.* Mimeographed, 1963.

29. Hoogengraad, R., "L'Evolution de la contrainte du contexte sur le processus de signification dans deux cas d'analyse de groupe. (The progress of contextual constraint on meaning in two cases of group analysis)," *Journal de Psychologie,* 1966, Vol. 63, pp. 437–62.

30. Vansina, L., "Training Groepen en Leidersidentiteit: Een studie over waardenwijzigingen en onderliggende psychische processen," *Nederl. Tijdschrift Psychol.,* 1967, Vol. XXII, pp. 7–30.

31. Moscow, D., "The influence of interpersonal variables on the transfer of learning from T-groups on the job situation." Paper read at the XVIth International Congress of Applied Psychology, Amsterdam, 1968.

Moscow, D., "T-Group training in the Netherlands: an evaluation and cross-cultural comparison," *Mens en Onderneming,* November 1969.

32. Smith, P. B., "Attitude changes associated with training in human relations," *British Journal of Social and Clinical Psychology,* 1963, pp. 105–13.

Smith, P. B., "The effects of T-group training," in *T-Group Training: Group Dynamics in Management Education,* edited by G. Whitaker, ATM Occasional Papers No. 2 (Oxford: Basil Blackwell, 1965).

33. Kuehn, J., and Crinella, F. M., "Sensitivity Training: Interpersonal Overkill and Other Problems," *American Journal of Psychiatry,* 1969, Vol. 126, p. 6.

Lakin, M., "Some Ethical Issues in Sensitivity Training," *American Psychologist,* 1969, Vol. 24, pp. 923–28.

34. At present one has to make such observations explicit. The professional code of ethics usually only had to *imply* that sexual behavior in a professional relationship was unacceptable. Now, with the turbulent changes in values, one has to write it down explicitly.

35. Lakin, M., op. cit.

36. Howard V. Perlmutter is today professor at the Wharton School of Finance and Commerce.

37. Alden Lank is a faculty member of CEI and is presently doing some special studies at Harvard University.

38. IMDP stands for International Management Development Programme, which is a ten-month course at CEI on a post-experience level.

Levelwise, it is comparable with an M.B.A. programme of a leading American university.

39. See also Houston, Thomas, "Belgian A.M.P. Is On-Line, Real-Time," *European Business,* July 1969, pp. 17–21. For more detailed information, see also Chapter Six in this book.

CHAPTER EIGHT
Developments in Methods of Management Training in the Eastern European Socialist Countries*

INTRODUCTION

This chapter is an attempt to show the progress in teaching and training methodology in a broad context of overall advancement of management education and training in the Eastern European socialist
countries. That is why it begins with a brief review of the development of managerial resources in these countries. This is followed by
a discussion of several factors that shape the management education
and development activities in the region and, consequently, are of
major significance for the methods and techniques used. The third
part of the chapter deals with recent experiences in the use of some
selected methods and the final part is devoted to problems of promoting effective teaching and training methods.

The chapter deals with experience of the following countries: Bulgaria, Czechoslovakia, German Democratic Republic, Hungary, Poland, Romania, U.S.S.R., and Yugoslavia. It is based on information
obtained from the countries themselves, on the author's personal
experience with management education and training, and on a number of visits to educational and training institutions in the region.

"Teaching and training methods" is not interpreted to mean only
those used in the classroom, since a substantial part of manager development takes place on the job where an appropriate choice of

* This chapter was prepared by Milan Kubr. Views expressed are those of
the author and not of the International Labour Organisation (ILO).

methods is also necessary. The chapter deals mainly with methods used in the development of practicing managers (general and functional) and staff specialists being trained for future managerial posts. However, as improvements in teaching methodology are no less urgent for university studies in management and related fields, references to methods used at universities have been included wherever possible and appropriate.

I. OVERALL SITUATION AND MAIN TRENDS

The history of management development in the Eastern European socialist countries is a young one. Although some conferences, seminars, and courses of interest to managers were available during the fifties, it was not until 1959–60 that the education and training of managers began to be introduced on a larger scale and on a more systematic basis, with clearly defined objectives and content and methods adapted to the nature of managerial functions. The 1960s were then a period of rapid advancement of management development in virtually all countries of the region, although not every one started at the same time or progressed at the same rate. In the course of this decade, networks of management development and training institutions were established and many new programmes commenced. To emphasize a systematic, continuous development of managers, in most countries governments adopted resolutions or decrees which indicated how this development should be planned and organized and determined the responsibilities of national and other institutions operating in this area.

Such progress in the development of managerial resources during the 1960s was made both possible and necessary by some socioeconomic and administrative realities:

1. Owing to accelerated industrialization, enterprises became larger and more complex.

2. The effective utilization of resources became a much more difficult goal for management to achieve.

3. Methods of planning and control used in the first phases of industrialization were no longer suitable and needed modification.

4. As a consequence, economic reforms were introduced; these reforms increased the decision-making power and responsibility of managers of enterprises and enhanced the part played in management by prices, credits, taxes, and other financial instruments.

It was only logical that these developments drew attention to the question of managerial competence. If men in strategically important managerial positions were not to become bottlenecks to further economic growth, measures were immediately necessary to broaden their capabilities.

While the short-term objective was to help practicing managers to cope with the requirements of the economic reforms, a long-term broader goal gradually evolved: that of developing a system which would keep managers continuously up to date and prepare them to face new situations at all stages of their professional careers.

Nobody contested the fact that managers acquire their competence primarily through practical experience. However, more people were emphasizing that not every experience molds good managers, and that managerial experience without further education and training does not suffice to cope with the present period of accelerated scientific, technological, and economic change.[1]

It does not seem appropriate to list, in the context of this chapter, all the new institutions and programmes established in the Eastern European socialist countries during this period. The process of growth is far from being completed and every month brings some new developments.[2] Presently it consists largely of building educational and training institutions and introducing suitable off-the-job programmes for managers and staff specialists in all sectors and at all levels of the national economy. Concerning the future, it can be expected that more emphasis will eventually be placed on such things as career planning for managers, management development schemes of enterprises and other organizations, on-the-job training and job rotation of talented young managers, without which formal education and training cannot produce full effect.

Turning to the newer teaching and training methods, it will be apparent from the above that their history in the Eastern European socialist countries also cannot be old. Before 1960, only a few enthusiasts in research institutes and universities were experimenting with participative methods.[3] Lectures, discussions, and exercises of the classical, i.e., university, style prevailed in the few management courses then available. In fact there was little difference between courses for adults with managerial experience and courses given to undergraduates.

During the 1960s considerable progress was made in teaching and training methodology. The subsequent sections of the chapter will analyze this process in greater detail and discuss the various factors which have accelerated or hindered the application of newer methods of teaching and training. Before doing this, however, it might be useful to take a look at the 1971 situation.

Presently, the various teaching and training methods in management education and training programmes are used in approximately the following percentages of classroom time:

Lectures	35–65 per cent
Discussions and group work	10–20 " "
Case studies	5–20 " "
Management exercises and games	5–15 " "

A smaller amount of time is spent on role-playing, training films with discussions, in-basket exercises, and some other methods.

These figures are based on information from a number of training programmes carried out in various countries of the region. The broad range shown for particular methods is intentional; it gives a truer representation of the present overall situation than averages or figures from a few programmes selected at random.

There is no doubt that in 1971 not only is the strength of participative methods fairly generally recognized, but these methods are more extensively used than they were five or ten years ago, when, for example, the use of case studies and management games was the exception rather than the rule. Most training institutions favor a mix of teaching and training methods. Programmes which would rely on one single method (intentionally or not) are rare.

There is growing agreement as to the limitations of the lecture method, especially in training programmes for adults; consequently many institutions have reduced its use considerably. In addition, a great deal of work has been done to improve the lecture technique itself through audio-visual aids and flexible combinations with other methods. Nevertheless, this has not led to a complete rejection of lecturing. For reasons which will be discussed further, lecturing is used and will certainly continue to be used, within sound limits (and in its "improved" versions), in the future.

The figures given above do not include practical work, which is done in connection with the training programmes but outside the training institutions, in the participants' own or in other enterprises and organizations. However, project assignments have become an important feature of a number of programmes for managers and students of management and are becoming increasingly popular. At many institutes and centers the project method is considered the most effective participative method.

II. REALITIES THAT INFLUENCE TEACHING AND TRAINING METHODS

1. Objectives of Training Programmes

Presently, the main objective of many training programmes for managers in Eastern Europe is to increase the knowledge of modern management concepts and techniques and to make the participants aware of the changes which need to be made in the management of enterprises, trusts, ministries, and other organizations in connection with economic reforms. Consequently, these courses endeavor to transmit a great deal of new information to the participants. As evaluation has shown, in some cases the amount of information is too great in proportion to the length of the programmes.

This is reflected in the choice of methods. In "knowledge" or "appreciation" programmes, lectures continue to be used extensively in view of their capacity to transmit a great deal of structured information in a short time. The use of participative classroom methods is restricted, although not completely neglected, and the programmes include little or no practical assignments.

At the same time, however, there are quite a few newer programmes which go further. They not only try to broaden a manager's horizon by supplying him with new information but also deal with the application of theoretical knowledge to practical situations, provide for exchange of experience among the participants, and attempt to influence the manager's attitudes. These programmes demonstrate a trend which is becoming fairly general—the effort to arrive at an optimum proportion and integration of theoretical teaching and practical training in management development programmes.[4]

In this type of programme the share of lectures tends to be reduced. Discussions and syndicates enable direct exchange of experience among participants; practical projects, exercises, and case studies are used to sharpen managerial skills. Recently, many management development programmes have become increasingly concerned with the human side of management and include exercises intended to improve the personnel management skills of the participants.

In the Eastern European socialist countries, most training programmes for managers devote a fairly large amount of time to problems of the national economy, central planning, governmental economic, technological, and social policies and other environmental factors, which every manager must understand in order to adjust planning and decision making at the enterprise level to the needs and requirements of a planned socialist economy. The procedure of adjusting the behavior of the enterprise to the environment is in some cases dealt with in case studies or planning exercises. However, most problems and principles of a macroeconomic and nationwide nature are explained in lectures and then analyzed in greater depth in subsequent discussions. The main reasons for this are that, first, it is undoubtedly much more difficult to prepare case studies, exercises, and projects dealing with macroeconomic and central planning problems than it is to prepare them for problems at the enterprise level. Second, in recent years central plans and planning and control systems have been evolving so rapidly that it has scarcely been possible to prepare teaching materials to handle these problems other than by lecture and discussion.

Another concept which is understood at many institutes in the region but not yet fully implemented is the inter-disciplinary approach to management training. Most management courses consist of several blocks or groups of subjects corresponding to various management functions or theoretical disciplines. Teaching methods are selected largely according to the requirements of each subject. Some courses, however, attempt to get into the discussion of multifunctional and multidisciplinary problems through the use of participative methods. Practical projects, planning exercises and games, and some complex case studies are used for this purpose. Moreover, discussion groups, syndicates, and panels are frequently structured in a way which brings together general and functional (economic, technical, commercial, personnel) managers and thus combines their expertise. Although first steps have been made, a long-term solution to this problem will require a complete restructuring of many courses, the retraining of teachers, as well as the development of new teaching material, all of which will be a matter of several years.

2. The Participants

A manager's attitude to methods he is exposed to in a training programme is a highly personal matter. It depends very much on his educational background, experience, personality, and expectations related to the programme in question. So far little research has been done on this problem in Eastern Europe. Nevertheless, a few comments can be made on the basis of observation and evaluation of various training programmes.

If asked to express their views, or even select training methods themselves, most managers in Eastern Europe prefer participative methods. For example, in the final evaluation of the general management courses at the Academy of Social Management in Sofia, Bulgarian managers repeatedly claim that the share of "active" methods used should be increased.

Also, in other countries of the region managers prefer discussions, simulation exercises, well-selected examples and cases, and, in particular, practical in-plant projects. They are, however, willing to listen to lectures if these deal with new management concepts, information from successful foreign enterprises, trends in the economic, technical, and social environment.

To get managers to participate actively in a training programme does not seem to be a problem. They are, however, sensitive to cases of wrong use of participative methods—most of them are competent enough to identify quickly case studies and exercises of low learning value and to know when a trainer is overemphasizing the method to make up for a meager content.

The fact that managers are able to learn from each other was recently re-emphasized by a survey in Great Britain,[5] and Eastern European managers are no exception. The conditions for exchange of experience among managers in the same trade or industrial sector (through teamwork, syndicates, discussions, factory visits, surveys, projects, etc.) are favorable in view of the fact that enterprises are government-owned and centrally controlled. Cases where a manager would not be prepared to unveil some information to a colleague having similar management problems are likely to be infrequent, although they may occur.

There are also cases when an appropriate training method may help to overcome a manager's resistance to learning. Some managers tend to be quite satisfied with their work methods and do not want to admit they may need further learning. In such cases, participative methods have to be utilized tactfully to shake the manager's excessive self-confidence and persuade him that he can learn a great deal from his colleagues and from the trainer.

3. Teachers and Trainers

The use of participative methods depends, above all, on teachers and trainers. However, at present no Eastern European country has enough management teachers and trainers with the right practical and teaching experience. As in other European countries, this hampers the advancement of management education and training and causes difficulties in the introduction of newer training methods and techniques.

In many institutes and centers the number of full-time professional teachers and trainers is too small and there are even centers with no such staff at all. To cope with the programmes demanded by industry, or even introduced by governmental decree, these institutes use a large number of part-time teachers, such as senior specialists from research institutions, governmental departments, and large enterprises.

While this practice helps training institutions to keep in touch with economic practice, if an excessively high number of external teachers contribute to one course (each giving one or a few sessions) this can become unsettling and it is difficult to ensure integrity, continuity, and proper methods for the whole programme. Consequently, the utilization of part-time teachers with rich practical experience sometimes does not give the desired results. It must be kept in mind that persons with valuable practical experience but without special pedagogic training need to prepare their training assignments in close collaboration with professional teachers and should be given the opportunity to perfect themselves in teaching and training methodology.

Turning to those professional management teachers and trainers who do exist, most of them were originally either university teachers or specialists in institutes, central administration, or enterprises. The university group is definitely aware of the importance of the methodological side of the training and learning process. However, in most cases they have been educated according to classical methods and then have used these methods themselves. It is not easy to change a method to which you are accustomed. Some teachers are therefore reluctant to widen the range of their methods of teaching. Furthermore, teachers who have only rare contact with practical life find it difficult to prepare and give cases, guide project work, or get involved in discussions on practical problems. No wonder that they prefer to stick to lectures and discussions of a theoretical nature.

The pedagogical problems of the second group—former practicing managers and staff specialists—are not too different from those of the part-time teachers. To become fully competent management teachers and trainers they need more teaching experience, some theoretical study, and guidance in teaching and training methodology.

In addition, many full-time management teachers and trainers find it difficult to prepare new cases, games, and other materials, or guide trainees during in-plant work, since this requires substantially more time than the traditional lecture or discussion. As their teaching load is often heavy, they sometimes have to choose the easier solution.

Despite these difficulties, the attitude of teachers and trainers to participative methods and their ability to use these methods are improving continuously. The best evidence for this lies in the improvements in teaching and training methodology which have occurred during the last decade.

In a number of Eastern European countries realistic appraisal of the teachers' and trainers' need to master quickly a broad range of modern didactic methods, including technical aids, has brought about various arrangements for methodological guidance and help to teachers, as will be discussed in Section IV, "Promotion of Participative Methods."

4. Duration and Organization of Training Programmes

The effect of time and organizational arrangements on teaching and training methods must not be overlooked. A number of methods can be used effectively only if enough time is available for preparation and discussion. If practical project work is to be included in course programmes, the duration of the course needs to be adjusted accordingly. Longer programmes not only provide for but usually require the use of a variety of methods in order to achieve various objectives of the programme and maintain participants' interest throughout the course.

In some countries in the region, there are still a number of short programmes in general and functional management (one to four weeks). As mentioned earlier, these courses suffer from being over-loaded with too many subjects. There is, however, a tendency to abandon short courses as a form of basic or introductory management training,[6] and to replace them with courses of longer or medium duration. Some examples are given in Table 1.

Table 1

INSTITUTIONS	PROGRAMME	
Institute of Management, Prague	Course for top managers	11–12 months
Faculty of Management, Prague	Postgraduate course for managers	3½ months
Academy of Social Management, Sofia	Courses for future higher managers (2 types)	6 months and 24 months
National Management Center (CEPECA), Bucharest	Course for management consultants	18 months
Institute of Management of National Economy, Moscow	Course for top managers	3 months
Faculties of Organizers of Production, U.S.S.R. (various cities)	Courses for future managers (middle level)	10 months

It can be foreseen that, in future, shorter programmes in general and functional management will be given as refresher or retraining programmes to managers, who will have previously passed through introductory or advanced programmes of longer duration. They will therefore be less loaded with factual material than most short programmes are in the present period.

Concerning organization of training programmes, preference is generally given to residential ones. Longer residential programmes are sometimes split into two or three phases with intermediate periods reserved for practical assignments (surveys, individual or group projects, practical exercises, etc.). It is a great advantage of residential programmes that they provide convenient conditions for individual study, careful preparation of case studies, teamwork, discussions, and frequent consultations with the trainer.

As yet, relatively little attention has been paid to organizing a preparatory phase to precede the course, during which the trainee is supplied with material for study and requested to prepare himself for discussions. The effectiveness of some shorter courses could be increased in this way.

The number of participants represents a problem in some programmes. Owing to the shortage of teachers, conference rooms, and technical aids, some institutes have relatively large classes (45–60 participants), which implies that syndicates and discussion groups are also overloaded. A more extensive use of modern technical aids (television, videotapes) and more adequate provision of teaching materials to participants will probably make this problem less urgent in the course of the next few years. Nevertheless, in some training programmes the size of groups will have to be reduced.

III. EXPERIENCE WITH THE USE OF SELECTED METHODS

1. The Discussion Method and Teamwork

In Eastern European management education and training programmes the discussion method has been widely used for a long time. However, the ways in which it is used have been changing.

Originally, discussions in courses and seminars were directly linked with lectures: most commonly they were question-and-discussion periods which immediately followed a lecture or seminar presentation by a participant. Now discussions are beginning to be used for other previously little known purposes, with greater attention being paid to the preparation and structuring of discussion. Completely unprepared discussions, in which participants talk about virtually anything that comes into their minds over a broad subject range, are disappearing.

In a number of institutes, discussion groups or syndicates are used in which teams of four to eight members are asked to prepare a short report or statement on a given problem; group reports are then transmitted to plenary sessions of all course participants.

In the National Management Training Center in Bucharest (CEPECA) good results have been obtained by conducting group and panel discussions in general management courses in the following way: three or four times a week smaller discussion groups work, as a rule after introductory lectures, to deal with selected subjects of particular interest to the participants. Next morning, this is followed by a panel discussion. The panel consists of the group rapporteurs and a few teachers and consultants, who represent various management functions. The panel discusses the group reports, and then there is a brief general discussion, in case other participants feel the necessity to contribute at this point. This application of panel discussions is considered to be a way of fostering a complex dynamic view of management problems, developing the participants' critical faculties, examining how similar problems are solved in various types of economies (in cases where international experts participate in panel discussions alongside Romanian experts and managers), and giving useful practical advice to participants.[7]

Panels have also been used in this Bucharest center to discuss questions which the participants pose beforehand in writing (these are called "free panels"). In other institutes, various alternatives of the discussion method are used to identify and handle problems of major practical interest to participants. Thus, for example, the Management Training Center at the Academy of Social Management in Sofia has been using a combination of group and plenary discussions called "Our Problem." In a broadly defined subject area, every participant is asked to propose three to five problems he would like to discuss. Problems which receive the most votes are then discussed in a cycle of group and plenary sessions.

2. Case Studies

Virtually all management courses in Eastern European socialist countries now include at least one, but more frequently several, case studies. This corresponds to the idea that the discussion of concrete cases of practical experience provides a good learning opportunity, especially if the case appeals to the manager's own experience and helps him to understand that the same practical problem may be approached in several different ways. There are, however, no institutes which rely exclusively, or even mainly, on case studies; they are always combined with other methods. They usually follow after lectures to demonstrate how the principles and methods which were explained theoretically have been, or could be, applied to a concrete situation. Their main purpose is, as elsewhere, to improve the trainee's analytical skills and ability to seek alternative solutions.

To promote a multifunctional approach to management, the Management Training Center in Budapest (OVK) and some other centers give priority to complex cases.

The shortage of suitable cases and the lack of experience with preparing cases and leading case discussions are the main difficulties connected with the use of this method at the present time.

For example, the national management centers in Bulgaria, Romania, and Hungary presently have between twenty-five and forty case studies each, prepared on the basis of local management experience. This number is still low. As mentioned earlier, most teachers do not have enough time to devote to the preparation of new cases. At the same time, experience with the use of foreign case studies has shown that these usually are not suited to the particular socioeconomic conditions of Eastern European socialist countries. A few of them can be used after adaptation, but others can only be helpful in stimulating ideas for the production of new local cases dealing with the solution of similar types of problems but in a different socioeconomic environment and under a different planning and control system.

The exchange of local case studies between centers in various Eastern European countries will certainly become more frequent in the near future. Nevertheless, between individual countries the differences in planning and control systems and in the economic role of enterprises are sufficiently important to make it difficult to transfer and use case studies without adapting them.

3. Management Exercises and Games

Many management courses in Eastern Europe include one or more exercises and games for the purpose of improving training in the skills of analysis, planning, decision making, and working with and through other people. Simulation, on a simple or complex level, can help course participants to view their own practical problems in a clearer light, and give them ideas as to how to solve them.

For a management exercise or game to achieve this effect, it should require from the participant a way of handling problems which is more systematic, disciplined, or sophisticated and which implies a better organization of professional teamwork than that to which he is accustomed. At the same time, it would defeat the purpose of the simulation if it were to create illusions or force participants to behave in a way which would be foreign to their actual managerial duties and environment.

That is why management institutes are searching for types of exercises and games which would be most appropriate to the nature of economic life and management in their countries. For example, the Scientific and Methodological Center for Organization of Work and Management of Production in Moscow has developed a number of "complex planning exercises" for use in management courses. Each exercise simulates a concrete management problem at the enterprise or plant level and its objective is to propose an optimum solution. The course participants are divided into small groups of three people, which compete with each other to find the best solution to the same problem. It must be pointed out, however, that they are not playing as if they were competing with each other commercially, i.e., by acquiring a greater share of the same market. Similar types of simulation exercises are being developed in other countries too.

This does not mean that games with elements of marketing and competition do not come into consideration at all. Many enterprises in Eastern European countries are essentially export-oriented. In a steadily growing number of cases, the profitability of enterprises depends on their ability to flexibly supply the market with goods of a high technical level and good quality. Publicity, advice to buyers, and after-sale services are becoming more important. The actual role of such factors in a game must, however, correspond to realities. Thus, for example, the effect of publicity or sales efforts in a game has to be evaluated in accordance with the actual role they are likely to play in economic practice. Information given to the players (including its cost) must correspond to information obtained in practice from planning organs, research institutes, foreign trade companies, and other existing sources.

4. The Project Method

As mentioned in Section I, the project method is probably the participative method for management education and training most widely used in the region. This reflects, first and foremost, the growing effort to link theory with practice in training programmes, in order to help the course participants to apply their newly acquired knowledge and, in so doing, to develop their skills.

It also reflects the particular way in which training methodology has evolved in Eastern Europe. At many management institutes and universities the project method was, in fact, the first really participative method to be used and to exert influence on the overall shape of educational and training programmes. Many teachers and trainers have had ten or more years' experience with it even if, in the meantime, they have made little use of case studies and other methods. It is even fair to say, on the whole, that the project method has been better known and more widely used in the Eastern European countries (especially in the U.S.S.R., Czechoslovakia, Poland, and Romania) than in some other regions.

The project method is generally used in combination with more theoretical teaching of management principles, methods, and techniques. The idea behind this is that the student or trainee ought to possess some background knowledge to be in a position to design and execute a useful project. Training programmes are organized so that a period of classroom teaching and training usually precedes a much longer period of project work. In some programmes this is followed by a third period, during which the participants come together again for collective discussion of completed projects.

Most practicing managers and staff specialists undergoing training do project work in their own enterprises. The projects are selected in such a way as to provide a learning opportunity and, simultaneously, to help in the solution of a real problem in the enterprise. Thus, through project work a formal off-the-job training programme can be integrated with on-the-job training, even in the case of senior and top managers.

Some institutions, like the Training Institute of the Ministry of Automobile Industry in the U.S.S.R., give priority to projects carried out in enterprises where the trainees are not employed.

Universities and colleges which use project work to give some practical training to the undergraduates, and at the same time test their abilities to apply what they have learned, also aim at selecting projects in which the host organizations are really interested. As a result, after graduation students are frequently offered employment by the enterprises in which they worked on projects.

Seen strictly from the point of view of a formal training programme or university management course, most projects are examined and approved at the point when a participant has drawn up proposals for implementation. Normally, the trainee's report with proposals is submitted to a commission in which all parties concerned are represented. If senior and top managers defend their projects before such a commission, higher representatives of central planning and control bodies are also invited to participate.

Consequently, most project proposals worked out in courses for practicing managers and specialists are put into effect by the trainees themselves after the completion of a formal course, which means that individual, on-the-job training continues. Those who approved the trainee's participation in a course, and the theme of his project (for example, higher management of the enterprise) must see to it that the project is really implemented and that the person concerned obtains the necessary support.

The trainers should guide project work in all its phases, which includes follow-up and advice on project implementation after the official end of a training programme. This principle is, unfortunately, only partially respected, since it is difficult to guide a number of participants who work on projects individually in different places.

Enterprises which object to project work are an exception. In such cases it is easy to find the reasons: the managers have not appreciated the value of training, or have been disappointed by some unsuccessful previous project, or are afraid that a training project will discover faults which they prefer to conceal.

Many institutes have realized that project work is an extremely valuable source of training material and feedback for the continuous improvement of course curricula.

IV. PROMOTION OF PARTICIPATIVE METHODS

The Eastern European countries use a range of measures to promote the use of participative methods and to help management teachers and trainers to master such methods.

The establishment of methodological units (departments, sections, centers, laboratories, cabinets) within management education and training institutions is a fairly common organizational measure. In the early sixties such a unit was established at the National Management Training Center (CODKK) in Warsaw, and similar units have been created since then in a number of training institutions in the region. Their purpose is to provide advice and guidance on teaching and training methodology, to promote modern concepts and methods of training, and to produce teaching materials adapted to local needs. These units, as a rule, include specialists in the psychology of learning and in training methodology. They collaborate with other teachers in applying modern methods to specific subjects and in preparing appropriate teaching material.

Some methodological units are assigned to serve only the teaching and training staff, including part-time teachers, of a given institute. Units in national management institutes, however, have a wider responsibility: their goal is to upgrade the methodological level of management education and training in the whole country.

Their competence is not confined to teaching and training methods. Such an approach would be too narrow and could lead to an overestimation of methods, which might become ends in themselves. Methodological units therefore deal with the design of overall training schemes and systems, preparation of course curricula, selection of subjects to be taught to various categories of managerial personnel, information on teaching methods, training of teachers and trainers in methodology, production of teaching materials and audio-visual aids, review and evaluation of training activities.

In certain cases, governmental decrees have made methodological guidance by a nationwide institution compulsory. An example is the Academy of Social Management in Sofia, which has to approve the curricula used by sectoral and other specialized institutions engaged in manager training in the country. In most instances, however, this guidance is carried out through advice and recommendations to trainers and directors of training on the content and methods of training programmes, and by disseminating information on new training concepts, methods, and techniques.

Presently, the most popular way to promote new methods as well as to improve schemes and organization of training are programmes in methodology for management teachers and trainers. At the academy in Sofia, fifteen short courses in teaching methods have been organized during the last two years. Whereas the first courses were organized internally for the academy staff, later courses were prepared for teachers and trainers from other institutions. A similar type of course has been available for some time at the National Management Training Center (CODKK) in Warsaw and at other institutes in the region.

Most of these methods courses do not exceed one or two weeks. They offer the minimum appreciation of participative methods, but they are too short to provide practice for every participant in the actual use of the methods or in the preparation of teaching materials. Gradually, these short courses will have to be supplemented by longer programmes, which will combine a several-week course in methodology with periods of teaching practice under the guidance of experienced senior teachers and trainers.

In a number of instances, conferences, symposia, and international seminars dealing essentially with modern concepts and methods of management training have been organized. The Czechoslovak Committee for Scientific Management has been active in this area since 1965. In 1970, the Committee organized, with the help of the International Labour Organisation, a high-level seminar for senior management teachers on management training practices of selected large international firms and on latest developments in training methods.[8]

Several countries in the region have had international technical cooperation projects in management development lasting three to five years: Bulgaria, Romania, and Hungary recently, Yugoslavia and Poland in the late fifties and early sixties. In the execution of the projects the governments have been assisted by the International Labour Organisation. These projects among others, have been utilized as a source of information on, and expertise in, organization and methods of management training, including institutional, formal training programmes and on-the-job training of managers and staff specialists.

The production and dissemination of teaching materials, including films and other audio-visual aids, is a further way of promoting modern teaching methods and techniques. This concerns case studies, management games and exercises, manuals for the use of individual methods, training films, etc. The methodological units gather materials, produced at their own institute and at other institutions, including the foreign ones, screen these materials, and prepare publications for use by management teachers and trainers in the whole country. The Scientific and Methodological Center for Organization of Work and Management of Production in Moscow has so far prepared three manuals with complex planning exercises for managers. Some new teaching materials are available from most national management institutes in the region.

Methodological guidance and centralized production of new teaching materials are easing the transition from classical to modern teaching and training methods. Their purpose is by no means to restrict or replace the individual teacher's initiative and imagination, without which there could be no real advancement in teaching and training methodology.

CHAPTER EIGHT—FOOTNOTES

1. "People have to be prepared for managerial jobs in a professional manner. . . . If management should be taught as a special field and systematically, we need a new network of training institutions" (V. Lisicyn, Vice-President of the State Planning Committee of the Russian Republic in the U.S.S.R., in *Literaturnaya Gazeta,* No. 11, 12.3.1969).

2. For example, in February 1971 a new institute for top managers from government and enterprises called Institute of Management of National Economy was opened in Moscow.

3. The term "active methods" is more common in Eastern Europe.

4. "In preparing training programmes it is very important to achieve optimum combination of studying theory and practical experience. . . . In courses for enterprise managers, no less than 30–40 per cent of time ought to be devoted to theory" (B. Melnikov, "Obutcheniye rukovoditelya," *Izvestiya,* Moscow, 5.12.1970).

5. See A. Mant, *The Experienced Manager—A Major Resource* (London: British Institute of Management, 1969).

6. The National Management Center in Bucharest (CEPECA) abandoned one- to two-week general management courses soon after the first year of its operation. Poland has had the same experience.

7. See "Designing Courses for Central Management" in *Management and Productivity* (ILO), No. 35 (1970/4).

8. See ILO, "Management Development in Practice," MAN DEV Series No. 9, Geneva 1970 (a short report on the seminar).

CHAPTER NINE
New Techniques of Training for Managers in the Polish Management Development Center and Other Training Centers in Socialist Countries*

Effective management demands the satisfaction of certain basic needs which have been generated by the extremely complex and sophisticated environment of our economic life today. The demand for continuous improvement of management is unceasing and the need for training increases year by year. This was foreseen soon after the Second World War, when programmes of training began to be more elaborate than any previously devised. Moreover, they were extended in time and diversified as to content, with a growing list of subjects soon longer than ever before.

It did not follow, however, that actual training methods became automatically more advanced and more adequate to the programmes that were being developed. On the contrary, teaching methods were rather neglected in comparison to the programmes themselves and to the prerequisites and recruitment policies governing admission to them.

During the past fifteen years the gap between programme requirements and training methods has narrowed. Many new training methods have been developed, modified, tested, and adapted to significant phases of the training process.

Closely related to the general improvement of training methods is

---

* This chapter was prepared by J. Goscinski.

the fact that managers are now much better educated than they were a few decades ago. They are more familiar with new processes in the economic environment as well as with social and technological processes within the enterprise. In fact, the overall level of education among managers is now relatively high, especially in developed countries where they are usually graduated from schools and have received training in junior and senior executive courses. Moreover, businessmen engaged in small business in these countries as well as managers from enterprises of varying size in the developing countries require considerable ability and knowledge in the field of management. The time is not long past when the life of a human being was divided into two distinct stages: the first one was his education period, and the second was devoted to working exclusively on professional problems. The simplicity of this style of life is now an anachronism. His counterpart today must continuously study and improve his knowledge; otherwise he will be replaced, sooner or later, by a person who is more dynamic. It would be just a question of time.

The elements of effective management are fourfold. They are (1) managerial knowledge, (2) the capability to use the knowledge, (3) managerial talent, and (4) an appropriate social attitude together with a responsiveness to events and problems which is conditioned by a relevant social background.

All training courses which seek to increase managerial effectiveness are, in fact, dealing with some or all of these elements. The first two can be dealt with in the formal education process. The other two components of effective management can be supported only by training. People are born with or without organizational talent and social orientation. An appropriate social attitude is associated with factors which are only partly under the control of the individual.

Modern training techniques have been developed to meet demands for the modification and updating of managerial knowledge, for better use of this knowledge by training in new techniques (technology of data processing, operations research, engineering methods), and for development of talent and new skills. New techniques derived from psychology, particularly its tools for the study of motivation and attitude formation—and from sociology—are introduced in order to assess attitudes and reactions emerging in the field of human relations and in problems arising from the social environment.

These numerous training techniques are of varying utility with respect to the elements of managerial effectiveness mentioned above. Some techniques are more appropriate and effective when applied to the areas of knowledge and of the ability to use it. Others are more suitable for developing and supporting the managerial talent and for fostering improved attitudes.

The Polish Management Development Center was founded in 1960 on the basis of an agreement between the Polish government, the International Labour Organisation, and the United Nations Special Fund. Two years later it started to provide courses for supervisors and for some kinds of specialists. Staff and top-level management problems were at that time beyond the interest of the Center. Management training centers in other socialist countries followed suit, developing in a similar fashion.

Gradually managers from higher levels of decision making became involved in the training process. Among the higher levels of managers in a structure, however, management is more a problem of talent, attitudes, and the ability to use them than a problem of knowledge. Specialized knowledge was increasingly superseded in the interests of general knowledge. Managerial philosophy, strategy, overall objectives, and forecasting became step by step the most relevant problems of management education, requiring different training techniques from those of narrow specialized subjects. On the other hand the vast growth of computer techniques and recently of systems analysis has increased to a fearsome degree the reservoirs of knowledge that can be made available to specialists and middle-level managers. To a great extent it has become impossible for all these new techniques in management to be learned as long as traditional training methods are employed.

As a result, our Center, as well as the other centers in Czechoslovakia, Romania, the Soviet Union, Hungary, and Bulgaria, started to introduce some participative training techniques in the 1960s. Practically all these methods were imported from Western European centers and from the United States. While at the outset case studies were the only advanced method applied in practical work, nowadays the list of modern training methods in current use is much longer. Since the effectiveness of the different methods varies, it would be useful to present observations on our experience with the most essential and best-known methods.

No one method can have a practical application without taking into consideration three important factors affecting the effectiveness of the techniques to be used. These are: (1) the results one assumes can be achieved in the training of programme participants; (2) the intellectual level of the participants as well as their experience and age; (3) the social and cultural conditions and the "rules of the game" which are valid in the environment.

The second and third factors were the cause of some misunderstanding and of a limiting of effects when, for example, American sensitivity training methods and certain psychological tests were applied. The negative response of the participants was sometimes very strong. The personality of our people differs from that of the American people. And again, because of educational differences, some more simple and others more sophisticated, case studies and decision-making simulations have had to be devised. Which of them are used depends on the intellectual level of programme participants and on their managerial experience.

Unlike training for specialists, programmes for managers, and especially for top-level management, are developed with four objectives in mind. They are intended to achieve (1) a better understanding of business development; (2) the updating of knowledge in managerial methods; (3) the creation of new needs for modern approaches to problem solving; (4) an improved ability to communicate with employees and specialists.

Effective training of managers requires clear and well-defined objectives, standards of performance, and a measurement (testing) system. The increasing capability of participants can be measured much better through the use of participative methods than by final examinations and other traditional testing methods.

In this connection a most interesting diagram has been presented by B. Hawrylyshyn from the Centre d'Etudes Industrielles in Geneva in an article entitled "Preparing Managers for International Operations" (*Business Quarterly,* Autumn 1967). The relationships between modern teaching methods and managerial skills are considered and displayed in this figure. Six techniques of training are discussed, namely, field studies, the incident method, case studies, decision simulation, role-playing, and group projects. The paper further deals with the managerial skills of observing, selecting pertinent data, diagnosis, formulating and solving of problems, deciding, communicating, and motivating.

All the modern methods observed by Hawrylyshyn as well as other methods not mentioned by him (T-group training, psychodrama, round-table and panel discussions) can be applied in order to involve participants, to increase their interest in learning, to develop their synthesis capability and at the same time to increase their analytical skills.

In place of Hawrylyshyn's diagram, I wish to show the three managerial skills most closely related to and developed by each particular modern teaching method. This involves a kind of ranking because the skills developed by the particular method are enumerated in accordance with the strength of relationship.

TEACHING METHODS	RANKING OF SKILLS		
field studies	observation	selection	diagnosis
incident method	selection	diagnosis	solving
case studies	diagnosis	solving	deciding
decision simulation	deciding	communicating	solving
role-playing	communicating	deciding	motivating
group projects	motivating	communicating	deciding

Adding some other methods, for example,

T-group training	motivating	communicating	observing
psychodrama	motivating	communicating	solving
panel discussion	solving	diagnosis	deciding

we can see that five skills—motivating, communicating, deciding, solution formulation, and diagnosis capability—are supported by the use of the additional techniques in almost the same way as those in the first group. A correct choice among modern teaching methods will therefore ensure that the skills most required in managing are developed.

Generally speaking, the new training techniques increase the effectiveness of the training process. They do, however, have the drawback of being time-consuming and expensive. Preparation of materials involves a lengthy testing process. Moreover, classwork requires contact not with a single lecturer but with as many as three or four—sometimes more—instructors. This in turn entails co-ordination activity before the class even meets. Implementation of modern techniques also is expensive in that it requires more facilities, such as the use of computers, which are necessary when employing games, simulations, and various other participative methods.

Group Dynamics

The principal advantage of this technique is that it affords an insight into group behavior, involving as it does the psychological make-up of a group, interactions among group members, and the search for a balance between conflicts among them. The tendency to dominate, the demand for power, the flight from responsibilities, the conflict between individual goals and group goals, and satisfaction are some of the more important phenomena which are usually brought to light in this type of training.

We do not have a great deal of experience on which to base our observations in this area at the Center. The results of a few experiments fell far short of our expectations. They did teach us that one should be very cautious in using this method. The individuals concerned, both participants and instructors, are under strong pressure. In such situations, the reactions of human beings can be unexpected, often irrational. There is another danger: relations between each pair of participants deteriorate during the training. Moreover, the effects of the experience outlasted the training session. We know of individuals who became unfriendly and in a few cases outright enemies for months thereafter.

Educational and cultural factors are very important here. The sensitivity of individuals—their ways of thinking, habits, ideas, and attitudes—calls for the use of very flexible, adaptive, and individual methods in order to be acceptable to the participants. The direct transfer of somebody else's methods onto a given group is simply self-defeating. Such methods can be of value only indirectly, once they are modified to suit the particular situation.

Successfully used, then, these methods serve to support and develop the motivation capability, to increase skill in communicating, and to promote the ability to observe other people and their reactions, attitudes, and motives of behavior. Where they are used without success, however, such methods can destroy existing skills. The hazards point up the need for experienced instructors in order to undertake a successful T-group training experience.

Psychodrama

This is a procedure which seeks to reconstruct in a dramatic way a situation or event which has caused conflicts among people. The participants play some assigned roles (or functions). The situation is reconstructed several times with participants playing different roles at each stage, exchanging roles, and evaluating the same problem from different points of view.

As is the case with T-group training, the method is useful in developing motivation capabilities. Communication and problem-solving skills are supported and developed with these types of training methods.

Case Studies

This technique, the oldest of the modern training methods, is effective only if certain conditions are met. We do not fully agree with those who have argued that only a real situation selected and reconstructed from an actual problem in an existing enterprise or other institution can create an input for a successful case study. An invented but probable situation can provide as good material for a case study as information gathered in an organization. The only condition is that the described situation must be typical and should be suggestive of many alternatives of problem solving.

One more problem needs to be pointed out, however. Courses at American universities and some European training centers supported by American institutions have tended to utilize a large number of case studies within the same course. Some instructors apparently believe that the provision of many different case studies simulating several situations and events will itself fulfill the need for new knowledge in management. They do not provide for a general discussion after a case study is finished because they do not think it is necessary.

We do not agree with this approach. The case-study method can be used for diagnosis, problem formulation, and guiding solutions but not as an end in itself. General conclusions should be formulated. Case study is an exercise undertaken to illustrate by practical problem solving the management philosophy, the decision-making process, and the use of more or less sophisticated managerial techniques. Its function is to illustrate by case analysis a more general approach to management.

Incident Method

This method is not so often employed now as it was some years ago and is seldom used as an independent method. The only area in which it is fruitfully applied is that of personnel conflicts. Human relations, personnel evaluation, conditions of frustration, and the problem of lack of identification of the individual and/or group with the goals of an organization as a whole are the most fertile fields for use of the incident method. Otherwise it is most often found combined with other modern methods, with decision simulation, for instance, or with industrial games. Sometimes the combination of case study and incident method is used to portray managerial problems more vividly.

Role-playing

What has been said about the incident method applies also to the use of the role-playing technique. In fact, the area within which effective role-playing is applicable is even narrower. Almost the same skills are exposed and developed when both role-playing method and decision simulation are considered. There are the same skills but not precisely in the same order: deciding, communicating, and problem solving.

Decision Games (Simulation)

This method is one of the two participative methods most often used at the Center with good results. Consultation with other training centers in socialist countries as well as with co-operating West European management development centers indicates that the use and effectiveness of this method increase year by year. Both manual and computerized games are involved in the training.

If a fairly sophisticated simulation is used—for example, a game with several markets, many production variables, cost calculations, pricing and investment alternatives, among other factors—the game tends to serve as an actual introduction to the course. All important problems are demonstrated during the game and after analyzing the results achieved, each particular topic is treated step by step in logical order. At this stage a number of other modern teaching methods are also advanced.

Occasionally, if enough time has elapsed during a programme, the same decision game is repeated at the end of the course. The purpose of this procedure is to test the effectiveness of the programme by comparing the results of the opening and closing games.

Decision simulation combined with role-playing also produces good results. This is accomplished when the decision simulation is divided into two stages. In the first stage decisions are taken by individual participants. The results are then compared and groups of decision makers are set up. The idea is to create groups in which participants with differing assumed policies (and achieved results) are put together. Now we have a good starting point for lively discussion within each group. The role-playing method can be used in groups. Two problems emerge. The first one is created by the need to reach a group decision based upon conflicting individual decisions. The second, which compounds an already complicated situation, is the task of reconciling the diverse viewpoints based on the roles to be played by the members of groups.

Group Projects

This is the second most effective method employed by our programme managers. A group project can be organized in two ways. The first is a matter of giving an assignment to students working as groups within the classroom. The second is accomplished by in-field training. In the latter case groups of participants are sent to an enterprise which is collaborating with the Center. They formulate a diagnosis, suggest ideas for improvement, and start to design a project. All projects are discussed with the board of directors in each enterprise, after which they are the subject of judgment by a jury. The jury normally consists of lecturers and managers from collaborating companies.

The second approach is especially useful in training consultants. The field designing is in this case contracted as a consulting service. Groups are led by experienced consultants from the Center.

In the case of classroom group projects the competitive factor is exploited as much as possible. All groups receive the same task and are supplied with the same data and ground rules. From the various projects—all prepared without the gathering of additional information outside the Center—the best is then selected.

Our experience is still somewhat limited in this field, especially when compared to such large projects as have been undertaken by Belgium's Inter-University Programme for Advanced Management in Brussels. The results, however, have been encouraging enough to persuade us to accept the group project approach as a highly effective and successful method and to lead us to develop new project assignments and tasks.

Our general experience, moreover, has convinced us that almost all the modern training techniques can be used even though the more sophisticated facilities may not be available. From this point of view they are relevant to all developing countries. More important than technical equipment are the requirements of experienced instructors, well-thought-out instructions and programmes, and an abiding respect for local conditions be they legal, intellectual, cultural, or psychological.

CHAPTER TEN
Soviet Experience in the Field of Management Training Methods*

INTRODUCTION

Through its more than fifty years of evolution the socialist economy has given ample evidence of its viability and power to solve complex historical problems—industrialization of a formerly backward country, building up of a war economy that ensured the defeat of Nazism, meeting the challenge of the constantly growing material and spiritual needs of the people, and assistance to the socialist and developing nations.

The key factors in the successful development of a socialist economy are the public ownership of the means of production, the predominance of the state sector, the development of the economy in keeping with the long-range and current directive plans, and the science-guided principle of the entire management system.

Of tremendous importance is the role played by the corps of managers in the national economy. The performance of a factory, association, industry, economic region, union republic, or of the entire national economy is largely predicated on the qualifications, knowledge, and managerial skills of the leading executives. The part played by these is becoming particularly great in the context of the current economic reform which has opened broad opportunities for expanding the competence of all managers, especially at the enterprise level.

The important role assigned to the manager explains the unrelent-

* This chapter was prepared by Gavriil Popov.

ing attention paid in the Soviet Union to an entire range of related problems—personnel selection and placement policies, efficiency assessment and training of managers, and so on.

The subject of the present chapter is the methods employed for the training of managers, but since these methods are organically connected with the general system of personnel selection and placement—which, in turn, is determined by the entire economic management system—these issues will also be dealt with in brief.

The plan of the chapter is as follows. First, we set forth our interpretations of the concepts of "economy managers," "training of economy managers," and "training methods" as accepted in the U.S.S.R. Thereafter the factors affecting the system of training managers are discussed. Finally, the body of the chapter describes the actual system of management training and the content and form of this training.

THE CONCEPT OF THE ECONOMY MANAGER

The concept of the "economy manager" as used in the U.S.S.R. is not equivalent to any of the concepts covered by the English terms "manager," "administrator," "chief," or "head."

Certain authors draw superficial parallels between the education and training of Soviet factory directors on the one hand and American company directors on the other, basing various conclusions on this comparison. But a director in the socialist economy is not the head of a hierarchy; he is only a link in the management chain, albeit a very essential link. Hence, to compare the educational standards of the managerial staff in the socialist economies with those of Western company and corporation managers, one should properly consider not only Soviet factory directors but also the senior staff of the industrial ministries, planning and financial agencies, banks, and like institutions. It is precisely to these posts that efficient enterprise directors are normally promoted. This framework of comparison is indispensable to the obtaining of an undistorted picture.

Soviet current statistics include the following in the national economy: industry, farming and forestry, construction, transports, trade, public catering, state purchases, material and technical supplies and marketing, housing and municipal utilities and public services, health services, sports and social maintenance, education, science, fine arts, administration, credits, state insurance, and Party, youth, trade union, co-operative, and other public organizations. By and large, this is the whole of the community.

Soviet statistics designate as "employees" all persons working in the national economy and engaged mainly in intellectual work. Three categories of employees are distinguished: managers, experts, and technical executives.

The group of managers is subdivided into heads of enterprises and establishments, and heads of services and departments of the enterprises and institutions.

Posts of managers are classified according to the *kind of object they manage.* Thus a post may be either "principal" (director, head, chief) or "secondary" (deputy, assistant, etc.).

The term "director" is applied to managers of production enterprises: plants, factories, mines, bore-wells, state farms, trading agencies, department stores. The term "head" is used to refer to managers of non-productive enterprises such as baths, shops, and hairdressing establishments. As to *institutions,* the term "director" is used to designate managers of educational and research institutes, publishing houses, observatories, or schools, etc., while the term "head" is applied to managers of holiday homes, boarding schools, etc. The term "chief" is employed when referring to managers of such undertakings as construction, geological, road, and transport enterprise, post offices, stations, etc., as well as the managers of computing centers, customhouses, agencies, etc.

As regards the structural *subdivisions* of enterprises and institutions, the term "chief" is used where *productive* enterprises and state administration bodies are concerned, and the term "head" in the case of *unproductive* enterprises and organizations (faculty chairs, bureaus, laboratories, etc.).

Appendix 1 gives a list of the posts of managers of enterprises and institutions together with a list of the heads of services and units of these enterprises and institutions.

Soviet statistics draw a distinction between the system of the organs of state administration as a special sector of the national economy and the administrative apparatus for managing industry, construction, and other economy sectors. Both mechanisms are run by the state, but the former is financed directly out of the state budget while the latter is provided for within the appropriations for each particular economy sector and its expenditures are often included in the production costs. In addition, there are administrative mechanisms in the co-operative sector and in the system of public organizations.

Accordingly, when a census is taken, part of the managerial staff is included in the number of employees of the particular economic sectors, and another part is counted as employees of the state administration bodies, treated as a special sector of the national economy. The latest general census in the U.S.S.R. was taken in 1970, but figures for the managerial staff have not been published yet. In the industrial sector, according to the 1959 census, there were, for instance, 472,000 managers of enterprises and of their structural units, 61,000 chief engineers, and 104,000 managers of supply and marketing organizations. The total number of managers of various ranks in the industry was 689,000. Data on the numbers of managers for the Soviet national economy in 1959 are given in Appendix 2, and data on dynamics of these figures in Appendix 3A and 3B. A breakdown of managerial staff according to age groups per 1,000 is given in Appendix 4.

Recently there have appeared papers in Soviet specialized literature advocating a narrower interpretation of the concept of economy manager. Specifically, it is proposed to apply the term only to enterprise and organization managers and their deputies and assistants but not to the heads of structural units, functional services, and the like. Since these proposals have not been adopted thus far, the present chapter employs the concept in the broader sense commonly accepted in Soviet statistics.

Training of Economy Managers

There is no single interpretation of the concept of "training of economy managers" that is universally accepted by all Soviet management scientists.

Two approaches may be taken: the broad and the narrow. Proponents of the narrow approach draw a distinction between *training* and *skill improvement*. They confine training to tuition provided at higher and/or secondary special learning establishments, postgraduate studies, and the special diploma-granting faculties, recently established at a number of institutions of higher learning, for management training of specialists with work experience. All other forms of instruction provided for managers through refresher courses and special schools at ministries and administrative boards are classified as skill improvement.

The broader approach draws no clear-cut demarcation line between the training of managers and their skill improvement. Training in this interpretation includes not only full-time studies but also all kinds of in-house and on-the-job conferences, seminars, and meetings. Moreover, training includes also a manager's self-education, the experience he gains through performance of various public responsibilities, and similar gains.

In this chapter we proceed from the standpoint that it is necessary to distinguish three concepts: (1) training a manager for his first administrative post (basic background training); (2) training a manager for a new, higher post; and (3) skill improvement for the manager who is to continue in his former post.

At the same time we favor the broad interpretations of management training and management skill improvement that include not only regular daytime studies at special educational establishments but also on-the-job instruction, self-education, and so on. Failure to take cognizance of this variety of forms is bound to distort the overall picture of management training and to make a mystery of the emergence of many an efficient director, official, or minister.

Management Training Methods

In seeking to define a "training method" there is likewise no unanimous interpretation. Some authors understand a training method as the totality of the teaching techniques used at this or that special learning institution. This is obviously an interpretation more associated with the means than with the contents of instruction and thus belongs within a pedagogical rather than a management-science framework. Moreover, this approach deals not with the whole of training but only with its educative aspects, in which case it would be more appropriate to speak of "teaching methods."

More pertinent is the interpretation of training methods which includes in the concept not only a description of the form of teaching but also that of the contents of the subject being studied. Although in this case, too, it is only the educative aspect which is taken into account, the picture of the training methods that emerges is fuller and more profound than in the former case. This approach makes it easier to understand the form of instruction since the latter largely depends on the subject matter to be learned.

However, the most adequate interpretation of "training methods" seems to be one that encompasses not just the contents and forms of teaching at a specialized educational institution but also the contents and form of all kinds of management training and skill improvement as well. In this case the concept embraces the form and contents of: education in daytime and evening classes and by correspondence; training in house and on discontinued-work basis; training on the job and in extra hours; special kinds of training and skill improvement— conferences, seminars, service trips within the country and abroad, participation in the work of various commissions and committees, and public activities.

So much for the significance of the concepts used in this chapter.

Factors Affecting the Management Training System

Methods of management training cannot be treated as purely a pedagogical problem of conveying certain knowledge and skills from the trainer to the trainee. The training methods are intricately connected with the system used to train managers. In turn, this system is bound up with the entire management system, and with the functions of managers within this system.

This makes it indispensable to any analysis that we identify the factors that exert an influence on the system of training managers. Disregard of these factors would make it quite difficult to explain why this or that country employs predominantly this or that method or why at a different time some other method prevailed in the same country. What are these factors that affect the system of training managers for the economy?

The Sociopolitical System

The political, economic, and social system obtaining in a given country is the primary factor exerting a decisive influence on the management training methods it employs.

The nature of the Soviet economic system makes it mandatory to implement all the components of the plan, including the plan for training managers, lest the eventual disproportions jeopardize the general plan fulfillment.

The planned nature of the whole Soviet economy dictates that the training of managerial staff for the economy be carried on according to plans. These plans—annual, five-year, and long-range—specify the numbers of students to be enrolled in higher-learning institutions and secondary technical schools, the list of educational specialties, and the total admissions for each specialty. The plan likewise specifies the composition of the graduates. It is known how many graduates for each specialty will leave schools and universities next year, and two or five years hence. The plans of specialized personnel training are tied in with the economic development plans and with the growth rates envisaged for the particular economy sectors.

To ensure the implementation of these plans the educational system is generously supported by the state: the government grants scholarships to all indigent students who make good progress, provides hostel accommodations, and so on. For their part, the graduate specialists carry the obligation of working for some two or three years on the job to which the state personnel distribution commission assigns them.

Corollaries to the socialist organization of the Soviet community are such features of the management training system as free tuition (the students pay no fee), absence of any national, racial, or sexual discrimination, and special attention to and promotion of training for members of those nationalities which were formerly backward as compared to other nations in the country.

The fact that there is no competition to plague prospective managers can hardly be ignored when choosing a method of management training. One should keep in mind that a manager is controlled not so much by the market as by the higher administrative agencies. The controlling role of the workers and public organization in the respective plant is also quite important. It is essential to take cognizance of these and many similar factors in order to understand the present Soviet system of training managers and the training methods it employs.

Stages in Economic Development

Another factor affecting the management training system is the current economic policy adopted by the nation at a given moment. The socialist nature of the economy does not mean that it is not susceptible to change. While remaining a socialist economy, the Soviet economic system continually evolves and passes through various stages of growth.

For instance, the economy of the industrialization period in the 1930s greatly differed from the war economy during World War II. Currently an economic reform is under way in the Soviet Union to bring the economy into harmony with the requirements of the scientific and technical revolution and with the needs of the present phase in the community's evolution.

The particular stage of economic development naturally has an important influence on the content and form of training specialists in general and managerial staff in particular. Specifically, the current stage poses economic issues as the prime requirement for study by the managers. These are issues, for instance, such as consumer demand, forecasting it, and measuring its volume. The forms and programmes of study are modified accordingly.

Personnel Selection and Placement System

A third factor affecting the management training system is personnel policy.

For instance, the principle of selecting managers according to business and political characteristics is a major Soviet personnel policy. An executive must possess a sound knowledge of his enterprise or industry, its technologies and hardware, its economics and organization, and he must be clever, practical, and thrifty—a true manager. But these business qualities are not enough in conditions of public ownership. Our manager is not just a factory director, he is a representative of the whole people and a confidential official of the state. He must be concerned not only with the interests of his "own" enterprise but with those of the industry and the whole economy as well. Moreover, he cannot be guided just by the economic criteria and nothing else; he has to consider also social and political factors.

Here are two examples. It might be economically more efficient to build a new plant near Moscow, but it is built in Central Asia so as to develop industry in a union republic that previously had no such plant. Again, young workers are likely to pose certain inconveniences, but in the interests of the community a "place in life" must be found as soon as possible for the younger generation, and they ought to be broadly represented at the plant.

These are the sorts of decisions that must be made by a manager who has not just economic but also political wisdom and who takes interest in the entire complex of social problems—from the natural environment to the younger generation. The principles of selecting managers for political and not just business considerations has an obvious and very strong impact on both the content and form of management training.

Or take another characteristic of Soviet personnel policy: the ab-

sence of any caste or elite in the managerial sector. Any capable
person has free access to a managerial post. Thousands of trainees
of worker and farmer origin are promoted to management every
year. This is a major merit of the soviet system, but it is bound to
affect the training methods used. Naturally, a manager from the
"lower" sections of the population could not have absorbed from his
"family tradition" much of what a manager ought to know and be
able to do. He must be taught all of this. These and other features of
Soviet personnel policy affect the methods of training managers.

Requirements for a Manager

The notion of what constitutes a manager in current usage is an
essential element in management training. Prior to deciding what and
how to teach a manager one must have a clear idea as to what kind of
manager one seeks to bring up, what is the "model" manager.

Certain authors think it impossible to state a general scheme of
the requirements to which a manager must conform. They find it
preferable to speak not of the manager in general but of the *particular
type* of manager—at a plant or a workshop, and not even at a plant in
general but at this or that particular plant.

More common, however, is the view that certain attributes exist
that must be possessed by each and every manager in the national
economy.

Early in the 1920s Lenin suggested that a manager could be judged
according to four criteria: (1) political characteristics; (2) knowledge in the particular field that is the object of management (industry,
agriculture, and so on); (3) administrative capabilities (managerial
knowledge and skills); and (4) reliability and other personal virtues.

The proper distribution of these qualities required of a manager
may depend on a multitude of factors. For instance, in the early
years of the emerging socialist system and acute class struggle priority was given to the political attitudes of the manager. As socialism
was consolidated, more and more importance was attached to business and administrative capabilities.

It is essential to take into account the manager's rank. As H. Fayol
has observed, the higher a manager's rank, the greater the weight
that must be given to the administrative aspect and the lesser the importance of specialized knowledge concerning the object of management. The functional properties of managerial activity likewise play
a certain role: the manager heading a planning agency makes greater

use of his knowledge, whereas the operative manager draws more heavily on his skill and personal affective qualities.

We believe that the present-day requirements of a manager can be represented by the following scheme. First, as to his personal qualities, one should distinguish his degree of (a) knowledge (what he knows), (b) skills and know-how (what he can do), and (c) affective properties (what kind of person he is). Secondly, one should assess his operational qualities: (a) political aspects of his work from the standpoint of the object of management (industry, science, trade, etc.), and (b) his work from the standpoint of the quality of management (well-organized, punctual operation, etc.).

The above general scheme clarifies our approach to the problem of management training. Knowledge is to be *taught;* skills and know-how can be *trained;* while personal qualities must be *developed.* Knowledge is the most dynamic and easily acquired, while training of a person's skills calls for greater effort. As to capabilities, these are to be regarded at the present stage of scientific development as something given and susceptible of but slight improvement through very long "exercise."

Therefore, proceeding from the above scheme, it is possible to distinguish between the things a manager can be taught and the things he must have innately and to determine what he can be given in terms of a certain amount of knowledge, on the one hand, and what special methods are required to develop his skills, on the other.

Development of Management Science

The system of management training also depends on the general level of our knowledge, the level reached by economic science in general and by management science in particular. "Science" has a broad sense in the Russian language: the term is applied not only to exact and natural sciences but to the humanities as well. It serves to denote the entire volume of knowledge we possess at a given point in time.

The development and successes achieved by the existing disciplines and the emergence of new sciences determine the content of the instruction provided for the managers. On the other hand, the progress of psychology, pedagogical science, and information and learning aids help to lead us toward a more effective and rational organization of the training process.

The above factors do not operate in isolation but rather in interaction and interdependence. *The adopted system of training and skill improvement of managers in the economy* is the embodiment and result of the joint action of all these factors. As this system in turn exerts a decisive influence on the training methods used, we shall discuss the system in the following section.

3. System of Training and Skill Improvement of Economy Managers

History of Soviet Management Training System

The following periods can be distinguished in the evolution of the system for management training in the U.S.S.R.:

(1) the early period of building up the managerial machinery in order to guide the socialist economy after the revolution;

(2) the period preceding World War II: practically all graduates of higher-learning institutions and secondary technical schools (both evening and correspondence courses) were assigned to managerial posts, while a number of managers appointed were workers with practical experience, who only afterward started to educate themselves in various ways;

(3) the period when only part of the graduates were appointed to managerial posts while a majority first worked as experts, some of whom were later promoted to managers;

(4) the current period, entered during the past few years: all higher-school graduates first work as experts and are promoted to managers only after having shown their capabilities. A characteristic development in this period is the establishment of special postgraduate faculties and institutes for future managers selected from among qualified experts with practical experience.

Now to some details:

Tsarist Russia was a nation of mediocre economic development. It possessed a certain corps of administrators, and Russian scientists made many important contributions to world technological progress. Still, there was an obvious general shortage of qualified personnel, acute enough to prevent the country from catching up with such developed nations as Germany or Britain.

After the revolution, a portion of the administrative staff left the country together with members of the bourgeoisie. But the more progressive elements, including prominent engineers, military experts, scholars, and state officials, took an active part in the building of the new state.

The main difficulties were due not so much to emigration as to the following factors: a general shortage of educated specialists in Russia; lack of experience in managing the economy of the whole country, which had become an integrated organism; the need for new management methods which would comply with the nature of the socialist system whereby workers and peasants had become both the object and subject of management.

The shortage of managerial personnel was offset in several ways:

(1) drawing into the economic management sphere those party, trade union, and youth leaders who had shown themselves to be capable organizers during the underground struggle against tsarism, the revolution, and the civil war;

(2) bold promotion to leading posts of workers and peasants possessing an organizational talent that could not have flourished under a monarchy based upon class privilege;

(3) employment of former Russian administrators who were neither sympathetic nor hostile toward Soviet power ("bourgeois experts," "specialists");

(4) enlistment of experts from abroad ("foreign experts"); some sympathized with socialism, but the majority were attracted by high salaries;

(5) organization of mass-scale training of experts in educational institutions, where special departments were quickly set up to prepare peasants and workers lacking a secondary school background for higher educational institutions ("Rabfaks").

Problems associated with mastering the art of managing a centralized economy with new methods were solved in a number of ways:

(1) by applying to the economy the experience accumulated by the Party in organizing the workers' struggle against tsarism and revolution and in organizing the Red Army (methods based on widespread revolutionary enthusiasm, propaganda, and revolutionary organization);

(2) by accumulation through study, theoretical analysis, and generalization of the practical experience gained in building up the Soviet economy and by adopting valuable economic tools developed in the former capitalist system;

(3) by introduction of an extensive system of control by workers and their organizations to supervise bourgeois and foreign experts;

(4) by introduction of the so-called "red director" system: a

Soviet leader was put to work side by side with bourgeois or foreign experts so as to supervise the latter and at the same time to learn their methods and to supplement these with revolutionary methods. This system was particularly effective in the army during the civil war, and it proved its value in the period of economic construction.

At that time there was no special management training, because the chief goal was to give a "red director" the knowledge of, say, an engineer or agronomist. To this end managers were trained both at the usual higher-learning institutions and at special higher and secondary manager colleges, which provided the managerial staff with special (technical, agriculture, etc.) education. The most famous of these was the "Industrial Academy." Its students were experienced managers lacking higher or even secondary education. Many renowned Soviet economists graduated from this academy. Gradually the need for such special managers' colleges disappeared, and the academies and courses of this kind were abolished one by one.

As the number of "red directors" lacking a special education gradually diminished and the output of graduates from Soviet institutes and technical schools increased, it became more and more usual to appoint a higher-school graduate (a university graduate) directly to the post of manager. The shortage of qualified personnel right up to the 1940s meant that virtually every graduate specialist was assigned to a managerial position. His work in this capacity was helped by the fact that, at the university, he attended, as a matter of course, classes on Marxism-Leninism and had an opportunity to gain managerial experience by participating in the work of public organizations. Local Party organizations and teachers at the higher-learning institutions played a major role in preparing students for their future managerial posts from their very first year.

After the war, in 1945, academies with classes in certain special subjects for particular sectors of the economy were temporarily established in order to refresh the qualifications of managers who had spent a long time in the army or to train those who had shown a capacity for managerial work at the front.

But later, university graduates became once more the main source of managerial personnel. In the 1950s, the typical case came to be that of a graduate who first worked a number of years as an expert prior to being promoted to a managerial post.

Certain new trends emerged in the 1950s. Rapid technological progress, the introduction of mathematical methods and electronic computers, and the strenuous effort to enhance product quality and labor productivity faced the managers with a great number of new problems for which they were not prepared at the university. All kinds of refresher courses were therefore intensively developed in order to afford study of these new problems during, and more frequently after, working hours.

Present Management Training System

The present system of management training is characterized by the following features:

(1) Some university graduates (particularly economists and jurists) are given managerial appointments immediately after they finish their studies (occasionally daytime but more frequently evening class or extramural). They are prepared for managerial work simultaneously with and in the process of mastering the special subjects.

(2) Some graduates work for a few years as experts and are then promoted to managerial posts after having shown their capability for organizational work. In this case their training comprises not just the educational background but also the practical working experience as well as self-educational study of management science papers, attendance at lectures and so on in the postgraduate period.

(3) Managers who are already in office upgrade their qualifications at various special institutes or courses created for that purpose. Management training at higher-learning institutions can be classified in four categories:

(1) economic education of two varieties: (a) general economics and (b) engineering (agrarian) economics;

(2) technical education (agricultural, medical, etc.);

(3) legal education;

(4) other kinds of humanistic studies.

The first two categories are the principal ones since a majority of Soviet economy managers have an engineering educational background, and a considerable part are experts in economics. The share of the other educational groups is insignificant.

At the higher-learning institutions education can be daytime (usually five years) or evening-class and extramural (usually six years). Higher education is provided by universities and institutes, with both categories of institutions enjoying equal rights in the U.S.S.R.

With the contributions of the different higher-education sectors to management training being as unequal as it is, the particular sectors take differing approaches to the specific issues of managerial work and to the development of the management mechanisms. These issues are especially taken into account in the training of economists and jurists, that is, in the spheres of economic and juridical education. These are the two categories of graduates that receive the greatest amount of knowledge at the university to support their future functioning as managers and to develop the organizational know-how and the art of management. A certain degree of such knowledge is given to future engineers and agronomists as well.

Analysis of current trends in the field indicates a marked growth in economic and juridical education. At present, economics is taught throughout the country at 41 special institutes and 190 economics faculties of universities, and at engineering and agricultural institutes. This education is provided through 39 special and multidisciplinary training specialties, including national economic planning, industrial planning, labor economics, finance, and the economics and organization of the individual industries and sectors of agriculture. Training of general-profile economists is of special importance for elevating managers who possess many-sided knowledge and are capable of unraveling intricate economic problems and of analyzing the economy variables in a profound manner so as to work out plans and measures for ensuring the optimum development of the social production.

As against 72,600 students in economics—5.6 per cent of the total undergraduates—in 1950, there were as many as 492,300 economics students—11 per cent of the total—in 1969. Meanwhile the annual output of graduate economists increased sevenfold, exceeding 70,000 in 1970. New admissions of students to the economics specialties surpassed the 100,000 mark in 1967 and have continued to grow since.

Similar trends can be found in higher juridical education, provided in 1967 by four law institutes and 29 university faculties. From 45,400 law students in 1950 the number of undergraduates rose to 70,500 in 1969. This growing number of graduates trained to work in the management sphere ensures a greater fulfillment of personnel requirements in the managerial system.

In response to the qualitative changes taking place in the management sphere and the need for higher qualifications of managers, Soviet higher education has been continually upgrading the training provided to specialists who will be engaged in managerial work. A major effort in this upgrading is to set up training facilities for new specialists and subjects which correspond to the new types of work and new career profiles emerging in the management sphere in pace with the scientific and technological revolution and with progress in the field of socialist production relations. A case in point was the recent large-scale introduction of mathematical economics and high-speed electronic computers into the national economy in general and the management sphere in particular; the higher institutions responded by setting up a new specialty of economic education, termed "economic cybernetics."

Another new specialty initiated to meet the requirements of the state machinery and of economic management is documentation science and management organization. The first graduation for this profile took place in 1965. Another important new specialty is "organization of the mechanized processing of economic data."

The system of higher juridical education responded to the increased requirements of the management apparatus by inaugurating a special faculty of Soviet construction at the All-Union Extramural Juridical Institute in 1967 and by providing similar specialization at the law faculties of a number of universities. The first admissions to the new faculty took place in 1968, when 750 persons were enrolled. Priorities of admission were granted to persons with recommendations from the executive committees of the territorial, regional, municipal, and district soviets, thus providing broader distribution of higher education to the executives of local administration.

In the past few years management training has been undertaken also in the system of engineering education (training of specialists in automated management systems). The students are taught the theory of operations research and control, information science, systems design and analysis, and related subjects. After graduation they will be experts in the art of operative and strategic management of an industry or even of the entire economy, capable of finding optimum solutions and equipped to apply to the system they manage corrective control actions based upon current circumstances. The specific objectives of industrial management training are also taken into account in the syllabi of such specialties as computer engineering, automatics and telemechanics, and measuring instruments.

The system of postgraduate management training takes a marked variety of forms. Skill improvement is now channeled in two main directions—political and economic. The political training is carried on by Party organizations—the local Party units at enterprises and institutions, and the district, urban, regional, and central Party committees. In the economic area, skill improvement of managers is organized by administrative bodies of the enterprises and institutions, and by their superiors—ministries, associations, administrative boards.

The contribution of public organizations to managerial skill improvement is great. These are: Znaniye Society, devoted to the popularization of science and enlightenment, the scientific and technical associations of chemical engineers, radio engineers, and metallurgists, all of which are to be found in the corresponding trade unions (associations which are united on a national scale within the framework of the All-Union Council of Scientific and Technical Associations under the aegis of the All-Union Trade Unions Council, abbreviated as VSNTO and VTSSPS), special "Science and Technology Propaganda" and similar groupings. Last but not least, universities and other higher educational institutions and the research institutes of the U.S.S.R. Academy of Sciences and the special ministries.

The following are the main educational institutions in the field at present:

Institutes of skill improvement, set up at each of the industrial ministries. The education is daytime (up to two months) and evening class (up to six months). Attendance is compulsory, the students being appointed by the personnel departments of the corresponding ministries.

Of a similar pattern are the refresher courses set up by the administrative boards and departments, for example, the Higher Course at the State Planning Committee of the U.S.S.R. and the Course of the Central Statistical Office.

Special management training is provided at the Academy of Social Science under the Central Committee of the CPSU Higher Party Schools; and in special and extramural postgraduate courses at higher-learning and research institutions.

The entire system of managerial skill improvement is guided by the Party organization. It is their direct responsibility to supervise Party education, although they also control the other forms of management training through various modes.

Recently efforts have been exerted to set up, within the economy management bodies, certain institutions to supervise the system for skill improvement of managers. An All-Union Center for the Scientific Organization of Labor has been instituted at the State Committee for Labor and Wages of the U.S.S.R. Council of Ministers, responsible for organizing skill improvement facilities for enterprise managers. A methods research laboratory has been organized at the Ministry of Higher and Special Secondary Education to render methods guidance and advice to the institutions of management skill improvement.

The system of management skill improvement has an important role to play in the development of the Soviet national economy. In a single year thousands of heads of ministries, departments, and enterprises attended compulsory courses in conformity with a government decision. The rapid introduction of mathematical methods is also largely associated with the efforts of the skill improvement institutions. At present, the principal goals of these are set in the interests of a rapid implementation of economic reform and of mastering the art of management in new conditions.

Trends in the Management Training System

Although in general terms the problem of management training has been effectively solved, specialists in the field still point out certain shortcomings in the present system.

For one thing, the greatest part of management training is provided by years of study at the university or institute. However, since the majority of graduates will work not as managers but as experts, the universities see as their prime function not management training but special education. Moreover, the syllabi are overloaded and leave no room for any significant expansion of the course in the direction of management sciences.

There are also certain drawbacks in the system of postgraduate management training:

(1) the predominance of individual study over organized training, voluntary attendance over compulsory attendance, and evening classes over daytime training;

(2) the overlapping of subject scopes in different training organizations, weaknesses of the training methods, inadequacies of the composition of the staff of teachers;

(3) failure of the skill improvement establishments to make a clear distinction between managers and other administrative staff, all the categories being quite often given the same course of studies;

(4) the lack of sufficient centralization in the overall guidance of skill improvement establishments.

Proposals for perfecting the management training and skill improvement system are numerous and diverse. We shall cite the main ideas.

The most important is probably the proposal to introduce a clear-cut separation of the system for training managers from the context of the system for training other categories of managerial staff, and—more significant—to remove managers from the general framework of skill improvement of employees in the national economy. It is proposed, further, to distinguish clearly between the system of *skill improvement* of managers, on the one hand, and their *background education* prior to their first managerial assignment on the other.

The point is that in future university graduates will no longer directly become managers, at least not to high managerial posts. To be appointed to such posts one will have to be a graduate of a special educational establishment—institute, school, faculty—the function of which is to provide the qualifications of managers to specialists with practical experience in the industry and attested managerial talent.

Such schools are being set up already. There are four faculties with yearlong postgraduate courses in the training of directors for industrial and construction enterprises (at the engineering economics institutes in Moscow, Leningrad, Sverdlovsk, and Kharkov). A faculty which is preparing managers for the planning agencies, for agencies dealing with material and technical supplies, and for marketing organizations has been set up at the Moscow Institute of National Economy. A special institute for training high-level managers is also being organized. The network of such faculties will continue to grow.

There are also proposals which are directed toward better organization of the skill improvement system through an increased share of compulsory and daytime studies and a reduction of self-education and optional courses.

Implementation of these proposals will lead to a four-stage system of management training progressing from (1) university graduation followed by (2) practical work as an expert and leading to (3) studies at a management school (faculty) prior to first nomination to a higher managerial office and finally (4) managerial work accompanied by regular periods of study at skill improvement institutes and in refresher courses.

The transition to such a system poses a range of difficult problems. First is the problem of recruitment. What sort of students should be admitted to a management school? Should they be only those who are recommended by an enterprise of a ministry or should all aspirants be accepted? The former alternative has the advantage of admitting persons who are already candidates to managerial posts and offers a means of saving expenses.

But such an approach involves a restricted entry to the rank of managers which contradicts the principles of socialist management and is at odds with the principle that the right to education is one to be enjoyed by every citizen.

This problem brings up a second, that of financing the management training institutions. One negative implication of state budgeting is that it encourages an enterprise to assign more people to study programs than are actually needed, and they are not always the ones who should be sent. The enterprise's control over the standards of training is weakened and the students tend to identify rather with the institution where they are being trained and where they continue to receive their salaries—but from the state. When it is the ministries and the enterprises that pay for the training, however, they are more discriminating in spending their own funds. An enterprise under this arrangement will send for study only a person it finds appropriate to its needs. But such a system automatically rules out the possibility of an open competition for entrance into the management school among all those aspiring to become managers.

Next we have the problem of career managers. The creation of a management training system will lead to the appearance of a contingent of individuals possessing definite and weighty advantages over other members of the community as regards nomination to positions of management. But this eventuality was proclaimed as a major goal of social development by the Communist parties in power in the socialist countries in that the state is to die off and be converted into Communist self-rule based on a broad democratization in promotion of its managers. Lenin wrote that every citizen will be given a turn to work as manager if he wants. This aspect of management training is likewise being explored in the socialist countries.

Western experience is naturally of little relevance to such issues because of the difference in social conditions. Indeed, it is precisely because of the growing expertise of the socialist countries in this area that there is reason to anticipate a future organizational unification of all management training within the planned economies. Specifically, in the Soviet Union it was argued that such organizational focus should be a management academy set up to teach the commanding staff of the economy and to train teachers for other management education institutions. A special governmental agency is likely to be formed to supervise this area of endeavor.

It is probably to be expected that, as at present, there will be institutes, schools, and faculties at universities and other higher-learning institutions to provide the primary background training of graduate experts with a practical work record for managerial positions with a one- or two-year course. The various refresher courses, on the other hand, are likely to become the responsibility of the respective specialized organizations—the various research institutes, ministries, planning bodies, and banks.

Beyond a doubt, also, the socialist countries will harmonize the problem of training career managers with the process of democratization of management, and they will do so by working out such methods for admission of students, financing of the training establishment, and remuneration of the students during the course of training, in a way that will conform to the principles of the socialist community and the goals of its gradual evolution into the Communist system.

4. *Contents of Management Training and Skill Improvement*

It has been mentioned that the contents of the training provided to economy managers are essentially affected by a great number of factors. In a way a process of selection takes place here. On the one hand, there is a totality of various items of knowledge about management. On the other hand, there is a system of requirements to be complied with by a prospective manager. At the interstices of these facts the crucial question arises: What is a manager taught? In discussing the problems of the system of management we were seeking answers to the question as to *where* managers are trained. We are now interested in the *contents* of that training.

System of Knowledge about Management

What is the armory of knowledge from which we have to choose the materials to be learned?

The entire system of knowledge about management comprises the following components:

(1) aspects of different sciences that bear a relation to management (managerial aspects);

(2) the particular disciplines dealing with various facets of management (management sciences);

(3) the science of management as an integral phenomenon (theory of socialist production guidance); and

(4) the science of the art of action in the management system (theory of management art).

To understand the four components of the store of management knowledge helps us to interpret such concepts as "scientific foundations of management" and "theory (science) of management," as being synonymous with the overall concept of the totality of management knowledge, bearing in mind that the term "theory of (science) management" can be used to refer only to two parts of the scientific foundation: the theory of guidance and the art of management.

A peculiarity of the "particular management sciences" is that they deal with specific aspects instead of with management in its entirety. The grouping of the particular management sciences should be based on a description of management activity as such. The first group of the particular disciplines are the sciences that explore the individual stages of the management process: planning and accounting. The particular sciences dealing with the management of socialist production include also the disciplines concerned with the managerial technologies—economic data processing, documentation, and so on. The methodology of mathematical economics constitutes a discipline in its own right which also belongs to the particular management sciences.

What is the subject matter of management theory? It appears to be a wrong approach if we seek to build up a science (theory) of management as a conglomerate of certain chapters of other sciences as has been suggested by some authors. The theory of management can be singled out as a special section in the scientific foundations of management only if management can be proved to possess laws that do not belong within the scope of any of the existing sciences. Do such laws exist in socialist production management?

Management is not just the amassing of planning, accounting, financing, and computer techniques. It also bears a framework that serves to cement and integrate all the aspects and sectors of management into a single whole. The whole has laws that cannot be reduced to mere laws governing its component parts only; they are laws peculiar to that whole only. It is the laws of the socialist production management arising from the interaction and synthesis of all elements, or the laws of management as an integrated, complex, and concrete social phenomenon, that constitute the subject matter of the theory of socialist management. This theory first of all makes use of the logical method and formulates logical laws. But such laws are by no means precepts to be elevated to absolute status, but rather principles to guide us in deriving a recommendation out of a range of alternatives. The logic of management decision making is susceptible of formalization, and research efforts toward that end should be encouraged. For the present and not too distant future, however, the domain of economy management (as Norbert Wiener has also stressed) can be described neither by algorithms nor even by logical principles alone. The theory of management is not exhausted by a logical arrangement of principles and rules, however relative, because the creative aspects of management cannot be completely fitted into such rules and principles.

The art of management is always down to earth and reflecting a particular situation. It is natural, therefore, that generalizations of the experience of this art are empirical in nature. This does not mean they should be thereby ignored by the theory of management.

Hence, the subject matter of management theory is comprised of two separate parts within the framework of one and the same subject. One of these parts is based on the logical method which formulates the principles of management and can be called theory of guidance. The other is formulated on the basis of empirical generalizations derived from the particular instances of managerial activity; this can be called the art of management. Mindful of this distinction, one can unite the two parts under the common name of "theory (science) of management of socialist public production."

Common Features of Management Training Programmes at Higher-Learning Establishments

The vast store of knowledge about management that has been accumulated so far requires strenuous efforts before training programmes can be worked out.

The profile of the educational institute is of prime importance in this respect. Future engineers study management sciences in a different volume than do future jurists or economists. Skill improvement syllabi should take into account the rank of the managers, their former specialties and fields of work. Later we shall dwell at length on the applications of management training in the principal groupings of higher-learning institutions. For the time being, the common features of management training at the institutes will be dealt with, for these are elements that are necessarily included in all management training curricula.

(1) General educational and cultural background: This is ensured by the system of secondary education, which is a ten-year school programme in the Soviet Union. A person lacking secondary education cannot be admitted to the higher school or hence to a managerial position; the latter can be assigned only to a graduate specialist.

(2) Ideological stand: This is formed through study of philosophy, political economy, and the science of Communism. These equip students with a scientific method of cognition and reveal to them the objective laws governing the evolution of society and the economy, the forms through which such laws are manifested, and the principles according to which the laws have practical application. The study of these disciplines helps a specialist to work out a realistic understanding of the relationships and interactions between managerial activity and the objective laws which govern economic development, enabling him to see things in a historical perspective and giving him a profound insight into facts and events which is free from biased or erroneous judgments.

(3) Economic knowledge: This is afforded by the study of a range of economic disciplines intended to familiarize the students with an understanding of the national economy and with related subjects such as economics of the individual industries and enterprises, statistics, accounting, and labor organization. Lectures and practical lessons in these disciplines deal with the economic structure of production and the economics of finance, credit, use of funds, labor remuneration, and so on. Study of these subjects is organized differently in the training of different categories of specialists.

(4) Juridical knowledge: This is provided through study of the juridical disciplines that acquaint the students with the state administration system, legislation, and the fundamentals of the state law.

(5) Mathematical and cybernetic knowledge: This is derived through study of a range of disciplines that include the major features

of higher mathematics, mathematical programming, essentials of computers, and computer programming.

(6) Historical knowledge: The students study civil and economic history in order to have an idea of the evolution of the various systems of state administration and of the changes of the state system, and to gain a deeper understanding of the factors leading to changes in the forms and methods of management.

(7) Psychological knowledge: The essentials of individual, social, and industrial psychology are included.

(8) Knowledge about the future domain of activity: This implies knowledge of the techniques and technologies of future fields of endeavor, manpower resources, and so on. It is of paramount importance for a prospective manager to master this system of knowledge, because the essence of management must correspond to the sphere where it is undertaken so that efficient performance and improvement of management can be achieved in harmony with the features peculiar to that sphere.

(9) Management knowledge: This is provided through a course on "fundamentals of productivity," which deals with the key problems of management science viewed as a discipline in its own right. The scope and programme of the course differ among institutes according to the specifics of training for the various categories of specialists. To organize courses in management sciences, special chairs of management science have been set up at a number of institutions throughout the country (for instance at the Moscow Institute of Engineering Economics) and a qualified staff of professors and teachers has been trained. The institutions have worked out programmes of management science training, texts and methods guidance papers, and open postgraduate studies in a new specialty, "organization of national economy management."

These features, taken together, make up a sound theoretical and methodological base for mastering a system of special scientific knowledge about management, managerial know-how, and the art of performing managerial work. While underscoring the importance of these aspects of advanced training for the future managerial staff of the Soviet national economy, it should be emphasized that such training does not thereby constitute the training of full-fledged managers. The task accomplished by higher-learning institutions is more modest—it is essentially to teach the students the fundamentals of management.

Specifics of Management Training at Various Institutions

We mentioned earlier that, from the standpoint of management training, the system of higher learning can be subdivided into four groups: economical (general economic and engineering economic); legal; engineering (agrarian, etc.); and the other humanities. Since the main body of economy managers receive economic or engineering education, it is of particular importance to analyze the practices of management science studies at the higher-learning institutions with respect to these two areas.

The disciplines relating to management are most developed in the area of higher economic education. A central place in the curriculum at economics institutes and university faculties is occupied by the course in national economic planning. In training personnel for this particular specialty the course at the industrial planning department comprises 190 hours; at the labor economic department, 140 hours. The course on national economy planning has been combined with the national economy management course at the department of economic cybernetics of Moscow University to make a total of 220 hours.

The course in national economic planning gives the students an introduction to such strategic management functions as mapping out long-range economic development trends, working out and implementing technical policies, and calculating the main proportions in the national economy and its growth rates. Lectures and seminars on planning convey information on organization and methods of guiding the nations' development, on the structure of the economic plans and of state planning agencies, on the function of the principal units of the planning system, and on methods of planning. They also reveal the system of measures utilized in setting targets for the national economy and its sectors and illuminate the combined methods and economic tools that ensure the achievement of these targets.

The second facet of economic education is the study of the economics of industry and agriculture. The students are familiarized with the structure and functions of management organs in these sectors, the forms and methods of their activity, the specific features of this or that sector, and the use of the principal economic tools of management. In the context of the current economic reform, special attention is given to the principles of implementing the reform in the various sectors, involving a detailed study of the principles of democratic centralism methods, combining centralized planned management with local initiatives, the sectoral and spatial aspects of management, and economic and administrative means of influencing economic development.

A course in scientific organization of labor occupies an important place in the management training of economists. This course provides students with information on the rational organization of the production process to be employed both in their work and in making recommendations to enterprises and units likely to be subordinated to them. A course in accounting acquaints the students with the organization of work and bookkeeping and with the management documentation and reporting information used in management of socialist enterprises and as aids in assessing the results of economic activity and the degree of plan fulfillment.

Another course teaches the methods and techniques of economic analysis, the primary data employed, and the related checkup procedures. This information is of utmost value in enabling a manager to appreciate the economic activities of enterprises and other units of economy, correctly to identify advanced and backward elements, to detect the various factors involved, and to elaborate remedies for such discrepancies.

The role of statistics in management is expounded in a course in theoretical and economic statistics which explores the structure and functions of the statistical agencies and their interrelations with other bodies in the state administration. This and similar courses offer training in statistical methods of analyzing economic and social processes and serve to clarify development trends and the use of statistical data in managerial work. Students are taught to decipher current statistics and to interpret statistical tables so as to understand their objective implications.

Students in economics are also given broad training in mathematics and cybernetics. They attend courses of the queing theory and in mathematical statistics which permit them to verify the objective regularities of the processes being studied, in terms of objects of organized control, a course of variance analysis, multiple correlation, etc. Much attention is given to providing the students with knowledge that permits them to calculate the exact measures of the actions they undertake and to set efficiency criteria of these actions, and also to introduce the all-round mechanization and automation of the process of acquisition, arrangement, processing, and utilization of the various types of information which are part and parcel of the management system at all of its levels and in all of its functional branches. At Moscow University these courses amount to 910 hours for mathematical economists and 690 for planning experts.

In the system of juridical education the same problems are tackled—but from a legal point of view, such as the courses devoted to theory and history of state law, Soviet state law, Soviet construction, and Soviet administrative law.

As regards engineering personnel, the scientific foundations, labor and management organizations are explored in a course on production organization and planning. Students in the specialty are also offered lectures on industrial psychology and physiology, industrial aesthetics, computer engineering, and economic calculations.

Besides the compulsory course, optional courses are offered at the higher school which differ from the former in that they usually deal with narrower and more special problems and are available only to students who have elected to specialize. The list of special courses may vary from year to year as they are delivered not only by the university teacher but also by outside lecturers from research institutes, administrative agencies, or enterprises.

Study of Management Problems in the Postgraduate Training of Managers

The granting of a diploma to a trained specialist closes only the first, undergraduate stage of the process that enables him to become a manager. At this stage, he does not yet possess a perfect command of the science and art of management nor is he a career manager. The knowledge he has gained serves merely as preparation for his service and promotion to a managerial position.

Postgraduate studies are helpful for gaining new knowledge. As mentioned above, the main types of postgraduate learning facilities at present are the production managers' faculties at higher-learning institutions and skill improvement institutes (refresher courses) at ministries and administrative boards.

The principal mission of the managers' faculties is to train highly skilled managers for industrial and construction enterprises. Admission is granted to persons aged under forty and having a higher education and a managerial service record of five years. Among the enrollees are assistant directors of factories, heads of departments and superintendents of larger workshops, chief engineers, and so on.

Courses at these faculties are organized according to a curriculum devised for discontinued work training for a term between six months and one year. The curriculum takes cognizance of Soviet and foreign development in the field and is drafted with a high degree of flexibility. It is adjusted and updated not only after every training year but even in the course of training of a single group of students.

The curriculum provides for a broad set of disciplines that acquaint the students with the latest advances in science, engineering and production management, organization and planning, applications of computers, and mathematical cybernetic methods. A special place is allotted to the newer techniques of problem solving in production and the latest management methods. The curriculum of the Moscow Institute of Engineering Economics embraces about 850 study hours, that of the Urals Polytechnical Institute 720 hours, of the Moscow Institute of National Economy, 620 hours.

The course in industrial management is central to any curriculum. This course is allotted 130 hours, i.e., sixteen per cent of the total at the Moscow Institute of Engineering Economics; 89 hours at the Urals Polytechnical Institute; 120 hours at the Moscow Institute of National Economy. All the faculties also give courses in the essentials of political economy (30–40) hours, mathematical planning methods and economic calculations (40–60) hours, computers and economic data processing (40–50) hours, and the fundamentals of statistics (40 hours).

Disciplines related to planning and the economics of the individual sectors are broadly represented in the curriculum. For instance, at the managers' faculty of the Moscow Institute of National Economy the course in planning is for 60 hours; national economy balance, 50 hours; principles and methods of planning and economic analysis of industrial enterprise activities, 90 hours.

For skill improvement of employees with a higher educational background a network of skill improvement institutes, institute branches, and refresher courses at the larger enterprises, organizations, and establishments has been created in compliance with a decree on "perfecting the system of skill improvement of managers and experts in industry, construction, transport, communications and trade," approved by the Council of Ministers in 1967. These institutes, numbering over thirty, are as a rule based on the principle of industrial specialization and organized within the framework of the corresponding ministries, apart from the sectoral skill improvement institutes.

There are also inter-disciplinary institutes responsible for training in subjects of interest to more than one ministry or administrative board. For instance, inter-disciplinary institutes have been created under the Council of Ministers by the Byelorussian, Latvian, and Lithuanian Union Republics. The term of study at the institutes and their branches is up to two months for the discontinued-work version and six months for the on-the-job version. The term of studies at refresher courses of enterprises, research and designing institutes, and establishments is about one month for the discontinued-work and three months for on-the-job version. The discontinued-work students in the skill improvement system retain their average salaries at their main place of work.

The institutes carry on their skill improvement activities in conformity with the long-range plans of the managerial staff and experts in the industry concerned. They familiarize the students with the latest accomplishments in Soviet and foreign science and technology, effective methods of planning and economic stimulation, and the scientific organization of production, labor, and management. The curricula and programs of students at the institutes are submitted for approval to the ministries and administrative boards to which these institutes are subordinated.

Skill improvement faculties created at many of the higher-learning establishments in the Soviet Union have many features in common with the skill improvement institutes. Each such faculty provides training facilities for at least 100 students enrolled, from managers to experts working in the national economy. Financial support to students at such faculties is the same as at the skill improvement institutes. The teachers are university professors and extramural economic experts working on a regular part-time basis. The curricula and programs are submitted for approval to the special ministries and administrative boards concerned and then endorsed by the superior agency to which the university or institute in question is subordinated. A central place in the curriculum of the faculties is given to introduction of scientific organization of labor into the production and management spheres, improvement of planning and management with the aid of mathematical techniques and automated management systems, network planning techniques, and related problems.

Special refresher courses for managerial staff have been organized at a number of higher-learning institutes. Daytime courses for managers and experts have been functioning since 1965 to train students in the network planning and management methods in industry and construction. Such courses are offered at the Bauman Higher Technical School in Moscow, the Moscow Aviation Institute, Latvian and Novosibirsk universities, and Kiev and Leningrad Polytechnical institutes.

Skill improvement of managers is also provided through various cycles of lectures and consultations on topical economic, juridical, and political issues. These are arranged by higher-learning institutions and science and engineering societies, which also organize scientific and theoretical conferences and publish textbooks and methods guidance papers. In addition, at the popular universities there are many skill improvement faculties created on the basis of volunteer teaching at state institutes and enterprises. A case in point is the Moscow University of People's Control, functioning at the Committee of People's Control of the Moscow Soviet. Classes at the university are held once every two weeks.

If we attempt to generalize about the extremely diversified and dynamic programs of all skill improvement activities, three major groupings can be distinguished. One deals with topics derived from the scientific and technical revolution, involving an analysis of its impact upon techniques and technologies and the problems of technological progress. The second deals with topics associated with the national economy and the branches of economic science, and the third comprises topics devoted to the management sciences, particularly management theory, the new methods and hardware of management, and social and psychological aspects of the management problem.

5. *Forms of Management Training*

The forms of management training are very varied. Depending on the relation of training to the day-to-day work of a manager, it may be obtained during his free time after work; within working hours (a few hours or even the whole day, once or twice a week); or during a certain period when the official is freed entirely from his work at the enterprises or institution (daytime training).

Such training may be at regular intervals, or it may be occasional, organized to meet the needs that arise. Depending on the teaching and lecturing staff, it may be obtained through self-study, study guided by on-staff teachers, or study aided by extramural specialists, researchers, university teachers, economics experts invited to deliver a course of lectures and consultations.

Depending on whether the training is compulsory or not, one can distinguish training with voluntary attendance and, correspondingly, non-fixed audience from training through compulsory attendance for certain groups of managers, participants being chosen by order of a superior body.

All these diverse forms of management training can be divided into the following basic groups: self-study by a manager; training in the course of a service career and through public activities; all kinds of meetings, conferences, symposia, and other forms of experience sharing; research and teaching activities; and study under guidance of a teacher on the basis of regular contacts.

These various forms are combined in a different way at different stages of management training, for example, at a university or through a refresher course. Self-study may be the only form of training, or it may support the training received through a course. Much depends on the subject of study, how comprehensively it is covered, and what its purpose is. However, in this section we shall describe only these forms without touching on problems of their application, since their practical use is determined by the system of personnel selection and placement and by the system and program of training and skill improvement described above.

Self-study

Self-study to expand one's knowledge, to improve skills, and to analyze one's own experience in terms of its successes and failures undoubtedly plays a major role in a manager's life and career. No matter how or what he is taught by even the most qualified teachers using the most sophisticated methods, a manager's continuing individual study throughout his career is of decisive importance.

Self-study can be undertaken even during the years of formal education but here we are interested in it as a special form of training through life experience, that is, as an independent phenomenon.

The unique advantage of self-study lies in its close relation to the manager's personal characteristics and the conditions peculiar to his work. One can say that the success of a manager depends on his capacity for analyzing his own experience, recognizing the pitfalls and his own weaknesses, exercising his natural gifts, and learning how to use them better. Self-study is intimately connected with life and practice and is to an extent a response to this practice.

The drawback of self-study is the absence of supervision from without and of external corrective influence. Self-study is often an internal, outwardly invisible, and perfectly voluntary personal effort. Another shortcoming is that it takes place at the expense of the manager's leisure time after work. Such study thus burdens the manager or at any rate his kith and kin.

Nevertheless, self-study has for a long time been our sole form of skill improvement after graduation. It has retained its exceptional importance despite surveys by Soviet authors which show that managers are so overloaded with work that they have little spare time for self-study. For example, self-study in the form of browsing through a special journal took up an average of two hours a week among directors of the Sverdlovsk factory. Interestingly enough, though, it is the busiest people who devote the greatest effort to self-study.

A whole range of measures has been undertaken in the Soviet Union to facilitate self-study for managers: programs of study in the different disciplines are published; courses of lectures are delivered through radio and TV (one TV channel has been dedicated specifically to transmission of lessons); libraries prepare all kinds of abridged and complete bibliographies for the benefit of those engaged in self-study; publishing houses issue so-called "manager's library" series; journals devote a special section to consultations; abstracts and information on foreign accomplishments are being published; and many others.

Usually self-study is not subject to supervision. The sole exception is the political self-study on the part of managers who are Party members. The Party organizations favor yearly programmes for the political self-education of managers and carry on a degree of supervision over these students.

The underlying assumption of the widespread self-study on the part of managers is that they are materially, morally, and formally committed to achieving the best possible results in their work, that they are interested in the successful operation of the factory, association, or industry they supervise. Acting as the spur to such achievement is the Soviet system of material, moral, and administrative rewards for successful fulfillment of managerial duties—and in conditions where private ownership does not exist, such incentives provide a vital stimulus to self-study.

Training in the Course of Work

Besides self-study, practical work experience is of utmost importance to management training. Practical service is the ultimate test of the adequacy of the training received; it either confirms the value of the training or reveals its uselessness. No form of training can substitute for practical managerial experience, and this explains the value of managers who, regardless of graduation diploma, possess a record of successful service for many years.

Quite a few forms of skill improvement are available to managers in the course of their work. These can involve a change of job without change of rank—horizontal shifts; probation work in various positions; extensions of responsibilities; periodical redistributions of responsibilities among the staff; and assignments of temporary tasks, extraordinary mandates, and the like.

In-service training can be provided by all kinds of in-house sessions, conferences at superior bodies, or inspection visits to subordinate organizations. As there are no commercial secrets in the socialist economy, visits to a related enterprise are normal avenues to learning about its experience and viewing the best samples of its work. Ministries take special steps to organize this mutual sharing of working experience. Experience-sharing plans are worked out to disseminate the experience of the advanced enterprises and institutions.

The skills of a manager are improved not only through his formal service duties but also in the public work he engages in. Soviet economy managers take an active part in the public life of the nation: they are elected deputies to local, republic, and supreme soviets and to the Party and trade union organs. They are on the boards of various scientific and technical, sportive, and enlightenment associations, on the editorial boards of special journals, and on the academic councils of higher educational establishments. This broad activity helps the manager gain a deeper insight into various problems, widens his economic outlook, and teaches him to harmonize the interests of the community with those of his "own" enterprise or institution.

Meetings, Conferences, Symposia, Congresses

Apart from working meetings that are a part of regular managerial service, a number of conferences, symposia, and other meetings are convened every year on topical aspects of management by the Party bodies, ministries, trade unions, or research and educational institutes. Essentially, these are various forms of experience sharing between the industries, departments of administration, or regions and republics. At these meetings the programmes for the future are mapped out and ideas and approaches to pressing problems are elaborated.

For example, the All-Union Conference on the Scientific Organization of Industrial Management took place in 1966. It was convened under the auspices of the State Committee for Science and Technology of the Council of Ministers of the U.S.S.R., the Ministry of Higher Education, the State Planning Committee, the Academy of Sciences, and the All-Union Council of Scientific and Technical Associations. More than 514 organizations took part in the proceedings of the conference, attended by more than 1,000 participants. Among the participants were 13 ministers and deputy ministers, 90 directors and assistant directors, and 60 academicians and doctors of science. There were six working sections at this conference, where 148 papers and 140 communications were delivered.[1] Even more impressive was the representation at the All-Union Economic Conference organized in 1968 by the State Planning Committee, the Ministry of Finance, the State Bank, and the Committee for Labor and Wages and other administrative bodies: the number of participants surpassed 5,000. The proceedings of this conference served as a basis for a number of resolutions passed by the U.S.S.R. Council of Ministers, the State Planning Committee, and ministries and administrative boards.[2]

Such conferences, congresses, and meetings are organized along varying lines. Reports may be presented orally or disseminated in advance in printed form; the conference may work in individual sections or in a general session; there may be speeches and discussions, or question-and-answer periods. Some of the conferences elect their chairmen, others have them nominated by the convening committee. The forms of organization are determined by the objectives and topics for these gatherings, which constitute, by any count, a universal school for managers.

Research and Educational Activities

Participation in research and educational work also has a bearing on the training of a manager. Its utility can be to some extent regarded as intermediate between education proper and training during a practical service career.

In fact, however, such participation plays a role in the shaping of a manager that justifies its being treated as a special form of training. In the course of research and teaching a manager is given wide opportunities for analyzing and for drawing generalizations based upon his own experience and the literature he has read. Many a manager has tangibly been able to perfect his performance once he began teaching other people or writing scientific papers and books. Enlistment of managers for such research and educational work, then, enables them to improve their own skills.

Forms of Education

Three categories of education are distinguished: daytime, evening class, and extramural. Employment in the economy is obligatory for both extramural and evening-class students, who lose their right of attendance if they cease to work. Extramural education in the U.S.S.R. is normally intended for employed persons on the basis of a profile of their future specialty. In other words, extramural education serves, as it were, to consolidate their positions in the pursuit they have already chosen and to permit them to advance to higher posts. Evening education is not so rigid as regards the profile of the daytime employment of the students. For example, at the economic faculties for the first two years the students need not be employees in the economic field, but beginning with the third year this becomes obligatory.

These rigid requirements are associated with the fact that in the U.S.S.R. such students receive obligatory support, fixed by legislation, from the enterprises and organizations where they work. They are given extra leaves to pass winter and summer examinations, reduced-price long-distance tickets, and similar benefits.

The advantage of evening and extramural education under such conditions is that a student knows why and for what purpose he is studying this or that subject. He is an employee in the field concerned and therefore he feels the tangible effects of his study in his practical work. A drawback of the system is that it involves an overburdening of the student; in addition, it takes longer to study a subject than with the daytime courses. Sometimes the scope of material studied is narrowed because it is assumed that a student will expand certain areas of knowledge during his work.

Similar teaching methods are used in all three categories of education, although their relative proportions may vary. In this section we shall deal with those forms of education which are under a teacher's guidance and in direct contact with him. The forms include lectures, seminars, practical lessons, the writing of course papers and diploma papers, and methods of assessing the results of learning (checkups and examinations). Let us give a brief description of these methods.

Lectures, whether delivered by one lecturer or a group of lecturers, are more efficacious when the subject of study has been elaborated into a clear logical scheme and its definition has been formulated in advance. Lectures help convey to the students the logic of the subject and its internal unity. They also give the lecturer an opportunity to express his personality and show his worth and potentialities. Lectures are directive by nature and call for a mastery of the truths of the subject matter, the validity of which is taken for granted.

The reading of lectures by more than one lecturer may infringe to some extent on this worthwhile feature of the lecture system, by turning a course into a series of oral communications. The sole advantage of a "group lecturer" is in the higher standards of exposition, owing to the fact that each subject is lectured upon by a relatively specialized, hence, usually a fairly competent expert. On the other hand, it is very difficult to provide for linkage between the lectures, with the result that the chief advantage of the lecture system—the conveyance of the logic and organic unity of the course—is quite often lost.

A special place among lectures is given to the "orientation" lectures delivered to extramural students to introduce them to the range of problems of the discipline at hand and to help their future self-study. These are, so to speak, consultative lectures.

Seminars are quite diverse in type, embracing a number of features known by various names in the West, but referred to in the U.S.S.R. by the general term "seminar." It will be worth while, therefore, to specify these types.

Discussion seminars. At such seminars, the teacher notifies the students in advance about the literature they are to study and subsequently poses a list of problems to be discussed. He may name the speakers himself or they may volunteer. While discussion among the students may illuminate all the aspects of the problem, the role of the teacher is to streamline the course of the discussion, seeking to enrich its contents.

Reporting seminar (or *checkup seminar,* which is very similar). The teacher simply calls on students to answer his questions, the traditional classroom technique serving mainly for the checkup purposes.

Problem seminar. At the beginning of the meeting the students are posed this or that practical task or problem to be solved or accomplished in class.

Documentation seminar. Also dedicated to solving a problem, but the solution is to be derived from the use of various documents—compiling accounts, tables, memoranda, or "findings" reports.

Each type of seminar has its strengths and weaknesses and they are accordingly used in the study of various subjects. The subjects that are studied for the purpose of general acquaintance require reporting or checkup seminars. The subjects that are concrete by nature gravitate to problem or task seminars. Theoretical and as yet insufficiently well shaped disciplines require discussion seminars. Of importance is whether the seminar is supplementary to lectures or deals with an independent subject. In the latter case the teacher spends more time on introduction and conclusions.

In recent years there has been a discernible tendency for certain types of seminar to evolve into forms quite similar to those used in the West, so that under the name of "seminar" we may have a typical Harvard case study or a management game, although these names are not usual in Soviet university practice. In management training at the skill improvement courses and faculties the terms "business game" and "case study" are sometimes applied, but the term "seminar" is still the one that most frequently serves to designate the diverse concepts it covers. This should be kept in mind when making comparisons of management training methods in the U.S.S.R. and in other countries.

Practical work holds an important place among the forms of study under teacher guidance. Public ownership makes it possible to arrange the practical work of students at any enterprise or organization where the conditions are suited to that purpose. Usually practical work is started from the third year of study. To give an example, students of economics have orientation practice (one month), production practice (one month), and undergraduate practice (three months). Practical work is conducted at factories, collective farms, and ministries. A student on practice has two tutors, one often the educational institute and the other from the enterprise (organization) where he is sent to work. Diverse programmes of practical work have been developed, specifying the subjects a practicing student has to study and the tasks he has to fulfill. The final undergraduate practice usually consists of the student working on probation as an expert; he has to submit a report on the results of this work. Practical work promotes the development of organizational capabilities, of skill in taking independent decisions and in working in contact with people, and of business efficiency and other practical skills necessary for a manager.

Course papers and diploma papers. A course paper is an independent study carried out by the student at the end of each academic year—a design project, a research study, critical literary survey, and so on. The chief purpose of a course paper is to encourage independent creative work and attract a student to research and development activity. The diploma paper is prepared during the last academic year and comes as the culmination of the course of studies. For the most part this is an independent creative research or development project dealing with a topical scientific or practical problem. The student has to defend his diploma paper at a session of the faculty chair. In some institutes the defense of the diploma paper replaces the passing of the final examination on the special subject, but more often the final assessment of a student's progress is provided by defense of the diploma paper and the graduation examination combined.

Diploma and course papers prepared on the basis of data collected during practical work, studies, research, and the reading of special literature are an efficacious method for drawing the students into the research and consultative work carried on by the educational establishment concerned. Often these papers are profound and original studies containing valuable practical and scientific information. Topics are approved by the faculty chairs, which appoint the scientific tutors responsible for them from among the teachers (usually chosen by the students themselves in agreement with the teachers). For proper orientation of the students the chairs work out the preliminary lists of topics for diploma and course papers. A course paper is written throughout the academic year, whereas for writing a diploma paper some two or three months during the fifth year of studies are assigned. It is essential that the topics of a given student's course papers be correctly tied in with the subject of his diploma paper, and that the volume of future work be estimated correctly. Many pedagogical problems arise in this context.

Supervision of studies such as by examinations (assessment by marks) and checkups should also be regarded as a form of management training. The nature of this supervision is very important. An examination may be intermediate (for part of the course of studies) or final (for the whole special subject). In addition, official graduation examinations are given at the end of a course. Checkups come in a variety of forms depending on their objectives.

SUMMARY AND CONCLUSIONS

The problem of effective management training is sometimes reduced to a discussion of the relative merits of the lecture, the seminar, the management game, or other methods of training. We believe this discussion to be based on a pedagogical rather than a managerial approach to the problem.

It has been our aim in the present chapter to show that a training method is not a matter of reduction to the form of conducting studies but includes the contents of those studies. Moreover, the form of studies is determined by the subject matter to be learned.

Further, we have tried to show that neither the forms nor the contents of management training exist by and for themselves, but that they are part and parcel of the system of management personnel selection and placement that is accepted in a given country and are determined by the requirements of that system. Unless one has studied the system of personnel policy, one will hardly be able to judge the efficiency of personnel training methods.

We have emphasized, moreover, that the system of managerial personnel policy is a component of the system of economy management and that as such it is affected by a broad range of factors—social, political, economic, cultural, both permanent and temporary. The experience of the Soviet Union shows that an effective choice of the appropriate system of management training and hence of training methods can be made only after taking into account the multitude of these diverse factors.

Hence, if the problem of effective management training is viewed not just as a pedagogical but also as a managerial problem, any analysis should follow this logical sequence: interpretation of the concept of a manager; factors affecting the choice of the system used to train managers; system of management training; and the contents and forms of this training. A pedagogical characterization of the forms of training occupies a subordinate place in this framework, which is to suggest that it would be an error to consider these forms in isolation from the principal and leading issue. This explains why the subject of management training methods as applied in the Soviet Union has been explored in this chapter as a complex aggregate of interrelated issues.

Appendix 1

List of Posts Classified as Managerial

Subgroup: *Managers of Enterprises and Institutions*

Ambassador
Chief
Chief arbitrator
Chief doctor
Chief state inspector
Chief captain
Commander
Consul
Director

Director general
First secretary
General designer
Head
Manager
Minister
Permanent representative
President
Rector

Subgroup: *Managers of Services and Departments in Enterprises and Institutions*

Artistic director
Captain
Commander
Chairman
Consular agent
Chief
Chief accountant
Chief administrator
Chief agronomist
Chief arbitrator
Chief architect
Chief artist
Chief artistic director
Chief auditor
Chief ballet master
Chief bibliographer
Chief brewer
Chief builder
Chief cashier
Chief champagne maker
Chief choirmaster
Chief cognac maker
Chief colorist
Chief commodities expert

Chief concentrator
Chief conductor
Chief consultant
Chief controller
Chief culinary expert
Chief custodian
Chief designer
Chief economist
Chief editor
Chief electrical engineer
Chief engineer
Chief expert
Chief expert steel producer
Chief flour expert
Chief forestry expert
Chief geologist
Chief grains expert
Chief inspector
Chief land-reclamation expert
Chief land surveyor
Chief legal advisor
Chief librarian
Chief mechanical engineer
Chief metallurgist

Chief mine surveyor
Chief modeler
Chief navigator
Chief perfumer
Chief pisciculturist
Chief power engineer
Chief producer
Chief roller
Chief soap boiler
Chief sound expert
Chief tea taster
Chief technologist
Chief tobacco expert

Chief transport controller
Chief veterinary doctor
Chief welder
Chief wine maker
Chief zoo technician
Dean
Director
Foreman
Head
Pro-rector
Secretary (qualified, scientific)
Technical expert

Appendix 2

Number of Managerial Staff in Various Sectors of the National Economy in the U.S.S.R. in 1959

INDUSTRY	NUMBER OF EMPLOYEES
Managers of industrial enterprises and their subdivisions	
Directors, heads, and chiefs	128,173
Chiefs of production—technical departments, sectors, groups, office	80,122
Heads of shops, lines, workshops, subsection	242,437
Ships' captains and navigators	21,890
Chief engineers	61,067
Heads of supply and market organizations	104,228
Chiefs of supply and market department in enterprises and institutions	28,430
Chiefs of planning, finance, accounting, and statistical departments in enterprises and institutions	22,941

CONSTRUCTION	
Managers of construction enterprises and their subdivisions	87,237
Directors, heads, and chiefs	44,630
Chiefs of production—technical departments, sectors, groups, officers	26,107
Heads of shops, lines, workshops, subsections	15,784
Chief engineers	32,284

| | NUMBER OF |
CONSTRUCTION	EMPLOYEES
Heads of supply and market organizations	20,885
Chiefs of supply and market departments in enterprises and institutions	10,884
Chiefs of planning, finance, accounting, and statistical departments in enterprises and institutions	7,854

AGRICULTURE

Managers of agricultural enterprises and their subdivisions	179,744
Directors, heads, and chiefs	43,882
Chiefs of production—technical departments, sectors, groups, offices	957
Heads of shops, lines, workshops, subsections	34,395
Presidents of *kolkhozes* and their deputies	101,291
Chief engineers	7,899
Chief agricultural experts	12,278
Heads of purchasing, supply, and marketing departments	52,217

FORESTRY HUSBANDRY

Managers of forestry enterprises and their subdivisions	4,898

TRANSPORT

Managers of transport enterprises and their subdivisions	110,142
Directors, heads, and chiefs	21,620
Chiefs of production—technical departments, sectors, groups, offices	8,381
Heads of shops, lines, workshops, subsections	44,609
Ships' captains and navigators	35,532
Chief engineers	7,353
Heads of supply and market organizations	15,256

COMMUNICATIONS

Managers of communications enterprise and their subdivisions	26,955
Directors, heads, and chiefs	22,528
Chiefs of production—technical departments, sectors, groups, and offices	2,457

TRADE, PUBLIC CATERING, PURCHASES, SUPPLY AND MARKETING	NUMBER OF EMPLOYEES
Directors and heads of shops, managers of trading organizations	325,811
Executives in catering establishments excluding buffets	55,230
Heads of purchasing, supply, and marketing	162,739
Chiefs of supply and market departments in enterprises and institutions	5,558

HOUSING AND PUBLIC UTILITIES AND SERVICES

Managers of housing and communal enterprises	20,121
Managers of houses	48,888
Chief engineers	1,741
Managers of supply and market organizations	5,008

PUBLIC HEALTH, PHYSICAL CULTURE, AND SOCIAL MAINTENANCE

Chief doctors and other heads in hospitals and sanitary institutions	38,353
Executives in other public health institutions	4,560

EDUCATION, SCIENCE, SCIENCE SERVICES, AND ARTS

Managers of scientific research institutes	25,613
(excluding heads of primary schools)	114,493
Chief engineers	11,079
Directors of theaters, cinemas, parks of culture and rest, museums, exhibitions	7,861

ADMINISTRATION, CREDIT, STATE INSURANCE, PARTY ORGANIZATIONS, YOUTH ORGANIZATIONS, TRADE UNIONS, CO-OPERATIVES, AND OTHER PUBLIC ORGANIZATIONS

Executives in state administrative bodies and their subdivisions	246,534
Executives in All-Union, republican, territorial, regional and district bodies and their subdivisions (including executives in towns with a population of 500,000 and over)	51,151

NUMBER OF
ADMINISTRATION, CREDIT, STATE *(cont'd)*   EMPLOYEES

Executives in district and town administrations and their subdivisions (excluding executives in towns with a population of 500,000 and over)	90,890
Chairmen and secretaries of the executive committees of village and settlement soviets	104,493
Executives in Party and youth (Komsomol) organizations, trade unions, co-operatives, and other public organizations and their subdivisions	145,597
Executives in All-Union, republican territorial, regional, and district bodies and their subdivisions (including executives in towns with a population of 500,000 and over)	25,912
Executives in regional and town organizations and their subdivisions (excluding executives in towns with a population of 500,000 and over)	61,728
Executives in local organizations	57,957
Chief engineers	9,002
Heads of purchasing, supply, and marketing organizations	10,822
Chiefs of planning, finance, accounting, and statistical departments in enterprises and institutions	6,779

Appendix 3A

Number of Managerial Staff in the National Economy of the U.S.S.R. in 1939 and 1959

	1939	1959	Index
Managers in state administration bodies, Party and youth organizations, trade unions, co-operatives, and other public organizations and their subdivisions	445,224	392,131	0.9
Managers in All-Union, republican, territorial, regional district, and town administrations, and Party, youth, trade union, co-operative, and other public organizations, and their subdivisions	244,834	229,681	0.9
Presidents and secretaries of the executive committees of village and settlement soviets	137,971	104,493	0.8
Executives of local Party, youth, trade union, and other public organizations	62,439	57,957	0.9

Managers of enterprises (industrial, construction, agricultural, forestry, transport, communications) and their subdivisions	757,010	955,224	1.3
Directors, heads, and chiefs	231,348	292,181	1.3
Chiefs of shops, lines, workshops, subsections	165,191	363,821	2.2
Presidents and deputy presidents of *kolkhozes*,	278,784	102,768	0.4
Ships' captains and navigators	20,388	61,449	3.0
Chief doctors and other executives in public health institutions	16,530	43,994	2.7
Directors and heads of shops, managers in trading organizations	244,887	334,780	1.4
Managers of catering establishments (excluding buffets)	48,463	57,139	1.2
Managers of communal service enterprises	12,111	24,377	2.0
Managers of houses	31,801	60,583	1.9

Appendix 3B

Managerial Staff in the National Economy of the U.S.S.R. in 1926 and 1959*

	1926	1959	Index
Managers of enterprises, construction sites, state farms, collective farms, administrative institutions, and their subdivisions	364,816	2,222,589	6.1
Chief doctors and other executives in public health institutions	3,772	43,994	12

* Not including managers in educational establishments, public health institutions, research establishments, publishers and editors' offices, clubs, libraries, and other cultural institutions, who are included in their corresponding occupational groups.

Appendix 4

		Age Groups per 1,000					
	under 20	20–29 yrs.	30–39 yrs.	40–49 yrs.	50–54 yrs.	55–59 yrs.	60 yrs. and over
Managers in state administrative bodies and their sub-divisions	5	136	405	266	103	62	63
Executives in All-Union, republican, territorial, regional, and district bodies and their subdivisions (incl. of towns with a pop. of 500,000 and over)	–	36	224	364	213	123	40
Executives in regional and town administrations and their subdivisions (excl. of 500,000 and over)	5	137	416	287	88	51	16
Presidents and secretaries of the executive committees of village and settlement soviets	9	185	484	198	63	42	19
Executives in Party, youth, trade union, co-operative, and other public organizations and their subdivisions	7	230	395	259	71	30	8
Executives in All-Union, republican, country, provincial, and district bodies and their subdivisions (incl. executives in towns with a pop. of 500,000 and over)	3	150	337	315	123	54	18
Executives in regional and town administrations and their subdivisions (towns with a pop. of 500,000 and over)	8	305	391	227	46	18	5
Executives in local organizations	8	186	424	269	75	31	7

Age Groups per 1,000

	under 20	20–29 yrs.	30–39 yrs.	40–49 yrs.	50–54 yrs.	55–59 yrs.	60 yrs. and over
Executives in enterprises (industrial, construction, agricultural, forestry, transport, communications) and their subdivisions	3	140	340	319	118	59	21
Directors, heads, and chiefs	5	108	306	345	139	72	27
Chiefs of production—technical departments, sectors, groups, offices	2	105	319	334	140	76	24
Heads of shops, lines, workshops, subsections	2	154	358	312	106	50	18
Presidents and deputy presidents of kholkozes	0	61	419	349	106	47	18
Ships' captains and navigators	15	424	301	163	56	33	9
Chief doctors and other executives in hospitals and sanitary institutions	3	170	400	233	75	57	62
Managers of other public health institutions	5	116	310	298	130	87	54
Managers of scientific research institutes	1	156	316	289	135	73	30
Managers of educational establishments (excluding heads of primary schools)	1	125	431	308	81	40	14
Directors and heads of shops, managers of trading organizations	16	198	408	235	77	43	23
Managers in catering establishments (excluding buffets)	10	141	368	317	102	46	16
Chiefs of planning, finance, accounting and statistical departments in enterprises and institutions	1	88	312	318	143	98	40

CHAPTER TEN—FOOTNOTES

1. See "Problemy nauchnoi organizastii upravleniya sotsialisticheskoi promyshlennost 'yu' (Problems of Scientific Organization of Socialist Industry Management)," *Ekonomika*, Moscow, 1968.

2. See "Sovershenstvovanie planirovaniya i uluchshenie ekonomicheskoi raboty v narodnom khozyaistve [Improvement of Planning and Enhancement of Economic Efforts in the National Economy]," *Ekonomika*, Moscow, 1969.

CHAPTER ELEVEN
The Training of Managers in the People's Republic of China*

Thus far, managerial motivation, attitudes, drive, zeal, pragmatism, and sheer hard work appear to have been significantly more important with regard to China's impressive general economic and industrial progress to date than management education or training. However, management training, as most readers view such activity, will become increasingly important in the future, and the Chinese seem to be aware of this.

There are really two basic types of managers in the People's Republic of China. One consists of the professional and semiprofessional managers and technicians who have obtained their positions primarily because of their formal education, training, functional skills, technical competence, and/or considerable practical experience. They are often referred to as the "experts." The other type is made up of Party cadres and other ideologists who have acquired their jobs primarily because of their service, dedication, and loyalty to the Chinese Communist Party and its ideology. They are commonly referred to as Communist Party ideologues. There are still not many Chinese managers and leaders in business and industry who are really both Communist Party ideologues and experts to a very high degree.

Ideological education and training is of utmost importance to the Party ideologues who hold executive positions in China. Not very many of them—although the number is growing quite steadily—have had the kinds and levels of training or practical experience that the

* This chapter was prepared by Barry Richman.

experts have had. However, ideology is also given a prominent place with regard to the education and training of experts, along with their technical, scientific, economic, business, and/or managerial training. Therefore, one should not ignore the nature and impacts—both positive and negative—of ideology in connection with the training of managers and leaders in China, whether they be primarily ideologues or experts. In general, ideology has a great deal to do with managerial motivation and attitudes in China.

Sources of Data

This chapter is based primarily on my own firsthand research in the People's Republic of China during the April–June period of 1966. Being a Canadian citizen, it was not difficult for me to get a visa from the Chinese to undertake this research project. I visited eleven major cities—most of them important industrial centers—and surveyed thirty-eight industrial enterprises in a wide range of industries. At enterprises, I met with managers at all levels, Communist Party cadres, union officials, workers, technicians, engineers, and other specialists. I also interviewed officials and workers at various national-, provincial-, and municipal-level planning, administrative, industrial and commercial organizations, retail stores, wholesale organizations, communes, educational institutions, and other types of organizations.

The primary focus of my research in and on China has been on industrial management and economic development, taking into account both the internal management, operations, and performance of individual enterprises studied and the critical external economic, political, legal, cultural, sociological, and educational environmental conditions within which they function.[1] It has been both macro- and micro- in nature, with the emphasis on linking these two key dimensions. Although management training in China has not been my only specific research interest, I have devoted particular attention to that topic.

This chapter is also based on various secondary sources in English, Chinese, Russian, French, German, and various other languages. While the firsthand data relate to the April–June period of 1966 (which covered both the time just before the Cultural Revolution and its initial phase), some consideration will also be given to what has happened—or seems to have been happening—with regard to management training since the Cultural Revolution in particular, and to some extent also before 1966. This kind of perspective seems to be essential since management training in China has tended to be closely related to ideological swings between extremism and moderation. I use the term "ideological extremism" only with regard to managerial, technical, and economic progress and rationality during a given period or point in time.

I have had the opportunity to discuss what has been going on in the sphere of management and economic development in China with a variety of informed Westerners who have been there more recently than I. These include scholars, businessmen, lawyers, journalists, government officials, etc. Some have visited organizations that I surveyed in 1966. I have also had the opportunity to talk informally with various citizens and residents of China who have been living in or visiting various Western countries in the last several years. All of this has contributed to this chapter as well.

Since I am neither from China nor Chinese, I am aware of the perceptual difficulties involved in presenting an accurate picture in depth of management training in China, especially with regard to its ideological dimension. No doubt some Chinese will feel that I view things too much from the vantage point of a foreigner and see things too much through Western eyes, values, and preconditioning. However, I have done my best to be as objective and honest as possible, and this includes a serious effort to try to see things through Chinese eyes to the best of my ability. I do feel that my presentation is essentially meaningful and reasonably accurate.

Since ideology has played such a vital role in all phases of life in China, it seems best to begin with a brief overview of the relationship between ideology and management in China.

Ideology and Management

Ideology has played a vital role in bringing Communist China into the modern industrial world in a remarkably short period of time. Pushed to extremes, ideology has also led and could again lead to severe problems with regard to China's system of business and industrial management, including the training of managers, and hinder general economic progress as well.

The Chinese approach to industrial and general economic management appears to have oscillated, with pure ideology implemented in practice most intensively when economic conditions have been relatively good, and relaxed when there has been a downturn. The regime has viewed the experiences of various other socialist countries as showing that economic progress and growing affluence can lead to revisionism and softness with regard to pure Communist ideology as interpreted by Chairman Mao and his key supporters. This appears to explain much about China's pattern of economic development and management since 1949; strongest emphasis on ideology has followed a period of substantial economic progress—and economic recovery. This in turn has led to serious economic and managerial problems which, in turn, has been followed by a relaxation of ideology.

Thus far, there have been two major periods of ideological extremism in this sense in China since 1949. First there was the Great Leap Forward and its aftermath which covered the 1958–62 period. More recently, there was the Great Proletarian Cultural Revolution of 1966–68.

I view this ideological pendulum as having four key prongs with regard to management training and practice in China. These are (1) "class struggle" and the elimination of class distinctions; (2) self-interest and material incentives vs. moral incentives, self-sacrifice, and altruism; (3) ideologues vs. experts; and (4) the amount of time spent in political and ideological education.

When these four ideological prongs have been pushed to the extreme, at least in the relative sense, it has been with the aim of creating rather rapidly a nation of selfless, altruistic, classless, equal, completely dedicated and pure Communist citizens, as defined by Chairman Mao—or at least in his name.

With regard to the first, during periods of ideological intensity, policies and programmes have been pursued with the aim of eliminating significant difference in the roles, status, privileges, and material benefits of managers and workers, leaders and followers, superiors and subordinates, Party cadres and the masses, generalists and specialists, the well-educated and the poorly educated, and so forth. For example, managers are required to spend considerable time in physical labor and workers are supposed to play a much greater role in the management and decision making of their organizations. In general, this tends to have significant implications for management training as well as practice. The informal organization tends to be more significant with regard to management training in China than in the West. This even tends to be the case during periods of relative ideological moderation in China.

Managers—especially the experts—tend to be significantly downgraded in role-authority and status. Ideological education takes precedence over training in managerial techniques, practices, concepts, and skills lacking a heavy ideological component. At the same time, some effort may be made at various organizations to teach workers—and the "masses" generally—techniques for managing their own enterprises. However, reliable cadres—reliable in terms of their perceived ideological purity—rather than those with the most suitable qualifications typically serve as the trainers in such situations, and such training probably does not generally prove to be very effective or durable, at least from the standpoint of expertise and management in the conventional sense.

As for the second, material incentives and self-interest as motivating forces tend to be downgraded markedly, with great emphasis given to moral stimuli and appeals to altruism and self-sacrifice for the sake of the collective and the state. This probably has greater implications for managerial motivation and practice than for the training of managers.

Third, the ideologues are seen as crucial for meeting the other three ideological requirements. It is thought that the experts cannot be counted on to implement them because they are professional managers and administrators, engineers, technicians, scientists, and other professionals who hold their positions largely because of educational qualifications, prior training, experience, and other acquired expertise. Hence, the ideologues take over many of the operating management and leadership functions normally performed by the experts. Normally the ideologues have been the regular Party cadres found at all levels and in all types of organizations. However, during the Cultural Revolution, numerous Party cadres were judged to be politically unreliable or too bureaucratic, and the Red Guards, the people's militia, military purists, and newly formed revolutionary committees took over their functions, as well as those of the experts, in numerous cases.

When the ideologues take over in this manner from the experts, politics and ideology tend to take precedence over managerial, technical, and economic considerations when a choice must be made—which typically is frequent. This ideological dimension tends to have a great impact on management training in China. During periods of relative extremism, the training of managers and potential managers as managers tends to be ignored except for certain ideological aspects of management. The appraisal of managerial performance tends to focus on ideologically correct behavior rather than on productive results from an economic or technical standpoint.

In relatively normal times in China, the ideologues tend to be primarily interested in broader policies and ends rather than in operational plans and means. Plans involve managerial, economic, and technical criteria and analysis, while policy tends to be intimately linked with ideology and the higher goals of the regime. Another important distinction is that the experts are typically chiefly concerned about transforming things—inputs into outputs—and the ideologues with the transformation of people in their attitudes and values. In this connection, the experts tend to stress technical and managerial feasibility and economic efficiency, while the ideologues are primarily interested in politics and theory. In general, the ideologues focus more on the more human-centered functions of motivation, personnel management, welfare, and political leadership, while the experts pay more attention to operational planning and control, organizational design, functional training, and managerial direction.

Political and ideological education, the fourth prong, becomes greatly intensified during the shift to extremism in an effort to support the implementation of the others and the broader ideological aims being pursued. Political education and study sessions are increased dramatically, stressing Mao's thoughts and works. At an early stage during such periods, this may be done chiefly after regular working hours, but eventually they come to occupy an increasing amount of time during working hours. In fact, in China's educational sector, universities and other schools were actually closed down on a widespread scale for several years during the Cultural Revolution. This final prong also can have and has had a major impact on management education and training in China.

It is interesting to comment briefly on those works of Mao which seemed to be the most commonly read, studied, and discussed by managers, Party cadres, and workers alike when I was in China in 1966. They are still apparently among the most popular of his works.

"On Contradictions" has been very popular among enterprise personnel and other groups. A major reason for having such personnel study this work seems to be to provide them with a "correct" and scientific view of reality and to increase their effectiveness in solving problems and overcoming obstacles. They are encouraged to persist in working out solutions to problems, even where seemingly conflicting or incompatible factors are involved—e.g., cost reduction vs. product quality.

One basic aim of devoting much time to "On Practice" is to get people to behave according to correct ideological standards through constant practice, experience, and evaluation, and in a manner based on correct thought. Another key aim is to merge theory—including non-ideological theories ranging from the physical sciences and engineering to bookkeeping and operating machines—with practice and application. Here, too, overcoming obstacles, problem solving, accepting challenges, and persistence are stressed in study sessions, as are self-improvement and better performance.

"The Foolish Old Man Who Removed the Mountains" is widely studied to encourage people to overcome difficulties and obstacles which confront them, however great they may seem. It is often studied along with phrases such as "learn from," "catch up to," "overtake," and surpass the advanced worker, group, collective, enterprise, region, or foreign country. It stresses such virtues as persistence, self-confidence, and effort. It can have positive effects in terms of risk taking and raising the achievement drive and aspiration levels of both managers and non-managers.

"In Memory of Norman Bethune" also receives much attention. Bethune, a Canadian surgeon, served with the People's Liberation Army in China in the 1930s and gave his life doing so. Mao's eulogy to him stresses his virtues of selflessness, response to moral stimuli, co-operation, classlessness, humility, altruism, and compassionate dedication to his fellow man. A major aim of studying this work is to replace self-interest and material gain as key motivating forces and to illustrate the value and correctness of a classless society.

Some of Mao's other most widely read works among managers, cadres, and the "masses" include "Among the People," "On the Correct Handling of Contradictions Among the People," "Where Do Correct Ideas Come From," and more recently, "On Absolute Equalitarianism" (the last Mao now acknowledges will probably not evolve for some time).

The study of Mao's *Thoughts* and works in China, along with efforts to implement them in practice, can and do have positive motivational and attitudinal effects on both managers and non-managers. This can also make the leadership, direction, and motivational functions of management vis-à-vis the work force easier and more effective. Moreover, up to a point, it can improve skills in connection with problem solving, decision making, planning, control, and various other managerial and productive functions.

Don't forget that China's managers, cadres, specialists, and workers have, on the average, considerably less formal education and training than their counterparts in the United States and other advanced industrial societies. And this type of ideological education, within the context of both Chinese culture and China's contemporary Communist society, can be and is beneficial—if not carried to extremes—in terms of managerial, economic, and technical progress and performance. Some of Mao's important works, as well as the ways in which they are studied and applied, have much in common with Chester Bernard's classic work on organization and management theory (*The Functions of the Executive,* Harvard University Press, 1938 and 1962). Both clearly recognize and emphasize the notion of "economy and incentives" in that social and psychological incentives can often prove both more effective and much less costly in economic terms than monetary or material incentives. Moreover, both emphasize the importance of the informal organization with regard to decision making, its potential for either constructive or destructive personnel development, and human behavior generally. The Chinese tend to capitalize on both the economy of incentives and the informal organization with regard to the training of managers and future managers and leaders, as long as the ideological pendulum does not swing too far to the extreme. When this has happened, the formal organization has tended to run completely out of control at numerous enterprises and, combined with the lack of attention paid to material incentives in lieu of extreme emphasis on moral or ideological stimuli, this has led to relatively poor economic, technical, and managerial performance. In relatively moderate times the Chinese have been able to generally achieve a pretty effective balance between the functioning of the informal and formal organization and material and non-material incentives. It often is difficult, if not impossible, for foreigners to take seriously ideological and political education in China, especially with regard to its positive managerial implications. This is because they typically do not really understand the nature and use of ideology in practice.

On the other hand, ideological and political education carried to extremes tends to diminish returns and eventually to have negative effects on managerial as well as economic and technical performance. When managers and other personnel are required to spend not only long hours after work but also much time on the job in both formal and informal ideological and political sessions, managerial effectiveness tends to suffer significantly. This happened on a wide scale in the Great Leap Forward period and the Great Proletarian Cultural Revolution.

Formal Educational Programmes Related to the Development of Managers

Most managers in China do not have a university or college degree. However, the number and proportion who do have increased greatly in the last two decades. Out of a total of 25,444 managerial and technical personnel at thirty-one industrial enterprises which I surveyed in 1966, about 18 per cent of them had completed a higher educational programme. This is a significantly greater proportion of higher educated graduates than for all enterprise personnel combined. Out of nearly 150,000 employees at thirty-seven industrial enterprises in a wide range of industries—this includes the above 31—which I surveyed, only 3.7 per cent had a higher education.

Only three managing directors out of thirty-six at enterprises I surveyed had a completed higher education, and one had some college education in law. These three studied education, political economy, and engineering respectively. Some of the others had a semiprofessional education—to be discussed later—but on the average the thirty-six directors had only about nine years of formal schooling. Out of thirty-five enterprise Party secretaries, only one had a higher degree—in civil engineering. The average formal schooling of the Party secretaries amounted to only about seven or eight years. On the other hand, at a majority of the enterprises surveyed, from 25 to 50 per cent of the vice-directors and chief engineers had a higher education, although at some firms none of them did. The top experts at enterprises are typically to be found in such positions.

Most middle-aged and older managers, in particular, with a university degree or its equivalent probably have obtained it on a part-time basis. The same may also be true for many potential managers. Part work-part study programmes at all levels of schooling have become increasingly popular and widespread in China in recent times. This method is applied in all studies from basic adult literacy training to the more advanced and complex forms of higher education. Such programmes are conducted by both regular educational institutions and schools operated by individual enterprises and other organizations. The latter type has been growing more rapidly than the former recently. Much of the training received in the part-time programmes is job-related—the aim to tie theory with practice. This is particularly the case in factory- or enterprise-run schools. However, even many of the regular higher educational institutions, especially those concentrating on technical fields, have their own factories and/or workshops in which they train both part- and full-time students.

The vast majority of professional managers and other experts in Chinese industry with a higher or professional education are concentrated in engineering and related technical fields. About one third to over half of all graduates annually, during the last two decades, have been in such fields, and an additional 6 per cent or so have been science majors. This kind of education and training is offered by polytechnical universities—such as Tsinghua, in Peking, which is considered to be the best of its kind—and specialized institutes. The former typically offer broader and somewhat more theoretical programmes, while the latter are more specialized and often focus on a particular branch of industry. Neither of these kinds of institutions offers very much in the way of management, business administration, or even economics training. A good part of what is offered focuses on ideology and description (largely in terms of what "ought to be" rather than what actually is) rather than on problem solving or analysis. Courses dealing with the economics and organization of various branches of industry stress primarily the descriptive and procedural aspects, regulations, industrial data, and the like. There are also courses in accounting, finance, labor regulations and wages, production planning, and a few other business-related subjects.

Some university departments of the social science type—e.g., at China People's University in Peking—as well as the institutes of economics and finance, offer considerably more in the way of management and business training. However, they have accounted for only about 2 to 6 per cent of the total number of higher graduates annually over the last two decades. The time devoted to ideology and politics in such programmes has typically been even significantly more than in engineering, technical, and scientific programmes. There has been no programme in China, to date, really comparable to American, Canadian, European, or even Japanese business administration and management programmes or schools.

The above types of institutes and universities in China offer such specializations as: industrial, agricultural, and trade economics, political economy, accounting, industrial statistics, finance and credit (banking), foreign trade and international finance, planning of the national economy, and a few others. There are also courses on labor and wages, supply and production planning, distribution and trade, and various other business topics. In all of the above specializations and courses, little attention has been paid to operational theory, explanation, prediction, or problem solving. They offer a mixture of description and what ought to be—who does what, when, and how. And of course considerable attention is devoted to ideology and politics even when the ideological swing has been relatively moderate.

The closest equivalent to U.S. courses in general management or policy is that called "management of industrial enterprises." It has not been offered very extensively and is usually found in departments of industrial economics. This type of course usually deals with formal organization structure, authority relationships, the role of the Party, planning and control procedures, participation of the masses in management, and various ideological issues.

In general, management as a system of processes and techniques is viewed in China as part of economics. But those aspects involving human motivation and behavior and personnel management tend to be viewed primarily as part of politics and ideology. As noted earlier, this dichotomy is also found in management practice with the division of functions between ideologues and experts.

As compared to programmes in the United States and other countries, little attention is given, in Chinese education and training, to the empirical aspects of organization or human behavior, or organizational theory and the behavioral sciences generally. Likewise, little attention is given to quantitative methods, tools, techniques, or models used for managerial problem solving and decision making compared to a growing number of programmes in other countries. Somewhat more attention is given to managerial functions and principles but, unlike American management courses, this is not in terms of an analytical or decision-making approach.

It is not surprising, therefore, that many of the modern pedological approaches used increasingly in other countries for managerial training are not yet found in China. Business and management games, simulation exercises, the Managerial Grid, etc., have not been introduced as yet. Lectures and discussions are the chief forms of education and learning in the classroom. Although a study of cases and incidents is used in some Chinese courses, the emphasis is again ideological. For example, the experiences of a "model" enterprise, work group, manager, or worker are considered, discussed, and analyzed in terms of their ideological implications. Similarly, the Chinese do not have sensitivity training, T-groups, group dynamics, psychodrama, role-playing, organizational development of the Western type in their programmes, although analogous approaches are used with stress on ideology and politics.

Virtually no use has been made of computers for management education or training in China to date, and few, if any, computers are used by business and industrial enterprises. This may be one key reason why modern training techniques such as simulation exercises and business and management games are not yet utilized by the Chinese.

Management textbooks of the kinds found in the West do not seem to be used for management education in China's educational system. For courses that deal with management per se the textbooks used are usually either primarily technical and engineering in nature, with some peripheral attention given to management, or strongly political and ideological in their emphasis. The same is true for articles and other course materials. There seems to be little in use that really resembles Western works on management or organization theory. This is also true with regard to management development and executive training programmes in China—which will be discussed shortly.

On the other hand, students do get exposure to and practical experience in managerial, technical, and especially worker-level problems and operations through their work assignments and special projects. Many students also gain practical experience in management and leadership through the many extracurricular activities—again, in large part ideological and political in nature—at their schools.

Semiprofessional education and training have provided a substantially larger share of China's managerial manpower in total numbers to date than higher or professional educational programmes. There is really no directly comparable equivalent to Chinese semiprofessional training in the United States. Many of the Chinese graduates of these specialized schools are roughly comparable to the graduates from vocational and technical high schools and institutes in America. Chinese graduates from the best and most advanced semiprofessional programmes may be roughly comparable to American graduates of various junior and community colleges and the better technical institutes. However, Chinese programmes are typically narrower and provide far more intensive specialized training than most of the comparable U.S. programmes. American schools typically combine, in one programme, several kinds of specialized training—as well as some broader core content—that would usually be offered separately in individual Chinese semiprofessional schools.

About 6.8 per cent of the nearly 150,000 employees in thirty-seven industrial enterprises that I surveyed in China in 1966 were semiprofessional graduates. However, 31 per cent of the 25,444 employees designated as administrative and technical personnel were graduates of this type, most of them in technical and vocational fields. A few of the technical specialties in which managers interviewed had majored included: metal cutting, blast furnace production, paper manufacturing, forging and pressing, maintenance and repair of equipment, various kinds of machine building, technology of fibers, processing and sorting of wool, and technology of leather products. Some of the more business- and managerial-related specialties that various managers had studied included: finance, accounting, trade and merchandising, material and technical supply, and planning and organization in a particular branch of industry.

Management Development Programmes

There is still very little in the way of formal non-degree and special management development or executive training programmes in China. There are occasional short-term courses and educational meetings involving managers run by central-, provincial-, and municipal-level agencies. These are typically related to a particular kind of industry or type of firm, and the emphasis is usually technical in nature. Sometimes such programmes are conducted by a leading firm in a particular industry. Very few such programmes are operated by regular educational institutions.

Political departments at various levels of the country, as well as higher and other Party schools, conduct programmes which stress ideology and politics, the motivation and mobilization of personnel, and related matters. The participants are primarily or exclusively Party cadres and aspiring Party members, although in some cases managers, technicians, and others who are not about to become Party members also attend, often with the purpose of increasing their ideological awareness.

Around the mid-1960s, it did seem that the Chinese were becoming seriously interested in Western types of management development programmes and training. In fact, in 1966, some high-level Chinese officials were seriously considering accepting an offer to send some managers to the Banff Management School in Canada. However, this was about the time that the Cultural Revolution erupted and the offer has not been taken up to date.

Management Training at Work

Most of the activities related to the training and development of managers and potential managers at work are informal in nature. There are many study and discussion sessions of various kinds. Often they are organized by the ideologues and focus on ideology and politics, although, as noted earlier, this can have positive motivational effects if not carried to extremes. Study sessions, discussions, and committee meetings also deal with technical problems in ways that serve some educational and training purpose. The same is true for sessions that deal with managerial problems per se, although there are probably fewer of this kind than of the others. Both formal and ad hoc or informal committee meetings provide some training benefits.

It is also quite common to have meetings and study sessions which focus on the dissemination of good and effective ideological, technical, and/or managerial experiences involving leading workers, work groups, managers, cadres, or other enterprises. Here a type of case study approach may be used, and also some form of role-playing. Something resembling Western group dynamics and sensitivity training is also used, particularly where ideological and political problems are the focus.

Occasionally, managerial and other personnel are exchanged among enterprises with the aim of more effective training and the transference of managerial and/or technical know-how. At times, enterprises run more formal kinds of training programmes with participants from other organizations. Here the more conventional forms of lectures and discussion are used as pedagogical approaches.

Managers and especially non-managers and potential leaders can gain considerable leadership and managerial experience and develop managerial skills through the many extracurricular activities commonly found at enterprises. These tend to be primarily, but by no means exclusively, ideological or political in nature. The off-the-job lives of Chinese employees tend to revolve much more around their organizations than is the case in the United States. This holds for recreation, welfare, education, health, and many kinds of social activities. The employees organize committees and administrative structures to deal with them.

On the job there tends to be a pretty high degree of general employee—including worker—participation in the management, problem-solving, and decision-making processes of industrial enterprises and other organizations. This is even true in relatively moderate times ideologically. This is often an informal but effective form of managerial training and development, especially since there is considerable opportunity for advancement up the managerial hierarchy in Chinese industry, even for workers. "Mass" participation in management takes such forms as both formal and informal committees and meetings, suggestions, study groups, and much informal communication up, down, and horizontally in the organization.

In general, management training at work in China relies primarily on doing, emulation, and example rather than on formal study sessions which utilize written management literature of the kinds used in the West.

Conversely, in recent years managers and other cadres have been required to spend about half a day or a day per week in physical labor alongside the workers. During the Cultural Revolution many were required to spend considerably more time. When this is not carried to extremes, it can have positive effects on managerial training and development. Managers get to know more about the needs, problems, and operations of the workers first hand, and this can lead to more effective communication, motivation, direction, leadership, staffing, co-operation, planning, and organization.

Informal on-the-job training, including the apprenticeship approach, is also used to develop managerial skills. This involves not only direct superior-subordinate interaction. Co-operation is regarded as a key virtue in China, and it is common for the formal chain of command to be by-passed in Chinese enterprises in connection with helping others less knowledgeable to develop various kinds of managerial and technical skills, as well as for other matters. This can be one effective though somewhat limited way to train managers.

The Chinese have introduced what may be a unique concept which can and often does prove effective with regard to the training of managers and future managers, although it is based in large part on ideological considerations. This is referred to as the "three-in-one method" or the "three-unification movement."

Teams consisting of a cadre (who can be either a Party cadre or manager), a technician, and a worker are formed. They work together, solving various kinds of technical and/or managerial problems, more frequently the former. They function essentially like task teams or small project groups. Apart from solving specific problems, a basic ideological aim is to get rid of "contradictory" relationships among managers, technical specialists, and workers, between leaders and the masses, generalists and specialists, and ideologues and experts. Each member of the team is supposed also to put himself in the position of the others in solving problems, and the learning process is supposed to be mutual. Cadres become technicians and also do some of the things workers do. Technicians play a role in managerial decision making and other managerial functions, and also perform worker tasks. Workers become managers and leaders to some extent, develop new skills, and acquire greater technical and potential managerial expertise.

These three-in-one teams can be found working on many kinds of problems, not only on the factory floor but at virtually all levels in many Chinese industrial enterprises and other organizations. This can be and often is an effective form of training, learning, cooperation, and participation.

Concluding Remarks

As noted at the outset of this chapter, the Chinese economy, industry in particular, has made significant progress more because of the motivation, resourcefulness, dedication, hard work, and other positive attitudes of its managers and cadres—indeed of its labor force as a whole—than because of its management education and training. The lack of modern managerial know-how, skills, and expertise shows up on a pretty wide scale and with regard to all of the managerial and productive functions.

Although modern managerial training has by no means been totally ignored, much greater stress has been placed on ideological and political education and technical training. It is true that this stress—including the stress on ideology when not carried to extremes—has benefited management development greatly to date. The emphasis on ideology explains much about the positive motivation, dedication, and hard work found among both managers and non-managers throughout China. And the Chinese have introduced some almost unique concepts, methods, and approaches, like the three-in-one method, which have proven to be effective in terms of the training and development of managers and future managers.

However, at this stage of China's development it seems that without considerably more basic and extensive managerial know-how and training the Chinese economy will undoubtedly run into serious problems as it continues to develop and grow more complex in the future. It is not too difficult to achieve substantial industrial and general economic progress in a poor country like China even with rather inefficient management in many areas, if the people have the basic drive, motivation, and resourcefulness to improve their productivity and performance. But at a certain point along the development spectrum, managerial know-how, skill, and training become just as important as motivation and attitudes. In my view, China is likely to face up to this problem and handle it quite effectively in the foreseeable future.

CHAPTER ELEVEN—FOOTNOTES

1. Those readers desiring documentation of the facts, figures, and analysis contained in this chapter, as well as a much fuller account of management and economic development in China, are referred to my book, *Industrial Society in Communist China* (New York: Random House, 1969; and Vintage Books, paperback edition, 1972).

CHAPTER TWELVE
Training Managers for Development:
Methods and Techniques

I. MAJOR ISSUES AND TRENDS

Developing countries, especially those at the relatively advanced and mid-stream stages of development, have realized during the United Nations First Development Decade that the shortage of good managers and low efficiency in the managerial and organizational setup have caused tremendous waste, losses, and difficulties in the optimum use of available resources or in creating productive employment. In fact, unless forcible action is taken, the "management gap" which has emerged as underlying the technical gap and gaps in other areas will greatly influence the capability of developing countries to cope with their developing goals and strategies in the Second Development Decade and subsequent years.

Although developing countries have been able through technical co-operation to increase gradually the number of good managers and administrators, the needs still outstrip their managerial resource requirements.[1] Moreover, as industrialization proceeds, more managers will be required. Managers should not only meet high professional standards but also should be strongly committed and be able to contribute to the country's economic and social development. Furthermore, managers will require new skills, additional advanced and suitably adapted techniques to face new and complex tasks and to develop a positive attitude in order to be effective agents of social change.

However, the time factor has to be taken into consideration. Some fifteen years' lead time of experience are usually required for a senior management position in industrialized countries. Many developing countries could not afford to wait that long, especially when they did not even have enough experienced managers who could train new managers on the job in the traditional way.

Furthermore, the formal educational system in most developing countries, whether at or below the university level, could not for obvious reasons make the necessary contribution in business and public administration.

Consequently, the ILO had to give priority in the 1950s to initiating programmes for upgrading the competence of practicing managers: firstly, to make existing enterprises more profitable through work study and basic industrial engineering techniques and consultancy, i.e., raising productivity; and, secondly, to create a nucleus of experienced managers who could later contribute to the training of future managers.

The improvements and satisfactory modest results achieved led to concentrating in the 1960s on institution building in the form of training staff for management development and productivity centers. The main objective was to create and strengthen facilities for basic management and entrepreneurial training—although some of the centers dealt with some of the more advanced and specialized management techniques or with the development of consultancy and other special services. During the First Development Decade few developing countries were able to have a sufficient number of experienced national management trainers and consultants to provide and to further extend basic management training without any or with only modest international assistance. In fact some of the trained national staff were in later years seconded as international experts to bring the benefits of their experience to other developing countries. However, there are still a few countries at the early stages of development which require direct assistance in the first basic phase of management training.

The Second Development Decade, marked by increased efforts of developing countries to arrive at optimum strategies for economic and social development, the areas of management education, management development, and public administration, would now require an integrated approach to ensure that the development process, especially with regard to industrialization, will not be jeopardized by the shortage of competent managers and administrators. It is necessary to bear in mind here that in the long run a fairly balanced level of managerial competence should be attained in all interrelated areas and sectors of economic and social life. Without such a balance, based on agreed priorities, the growth and effectiveness of one sector would be prejudiced because of mismanagement in related sectors (e.g., the management of manufacturing enterprises could hardly reach and maintain high standards if management of distribution, banking, central administration, and other areas lagged behind). With respect to accelerated industrialization, the following areas have been identified as requiring special attention during this decade:

(a) advanced management and consultancy training;

(b) identification of managerial and entrepreneurial talents and mobilization of human resources for development (including achievement motivation);

(c) management development in special sectors and functional areas.

A. National Training: Approaches and Content

Approaches, methods, and contents of management development and training will differ in accordance with the situation to which they should be applied. It should, however, be recognized that simple and basic techniques and concepts of good management such as setting suitable organization for a specific purpose, delegation, budgets, and standards of performance and above all clear and accepted statement of objectives are prerequisites to the more complex advanced management techniques.

A management development and training programme should also be flexible and diversified owing to its orientation to the practical needs of various categories of management personnel and of specific jobs. Today's needs may be tomorrow's obsolescence. Accordingly, enterprises and organizations need to adopt a comprehensive approach to management development which combines individual career plans and training opportunities with a systematic assignment of managers to new tasks in preparation for future work and with proper motivation for personal growth. Such an approach, based on a recognition of the need for continuous training and the high mobility of managers, should concentrate on:

(a) training in general management, especially in connection with a promotion to higher managerial positions, e.g., in middle and senior management;

(b) training in functional management, e.g., management accounting, marketing, personnel, and industrial relations, etc., in order to keep abreast with recent developments in the respective professional fields;

(c) specialist training, e.g., work study.

It should be stressed here that as managers move from functional to general management they should undertake training in the latter. The main tasks of such training are "despecialization," the promotion of a broader and inter-disciplinary view of the enterprise and the management process, and to demonstrate how general management could make good use of new management concepts, methods, tools, and services, e.g., management by objectives, strategic planning, operations research, computer-based management information systems, etc.

B. Venue of Training

In principle, management education and training should embrace both internal training—i.e., for a particular enterprise or organization—and external training—i.e., carried out by institutions for managers from different enterprises.

Internal training programmes can be tailor-made for the specific needs and development strategy of an enterprise. Courses will concentrate on relevant knowledge and skills and be combined with practical assignments. It is possible, furthermore, to co-ordinate training of managers and staff specialists at various levels of the enterprise, e.g., three-tier programme; to schedule training for individuals according to their career plans; and to improve management methods. In this instance, management development is simultaneously organization development.

There are several reasons, however, why all management development needs cannot be covered at enterprise level. Small and medium-sized enterprises can only afford to organize a relatively modest part of management training. Even large enterprises have various special training needs that can be met more economically by the programme of external institutions. Finally, external management training brings together managers from different enterprises and gives them a valuable opportunity to exchange views and experiences. The higher the level of management, the greater the interest and value in external training for the manager.

In developing countries, the best use should be made of whatever few training facilities are available and internal and external efforts should be combined whenever this is feasible.

C. Management Training Cycle

The main lesson drawn from ILO field experience in management development showed that there is a marked difference between the *knowledge* of a management subject or technique and the *ability* to use it properly in a practical management situation. This ability can be defined as a *management skill*. In most cases, knowledge of the technique can be acquired through theoretical study and through simulation exercises in the classroom or laboratory. But the essential skills in practical use and application of the technique cannot be acquired in the same way as the theory. Acquisition of these skills involves identification of practical situations to which the technique can be applied, the adaptation of the technique to the requirements of these situations, co-ordination of the efforts of those people concerned with introduction of the technique, and the overcoming of diverse obstacles. Such skills are only developed and refined through practice and firsthand experience. The aptitudes and efforts of the individuals concerned as well as opportunities provided by the environment greatly influence the process of acquiring management skills.

In technical assistance in the management development field, the upgrading of the *theoretical knowledge of management subjects or techniques,* including the most advanced and sophisticated ones, does not represent a major problem. Today in many developing countries there are a number of capable young university graduates who have studied management techniques and other aspects of management theory in their countries or abroad. Normally they are able to understand quickly the theoretical aspects of any new technique.

On the other hand, the *skills of effective practical application of management techniques* to work situations are a major problem. Coupled with motivation, this is, in fact, *the* major problem of technical co-operation in management development. To be really useful, however, to countries which have requested assistance in building up their national management development services, the transfer of management skills and the whole range of personal, organizational, cultural, and other problems of application of management techniques and theories to the practice of developing countries must be consid-

ered collectively. Properly designed and executed training programmes can reduce the period of learning the practical skills which
would otherwise be needed, and thus help developing countries to
acquire the necessary managerial and administrative competence in
a *shorter* time than that required for industrialized countries. A
shorter development period is essential if we are to contribute to
closing the much-publicized gaps between the developing and the industrialized countries.

Most commonly, the first activities in which the managers, or young
people trained for future management jobs, participate are *training
courses*. To the extent that is necessary, these courses deal with management techniques and concepts in a theoretical way. This is only
the initial step, however, because as soon as possible, and normally
right from the very beginning of the course, many practical exercises
and case studies are used to bring the theory closer to practice and
present it in a form which appeals to the practitioner/trainee.

The next activity in the training cycle is *guided practical application* of the new techniques and concepts. In some cases, this is done
during the training programme concerned, which consists thus of two
major phases: the first, as a rule shorter, phase of classroom or laboratory training is followed by a phase during which the participants
work as individuals or in groups on practical projects. In other cases,
the formal training programme does not include this second phase.
But it is almost invariably followed by a follow-up period which is
very similar in objectives and scope. Before the end of the course,
each participant is assisted in selecting a *practical problem-solving
task* in which he will apply, in the conditions of his enterprise, what
he has learned in the course. The professional training staff (the
international experts and national staff) keep in touch with the participants and work with them in their enterprises long enough to ensure that each participant does, in fact, produce practical results. It
is considered that this approach is the only way to ensure that participants receive adequate training in, and exposure to, practical management skills. Further, top management is unlikely to accept any
alternative approach to training which excludes the practical application of new techniques.

At the end of this practical in-plant application phase (whether
part of a general course or follow-up phase after the completion of a
course) participants present to the group the description of the problem he tackled, the methods used to solve it, and the obtained or

expected results. Through such *"evaluation seminars"* everyone has a further opportunity to learn about additional practical applications.

For many years the ILO Programme of Technical Co-operation in Management Development has incorporated this *in-plant training feature* in most training courses. A subsequent and logical step relating to the improvement of management practice and to the building of national management development centers or institutes is the introduction of management consultancy services of all types to enterprises and organizations. Several major advantages accrue from this key activity. First, the center's international and national staff are able to provide direct beneficial assistance to enterprises and organizations where consultancy assignments are undertaken. Secondly, consultancy assignments provide a "feedback" of local knowledge and expertise to the center, thus facilitating the acquisition of national experience and outlook for the center and its staff. Thirdly, consultancy assignments facilitate the maintenance of a practical orientation to the related training courses. Lastly, they originate demand for further training and stimulate its continuity. This additional training, whether provided in plant or at the management center, usually confers two additional important benefits: it prepares the staff of the enterprise to assume responsibility for a significant part of the implementation phase of consultancy; and it assists the enterprise in building up its ability to solve its own problems in the future.

A very important feature of management methods and techniques is that most of them affect several departments in the enterprise and, above all, more than one level in the management hierarchy. Techniques, which could be introduced and effectively adapted and applied as a matter for a few specialists without involvement and support of general management, are rare and their real role in management is often marginal. Training in modern management techniques has to be provided, therefore, both to the *specialists* who will be actually working with a given technique and to *managers* responsible for the overall operation of organizations, which includes the effective use of management techniques.

There are at least three very important reasons why managers, including those in *senior and top positions,* need—and appreciate—training in management techniques:

(a) to be willing to send specialists from the management staff to training courses in management techniques and to know where to send them;

(b) to understand the actual potential of each technique and to properly combine various techniques in the overall process of management;

(c) to play a leading role in the introduction of appropriate management techniques and give personal support to specialists and other managerial staff who are directly concerned with the introduction of new techniques.

If training in advanced management concepts and techniques should be effectively introduced in an enterprise or any other organization, it is essential to provide *orientation training* to top managers (preferably through short and very well prepared seminars).

Frequently the top and other general managers who have participated in orientation seminars ask for more training for themselves in the use of management techniques. This may be provided through simulation exercises, application projects, or other training opportunities, in which the general manager handles a particular technique just as he would in his actual job and can, therefore, obtain help from specialists with the necessary mathematical, statistical, systems design, psychological, or another specialized background.

D. The Multiplier Effect in Training

In technical co-operation projects for which the ILO is responsible, the training cycle mentioned earlier serves as a basis for the training and development of national management trainers and consultants. As a rule, when a project of technical co-operation commences, the first cycle is executed largely by international experts. Step by step, the national staff assigned to the management institute becomes increasingly involved in training, guided practical applications, consultancy, preparation of original training materials, and design of new courses and seminars. The objective of each project is that the management development center or institute (national, sectoral, regional, or other) in a developing country should be in a position to assume the complete training and consultancy cycle and steadily improve its quality without depending on foreign specialists—though they may still use foreign specialists, if necessary, for new and special management techniques, as is usual in any industrial country interested in rapidly improving its management.

Whereas the same principles and processes apply to the training of national management trainers and management consultants, a certain difference lies in the emphasis given to the various elements in the cycle. Management trainers are required to do some consultancy so that they can assist and supervise during follow-up and prepare live cases for use in subsequent training activities. Management consultants, on the other hand, are required to do enough training so that they can assist those with whom they consult. Their in-plant collaborators must be trained to implement the consultant's recommendations effectively and to solve similar problems in the future without indefinite external assistance.

For example, the expert who devotes his time exclusively to ten consultancy assignments, no matter how successful these may be, will rarely make a significant *long-term* contribution to the social and economic development of the country as a whole. Consider now the expert who does only five such assignments and, in the course of them, trains five full-time and fifteen part-time national staff who can carry on his work. This expert may well make a much greater long-term impact. But, if this last expert can, in addition, ensure that five members of the national staff can also continue training others, his "multiplier strategy" has a greater chance to continue spreading improvements throughout the economy.

The provision of *training expertise* to international experts in management and administration is extremely important. It must be recognized that these experts are generally selected on the basis of qualifications and experience in other than the training field. It is unreasonable, therefore, to expect that they will automatically be effective trainers or organizers of training, especially in cultural and social contexts which differ from their own. Three main contributions toward providing this essential training competence can be suggested:

(a) provision of at least the fundamental skills and knowledge of training methods, design and organization of training programmes and their effective combination with other forms of assistance to managers and administrators in developing countries;

(b) making special experts in training methodology ("trainers of trainers") available to advise and assist virtually all officials, experts, and counterparts in the field projects;

(c) providing a series of carefully prepared manuals on training methods and organization.

In many cases, training and advice have to be provided over a *wide geographical area*. For this and similar requirements, there is a need for further development of methods of "mass transfer." The ILO is already experimenting with integrated mass transfer programmes involving the use of radio plays, bulletins and programmed learning texts, mobile training teams (using the training and consultancy cycle discussed earlier), and central or mobile advisory business clinics or training schemes. It would appear desirable for an appropriate interagency team to work on these and similar developments.

Consideration must also be given to encouraging the preparation of various categories of national training staff which would include *part-time* and *short-term* counterparts, in addition to the more conventional *permanent* or *long-term* counterparts.

In some projects, nominees of enterprises work as counterparts to the expert in the project for six to twelve months. They then return to apply their experience in their own enterprise and to *train others*. They are, in fact, short-term counterparts. The part-time counterpart group comprises all national personnel who have worked with the project long enough to be able to contribute to its objectives. It covers the range from an enthusiastic minister of government to the group of training-course participants who form an association to further their studies and, hopefully, train others as well.

Given a corps of suitably motivated and trained national staff, there may be no real need for a formal bricks-and-mortar-and-equipment institution. *The corps* can well be *the institution.*

A generalized pattern for creating an effective corps of long-term national staff/multipliers should include:

(a) The selection and initial training of one or more counterparts at the initial "survey stage."

(b) The early provision of extra training for one or a small number of counterparts at the pre-project stage. These men would be mainly trained so that they could help their government (or the counterpart agency) in the developmental stages of the project.

(c) The pre-project training of very carefully selected and proven counterparts so that they are ready to act as "assistant experts" (or even as the only experts in some cases) right from the beginning of the project. For example, they can reduce the number and duration of international expert posts required and help to overcome social, cultural, and language barriers from the start.

(d) The subsequent addition of sufficient national staff to bring the national staff up to full establishment fairly quickly after the project begins. Given successful application of the pre-project training approach discussed above, the training of subsequent additional counterparts will be greatly simplified.

(e) The addition of more counterparts for six months to one year before the departure of the experts (where involved) will, in part, alleviate the problems otherwise experienced when the activity enters its most important testing time, namely, after the international advisers have left the project.

(f) Provision of planned follow-up and guidance, sometimes with additional fellowships, for some time after the experts' departure.

In many cases the appropriate *pre-project training* would involve special courses rather than conventional fellowships. More use could be made of pilot projects as training grounds for "pre-project fellows" for subsequent projects.

A competent expert can usually train effectively many more multipliers than are established in the average activity plan, let alone actually provided. In too many cases today, expert/national staff ratios of 1:1 are accepted where 1:6 long-term (plus many more short-term) would be more in line with real needs in order to secure continuity and achieve the reasoning multiplier effect. It is a serious waste of scarce resources for experts to be placed in activities where they have little hope of working with an adequate number and quality of counterparts. More consideration will have to be given, too, to systems for supplementing national salaries for counterparts in order to retain them on the staff of the center in the face of competition from industry for well-trained managerial personnel.

To obtain and maintain the multiplier effect, more attention will have to be paid to the follow-up of completed technical co-operation projects. In the earlier days of technical co-operation, very little provision was made for either pre-project or post-project activities. Today, there is increasing provision of funds and personal effort for ensuring adequate pre-project preparation. More formal provision will now have to be made for post-project inputs of funds and further expertise. The main point is that in too many cases all the investment in funds, effort, and know-how fails to yield commensurate results unless provision is made to ensure that the work done is followed up and periodically re-energized.

A variety of ways and methods of follow-up of projects in management and administration will be needed. They may involve, for example, seminars for the directors of national training and consultancy centers or institutes; special courses and seminars on new management concepts and techniques; continuous information services to institutes, centers, and schools in developing countries; and the organization of regional or subregional institutes.

II. RECENT ILO EXPERIENCE IN THE USE OF TRAINING AND TEACHING METHODS IN MANAGEMENT DEVELOPMENT

As it had already become evident to the ILO that there would be an increasing need for management development programmes in developing countries, which should be maintained at a high level, a study was conducted in 1964 of the effectiveness of the ILO projects in the field.[2] One of the points emphasized by the technical meeting which discussed the study was the "need to adopt as far as possible participative methods of teaching, adapting them to the needs of different countries and conditions with special emphasis on content and conduct of the participants over the programme."[3] Meanwhile, ILO individual expert briefing was conducted on a group basis providing *inter alia* for a week's review of the principles of learning and refresher training in the following methods: lecture presentation, discussion methods, case study, incident methods, role-play, in-basket exercise, business games, programmed learning, consultancy assignments, etc. Practice sessions were also included in most cases.

The question is not to overemphasize teaching methods or techniques at the cost of the subject matter to be learned. Rather to make sure that an effective assimilation of the required knowledge and skills has taken place through the use of the most appropriate methods. One of the shortcomings which some of the national staff observed after a period of a study in the more advanced industrial countries was that teaching methods and techniques are sometimes so perfected that they become an end in themselves. In their enthusiasm to apply such methods on return to their home countries, they are met, to their disappointment, with the frustrating experience that some methods could not easily integrate with the local setting. Similar remarks are often made by experts during their initial assignment when they first experience what is known as the "cultural shock."

In order to gain a deeper insight into the influence of social or cultural factors on management as the development of managers, the ILO convened a technical meeting in 1965 to discuss the subject. Of the six points which were discussed the following two are specially relevant to this study:

—the relevant social and cultural factors for planning and administering management development programmes in a culture in which their basic ingredients did not originate;

—the main measures to be considered to ensure that new techniques and methods will be accepted and integrated.

The meeting agreed that many of the social and cultural factors affecting management development, which were difficult to identify precisely, were found in both advanced industrial countries and in developing countries. However, the extent to which they operated in the latter countries made it the more necessary to take them into serious account.[4]

In addition to the general factors related to ideological, political, economic, and educational systems, which should be clearly understood, the following factors were considered of significant importance to management and management development:

(a) group and personal relations and loyalties;
(b) attitudes to authority and responsibility;
(c) status and prestige;
(d) educational and intellectual traditions;
(e) attitudes to work;
(f) attitudes to property;
(g) attitudes to women;
(h) attitudes to public authorities;
(i) concepts of justice.

These factors could either promote or hinder the application of modern management techniques and related teaching methods; but they were susceptible to change through education, the way they are approached, or changes in the prevailing social, economic, or political conditions.

The meeting concluded that the important thing in the development of managerial personnel is to understand the nature of these factors by being more sensitive to differences in cultures and to adapt the manner of dealing with them so as to achieve the greatest advantage to the individual enterprise and to the society as a whole.

This is one of the most important subjects to which the ILO gives special attention when designing management development projects, in their implementation and through the technical support given to experts.

In conjunction with the UNITAR study on "Newer Teaching Techniques for Training Managers," the ILO carried out in 1970 a survey of teaching methods as applied in ILO-assisted management development projects in thirty-two countries (twelve in Africa, five in Asia, eight in Latin America, three in the Middle East, and four in Europe).

A. A Survey of Teaching Methods

The survey was primarily based on the returns of a questionnaire which was sent to ILO experts in the field soliciting their comments and those of national staff attached to management development centers. The questionnaire was designed to analyze the experience gained in the field with appropriate cross reference to subject area. It was first discussed with some experts during their visits to ILO headquarters to clarify any apparent ambiguities in the wording and was dispatched to projects in February 1970. The number of the replies received was 137 (the average teaching experience by expert ranged from eight to eighteen years) classified by subjects as follows:

1. SUBJECT AREA   NUMBER OF REPLIES RECEIVED
   —General management   41
   —Marketing and sales   14
   —Production management and
     industrial engineering   33
   —Personnel management   11
   —Financial management and
     accounting   24
   —Management sciences and EDP   14
                  Total   137

2. TYPE OF COURSE PARTICIPANTS
   —Future managers
   —Top and senior managers
   —Middle managers
   —Lower management (supervisor)
   —Functional specialists

3. TEACHING METHODS IN THE CLASSROOM
   (An operational definition of each method
   was attached to the questionnaire.)
   —Lecture presentation
   —Group discussion and syndicates
   —Case study
   —Business games
   —Role-play

—In-basket exercise
—Programmed learning
—Other methods

4. TEACHING METHODS USED OUTSIDE THE CLASS-ROOM

(An operational definition of each method was attached to the questionnaire.)

—Field visits
—Application projects
—Consultancy assignments
—Programmed books
—Other methods

5. SOURCES OF TEACHING AIDS AND MATERIAL

6. AREAS WHERE ADDITIONAL TECHNICAL SUPPORT IS DESIRED BY PROJECTS

The analysis which follows is based primarily on the replies received. It was, however, supplemented or interpreted in the light of discussions with ILO experts on the termination of their assignment, teaching material received from projects, and the cumulative experience of the Management Development Branch.

B. Requisite conditions for effective use of Participative Teaching Methods

Experts (together with the national staff of the centers when possible) were requested to make comments in the light of their experience as to any special requirements for the use of particular methods for management training. While the question on requirements may not have been clearly understood by the respondents (only 89 respondents made comments), their answers could be classified under two related categories:

—the more appropriate methods to be used;
—requirements for effective training.

Regardless of the subject area to be taught, the respondents emphasized the following requisite conditions for effective training by order of priority:

1. *Relating training to practical situations*

Whatever teaching method is used, the substance and content of training should be based on and related to practical situations which participants have encountered or are apt to encounter. They emphasized the point that examples and problems discussed in the course should be from real life in the particular country so that trainees, after course termination, could bridge the knowledge gap and translate theory into practice. Furthermore, training material should also be culture-oriented, taking into account the relevant socioeconomic and political factors which impinge on the management practices in the countries concerned.

On the other hand, experts felt strongly that course participants should have a minimum level of managerial experience so that, together with the instructor, they could develop "knowledge of acquaintance" instead of remaining in the realm of the "knowledge about." This was indeed a prerequisite to developing perception and to improving managers' ability to assess situations quickly before taking a decision or making a choice between alternative courses of action. This is much more necessary in developing countries where the level of academic knowledge is relatively high but its application is hindered by the lack of "deeply rooted prerequisite management skills" usually available in advanced industrial countries.

Such penury of elementary management skills makes it much more demanding for courses not to be only "knowledge-focused" but to be as practically oriented, i.e., skill practice, as possible and based on concrete examples so that trainees gain the necessary additional confidence. It was also found that examples properly chosen by the expert on the basis of his experience in other countries arouse participants' curiosity, improve their analytical ability, and broaden their horizons and perceptions. Though some experts have expressed their difficulties in finding readily available pertinent local educational material, the tendency seems to be that teaching is 70 per cent practical and 30 per cent theoretical.

2. *Developing an overall perspective of management*

While the great majority of experts were engaged in training in functional management subjects (96 of 137; the remainder were in general management), there was a general feeling that participants in their respective courses should also be exposed to a better understanding of management and organization in general. Technical training is indeed important for the specialist but unless it is placed in an overall perspective of the management process participants will not be able to draw the full benefit of their functional training. For instance, they will not be able to relate in a coherent manner the relationship between marketing and overall planning of the resources of the enterprise. With increasing emphasis on systems approaches through computer-based management information, decentralization, etc., when the earlier specialized managerial staff, whether at the lower or middle echelons of management, are exposed to the overall management picture, they have a better chance to make a worthwhile contribution to the profitability and effectiveness of their respective organizations.

3. *Visual aids support*

Use of visual aids to reinforce the learning process, especially when combined with lecture presentations, was found an excellent asset in putting the message across. In discussing the matter further with experts, some felt that, while such an observation also held true for industrially advanced countries, it was much more so in the case of developing countries. There, where memorizing lecture notes or textbooks was the traditional way of learning, visual aids in the form of graphs, drawings, slides, films, tapes, etc., helped to break this method. By means of skilled use of visual aids, the participants were enabled to concentrate on interrelations between variables, conceive the various dimensions of a practical problem, concentrate on approaches to problem solving and the like instead of retention of factual or theoretical data. Furthermore, use of visual aids could help the management instructor to recapitulate the main points of the session, thus assuring that these were well understood. This was found particularly relevant in countries where a foreign language was used as a media of instruction.

4. *Language media*

Technical literature on modern approaches to methods and techniques of management development is mostly in English, some in French and German or Spanish. In many developing countries where none of these languages is the national language or even the media of instruction, an additional dimension is added to the problem of promoting effective communication between the expert and the participants. In the written form, this requires translation, sometimes two-way translation, so that the expert may appreciate the value of teaching material available or adapt existing foreign sources. The problem is further aggravated by the lack of standard management technology (even in English). Those who are aware of the difficulty of translating English terms or concepts into French will certainly appreciate how difficult it can be to find corresponding terms in other languages such as Amharic, Turkish, Swahili, or Urdu, to mention but a few. When it comes to oral usage, there is the additional problem of fluency of language, easiness of expression, precision—all that is related to making one's point clearly understood in a language other than his own especially if one is not in full command. Shades of meaning, connotations, and perception, so essential to management development, have to be doubly clarified, in order to ensure that the instructor and participants are on the same wave length. If initial training should be given through consecutive or simultaneous interpretation, an additional difficulty must be overcome, i.e., training of both the instructor and local interpreters (who are not usually prepared for the task) to work together to make sure that they pass the message across. Successful experts have learned to present their material in plain words which most of the participants will understand—thus removing one of the stumbling blocks in learning. Moreover, they encourage national staff to prepare the basic material of some future training sessions in the local language, hence providing them with the opportunity of thinking through some of the problems in that language. As the national staff gains additional confidence, they can conduct some of the sessions in the local language in the presence of the expert and later on present it on their own.

5. *Assessment of the level of participants*

Participants in a management training course should normally have a certain level of qualifications with regard to age, proficiency in one or two languages, length and quality of past experience, educational background, present and potential position in the management organization. This does not mean that members of a particular course should be completely homogeneous and similar to one another. They should rather have enough common base to make their participation meaningful and not frustrating or retarding the learning process so each can attain the desired level of confidence.

This may be taken for granted in management training courses in advanced industrialized countries where it is possible to make a better selection from a greater number of candidates who possess the minimum qualification than the course could accommodate. In developing countries, such an opportunity, especially in the early stages of the programme, does not lend itself readily. To start with, there are not enough candidates of the right caliber and, secondly, those who would benefit by the little additional training are those who are already overburdened with responsibilities and can hardly spare the time.

Experts have found it necessary to assess what basic knowledge and experience participants have before they finalize the course programme—including syllabi. This helps them later to establish realistic requirements for future courses. This is no easy task in developing countries, partly because of communication difficulties and partly due to lack of sufficient knowledge of relevant socioeconomic variables to management development. However, some experts had to learn the hard way that such assessment of participants' level should be made first instead of working on given assumptions. This helped them to decide on appropriate teaching methods and, in certain cases, to divide the course participants into more coherent, homogeneous groups. In this case, participative methods were in fact most helpful in identifying points of strength and weakness in individual participants to compose groups which were most conducive to learning.

Account had also to be taken of the participants' level of experience in participative methods. If they had not been previously exposed to such methods, experts found that they should prepare the ground carefully in order to establish common language, simple but agreed-upon procedures and practices. Furthermore, a gradual approach should be followed to ensure that participants are deriving the optimum benefit of the course through new teaching methods.

6. *Experts should have adequate teaching and training experience*

In selecting experts for field projects, the ILO made it a point that they should have managerial, consultancy, or management training experience in their respective fields of competence. It should be recalled that at the early stages of the Management Development Programme greater emphasis was given to experience in management and consultancy (including coaching in implementing recommendations) since experts had to work more with practicing managers on the spot in order to assist them in raising productivity. As the programme developed and developing countries showed more interest in integrated management development programmes, experts' ability to teach became of primary importance. That is why the ILO started in 1964 group briefing courses which included one-week teaching methods for experts before they started their field assignments.

In training of national staff, experts felt that developing pedagogical, i.e., instruction and teaching, ability was as important as having a good command of the subject matter to be taught and the skill to be learned. This in fact was the base of the multiplier effect in the transfer of management skills and knowledge in developing countries.

7. *Participants should have clearly understood course objectives*

Some experts indicated that it was necessary to make sure that participants, from the start, understood clearly the objectives of the course. This was more than simply a question of having a written statement of objectives of the course. As might be expected, the meaning given to these objectives by participants was related to their past experience and to what they thought their own management perceived them to be. Unless this was clarified from the very beginning, experts felt that there would be no focal point of direction for the participants to reach as a group or as individuals. Moreover, an individual participant could not benefit from all the necessary support to achieve his own objectives. In the absence of clearly defined goals, it is not possible to establish measurable criteria to determine later whether and to what degree these objectives have been attained.

Since most training courses had a follow-through (in-plant) component at the enterprise or the organization from which the participant was sent, lack of agreed-upon objectives made it more difficult to relate the value of training to work and to conceive what additional training would be required in the future. This latter part is particularly important within the concept of continuous education and training.

The fact that this requirement was the last to be mentioned does not mean that it was the least important. On the basis of their briefing, experts are required to set clear work objectives in consultation with national staff and on the basis of their job description. It could therefore be assumed that all experts give adequate attention to goal and objective setting and that only a few of them chose to make comments on their experience in this regard.

C. Sources of teaching material

The very interesting aspect of the sources report by the respondents is the high use of books originating in Europe. American books were reported more as primer sources of teaching material than were volumes from the old continent.

This small advantage of European books seems to be due to the following factors:

(a) Language factor: all the respondents whose native language was French classified French books before other ones.

(b) Cultural problems: the former British colonies often rely more on books from the U.K. than on others.

Twenty-nine experts cited "My Experience as Management Consultant" or "My Notes" as a source of training material and in the overall picture it appears as third in the classification of the first training sources: 19 experts ranked it as their first source and 25 as one of their first three.

Local unpublished material, as a source for training material, took a relatively modest place: it was reported in 50 per cent of the answers (fifth rank), but in only 12 per cent as the first source (fourth rank) and 25 per cent as one of the three primer sources (fifth). This can be explained by the relatively important preparational work involved in local material, for which many experts cannot find enough time.

Within the different groups, the picture of the sources employed is generally not different: the two first places (by number of users, or by number of first ranks, or by number of three first ranks) are occupied by the books from U.S.A. and Europe. They are generally followed by the "own experience" and "the local unpublished" material in the reports of primer sources, and by enterprises and banks or business schools in the total number of users. The gap between books from the U.S.A. and Europe and other sources is in general relatively large, except in the case of management science where material provided by enterprises and firms is quite often used and ranks second before books from the U.S.A. by number of users.

Comments made by the experts

Two major comments arose in a lot of answers. Generally training is never based on a specific alien source but on a combination of sources adapted to every case. For this purpose the knowledge and experience accumulated by the experts during their management consulting activities is of prime importance, and for a lot of experts the other sources are only complements to their experience, mostly to inspire different methods of presenting the problems. This should not deny the importance of books and periodicals, which are essential sources for sources development and for teaching material, but signifies that a stronger accent is put on the development of local, unpublished material.

This leads us to the second remark, that in the opinion of the respondents the foreign material had generally to be adapted to local conditions (this was encountered particularly often in the answers in the French language). Adaptation means not only a translation in local language but also changes in the examples and simplification in the text. The better adaptability of the European sources to local conditions of developing countries was reported several times as a reason for their relative success, which was not the opinion of the expert reporting that European books only slant on American ones. As a matter of fact, the value of the sources depend mainly on their relevance to the specific economic and social circumstances. In many cases self-developed and self-adapted materials are much more relevant.

In addition to these remarks, several experts reported that their biggest problem concerning teaching sources was the lack of material in local language, be it Spanish, Turkish, or Swahili. They had to develop their own material on the spot and in the light of local conditions. Transcripts from books or previous assignments could thus be useful only as sources of material.

D. Additional Technical Support Desired by Experts in the Use of Participative Teaching Methods

The ILO, within the limits of its budgetary resources, provided experts with some 35 management development manuals, 9 Management Development Series papers, and 5 printed books.[5] Moreover, experts had access to a film library and to technical support as requested by individual experts. However, experts expressed their desire that the ILO provide them with additional support in the following areas to improve their teaching ability:

—more training materials in the form of training guides;

—more cross-fertilization of existing material among projects;

—more information on how to develop teaching materials or on research and studies;

—more training in teaching methods or more trained experts in this field;

—abstracts, bibliographies, course programmes, etc., which could be disseminated through the ILO newssheet *Management and Productivity.*

These are being studied and a priority list of further publications is under consideration.

III. TEACHING METHODS USED

With regard to the approximate time allocated by experts to the use of various teaching methods, it should be noted first that there is no assurance that respondents based their calculations on methods measuring actual time spent. It is possible that a great number made their calculations in retrospect. Secondly, no specific period of time was designated for which observations were made. Some respondents might have based their observations on courses conducted in 1970 while others might have included 1969 or even earlier years. Thirdly, some of the replies did not indicate time percentage but only an indication as to whether a teaching method was used or not.

All these points were anticipated before sending the questionnaire but it was thought worth while to get the maximum quantitative information available on the use of teaching methods in field projects which will later help in designing more reliable tools of measurement. Accordingly, the figures should be taken as rough estimates giving an indication of the relative time spent on the use of each teaching method.

While the number of replies received was 137, consideration must be given to the assumption that the relative use of teaching methods may have varied according to the particular subject and the level of participants attending. Accordingly if an expert conducted three courses for three management levels separately, he was counted as three teachers in relation to use of teaching methods. On that basis the number of teachers rose to 402, i.e., equal to the total number of courses.

Methods used within the center

Without taking into consideration the subject matter or the level of participants, there was a heavier reliance on participative teaching methods—59 per cent of the time in comparison to the lecture method, which was used 41 per cent of the time. The main participative methods used were:

- —discussion and syndicates   19 per cent
- —classroom exercises   14 per cent
- —case studies   13 per cent
- —business games   4 per cent
- —role-play   3 per cent
- —in-basket exercise   1 per cent
- —programmed learning   1 per cent
- —other methods   4 per cent

However, variations will be noted when cross reference is made to the subject matter and level of participants. On the whole, one could note that, regardless of the participants' level, the more established the theoretical basis of the subject, the more reliance there was on lecture presentations. More time than the total average was spent on lecture sessions related to management sciences and management information systems, financial management, production management, and industrial engineering—while less time than the general average was devoted to marketing, general management, and personnel administration. The first category of subjects in this context may be considered as "knowledge-focused" while the other category are more "problem- and experience-oriented."

The level of participants was not a very significant factor except in the case of top and senior management where there was slightly less emphasis on the use of lectures than in the case of other levels of management.

The heavier emphasis on the use of the lecture method in the knowledge-focused subjects may have been due to the fact that management and business education in most developing countries is but a recent endeavor. Consequently, additional input has to be provided to strengthen the knowledge base. Since there is very little published material, correspondence courses, or evening classes catering for those who would need to improve their knowledge on fundamental subjects related to management, experts must provide such knowledge through lectures.

Methods used outside the center

Management development programmes used one or more training methods outside the classroom in 92 per cent of the courses as follows: field visits, 70 per cent; application projects, 62 per cent; consultancy assignments, 51 per cent; and programmed books, 15 per cent. While there is no indication as to the percentage of time devoted to these methods, it is evident that substantial weight was given to providing trainees with reasonably good opportunities of relating knowledge and skills to work situations.

About 60 per cent of the experts indicated that there has been a steady increase in the use of participative teaching methods in the following order: case studies, group discussions and syndicates, application projects, business games, role-play, classroom exercises, field visits, consultancy assignments, outside classroom exercises, e.g., analysis of a relevant work problem, and in-basket exercises.

The previous section provided a bird's-eye view of recent developments in the teaching methods in management training and has indicated the relative emphasis on lectures vis-à-vis participative methods, whether in or outside the classroom.

In the following sections, an analysis will be made on the use of each method as viewed by the experts.

A. Methods Used in Lieu of a Management Development Center

1. *Group discussions, syndicates, and similar methods*

Discussions and syndicates are the most widely used participative method. This method is used in various ways, particularly syndicates of three to ten members (mostly four to six) all working on the same topic or each on different topics under usually elected or sometimes designated chairmen. The participants are then regrouped in a plenary session to which each syndicate's spokesman has to report, with eventual use of blackboard or flip charts. The conclusions are compared and commented on in a general discussion in which each syndicate has to defend its conclusions and argue about deviating viewpoints. Other used ways are unstructured discussions with the whole group of participants and panels with guest speakers. Generally, discussions are integrated with other methods, in particular case studies, business games, role-play, field visits, problem solving as application of the lectures.

The method is recorded to be particularly useful:

—to acquaint participants with each other (and the instructor);

—to define problem areas, examine methods of solutions, report findings, and offer conclusions and recommendations;

—to analyze situations involving interpersonal relations and their effect on productivity;

—to discuss policies and strategies arising in business games and other simulated activities;

—as a method of self-analysis, i.e., strengths and weaknesses, evaluation and planning of future career goals.

The bases of discussion are various, related to the various aims to attain, but they do not differ from one group of teaching to the others. Mostly mentioned were actual problems of participants' experience, practical problems following introductory lectures, particular or general questions arising during case studies, mostly actual.

The reactions of the trainees range from many "always enthusiastic" over many "excellent" and "very good" to a few "rather bad," as it has been shown that, after a first hesitance due to many factors (shyness, accommodation to the method, etc.), the reaction of the trainees became strongly positive, co-operative, enthusiastic, and eager. Many consider it to be the best way of keeping the subjects topical, by personal experience dictating personal observation, deepening understanding, and removing misconceptions. Nevertheless some experts record that the reaction to the method (and its effectiveness) depends essentially on the level of the participants and thus becomes poorer if the quality of participants drops, until it is of doubtful use to the average working class (supervisors and operators). Anyway, a favorable or enthusiastic reaction may not be an indication of effective learning, unless a logical relationship exists between themes discussed and things to apply, initial learning and implementation follow-up, and means to achieve the objectives in view. A solid evaluation in the assessment of the achievement of objectives is therefore as indispensable for the trainees as for the trainer.

Different methods are used, particularly group evaluation (each syndicate is scored by the rest of the plenary session), evaluation by the trainer of those aspects not correctly dealt with by the groups (an assessment is made of the failures so that they can be corrected), or evaluation by means of a questionnaire at the conclusion of the course or seminar.

Only very few experts agree that no problem has arisen with the use of the discussion method—in fact, the problems are various but can be classified into a few important groups, the first of which is to *create a participative climate* for trainees who were not used to it in their previous schooling. Lack of participation, slow starting, trying to get everyone involved, etc.—these were the comments in each expert's answer. The problem was said to be due to psychological factors such as shyness, resentment of being put "on the spot," ignorance which participants were reluctant to admit, and sociological factors (previous teaching systems, rank consciousness, opposition between members of different companies, over-dependence on authority, etc.). These factors are accentuated particularly on the lower levels by language problems, which are overcome partly by means of translation through a counterpart or being allowed to work partly in a native language. To create a participative climate requires first a certain personal contact among the participants and many interventions and encouragement by the trainer to disrupt the shyness barriers.

Once this is done, there often appears the opposite problem of domination of the groups or syndicates by strong individuals or endless talkers who tend to overelaborate and to stray from the subject, carrying the discussion over to personal questions. This is partly overcome when experts sit in the groups as observers and report at the end of the sessions on the good points and shortcomings of each group.

Another widely cited problem was that of *homogeneity of the groups,* which in some answers was said to be insoluble and often considered to be the most important. For the experts, homogeneity does not signify that each member of the groups or syndicates should have the same background or come from the same business area, it rather means that the professional level of all participants should be the same so as to ensure a homogeneous discussion and understanding. Only a careful selection of participants before beginning the session, including the composition of the syndicates, can be of help with that problem. It is also very important to obtain a good degree of homogeneity among the syndicates, i.e., to avoid building quiet groups beside very enthusiastic ones, though it was generally mentioned that enthusiastic groups are more difficult to control than quiet ones, for their discussion sometimes tends to stray from the subject.

A structuring of the subject matter, indicating the key points to discuss, will be of great help in that concern.

Several experts cited the *lack of knowledge* as an important problem, not just with discussions but with any participative method. They suggested therefore that knowledge be given in an introductory lecture, the discussion being regarded as exercise, practice, or application of the theory received before.

On the whole group discussions, syndicates, and similar methods were found effective in most countries. They had the additional advantage that they could be conducted by members of the national staff in the local language. Moreover, participants achieve deeper insight into the subject matter and the instructor is provided with instant feedback.

The solutions reached during discussions, which are usually in the form of approaches, are more adapted to the economic and social conditions of the country and hence more meaningful.

2. *Case studies*

While in general half of the courses use locally developed cases, these are often used in combination with case studies of the more complex type, with foreign cases, which are usually adapted, etc. (There are ten to fifteen experts who use Harvard-type cases.) Many of the locally developed cases are drawn from consultancy assignments which the expert has undertaken at one time or another. Most experts *plan* to use locally developed cases when they have the time to do so.

As a general rule a combination of locally developed cases and adapted foreign cases are used. However, the term "adapted" meant different things to different people. Most experts did not clarify how they used the word but in the majority of the cases where it was explained "adapted" meant mostly changing the names, currency, etc., to fit the particular locale. In a minority of cases it seems that "adapted" meant a fairly major revision of the material.

Uses

Case study as a method was used by many experts as a means to introduce concepts or techniques or as analytical approach to problem solving.

Some experts said that they could not use the case study to introduce a technique. By most, it was used to introduce the participants to the concept of analyzing a situation from various perspectives in order to show that there be more than one solution to a problem.

The case study was usually introduced midway through the course. Some said about a third of the way into the course and others about halfway into the course and a few waited until the end to introduce it. It was often used to reinforce the lecture. One expert made the interesting comment that case study should not be used prematurely in a course—only after a certain amount of knowledge absorption had been reached. In a few cases it was stated that simple cases were used except for top and senior management, for whom more complex ones were given. In fact, it was surprising how important principles involved in simple cases encouraged a serious attitude to learning. On the other hand, one expert said that he did not use simple cases as they tended to oversimplify the problem.

Reactions of Course Participants

According to the experts, the majority of their participants, regardless of the subject matter, had a positive reaction to the use of the case study which was described as: excellent, good, enthusiastic, favorably received, stimulating, or more popular.

Approximately 25 per cent of the experts qualified this to mean that reaction is positive when the participants can identify themselves with the situation presented (a good reason to use locally developed cases). Others said that the reaction was generally favorable but depended on the particular case, method of presentation, or steering the discussion (discouraging, for instance, those who had a tendency to talk too much).

On the whole, participants seem to favor the case study because they like active methods. It gives them the opportunity to discover for themselves solutions (or that there is no one solution to a problem) or reveals an angle which they had not thought of before.

On the other hand, some course participants express a feeling of bewilderment and sometimes reluctance to understand our difficulty in seeing the wood for the trees. Some are disappointed when the lecturer does not give a "model" answer at the end of the session. In one country participants found the case study strange to their traditional ways of learning and were reluctant to talk at the beginning. In another country, participants remained removed from the problem or were reluctant to offer a solution because, being used to taking orders, they were lost when it came to taking a decision.

Major Problems Encountered and How Resolved

(a) There is a lack of local material and it is very time-consuming to prepare good case studies. As indicated earlier, foreign cases are generally much preferred for direct use but have occasionally to be used, with little adaptation of names and currencies, due to lack of preparation time in producing local cases.

(b) It is difficult to get the participants to visualize and conceive a situation and to be able to relate or identify it with the case. In order to solve this problem experts often use simple cases which they have developed locally and combine them with audio-visual aids. To make the case effective, experts have found it necessary to personalize a situation and relate it to the extent possible to the field of the participants. Some experts who developed case studies from their own consultancy experience in other countries found participants more responsive and they enjoyed dealing with something they knew had happened instead of with fictitious situations. When using foreign cases, successful experts found it necessary not only to change names or currencies but also to relate principles and concepts to the local environment, e.g., a case study film shown and later re-enacted under local working conditions, thus modifying the case study to make a new film. The same principle was used in some projects to get the participants' co-operation in writing suitable cases.

(c) The participants too often lack basic technical knowledge to analyze the case properly. To overcome this difficulty the experts made themselves available as a technical resource to answer questions. But this solution cannot be attempted where many participants take part in basic mathematical and calculating problems as it may result in the decision-making element being lost to the greater part of the group. It is not clear whether such experts were using the case study as a supplement to the lecture method, where this basic knowledge could perhaps be imparted. Some of course may have introduced the cases earlier than necessary and before having assessed the level of the participants.

The answer to this problem, as one expert noted, may be to require the participants to have a basic course, e.g., in business mathematics, prior to the course, when such knowledge is necessary. But this is not an easy matter to organize.

(d) There is a tendency to get off the track. It was observed that some participants were too talkative and kept losing sight of the objective. Experts who faced such a situation could have it improved through a skilled and tactful leader who might lend a guiding hand without imposing his view. Experts found it necessary to encourage the group to establish certain procedures, such as putting time limits on discussions, avoiding repetition of points of view already expressed, and, on some occasions, practicing voting.

Some experts felt it was necessary to provide supplementary programmes, together with the group discussion method, to train participants in chairing meetings.

(e) Participants want the model or the right answer. Some experts noted that participants felt on occasion that the expert was not up to the standard if he could not supply a *correct* answer. In a way, as one expert put it, this in itself can be a good situation. With persistence and patience the participants can see that there is more than one answer. The expert keeps working until this very point sifts in: that there is no correct answer—there may be several.

(f) Some participants do not respond. When experts were met with this situation they used case studies which stimulated and challenged and which emphasized key points worth thinking about. In some instances, especially if the group was too big or too heterogeneous, it was better to split the group into teams of four participants —each playing one of the four roles of the main section of the case study. Participants then reported to the whole group.

This method, which is a combination of case studies and role-play, created an atmosphere of confidence and ensured active involvement of all participants.

If lack of sufficient involvement is due to language problems, especially of technical terms which have no translation, a provisional glossary of terms may be issued as a temporary measure. This was found effective by a production management expert.

3. *Business games*

Which Business Games Are Being Used?

It appears difficult to classify the users of business games in very definite groups. This is due to the different answers and partly to their lack of precision. Of the 53 answers of experts using this technique, it can summarily be said that some ten experts use one, two, or more ILO business games alone, without major modification. Two experts employ these games plus one more non-ILO complex game. Sixteen experts used other well-known simple functional games of, for instance, the stockholding, inventory-control type. Two experts used games of such types plus complex, computer-based games, while the latter alone were used by nineteen experts, among whom the most used games established by computer firms or business schools. Three experts were not precise enough in their answers, so it was impossible to determine what type of game they used. Three experts said they preferred using their own developed games, and some recorded having modified ILO games to bring out special points.

In What Part of the Course Are They Used?

It appears from the replies received that business games were mainly used only with middle and senior management trainees, but it is difficult to picture in a few words at which moment of the courses they were introduced; a difference must be made between the diverse type of games. The greatest use, particularly of simple functional games, was in the middle of the courses, in combination or directly following lecture and discussion on the particular subjects; 74 answered, "As a way to enlighten the subject" or "To support and consolidate important components of management," to demonstrate the need of quick decisions, the spirit of competitiveness.

Seventeen used the technique toward the end or as a conclusion to the course, or even following the course. This was more particularly true of the complex games, which require special knowledge and are precisely meant to provide practical issues of theoretical concepts developed during the courses. One expert used a simple game at the end of his courses as a means to detect lack of knowledge and mistakes in teaching.

Eight experts affirmed using this method in the very beginning of their course or seminar, as a means to reveal knowledge and attitudes, to create an atmosphere of concern and interest, and to show the interdependence of decisions and the necessity of forecasting and planning.

In four cases, business games were used on their own, being the subject of a seminar. In summation, it can be said that business games are sometimes used in approximately the same way as case methods.

Reaction of Participants

The general reaction ranked from a very good to an extremely enthusiastic one (35 answers), because the participants felt the result depended mainly on themselves. They were eager for similar exercises, zealous in rivalry groups and bettering performance.

Some participant groups voted this technique to be the most revealing way to highlight shortcomings and weaknesses of their business thinking, because of the "doing" properties of the games as well as the competitive atmosphere. Nevertheless, five experts said the reaction was not immediately positive, but first astonished or defensive and reluctant. This slow start, due to unfamiliarity, wears off as the participants find themselves in plenty of company and is then transformed into the favorable reaction stated above. One expert recorded that his participants even provided prizes for the winning team!

Seven other statements recorded that the participants' reactions were not always good or only variable. One expert said the reaction was good only if the game was kept simple with no more than one or two variables to be dealt with, the interest varying inversely with the number of variables. Another analogic statement was made that interest is great in the beginning but decreases with the difficulties, leading sometimes to confusion, due to view-staleness and poor value judgment. Thus, only participants with experience gain the full benefit of the method. The less experience the participant possesses, the less gain he makes.

Some participants complained about the calculations with which a few seemed more concerned than with the principles involved or of not presenting a ranking of the diverse performances.

Problems Encountered

Most are related to *material difficulties:* lack of time, of adequate material (subject or locality), big amount of calculations, difficulties of finding personnel. The next important problem is the *artificial nature of the games* which makes it difficult to establish understandable relations between the subject matter of the game and the management procedures. This is overcome by follow-up lectures.

Other minor problems were cited, such as the difficulty of composing homogeneous groups or bringing participants to adhere to rules and the low educational standard of participants (slow reading and poor arithmetic even for top management level).

4. *Role-playing*

Role-play is mostly used by experts for salesmanship training, supervisory training, human relations, and training methods courses. It is also used for personnel management and industrial relations, interviewing, communications, job analysis and selection purposes, decision making, merchandising, work study, management accounting.

When Is Role-play Used?

It is mostly used at the end of a course when experts know the participants better and the participants become better acquainted with one another. In a few cases, role-play is used both at the beginning and at the end of the same course. The purpose then is to re-enact the exercise after experience has been gained. A few experts use role-play in all phases of a course depending on the level of the participants.

How Is Role-play Performed?

Role-play differs depending on factors such as the subject matter, size of the group, managerial level, and quality of experience of the participants, etc. In most cases, once the subject matter or problem has been identified, the group allocates specific roles to the participants: manager, workers' representative, salesman, customer, consultant. Part of the material is usually prepared in advance in script or list-of-points form, while the rest is left to improvisation on the spot. Participants are also given time to rehearse beforehand. They are usually given roles different from their usual work activity, for example a supervisor may be given the role of shop steward, a salesman the role of a customer. The expert and the national instructor may play the more difficult roles related to the subject or may remain available for consultation or to clarify certain technical points.

If the group is sufficiently large, it is usually divided into subgroups, each of which may deal with the same problem though using a different approach, or with a related problem. In a few cases, especially in salesmanship training, where a salesman and a customer play, outsiders are invited to join the audience. A role-play is usually given a limited period of time (about fifteen minutes) so that it terminates while participation is still high.

An appraisal or evaluation of the group's performance is done either by members of the acting group or by other groups who observed the presentation. Sometimes a combination of both methods is used and supplemented by a discussion so that participants and observers may share their impressions and analyze the situation. Some projects use the tape recorder as a feedback device for self-correction. One expert suggested the use of video recording.

In all events, the role of the instructor is predominant, through his skill in steering the evaluation session and because of the comments he may offer.

Integration with Other Teaching Methods

In most cases, role-play is used after a lecture, especially lectures on communications, human relations, decision making. It is sometimes integrated with a case study or followed by film or a business game.

Reactions of Participants

In the majority of cases, the reactions of the participants were classified as positive, i.e., enthusiastic, very good, good, and satisfactory. Out of 63 replies on this method, only 10 indicated some difficulty on the part of the participants in using this method as a teaching aid.

Problems Encountered

There were two major problems which experts faced with regard to this method. First, how to overcome the feeling of shyness and reluctance to play for fear of embarrassment, being ridiculed or criticized, and, secondly, how to avoid overexcitement or zeal on the part of some participants who had a tendency to be overdramatic in their play.

In most cases these problems can be avoided or controlled through careful preparation (including use of a written script and repeated rehearsals, especially for the shy participants), prior demonstration of the technique, and the use of small groups at the beginning. The objective of the role-play should be made clear to the participants from the outset. Should things go wrong, the instructor should not hesitate to find a suitable way of stopping the play and starting again. If a player finds it difficult to fit in a particular role the instructor can help him to play another more suitable role. Here again the role of the instructor is vital, otherwise he may either lose control of the situation or the participants may depart from the objective of the exercise and concentrate on the drama aspect of the session.

Other minor problems were cited, such as being time-consuming, lack of adequate room facilities for acting, language problems at the beginning, especially when the expert did not have adequate support of national staff.

5. *In-basket exercise*

Value of the Exercise

This technique, although used very little, is very flexible. Experts primarily use it to assess quality of management thinking, perceiving, and behavior through self-discovery, by training in decision-making concepts and skills such as: ability to determine task priorities, use of personal initiative and thinking, reaction to difficult or irritating situations, reactions to forcing load and speed stress, acceptance of authority, responsibility and delegation.

The use of this technique enables them to evaluate performance resulting from the training of the participants in the skills cited above, as it provides them with immediate feedback on the level of the participants. Further uses are: to loosen up as a beginning of a course, initiating participation, and leading into subsequent material. Some experts use it as a change of activity rather than teaching.

"In-basket exercise" appears to be a highly flexible training tool, mainly as decision-making practice, when used in supervisory training, sales management courses, general management courses, office management courses. The opinion of instructors concerning the level of the trainees at which to apply the method successfully varies considerably: one expert says it is not for top managers, four others say it is only for top. Most of them use it for senior and middle managers, although some report it to be very effective for future and lower managers and for supervisors. A great variety of use appears also in the phasing of the courses: in-basket exercise is employed equally in the beginning (to loosen up or test participant's level) and in the middle (to evaluate performance); it is integrated with lectures, case studies, and business games, or at the end of the course also for appreciation.

It was rather difficult to determine which kind of exercises are used from the answers of the experts, but it appears mostly that the exercises have to fit in with local conditions. Therefore the experts use examples from the ILO manual, translated and adapted to local conditions, or ready-made, locally produced exercises, delivered from actual experience within local enterprises.

Interesting remarks concerning the use of the method were made by some experts: while some experts agreed not to use it as such, but in the way that documents were turned into a kind of background information, on the basis of which the participants had to produce individually a report on recommendations in a limited time; other experts saw a great advantage in having several trainees, individually or in small groups, exercising with the same set of materials. Their different reasonings and views on how to handle the same situation were put to good use by the instructor in exploring management practice from a variety of angles. At the same time they provided some interesting insights into attitudes and approaches of the participants.

One expert preferred as a method for top managers case studies on priorities in dealing with a number of matters simultaneously rather than in-basket exercises. For another trainer one exercise was not enough. The problem associated with decision making had to be introduced in advance, and at least two or three exercises had to be experienced before building on the experience of the groups in further examination of the subject.

Reaction of the Participants

The reaction of the participants ranked from highly positive to rather negative, covering a broad range of opinions. Among the many "pros," most experts said the reaction was enthusiastic, highly successful, and participative, creating a mood of personal involvement and generating a lively discussion. The method is being well accepted by experienced managers, due to high interest and spirit of competition, which makes them work harder and faster. One expert said that it created more spontaneity than the other participative methods he was using; another one recorded that a certain element of humor attached to the exercise invariably provided light relief from the intensive nature of the course, without detracting in any way from its instructional value. Among the few "cons," the technique was said to be regarded as less popular than, for instance, case studies, and was felt to be time-consuming by the participants. One expert said there was only superficial acceptance at first, the lessons of priority, relevance, immediacy of decisions becoming apparent only by pressing techniques.

Problems Encountered

The exercises have to be oriented to local conditions, practices, and customs if they are to be meaningful to the participants. A lot of the documents which would be applicable in other countries have to be modified to suit local practices, and great care has to be taken to select and write the in-basket documents in such a manner that they are correct for using as a basis for making the required assessment. The introductory story must be interesting, realistic, and also contain a touch of humor. All this requires a great amount of time, and thus the major problem reported by the respondents was the lack of time to translate and prepare locally suitable material, as well as to schedule the preliminary briefing, the exercise itself, and the evaluation session.

Other less significant problems reported were the lack of personal involvement until the novelty of the techniques was overcome, the maintenance of a balanced atmosphere in order to create the necessary reality in the participants' thinking and approach to the in-basket, the tendency to ignore the objectives of the method and the difficulty to express in English.

One particular point reported by one expert was that, after training, participants are not given jobs involving making decisions, the results of which they will be held responsible for. Follow-up visits have helped, as well as pre-course visits to superiors who must be "prepared" before their participants return, in order to discuss how new ideas can be applied to this work or the organizations and consolidate the training and plan future development.

6. *Programmed learning*

Programmed books are scarce, especially in the local language of many developing countries, and they are also very costly to produce. This explains why only 1 per cent of the teaching time, according to the survey, was devoted to programmed learning. The ILO has produced only two basic books in this form, namely, *How to Read a Balance Sheet* and *Creating a Market*.

Use of programmed books in projects varied according to subject;

for instance, 50 per cent of experts in general management and financial management used them, while 25 per cent in management sciences did, 20 per cent in marketing and sales, production management, and industrial engineering, and only 15 per cent in personnel management. This may be due to the availability of more and wider choice of programmed books in the first two subjects. Many experts asked for more programmed books aimed at developing countries, which should concentrate on specific subjects rather than general fields—and in local languages.

Use of Programmed Books

Programmed books proved most effective for use in the following manner by order of priority:
- —presession;
- —optional home reading;
- —postsession;
- —directly in classroom.

However, unless participants were highly motivated to learn on their own, many instructors found that when they assigned chapters from programmed books to be read prior to the session, or for homework, a number of participants did not carry out the exercise. The problem was sometimes related to the difficulty of using programmed texts by those who had not been exposed to the method before. It took some time to learn the method itself.

Experts found that they could get more effective use of this method if they combined it with short introductory lectures, guidance, and supervision—and later with discussions. Participants immediately showed eagerness and greater interest and the programmed books became a more lively task for reinforcing learning.

B. Methods Used Outside the Center

These are discussed under three headings: field visits, application projects, and consultancy assignments. It should be recalled that none of these methods is used exclusively and that many experts reported using all three methods, as in-plant training, in one form or another.

1. *Field visits*

On the basis of the replies received, field visits can be grouped into two types:

General field visits: organized with the intention of acquiring first-hand information and knowledge of the industry or branch of economic activity with which participants should be familiar. The need for this type of visit is rather limited since most participants have had some practical work experience which needs only to be broadened.

Illustration field visits: more closely related to the work done in classrooms, with which they are generally co-ordinated in order to supplement and complement the course. Visits are generally concentrated on a specific theme serving as illustration of practical application of knowledge and skills dealt with in the course. This type of visit is said to be a must in courses on production engineering, for it is the most valuable demonstration of techniques discussed in the course. It helps the expert to break down the attitude that "that is not possible in . . ." and is therefore of good training value, although some respondents regard its training value as limited.

In connection with his industrial relations course one expert invites the personnel manager of a company involved in a dispute to demonstrate how he prepared his brief to present to the Industrial Court. After that, when possible, the whole class is taken to the court to witness the presentation and procedure. This expert is supported in his efforts by the president and by members of the court. The problem in this kind of visit is that one cannot foresee whether there will be a case in the Industrial Court during the course, but on two occasions, sponsoring management and sponsored participants agreed to attend a session after the course was over.

Both types of visits are done either in whole classes (groups), in syndicates of four to five participants, or even individually. After field visits of that type some experts ask their trainees to write short individual or group reports, which are compared in a general discussion for evaluation purposes.

2. *Application projects*

It is difficult to give an overall picture of the use of the application projects as a teaching device since a great variety of duration, themes, importance, and ways to perform appeared in the respondents' answers.

For most of their users, application projects are the essential component of the training and are considered an integral part of the course, for which a large portion of available time, varying from 20 to more than 75 per cent, is allotted. Only some of the respondents consider it only as a follow-up technique after the course.

Hence, generally, the training is done in a sandwich approach, beginning with an instruction period, followed by application, and concluding with an evaluation and follow-up period. Where the training differs considerably is in the duration of these periods, in particular in the duration and size of the application projects. Projects from one day to up to three months have been reported, the most frequent length being three to six weeks, which signifies that the projects are usually rather small or medium-sized, to be workable during time allotted. More important projects were reported only in the management sciences, where the practical work is particularly essential.

According to most of the respondents, great emphasis is put on the choice of the subject of the project, which should be in line with the objectives of the course and have a bearing on the actual work of the trainees. In most cases it is proposed by the participants and submitted for the approval of the expert, although there were frequent reports of choice of the theme by the expert himself (before the beginning of the course), by the participants' superiors, or by the participant in a list established by the expert. Some experts assign the tasks to be carried out by the trainee in relation with his performance in the previous part of the course, and one expert assigns application projects (as follow-up devices) only to those who did *not* do well on the course, as the application projects should help to put studies into practice and implement what has been learned.

Generally, relatively simple individual assignments were preferred to more complex assignments carried out in syndicates of three to four members, but these were also reported (about one sixth of the cases). Most of the projects, chosen by the trainees themselves, are carried out at their usual working place in their own companies, where one important problem is to gain the support of the trainees' management to coach them and facilitate the implementation work.

During the project, the participants are generally helped in their work by frequent visits of the expert and the national staff, but most of the experts said these visits should not be too frequent (approximately weekly) so that the trainees will really carry out the assignment themselves and not rely too much on the teachers. One expert even reported that he never coaches during his visits to premises, but establishes training and evaluation sessions between his visits.

At the end of the time allotted to the trainees, in nearly all cases, they have to present a written (and also sometimes oral) report on their individual or group project to the entire group of participants regrouped in a plenary follow-up evaluation session of three days to one week during which the reports are discussed and criticized, and thus the entire class benefits. The evaluation of the work done is left to the class, to the experts and counterparts, to the trainees' management, or to visiting critics. Two experts said that the reports, accompanied by written evaluations and recommendations regarding further development, are forwarded to the sponsoring firm with the hope that they will be carried out . . . while some instructors use the reports as case studies material for future courses and one expert uses them as final evaluations for teaching.

3. *Consultancy assignments*

Consultancy assignments are the major medium of instruction in the development of national staff to be management consultants. They are required to be used to the maximum extent in this application because of the often highly theoretical background of the counterparts (university level), with a view to improving their abilities at the practical level and to learn the real meaning of management. Therefore, the major requirement placed on the assignments is that they be realistic, well programmed, so as to give the trainees a full sense of responsibility for results and a strong sense of satisfaction from achievements. To increase the realism, a fee, even if only nominal, should be charged and the trainees should be rated on performance, ability, application, report writing, and the savings calculated in the same manner as for professional consultants (cash or time benefit).

The sizes of the consultancy assignments vary considerably, as do the sizes of the enterprises where they are carried out. This is due to a great extent to the client relationship which takes place between the management development institutes or centers and the enterprises, on which depend the numbers of persons they will apply to the projects and how many national staff will participate. Requirements reported by respondents are that the projects should be full time, not too big, realistic, and well prepared. Assignments in individual enterprises, small, medium, large, and very large enterprises were reported, carried out individually or in groups up to ten, depending on the size of the project, although it is not possible to make a breakdown from the data obtained.

The assignment generally takes place in the following stages, during which experts are called for supervision:

—job definition in common (expert, national staff, client);

—diagnosis, investigation of actual situation by national staff with some help from expert;

—evaluation of situation, detailed analysis of problems;

—developing recommendations, discussions;

—implementation through national staff;

—eventual follow-up visits.

Very few data have been made available on the duration of such assignments, due partly to their variety, but projects of more than one year's duration have been reported.

The fields of application are also very variable and consultancy assignments are thus reported in all groups although their use is particularly extensive in production management, management sciences, marketing, while for some experts, many enterprises do not seem too open-minded about help in the financial field.

Reactions of the Participants to Field Visits, Application Projects, and Consultancy Assignments

The general reaction of the trainees to the methods described above was very favorable, although the "enthusiasm" or "most popular teaching method" comments were fewer than those in connection with some other methods. One expert said this is the case because participants are thrown on their own resources. Under the favorable comments are regrouped all the positive, interested, ready, invaluable, most beneficial, responsive, team-involving, challenging, etc., comments and their superlatives.

Among the responses were:

—"They welcome the visits, are quite frank with their problems and in most cases have taken specific steps to improve their company's marketing."

—"They consider practical work as very important and useful, and very often the completion of a project under the conditions of a developing country give them promotion."

Some experts, about a tenth of all, agreed that the reaction of their participants was good under certain conditions, or with certain exceptions:

—apprehensive, hesitant approach;
—always "sleeping partners" in the groups;
—slow progress;
—lack of concrete experience;
—not very keen on implementation of their proposals;
—mixing up functions: the coach should do their work;
—favorable if adequate service maintained.

Some more negative appreciations were given by a very few experts, who reported that the reactions were good *because* the experts helped the trainees at visits, or were good by those who were able, and therefore bad by the others.

Problems Encountered, Ways They Are Overcome

A great majority of respondents replied that there are problems with the visits, projects, and consulting teaching methods. These can be divided into three groups of different importance.

Most important problems are of an external nature, i.e., to find a suitable environment to carry out visits, application projects, and consultancy assignments. The other groups of problems are those related to the internal organization of the courses (practical questions) and those related to the participants' behavior.

The most important groups of problems, the choice of adequate enterprises and type of work related to the needs of the country and participants, and the requirements of the courses, result from two possible causes: the lack of valuable enterprises to that purpose in the environmental economy and first of all the *reluctance of the local managers* to support projects of that kind within their enterprises. This was reported in many various ways: "top management inertia," "owner/managers are very suspicious of fellows from outside," "strong feelings against the presentation of accounts," etc. Several experts claimed that managers of higher level did not allow their subordinate participants to apply what they had learned, for instance, by overloading them with current work. Thus it would be helpful if the participants were assigned to organizations other than their own for this purpose, but there the practical difficulties seemed to the experts extremely difficult to overcome. Other experts said that the managers fear government intervention if faults are found or are reluctant to introduce new accounting methods for fear these will lead to higher taxation.

This very important problem is difficult to overcome. Top managers of the old school must be persuaded to co-operate, to let their subordinates implement the knowledge they have gained during the courses. This can only be done in top management seminars showing the advantage of demonstration, delegation, and participation, through proper coaching and in personal meetings of the trainees with their managers.

For some experts, there was an important problem in the reintegration of the trainees with the personnel of the enterprise, in the case of traineeship which does not take place at the participant's usual working place. This requires a particular amount of preparation: the reasons, objectives, work, and responsibilities of the participant must be made quite clear and fully accepted by himself, his management, and his colleagues.

The problems internal to the institutes are less important and were only reported occasionally. They are:

a. the high time consumption and the requirement to concentrate on all trainees;

b. the need for suitable facilities to do the coaching, which takes place generally out of the office (car, hotel);

c. the inter-disciplinary nature of the work, which requires co-ordination of objectives of different experts;

d. the loss of good national staff after consultancy assignments done in enterprises.

Some important problems related to the behavior of the trainees arise with the use of these methods as teaching devices. They are due to inexperience, the shortage of knowledge, and a certain lack of drive on the part of participants which results in particular in reluctance to implement the findings, tendency to think only theoretically, time spent in discussions of what should be done without doing it, lack of thoroughness of the quality of the work, and projects left halfway. This requires constant attention from the instructor to persuade the participants of the teaching value of their kind of work.

Two problems due specifically to the lack of experience of the trainees are the acceptance of information uncritically and inadequate criticism made during visits. These can be avoided by good preparatory work.

Role of Experts and National Training Staff

If field visits, application projects, and consultancy assignments are to be effective teaching methods, experts and national staff should undertake preparatory and follow-through visits. These are undertaken at the work place of participants before, during, or after the course in order to meet the following objectives:

—initial visits to familiarize themselves with the enterprise;

—to recruit suitable participants;

—to learn about problems and develop cases;

—to coach and assist participants during practical projects and to follow them up;

—to appreciate the participants' work with superiors and employees;

—to give the expert evaluation of the training, particularly in:

(a) assessing to what extent innovation has taken place;

(b) learning to what extent the seminars have weaknesses;

(c) learning in which field further seminars should be directed;

—to widen the experience of national staff.

IV. CONCLUSION

The survey clearly indicated that in management development programmes ILO experts had to rely heavily on participative teaching methods. However, these methods could not be adopted; they had to be adapted in the light of the specific conditions of a particular country.

The study also showed that in developing countries a management training programme could not rely exclusively on one teaching method, e.g., case study, but on a methods mix most appropriate to the subject matter and the level of participants.

CHAPTER TWELVE—FOOTNOTES

1. The concepts and policy issues were the subject matter of two ILO papers: *Management Education and Management Development: An Institutional Partnership for Bridging the Management Gap* (Geneva, 1970), which was submitted to the UNESCO expert meeting on Management Education at University Level in Developing Countries, Paris, September 1970; and *Improving Training in Modern Management Techniques* (Geneva, 1970), which was prepared for the United Nations Inter-Regional Seminar on the Use of Modern Management Techniques in the Public Administration of Developing Countries, Washington, D.C., October 1970.

2. ILO: *The Effectiveness of ILO Management Development and Productivity Projects*, Management Development Series, No. 3 (Geneva, 1965).

3. Ibid., p. 94.

4. For a further discussion of the subject, reference may be made to ILO: *Social and Cultural Factors in Management Development*, Management Development Service, No. 5 (Geneva, 1966).

5. A list is available on request.

CHAPTER THIRTEEN
The Use of Modern Training Techniques in Administration for Development: Some Lessons of International Experience*

Training represents the most important component of international technical co-operation programmes in the field of public administration. Since its establishment in 1951, the United Nations Public Administration Division (PAD) has placed great emphasis on training for public service in developing countries. Training is important because public administration, which occupies a central role in national development, depends on the quality of the civil servants functioning in organizational settings. This quality factor is strongly influenced by the nature and effectiveness of their education and training.

Field experience to date suggests that success in any training programme depends upon its relevance to (a) the organizational goals and (b) the environment, particularly the stage of development reached by the country where the training is conducted. Field experience also indicates (c) the need to link training with career development and manpower planning and (d) the importance of adopting a systems approach to training.

Traditional training schemes consisted of a series of steps such as the following: (a) determination of training needs; (b) definition of training objectives; (c) design of a training programme to meet the objectives; (d) identification of the individuals to be trained; (e) con-

---

* This chapter was prepared by Chi-Yuen Wu. The views expressed herein are the author's and do not necessarily represent those of the United Nations.

ducting the training; and (f) evaluation of the degree to which the training has met its objectives. In the modern approach to training, these steps are conceptualized from a systems viewpoint. The determination of training needs is analyzed in the context of organizational goals, taking fully into account the environmental factors. The training objectives and the programming of a suitable course to meet them are both derived from organizational goals. Attention is paid not only to identifying the individuals to be trained but to coming to understand trainees through planned information retrieval before, during, and after course. Although environmental factors are of great importance in making selective decisions throughout the training process, they are of special significance in three problem areas: the selection of qualified trainers, the selection of current training materials, and the selection of training methods and techniques. According to the modern approach, training is seen as a continuing, dynamic, self-correcting process, being neither isolated nor static. Consequently, the extent to which the objectives are achieved is not measurable within a set period of time; such measurement requires a feedback of information based on the criteria of continuity and relevancy.

United Nations Projects Relating to Training Techniques[1]

The PAD has been concerned with improving public administration training and with modernizing training methods and techniques in three main ways. First of all, various training methods and techniques have been used and experimented with in the schools or institutes of public administration with which the United Nations has cooperative arrangements; these include about half of the eighty or so institutes or schools of public administration which have emerged in developing countries within the last two decades. In spite of the diversity of these institutions, certain trends have emerged from their common experience which are representative of the developing countries. Three of those trends pertinent to this material are (a) the growing interest in introducing training techniques that depart from traditional classroom instruction methods, (b) the recognition of a more diversified trainee population, and (c) the need for an expanded curriculum.

Second, attention has been focused on training methods and techniques in the various "training of trainers" projects. In the last two years the United Nations has markedly increased its efforts to "train trainers" for civil service training in developing countries. An accelerated programme of fellowships to train trainers outside the countries now forms an integral part of many of the UNDP Special Fund projects backstopped by the Public Administration Division. Many trainers in developing countries are former United Nations fellows. Some of the schools or institutes of public administration, especially those which are university-based, have undertaken programmes to train trainers for other schools and institutes. Expert assistance has recently been given to some institutions in formulating or strengthening their training-of-trainers programmes. Furthermore, a number of pilot projects have been undertaken: (a) The Training Officers' Course for the East African countries, also known as the Workshop on Modern Training Methods and Teaching Aids, was organized by the Economic Commission for Africa and the Institute of Public Administration at Lusaka, Zambia, in January/February 1970. Those attending this four-week course included twenty-four instructors selected from among officials in central and local government establishments and parastatal organizations. (b) In August 1970 the Economic Commission for Africa convened in Nairobi, Kenya, a Seminar on Training Methods and Programmes for Directors of Training Institutes and Civil Service Training Centres. (c) The Public Administration Division organized a Pilot Training Officers Development Course in the English-speaking Caribbean. This course was part of a major interregional project to improve the effectiveness of the training functions, through the training of trainers. Cosponsored by the Economic Commission for Latin America (ECLA) and the University of the West Indies, it took place on the campus of St. Augustine's University in August/September 1970.[2] (d) Further pilot projects will be organized in other subregions by the Public Administration Division and by the regional commissions. Training of trainers will form an important part of the work programmes of such regional public administration institutions as the African Centre for Research and Development (CAFRAD) and the proposed Asian Centre for Development Administration. (e) In the public administration programmes of the United Nations family of organizations proposed for the Second United Nations Development Decade, "improving training techniques and methods" has been included as a major item.

Third, in the interregional seminars and some other projects organized on a world-wide basis by PAD, as well as in some regional projects organized by the regional economic commissions, not only were questions relating to modern training techniques discussed but some techniques were experimented with in the design of the seminar or project. The resulting recommendations and experience regarding training techniques proved instructive and will be useful for the future. The Interregional Seminar on the Development of Senior Administrators in the Public Service of Developing Countries included a description and analysis of a number of new methods and techniques used in the training and the development of administrators specifically management games, in-basket technique, human relations laboratory training, role-playing techniques, coaching, and incident process.[3] Some modern training concepts in regard to the use of participation, feedback, and observation were also built into the design of that seminar and all subsequent seminars. Plenary sessions were supplemented by daily work group sessions. A feedback model was followed in the structure of work groups using small group participative methods and problem analysis. The composition of work groups was heterogeneous. The source of feedback was oral and written, and individual and group. For feedback purposes, participants served as rapporteurs on a daily rotation basis. Participant reactions were retrieved by a participant reaction sheet. Discussion questions in terms of specific issues were prepared in advance for work groups based on plenary session agenda items. In the Seminar on the Development of Senior Administrators, one of the work groups as a special project developed "Operational Guidelines for a National Programme for the Development of Senior Administrators." Techniques for systematic observation at that seminar included field visits and field consultation at two contrasting international management development institutes, one which was quantitatively oriented and one which was behaviorally oriented.

The Role of Training Techniques in Training[4]

It is not planned in this chapter to elaborate on the details of the use of various training techniques in the United Nations projects mentioned. An attempt will be made to draw certain broad conclusions from personal observations and analyses of the experience of these projects. In order to assist the readers to understand fully the PAD use of modern training techniques, it would be useful first to give a description of certain experience-based general considerations underlying the PAD approaches, taking fully into account the characteristics of modern training methods, particularly in regard to their potentialities and limitation in the international settings.

It is important to emphasize, at the outset, that training methods and techniques are only a means to an end. The means of training must not be mistaken for the end nor the form for the substance. Training is never an end in itself. Before any decision on the training method(s) or technique(s) to adopt for a specific training programme is made, training objectives (performance goals of the programme) require definition: for example, if the objective is to improve attitudes or to develop new attitudes, to instill a sense of urgency or a sense of mission in the development effort, or to bring about a change in orientation and motivation; then the training methods and techniques used must make full use of the findings of behavioral sciences in these areas, e.g., attitude formation and change. If the objective is to train the trainees to acquire certain technical skills or to perform certain technical jobs as in the case of technical or vocational training, then the training objectives should be determined through job-task analysis or other means to identify the steps required to acquire the skill or perform the particular job. The methods or techniques to be used should be those that help the trainees gain and retain the skill to perform all necessary steps effectively and efficiently.

Regardless of the training techniques used, they are effective only to the extent that they assist in meeting real or actual needs. Many training designs are launched without adequate identification of the real needs of the trainees at whom the programmes are aimed. Such needs should be identified through information for administrative personnel, which should come from the examination of organization performance records; analysis of actual administrative behavior; assessment of the problem-solving capability of public administrators, their social background and career patterns; and the conditioning influence of the environment in which administrators operate. Training programmes that fail to reflect the dilemmas and problems which public administrators really face in their actual work situations have proved worse than useless.

A training technique per se cannot be said to be good or excellent or considered superior to other techniques. A training technique that is good for achieving one objective may not be good for another. For example, a technique that is effective in imparting information may not be effective in improving interpersonal relationships. An effective technique for developing decision-making skills may be ineffective in accomplishing attitudinal changes. Training techniques need to be evaluated in relation to the training objective(s) as well as to the environmental factors.

As indicated above, one should adopt a holistic and system approach to training. Training techniques cannot be considered in isolation from other aspects of a training programme. In fact, training per se can become a wasted effort if not harmonized with all the other personnel activities that form the personnel system. The skills or attitudes acquired through training need to be put to use, and successful performance in training of a trainee should help his career development or advancement. Furthermore training in the public service needs to be linked to administrative improvement and reform programmes. Training is most effective when perceived as a component of an integrated administrative improvement programme; when integrated with changes in administrative systems; and when sensitized to the impact of systematic changes on the anticipated effect of training. Situations do exist, however, in which a training programme cannot be effective without at the same time contemplating certain changes in the system of national administration. Certain features of a national administrative system may reinforce, while others may nullify and extinguish, the effects of even the highest-quality training programmes. At times, effective training calls for promoting new values and attitudes incompatible with norms officially embodied in an administrative system, and quite disruptive of the status quo. To enhance the effectiveness of such training, certain reinforcing changes in the features of the system have to be readily forthcoming. In the selection of training methods, especially the training material to go with the methods chosen, these wider aspects need to be borne in mind.

Training Methods and the Trainees

Training methods and techniques have to be adapted to the trainees. The necessity for the adequate identification of the real needs of trainees has been mentioned. Different types of trainees require different training methods.

Since the trainees in civil service training are all adults, methods suitable for *adult learning* are mandatory. It is generally recognized that age per se is not a barrier to learning, although adult learning differs from childhood learning in many ways. An important difference is the relationship between the trainer (teacher) and the trainee(s). In childhood learning, the teacher is an adult and the trainee is a child. The authority of the teacher is well established by his maturity, by community sanction, and even by law. In adult learning, since both the trainer and the trainee are adults, the trainer-trainee relationships become supportive rather than authoritative in nature, not unlike that of host and guest. It is important that each respect the other's maturity and that both should participate in the learning process as partners. Responsibility for learning should be shared, with the trainer helping the trainee to learn and the trainee helping the trainer to teach. Two additional factors that distinguish adult learning from childhood learning should also be mentioned. One concerns what is called the "reality potential" or the need for learning to be perceived by the adult as meaningful in terms of past experience and/or future expectations. This factor is especially important for civil service training and failure to take it fully into account has often been the source of disappointment and frustration. The other factor concerns the time dimension. The use of time by an adult, especially a civil servant, is highly competitive. Because of this, the training programme must be perceived as meaningful by the learner and appeal to him as helpful in achieving objectives that are relevant to his needs. Because of the time factor, special emphasis needs to be placed on short-term and intensive training programmes.

A significant development in recent years in the United Nations public administration programme is the increasing emphasis on the *development of senior administrators*. Underlying this is the recognition that "training" the topmost-level administrators should receive the highest priority, and that management development within the public service in developing countries should proceed from the top downward, rather than vice versa. Ample experiential as well as research evidence supports the validity of this approach. Indeed, the reverse of this sequence has often led to undue frustrations, higher turnover, lack of sustained change, conflicts, and limited transfer of learnings from the training situation. Attempts at evaluation have frequently revealed that the effectiveness of a training programme often relates to the very sequence of training programmes. By and large, adequate "appreciation" training for senior administrators, as well as policy makers, has proved to be a precondition for effective training at middle and lower levels.

Training Methods and Programme Contents

From the standpoint of substantive content, there are broadly four kinds of training in public administration. One is to train the generalists in the traditional sense. This is normally done through the system of higher education and through continuous self-development during one's career. Another is to provide training facilities to teach, improve, and update necessary professional qualifications in scientific and other specialized fields. This is normally done through existing institutions of higher education and research. The third is to provide public employees with the necessary technical skills that they need for their jobs. Many vocational schools and government institutions provide this kind of training. The greatest emphasis in civil service training is on administration and management. This is necessary for the generalists as well as the scientific and technical personnel. The training approaches and techniques for each of these four types of training should be different. In this chapter, attention is devoted mainly to administrative and management training. The objective of this kind of training is to increase the capability of administrative and managerial personnel to produce results. Emphasis is placed on their ability to relate and apply their knowledge to problems of national development (especially economic and social development), to develop proper attitudes and high ethical standards for effective functioning as development administrators, and to foster the requisite human relations and conceptual skills needed for their administrative tasks.

Programme content, previously concentrated in knowledge or cognitive subject matter areas, is being expanded to include more sophisticated content such as that pertinent to behavioral and experiential development and modern decision theories and information systems. These new categories take a markedly different approach to training from the traditional approach. Here the active involvement of participants in a developmental process becomes the key focus of training. Training in this context is not perceived as a process of learning how things should be done through the traditional teacher-pupil or trainer-trainee relationship. Training becomes the means to stimulate and sustain a conscious effort by those in responsible positions to refine and renew their intellectual and interpersonal capacities. The training techniques required for this type of training should be adjusted accordingly.

A word of caution may be given here. Training objectives should be based on realistic assumptions. More than one case has been found in which a training expert, skilled in the use of modern management techniques and modern training methods, comes to a developing country with preconceived notions about the training of generalist administrators at the middle or senior levels. A training programme, reflecting up-to-date management and training knowledge and methods, is set up that is expected to achieve the following results: that the practicing administrator will emerge from the training programme with a new orientation, different attitudes, and changed motivation; that these changes will be assimilated sufficiently to produce significant alteration in administrative behavior; that the administrator will be able to adapt himself after training to the realities of his work situation; and that he will be able to persuade his superiors, colleagues, and subordinates to accept the change and to experiment with newer ways of responding, relating, and doing things, as well as making complementary organizational change. A training specialist with these notions is likely to face disappointment with the results. Such a series of assumptions will frequently be proven, at some points or others, to be overly optimistic, but also certain assumptions will remain questionable and require rigorous testing.

The Nature and Significance of Modern Training Techniques

The basic aim of any training technique is to enhance learning. The training techniques required for civil service training should be those that (a) facilitate, stimulate, and sustain the full participation of the trainees, (b) reflect the problems and situations that public administrators really face in their actual work situations, (c) meet the training objectives within a reasonable time limit, and (d) bring about a change in orientation, attitude, and motivation on the part of the trainees. Techniques characterized as being participative, relevant, objective-oriented, and sophisticated fall in the category of "modern" management techniques. They represent a shift from the instructional type of training to involvement or participative training. Instead of learning by being told what to do and how to do it, "participants" learn by actually doing, by generating behavior, and by receiving feedback. The training situation is designed to approximate the actual work situation (through the simulation of real life, the sampling of real life, or through other means), resulting in a greater possibility for a meaningful transfer of learning. Considerable emphasis is placed on the dynamics of individual behavior, interpersonal and intergroup relations.

These modern training techniques are designed to meet certain specific training objectives, such as imparting information on selected modern management techniques, developing decision-making skills, changing of attitude and motivation, or improving interpersonal relationships.

The existence of modern training techniques does not mean that the so-called conventional techniques, i.e., methods commonly used in current practice, should be discarded. Many of the conventional techniques should be continued and improved, and used in combination with the newer techniques. Some conventional techniques not only tend toward greater participation but also take into consideration time and reality factors. In a field which is susceptible to fads, untested innovations, and a considerable amount of fancy, the more glamorous newer techniques may tempt a hasty discarding of the conventional. Advocates of specific techniques may be so involved in the techniques they try to promote that they lose sight of other alternatives or combinations. Trainers tend to support the use of the techniques with which they are most familiar and feel most comfortable. Some trainers become so enamored of a new method that they cling to it for its own sake and, in a sense, become slaves to it as their pet technique.

Many new training techniques have not yet been subjected to experimental testing or evaluation research to such an extent that valid conclusions about their effectiveness can be drawn. As indicated in the paragraph above, a training technique that is effective for one purpose may not be so for another. Rather than clinging to the conventional or overselling the new, the real problem for programme planners is to discover for themselves the "right combination" of techniques for meeting well-defined training needs in a particular situation. The indiscriminate adoption of the new techniques is as unsound as their complete rejection.

The attitude of most of the training institutions in developing countries with which the PAD has co-operative relations lies between a position of undue resistance and blind advocacy of new techniques. They are generally open-minded, forward-looking, and willing to experiment with new approaches to training. The modern training techniques discussed later in this paper have been tried by one or another of such institutions. The general finding is that, although certain modern training techniques enlarge and enrich their training programmes, the lack of training material prepared specifically for their own respective environment or for developing countries handicaps their use. They also find that the new techniques do not make the conventional techniques obsolete but rather the subject of modifications to make them more participative and nearer to real life. Experiences to date with individual modern techniques tend to be mixed and far from conclusive. This is sometimes due to the lack of suitable training material for the individual countries or to the lack of well-qualified and experienced trainers. Indications are that, so far as application to developing countries is concerned, the controversy concerning the potentialities and limitations of the modern management techniques will continue for some time. Rather than adding to the current controversy, this chapter will attempt to mirror some experiential insights into some of these techniques as gained from PAD field experience.

Conventional and Modern Training Techniques[5]

Clarification appears desirable on what training techniques are considered as conventional and what as modern. For formal training in administration and management, conventional methods generally include information presentation techniques such as instructional talk (lecture), Socratic method (question and answer), discussion, conference, seminar and syndicate, and the case method.[6] The "modern" training techniques include participative training techniques, management games, role-playing, in-basket exercise, new variations of the case method such as incident processes, laboratory training or sensitivity training, organization development, as well as programmed instruction and use of modern teaching aids.

Management games, role-playing, in-basket exercise, and certain new case methods are all simulation exercises in which the trainee is expected to act as if he were in a real-life situation. They are more than sampling real life, as in the case of conventional case and discussion methods.

On the whole the PAD has had considerable successful experience in using participative techniques. In addition to the experience of the national institutes having co-operative relations with it, the PAD has utilized this new approach in its interregional seminars and in its assistance to public enterprises in certain developing countries in improving their performance. In the paragraphs below, the conclusions reached from the experimentation in some of the simulation techniques mentioned in the paragraph above are summarized.

Management Games

Like the war games long used in military training, management games hold certain potential for training senior administrators in strategic planning and decision making in competitive situations. Several kinds of games, differentiated by subject matter, complexity, participation, scoring, and method of computation, are already available to public administration institutes in some developing countries. Although they may not be as valuable as when an institute builds its own game to meet its own programme objective and fit its own environment, standard games when properly selected and judiciously used have proved valuable. While manual games cost less to design and construct, games that are programmed for an electronic computer, to which participants' decisions are relayed and from which printed reports are returned, often serve the additional purpose of enhancing the participants' familiarity with and appreciation of the computer possibilities in problem solving and decision making.

When used properly, and particularly when incorporated into a total programme, a game has a many-sided training value. The awareness of participants of the key factors to observe in actual decision situations is enhanced. Although management games do not and should not copy real-life situations in every detail, and are usually based on a condensed and simplified version of such situations, they have enough of the aspects of reality to provide insights into the complexities and the interrelationships involved in actual decision situations. A game provides a larger variety and number of decision-making opportunities than would obtain in an equal amount of time at work. The competitive and interactive aspects of the games enhance their training value.

In contrast to the experience in actual work situations, which tend to force emphasis on dealing with a series of crisis or near-crisis situations, a game demonstrates the need for establishing policies and strategies and drives home the importance of longer-range planning. As decisions are made, processed, and scored and then fed back to the training groups, the relationships between different ways of decision making and the outcomes of these decisions are vividly illustrated. Time is so compressed that many years of operations may be covered in one day, and the quick feedback received makes it possible for participants to ascertain readily the consequences of action or inaction. One group is able to compare its performance against the performance of others, and to evaluate the relative effectiveness of its style of decision making.

Furthermore, game playing demonstrates the use of analytic tools in problem solving in a given situation. Because of the number of interacting variables that can be built into the game, a greater appreciation of the value of such tools is readily assimilated. Last but not least, a management game generates both rational and emotional behavior. The effectiveness of a training group relates equally well to its problem-solving skills in tackling the structured tasks and to the way members of the group relate to each other and work effectively together as a task-oriented team. Observing team building in groups and group behavior provides valuable insights into the human side of the management process.

Valuable as they are, management games are not free from certain limitations. Good games take more time, money, and professional manpower to develop than most public administration institutes can muster. Even standard games require considerably more planning and adapting to the particular environment than is usually forthcoming. When a computer is involved, scheduling can create practical difficulties. The tensions, interpersonal and intergroup rivalries the games create may sometimes give rise to emotional difficulties. In some cultures, the attitude to competition may be so unfavorable that considerable stress results from the use of this technique. In some developing countries, however, considerable enthusiasm has been shown by the participants for this training technique. By and large, the experience to date, though spotty and scattered, points to a serious potential in this field, especially if the games used are relevant to the environment.

Role-playing

While games, particularly the computerized variety, are highly sophisticated and very costly to tailor-make to the needs of different groups of participants, some simulations may be less sophisticated, less costly to develop, and yet often no less useful, especially for developing countries. Among these less sophisticated simulated exercises are role-playing and in-basket. They have a much wider use in developing countries than management games.

In a role-playing exercise, each trainee or participant is assigned a specific role to play. Each participant should have a clear understanding of the nature of his role. Each is expected to play or act as if in an actual life situation. Role-playing thus enables the trainees (players) to experiment with how they would handle a given situation. Those trainees who do not play a role can analyze the behavior of the players. Both groups often are able to develop meaningful insights into their own behavior pattern and others'. As role-players act spontaneously, feelings and attitudes that would not otherwise emerge are often brought out.

There are a number of devices to increase the effectiveness of role-playing. These include "replay" (role-players going back to do the act again and try to improve the initial performance), role reversal (i.e., exchanging the roles of different players so that one can react to a different point of view), progressive and multiple role-playing, and the use of videotape to enable the players to have instant feedback to strengthen the impact on behavior.

Experience shows that role-playing is a useful technique for the teaching of complex physical procedures or for that of certain human relations questions such as interviewing a difficult staff member.

In-Basket Technique

The in-basket training technique, so named from the way in which it is conducted, is used to stimulate the handling of day-to-day administrative matters that reach the practicing administrator as a series of written communications (e.g., letters, memoranda, or documents from various sources). As he is asked to act upon these communications just as he would if they were actually on his desk in his incoming box, he generates certain aspects of administrative behavior that can be looked into for the purpose of learning. The in-basket technique is therefore designed to focus on individual decision making on the material available to see what action to take, to indicate the reason for taking it, and to examine the content and tone of the replies.

As a simulated exercise in decision making, the in-basket technique places the practicing administrator in a situation structured around the way he processes the inputs of information he receives. The purpose, design, and emphasis of the exercise are to explore what constitutes effective performance in responding to such a flow of inputs of imperfect information, as is usually the case. Each incoming item he has to handle involves a choice from an array of alternatives to which the administrator could commit himself. The patterns of responses generated usually reveal varying styles of managing which can be profitably identified, characterized, and contrasted in search for a reasoned assessment of their relative effectiveness. Such effectiveness can be evaluated in terms of certain criteria as appropriate, e.g., impact of response on the organization's operations, on its public image, risk taking, social responsibility, its politicosocial consequences, cost, time consumed, adequacy of information on which it is based, and its soundness in comparison with other alternatives.

Field experience suggests that such a technique has often proven particularly valuable in exposing what some researchers refer to as the bureaupathic response. Such a response is often noncommittal, evasive, procrastinating, pettifogging, and implying risk aversion. While minimizing the risk of making mistakes for which the administrator may be subsequently held accountable, it is usually less mindful of the broader social consequences and the cost to the organization in terms of its image and the effectiveness it projects. This technique has also proved useful in exposing the varying abilities of participants to generate meaningful and appreciable numbers of responses to a series of stimuli in a specified period of time; to arrive at a decision by discriminating between the relevant and irrelevant information; to exercise judgment as they are confronted with less than perfect information; and to appreciate the social consequences of their actions. In the replies received from our inquiries, several training institutions state that they have found the technique more useful in middle management and lower levels than at the senior level. Some have indicated that the high degree of personal involvement experienced by the participants tends to make the learning more enduring than otherwise would be the case.

Its value, however, as a training technique directly relates to the relevance of the simulated exercise to the realities of the administrator's job. If the simulation is a realistic sampling of an administrative role and environment, the result will offer a practical basis for a meaningful discussion of administrative behavior and effectiveness. Again, if the in-basket materials are carefully written to illustrate specific problems of day-to-day decisions, they may be more valuable in changing behaviors and attitudes than would comparable material included in a traditional case. Otherwise, the technique can only result in superficiality.

Other Variants of Simulated Exercises

Other variants of simulated exercises which are more difficult to categorize have been developed and tried by some public administration institutes in developing countries. Some variants involve the utilization of a sequence of cases and incidents to which trainees may react. Such exercises may be individually tailor-made to the needs of particular training groups or client organizations. Others are focused on generating particular aspects of administrative behavior of significance in a given situation. These may include leadership styles, testing the effectiveness of different organization structures, coping with crisis situations, and the like. In general, simulated exercises have proved to be a flexible enough training technique to make adaptation to the training needs of different groups and situations possible.

Laboratory (Sensitivity) Training

While the experience with participative techniques and simulation techniques appears to be, on the whole, positive, experimentation with laboratory training has led to questions and doubts, so far as application to the training of civil servants in developing countries is concerned.

Laboratory training or sensitivity training or T-group training is a process-oriented (instead of content-oriented) technique to re-educate the trainees through the working of face-to-face groups (often without any agenda). The initiative for discussion emerges from the group itself. The participants are given an opportunity to learn more about their own behavior (including also feelings, reactions, and perceptions) in its conscious and unconscious motivation and about the way their behavior is perceived by others, to observe and react to the behavior of other members of the group, and thus to improve their understanding of interpersonal relations. The object of the training is to increase the trainee's insight into himself, his sensitivity to others and their behavior, his awareness of the processes which help or hinder group function, his understanding of leadership, his skills in communication, and his acceptance of change or his effectiveness as a change agent. The goal is to make the trainee more effective in his organizational and job performance. In a number of developing countries, because of the growing concern for effecting change in administrative behavior through training, there exists definite interest in the potentialities of laboratory training. A start has already been made during the last five years in experimenting with this training innovation in some countries, e.g., India, U.A.R., and Ghana. Evaluation research on the effectiveness of this technique is still largely under way. But some experiential insights may be worth recording at this stage of the experiment.

Several of these initial experiments have been designed as "unstructured laboratories." As no agenda or task is being presented to participants, a vacuum is created in the training group which induces the participants to expose their behaviors. In dealing with the anxieties generated by an unstructured situation the participant inhibits something of his real self. As his behavior in the group elicits reactions from others, he receives feedback which starts a process of learning that may induce changed behavior. In the psychological climate of safety provided by a "strangers group" he is encouraged to experiment with new behavior which is hoped to be transferred to his work situation. The value of the learning generated through this unstructured group interaction depends, to a considerable extent, on the trainer's interventions. Well done, such a learning experience may sharpen self-awareness and sensitivity to others; may provide better insights into interpersonal relations and group dynamics; and may result in a growth experience and improved human relations skills.

The very "culture" that does make such learning experience meaningful and rewarding seems to reinforce certain values and norms which may not be altogether congruent with what may obtain in an oriental setting. It could shock blind faith in the wisdom of authority; encourage talking back to authority figures; foster openness and cast doubt on the conventional value of politeness as it runs counter to openness; discourage suppression of interpersonal conflicts and reward confronting behavior. To the extent that laboratory training inculcates such values and fosters such norms, and to the extent that these values and norms are incongruent with the prevailing organizational norms, laboratory training can be conceived as subversive of the status quo, or as responsible for radical change in the organizational culture. The question is to what extent would such values and norms be transferrable to public services where the organizational climate, as is frequently the case, may not be altogether congenial to them? It is not uncommon to find serious frustrations and tensions that laboratory trainees with changed values and norms experience as they get back to their organizations. Facing the hard choice of either becoming organizational misfits or reverting back to pretraining ways of relating to others, the chance may be considerable for a subsequent washout effect. At times, such training experience may induce voluntary separation and a higher turnover among the laboratory-trained personnel.

This, however, is not the only difficulty attendant upon laboratory training. While it could provide a healthy growth experience for a normal person, it can expose a maladjusted person to a traumatic experience. Since this kind of training, in the form of unstructured laboratories, is not meant to be therapeutic, it would be important to weed out those who really need therapy. In any case, such training laboratories have to be conducted under the supervision of highly skilled trainers with advanced training in behavioral sciences and with professional training required of laboratory trainers. In this connection it may be noted that limited evidence is reported in North America that T-group training laboratory methods induce behavioral changes in an organizational setting. Although the PAD has no data either to contradict or to support this finding, its experience confirms the difficulties encountered in trying to specify the nature of any changes, how changes relate to job effectiveness, and the relative proportion of changes detrimental rather than beneficial to performance.

On the whole, the experience of developing countries with laboratory training in the field of public administration has not been a fruitful one so far.[7] This is the case of training not only inside but outside the country. While it cannot be conclusively stated from this very limited experience that laboratory training is not suitable for developing countries, it can be said without hesitation that when used in developing countries it should be carefully planned and organized. New approaches and adaptations may have to be adopted, taking fully into account what was described in preceding paragraphs. The usefulness of unstructured laboratory training is further reduced because it does not lend itself to a predictive model concerning training outcome; the degree of its success cannot be predicted to any reasonable degree of certainty. One possibility is to inject structure into the training design and to maintain a balance between task-oriented issues and process-oriented issues. While the participants are grappling with meaningful tasks in their groups, they are generating problem-solving behaviors which they are taught to observe and analyze.

Individual-oriented or Group-oriented Techniques

The discussion so far has dealt with individual-oriented or group-oriented training techniques. The experience of the PAD in developing countries so far shows that participative techniques (often used in conjunction with conventional techniques) yield fruitful results, simulation techniques show positive results when the teaching materials used are relevant and suitable to the environment or prepared for the particular country, but laboratory training raises many questions and is of doubtful value (especially if unstructured) for the training of civil servants in developing countries.

There are also other individual- or group-oriented training techniques. The PAD has sponsored a number of *study tours* to foreign countries to learn their experience and with very positive results. Very little has been done in using *programmed learning,* which can be an important instrument especially for countries with inadequate training institutions and trainers. The major questions here are the writing of programmes for the specific country or group of countries and often also the high costs involved. The PAD did assist developing countries (in East Africa) in using *correspondence courses* to train local government personnel. This is a promising area, especially for local government and for countries sparsely populated.

For all training, it has been found fruitful to use as appropriate various *training aids.* Special attention has been given by some of the institutions with co-operative relations with PAD to audio-visual aids.

Organization Development (OD)

Time and again, experience has shown the need for organization-oriented training. In this connection, the PAD has paid increasing attention to the question of organization development (OD).[8] In the course of its development, the concept of OD has acquired a number of definitions and operational characteristics. Most of these, however, share an emphasis on situational training, mostly for managers, in relation to organizational objectives, problems, and dynamics. While some practitioners of OD concern themselves primarily with the human relations aspects of organization, others equate it with total management development. More recently, OD has come to be viewed as organizational improvement in its totality, or improvement of the effectiveness of the total organization. This implies attention to total configuration of all relevant parts of an organization. From PAD's limited experience in OD, it would seem that, while its use in developing countries is more effective when viewed as organizational development in its totality, the OD approach could lead to considerable difficulties if viewed only from the human relations angle without taking fully into account the legal and structural attributes of public organizations. Taking organizational performance as the major objective, it brings out not only the role of operating management and the need for management development but also the importance of simultaneous improvement in other elements of organization for improving its performance. This approach normally requires a combination of research, training, and consulting activities aimed at organizational improvement.

Workshops for Improving Organizational Performance

Organization-oriented training needs often get recognition in the context of a performance shortfall of certain government agencies in particular situations. For example, a family planning programme is not making sufficient impact, communications break down between the National Planning Commission and the Ministry of Finance, certain public services fail because of bad programming practices and inadequate preventive maintenance, a crisis develops in school administration due to shortages of paper and pencils that might well have been anticipated, or chronic administrative problems recur and linger over a long time. When such conditions occur, there is certainly an urgent need for improving organizational performance. The PAD has responded to government requests to remedy such organizational deficiencies and has, in a number of cases, established workshops for improving organizational performance as part of the action programme. Although an organization-in-crisis may not be in the best posture for assimilating new learning, the call for help that comes from such situations (frequent as they are in developing countries) presents professional trainers with challenging opportunities. The trainers' interventions are apt to be judged by their immediate impact on organizational performance. Whether or not such expectations can be deemed realistic, the trainers operate under exceptional pressures to deliver results.

A training methodology that proved effective in dealing with such situations has been evolved by the Public Administration Division in handling a number of advisory requests in the Far East, the Middle East, East Africa, and Latin America. Almost invariably the request originated from a problem of organizational performance. In Ceylon, for example, the problem was that the performance of the state corporations has been falling short of the expectations of planning authorities.[9] In Jordan, it was a problem of effecting administrative improvement to cope with the demands and pressures of a new situation.[10] In Venezuela, it was the need for accelerating the development of managerial capabilities of municipal councils to cope with expanding responsibilities in the field of municipal services, in line with an established policy of decentralization.[11]

Although a tailor-made design could only speak to the problem in each case, certain commonalities run through these training episodes geared, according to PAD's approach, to improve the performance of a particular organization. A diagnostic study of the target organizations has to be undertaken using several action-research techniques, as appropriate, including examination of performance records; structured interviews with policy makers and senior administrators; survey technique whenever needed to illuminate certain problems; and contrasting cases of high and low performance. The overall purpose of this preliminary diagnostic study is to make a "before" reading of the state of organizational health of the target organizations. In addition to defining the problem of performance to be tackled, such a study has proved valuable in generating a problem census to be used for agenda building; in furnishing clues as to training needs to be incorporated in any subsequent training design; in evaluating the information available on performance; in yielding some insights and hypotheses as to what accounts for effective performance or for the lack of it; and checking on the perceptions of key groups involved in the contemplated task of performance improvement.

The results of the diagnostic study are to be fed back to a conference of the topmost policy makers and senior administrators of supervisory authorities involved in the problem. The purposes of this feedback discussion in conference are to check further such results, to help develop some working consensus or near consensus over the definition of the problem and its diagnosis, to make sure that the perceptions of key individuals at that level are not far apart, to stimulate their thinking in the direction of problem solving, and to elicit their involvement in planning the training intervention. Such an involvement on the part of supervisory authorities marks the closure of the first phase in the plan of operations in this kind of PAD methodology.

The training intervention is, then, directed at the top administrators on the operating or executive level, and their senior subordinates who directly report to them. A workshop, or a series of workshops depending on the number, size, and heterogeneity of the target organizations, is instituted to pool together these participants for three to five working days to begin with. Although the participants are physically extracted from their work situations, they are directed to focus on their own organizations throughout the training experience. To the maximum extent possible, the training situation is meant to be an extension of their work situations. This meaning can be psychologically reinforced by making the opening of the workshop an encounter session with representatives of supervisory authorities in which the task ahead is clarified and the time is set for the workshop. Indeed, one main feature of the workshop design, as will be taken up further, is to bridge the gap between the "training situation" and the "work situation" and to ensure the immediate transfer of the newly acquired skills to the actual administrative practices in the target organizations.

The first portion of the workshop (three to six days as mentioned before) is designed to walk the participants through a multiphased simulated exercise. The phases of that exercise involve: defining performance problems; performance measurement, including the actual and the attainable levels of performance within a certain time horizon; performance analysis, i.e., identification of the forces impeding, and those that could impel the movement of the organization from where it is to where it could be; evolving a strategy for performance improvement by indicating which forces to manipulate and how; and translating that strategy into an action programme.

The exercise is presented to the participants as a working instrument tentatively built up by the trainers with a view to be a starter that is to be critiqued and redesigned. The essence of such a posture is to test the realism and relevance of the instrument; to elicit participants' involvement; to set an example of openness to criticism; and to provide an opportunity, through participative discussion of the tentative instrument, for assimilating the underlying concepts and techniques. Instead of posing as a lecturer, the trainer makes short interventions, at appropriate points in the flow of the discussion, to clarify a concept or explain a technique. As he senses certain gaps in the knowledge of the participants, such interventions are usually timely and well received.

In addition to substantive concepts and techniques, directly related to the task at hand—such as constructing composite indices of organization performance, identifying significant performance indicators, stochastic models of organization performance, understanding the interrelations between variables, force-field analysis, maximizing versus satisficing versus optimizing in a practical sense; action programming using new tools like CPM, PERT, and the like—some behavioral concepts pertaining to observing group processes, effective team building, and evaluating group performance are also introduced. In this respect, some simple instruments for recording observations and facilitating evaluation may prove handy. The idea is to drive home to the participants the point that, while the task involved in the main instrument is being tackled, sight should not be lost of group behavior as a major determinant of group effectiveness in problem solving.

With the closure of that orientation segment of the workshop, the participants move back to their work situation to work out their responses to the main instrument, described above, involving as many as possible of their direct assistants. They are to be reporting back, organization by organization, on the programmes, structured around the instrument, that they have developed for performance improvement in their respective organizations. An element of exposure and competitiveness is already built into the procedures to add to their motivation for investing themselves in the exercise. In fact, the reporting sessions are usually designed on the model of a fishbowl arrangement, with the members of the reporting organization placed in the middle, and with other representatives around to critique their programme and to feed back substantive as well as process observations.

An exercise in giving and receiving help could also be built into the design of these reporting sessions. The role-playing technique could come in handy at this point. The "helpers" are preferably drawn from representatives of supervisory authorities and other organizations whose roles encompass rendering help and support to operating managers. An adequate interaction between the operating and the supervisory levels of administration around the actual performance problems of particular organizations is a basic feature of the training procedures. In fact, the main instrument is designed to feed back to the supervisory authorities meaningful information, generated at the operating level, as to what systematic changes should be forthcoming to help improve the performance of particular organizations and to reinforce the effect of training. At times, it might be useful and particularly relevant to the problem at hand to design the final segment of the workshop on the model of a "confrontation meeting"[12] between operating managers and representatives of supervisory authorities.

Although this sequence of happenings in the workshop, namely, orientation-practice-reporting-receiving-feedback, has proved necessary to ensure the "internationalization" of the newly acquired skills, some post-workshop follow-up has also proved necessary to ensure the transfer of learning to the actual administrative practices of the target organizations. Several follow-up procedures have proved meaningful in different situations. Post-workshop counseling sessions to be held with the senior staff of some target organizations may seem to be adequate. Special arrangements may be worked out with some other target organizations to call in some consulting help for a protracted period of time. Special sessions could be held between the trainers and the representatives of supervisory authorities to relay certain relevant information and to stress the need for changes that may be beyond the realm of authority of operating managers. Similarly, sessions could be arranged between the trainers and the counterpart staff of local institutions that could extend further help, e.g., institutes of public administration, professional associations, and the like, to exchange experiences that may orient these institutions to the task envisioned by the workshop. Finally would come the independent reporting by the trainers-advisers to supervisory authorities on the meaning and implications of the workshop experience and on what could be done by these authorities to effect supportive change. Although these varieties of workshop have yet to be subjected to comprehensive evaluation research, some experiential insights and some partial evaluations do affirm their relative effectiveness in comparison with the regular individual- or group-oriented training programmes. Their strength derives from a combination of features that seem to counter the weaknesses of the regular variety of training programmes described above. For they focus on particular target organizations rather than participants drawn from a variety of sources. Nor are the participants being extracted from their work situations. Indeed, they bring their work problems to the training situation and they are made to move back and forth between their training and work situations.

Bridgebuilding between the two is the hallmark of the training design.

The training intervention is specifically and directly aimed at certain problems of organizational performance which are identified, in advance, through action-research techniques. While it is mainly addressed to the operating managers who are grappling with the real problems and whose actions relate directly to performance results, supervisory authorities, as a part of the problem, are not lost sight of.

To effect change in administrative behavior commensurate with some attainable level of organizational performance, through the balanced acquisition of problem-solving, substantive skills as well as the behavioral skills relevant to the task at hand, is the very object of the training exercise. The design is not made captive to a particular training technique, nor does it presuppose the superiority or the validity of any single technique. Rather, the presupposition is that to assault the problems of ineffective, and at times dismal, performance trainers need to draw upon an enlarged kit of armory. At the core of any blend of techniques that may be deemed appropriate to the problem at hand is an instrumented workshop built around a multiphased simulated exercise. The premise being that practicing administrators can best learn by being oriented to use new substantive and behavioral skills which they put into practice as an actual assignment in their work situations. By demonstrating their newly acquired skills and by exposing their new behavior in going about the task of improving organizational performance, they receive feedback which reinforces their learning.

The transfer of such learning to actual administrative practices is a serious concern of the trainer-adviser from the very start of his intervention. So is the problem of bringing about changes in the administrative system and the environment in which practicing administrators operate in order to reinforce the learning, counter the washout effect, and ensure that the impact of training will carry over into actual performance results. Such variables are not left out of his calculations; neither does he make any implicit assumptions as to the eventual outcomes of training in terms of organizational performance results; nor is he content with "happiness data" and the satisfactions of the participants as an index of the success of his intervention.

Such a training programme, getting to be known as a Performance Improvement Programme (PIP), has proven to be useful and innovative when used in a number of public enterprises in developing countries. In essence, PIP is an organization development (OD) intervention designed to improve the process of programming for performance improvement through better measurement. Its starting premise is that the performance of a public enterprise is more amenable to measurement than is usually realized. The problem is to initiate the process of improved measurement at the level of the enterprise itself by eliciting the involvement and participation of the practicing managers themselves.[18] The PIP is so designed as to include a practice phase, immediately following the training sessions, whereby the management team, back in their work situation, carry out the exercise, with appropriate coaching from the trainer-consultant. As better measurement practice takes hold, a more programmatic approach to performance improvement can be built into the management process, thus making possible a system of management by objectives and control by results. And that is the system most geared to sustained improvement in administrative performance and to continuing appraisal of administrative capability.

Concluding Remarks

In this emerging field, the United Nations Public Administration Division perceives of its role as that of enhancing the effectiveness of training for public administrators through backstopping the efforts of developing countries to assimilate, adapt, and utilize modern training techniques. By strengthening the national institutions having cooperative relations and assisting regional units in this field, the PAD hopes to be able to make a contribution in this area.

No training techniques can by themselves be successful without good trainers and/or good training material. It is not enough that trainers are qualified professionally or training material measure up to the standard of the academic world of the developed countries. Public administration is culture-bound. Effective training hinges on the availability of trainers who have a deep insight into the national environment as well as training materials which are indigent and relevant. This is the reason why the PAD has given increasing attention to its training-of-trainers project and has given increasing support to national institutions in developing their own training material.

The conclusions drawn from the limited experience of PAD and the institutions having relations with it on the use of modern training techniques, it should be emphasized, must be considered as of only a tentative nature. Much more experience and deeper appreciation studies and evaluation would be required to draw definite conclusions. All I can say very definitely is that this is an important field in which additional investment and experimentation would yield fruitful results.

CHAPTER THIRTEEN—FOOTNOTES

1. For a description of the United Nations projects relating to training and training techniques, see Public Administration Newsletter No. 29, January 1970, pp. 30–31. Reference should also be made to the following two United Nations (PAD) publications: *Handbook of Training in the Public Service* (ST/TAO/M/28) and *Report of the Interregional Seminar on the Development of Senior Administrators in the Public Service of Development Countries* (ST/TAO/M/45).

2. For an illustration of the kinds of material prepared for such projects see *Guidelines for the Training of Professional and Technical Personnel in the Administration and Management of Development Functions,* which will be published in the PAD ST/TAO/M series.

3. See Technical Paper V in part two of Vol. 1 of the *Report of the Interregional Seminar on the Development of Senior Administrators in the Public Service of Developing Countries.*

4. For a background of international experience in training, see Chi-Yuen Wu, "Training in Public Administration for Development: Some Lessons of International Co-operation," a paper presented to the Sixth Inter-University Conference on Special Training Programmes for Overseas Students, Leeds, U.K., April 8, 1970.

5. For a description of various training techniques, see United Nations Public Administration Division, *Handbook of Training in the Public Service* (ST/TAO/M/28), pp. 235–73; *Report of the Interregional Seminar on the Development of Senior Administrators in the Public Service of Developing Countries* (ST/TAO/M/45), Vol. 1, pp. 22–25, 113–34. There are other PAD documents dealing with training methods, including those for training-of-trainers projects.

6. We do not include here individualized training (such as tutoring, coaching, counseling), field trips.

7. There are a small number of cases in which laboratory training (of

short duration and/or structured) has been found to have useful results.

8. Reference should also be made to a number of technical papers dealing with the subject of organization development presented to the Interregional Seminar on the Use of Modern Management Techniques, organized by PAD in Washington, D.C., in October/November 1970.

9. For a detailed description, see United Nations Public Administration Division, *Report on Performance-Improvement in the State Corporations of Ceylon,* by A. Fouad Sherif, 6 May–16 June 1968.

10. See United Nations Public Administration Division, *Report on Public Administration in Jordan* (with special reference to the role of the newly established Institute of Public Administration), December 1968.

11. See United Nations Public Administration Division, *Report on the Management of Municipal Public Services in Venezuela* (with special reference to the role of FUNDACOMUN), by A. Fouad Sherif, December 1969.

12. For a description of this technique, see Richard Beckhard, "Confrontation Meetings," *Harvard Business Review,* 1964.

13. For further details on PIP workshops, see *Public Administration Newsletter* (issued by PAD), July 1968, pp. 5–6; March 1969, pp. 4–7; April 1971, pp. 7–8; and October 1971, pp. 23–24. Mr. A. Fouad Sherif was the PAD consultant responsible for developing PIP.

CHAPTER FOURTEEN
Methods and Techniques for Training
Senior Administrators*

INTRODUCTION

There is a growing awareness in the developing countries today that the remedy for several current administrative ills and maladies lies in improving the quality of higher administrative personnel or what may be called "senior management" in government. Improvement of senior management is essential to the success of the new role of the administration as a catalyst of economic and social change and to building into the administrative system increased capacity and competence to meet new challenges and demands.

Apart from proper selection, the effectiveness of senior administrative personnel lies in their being well groomed for their duties and responsibilities. There is a paucity among the middle-level administrators of persons fully qualified for higher positions. Retraining of the senior administrators in terms of the requirements of new problems and challenges is equally essential. Earlier training and experience are not always adequate to cope fully with new situations and circumstances. Retraining is also needed for modernizing old law-and-order-oriented attitudes and increasing responsiveness toward the citizens' legitimate demands and difficulties. Programmes of training

* This chapter was prepared by J. N. Khosla. It was originally contributed to the United Nations Interregional Seminar on the Development of Senior Administrators in the Public Service of Developing Countries. It is published with the permission of the United Nations, Public Administration Division. Its contents do not necessarily reflect the views of the United Nations.

for senior administrative assignments have, therefore, today, special significance.

The right choice of methods and techniques for training administrative personnel, particularly for the senior level, is vital to the effectiveness of such training. This choice is, by and large, determined by the objectives and contents of the proposed training and the character and number of trainees. It is essential, therefore, to determine, first, the specific training requirements and priorities in the context of organizational goals; secondly, to make an analysis of the types of skills and attitudes needed to achieve those goals; and, thirdly, to design suitable programmes and provide resources for the purpose. These aspects of training are covered elsewhere in the documentation in this volume.

This chapter deals with various methods of institutional training and practice, individual-oriented training methods and techniques, study and training abroad, and training aids. A conclusion is presented in the last section.

This chapter is based on the methods commonly used in the developing countries of East and South Asia.

A. METHODS OF INSTITUTIONAL TRAINING

Lecture Method and Guest Speakers

The lecture method is a classical teaching technique. It is simple, comprehensive, and the least expensive and time-consuming device. It may also be the least effective for executive development programmes. The participants have only a passive role to play. They are expected to imbibe through exercising rather than by doing something or cogitating their minds in a work situation. The method tends to increase information rather than understanding. It is, therefore, more suited to orientation or introduction lessons for large groups of participants. Except for learning of new techniques, e.g., operations research, systems management, etc., the lecture method is hardly suited to institutional training of administrators who already possess some firsthand, worthwhile experience of administration. For most of them, it is wearying to listen to somebody else for increase of knowledge in a certain area of administration. Study of the relevant administrative literature, provided an administrator can take time off to do it, has an edge over the lecture method for this purpose. But as already mentioned the lecture method cannot be dispensed with for learning of new techniques.

Public lectures by eminent scholars or practitioners of public administration, however, have been found more useful. Administrators are too preoccupied with their official work and other responsibilities in life to find time for a continuous study of periodicals, reports, and new original works. Public lectures are generally arranged on an ad hoc basis by the professional institutes or university centers of public administration or other similar bodies. This greatly limits their utility. Also all the public lectures may not be of high enough quality or of wide enough range to be of interest to the senior administrators or promising junior officials. The solution lies in arranging the public lectures as a series on selected relevant themes or subjects and at a time or on days which are likely to be convenient to the senior administrators.

An instructional device frequently used in institutional training programmes for higher administration is visiting or guest lectures. This method is used in almost all institutional training programmes. The main difficulty here is the varying quality of the content of the lecture, depending upon the interest, aptitude, and scholarship of the lecturer. There is also the problem of integrating these lectures into an overall scheme of training.

At the National Academy of Administration in India, a certain number of topics are covered each year by visiting lecturers. The speakers are drawn from various sources—from among senior civil servants, from top management of public-sector undertakings, and from academic institutions including universities. The Academy has found that a detailed briefing of the guest speaker is essential if the talk is to be pitched at the appropriate level for the trainees. The guest speaker has to have a clear idea of how much of the subject the trainees are familiar with and in what aspects of it they would particularly be interested. However, a detailed briefing is not possible in many cases. There is little opportunity to meet the visiting lecturer sufficiently in advance of the talk. Some briefing is done through written communications.

It has also been the experience at the National Academy that a visiting lecturer has considerably more impact if he can afford the time after the lecture to meet trainees in small groups for discussion. But as those lectures are delivered to a body of 200 to 300 probationers, the group is too large for a useful discussion to be held after the talk. On the other hand, the guest lecturers are unable, generally, to spare the additional time required for such discussions with the probationers divided into suitable groups.

The Institute of Management, Ahmedabad (India), invites outsiders to conduct courses of between twenty and thirty-five sessions. The participants may visit the Institute for a week at a time, or for longer periods, and reside at the Institute. It has been found that the visiting lecturers are most effective if they are given an opportunity to live in the culture in which they are going to teach and are provided adequate time and facilities for preparation. The Institute invites only those who have proved their worth through academic or practical output and who have been known to members of the faculty over a considerable period of time.

The Administrative Staff College of India invites top-level administrators and executives from government, private-sector companies, or public-sector undertakings to discuss their organizations' policies and practices. The college also invites trade union leaders of national standing, and occasionally university professors of special distinction.

Conferences, Seminars, and Group Discussions

The last decade has witnessed a growing use of conferences, seminars, and discussion groups as tools for promoting exchange of ideas and interaction between the administrators themselves and between the practitioners and scholars of public administration. These meetings may be organized to discuss specific administrative problems which call for concerted collective thinking for their solution, or they may form part of an executive development or training programme for the civil servants. The meetings may be convened by a university center, a government department, a national institute/training school, or an international agency.

Broadly speaking, participation in conferences and seminars is becoming a fashion in administrative life. The United Nations considers seminars and conferences the most useful tools of training for senior management. International seminars provide an opportunity to establish contacts with eminent scholars and practitioners and for exchange of ideas. There is a growing feeling, however, amounting to a general consensus, among the developing countries that seminars and round tables are not of much help in deepening knowledge and learning new techniques. While the conference method is useful for analyzing problems, programmes, procedures, and practices, it is inadequate for developing new attitudes, leadership or supervisory skills, or ability to adjust to rapid social and economic changes.

Past experience with national and local seminars and conferences in developing countries has been still more disheartening. Working papers are not always prepared and seldom circulated in time for promoting fruitful discussion. Seldom are the papers of high quality. The steering of discussions is generally poor. Regularity in attendance is also lacking. In any case, the individual tends to be lost in the group, and one or two of the participants may dominate the discussions. There is also the difficulty of finding conference leaders competent enough to lead and guide discussions in a meaningful way and at the same time encourage every participant to contribute his best. Many foreign experts visiting the developing countries still favor this method for training of senior administrators, possibly because this is the only way to begin the process of involvement of senior administrators in training programmes.

Participation in meetings of official committees has shown greater promise in preparing administrators for senior responsibilities. There is generally a tightly set agenda for these meetings and a compulsion to arrive at some agreement or conclusion, which implies a heightening of sensitivity on the part of each participant to the views and feelings of the other participants. This setup also helps sharpen the participant's ability to express himself, to interact with his senior colleagues, and to organize his thinking toward a logical conclusion.

Syndicate Method

There is a manifest trend toward use of the syndicate method in programmes of executive development for senior administrators. It is used in Japan in combination with the lecture method in the administrative training course run by the Institute of Public Administration under the administrative control of the National Personnel Authority. Syndicate studies consist of exercises in tasks relating to the contents of lectures given on administrative management, law, economics, and social policies. Each syndicate usually consists of fifteen or sixteen persons and has two to four watch-leaders. Each trainee acts as a watch-leader of the syndicate in at least one of the exercises. Individual trainees do a considerable amount of voluntary study related to the exercise. After the material has been collected and arranged, preliminary discussions are held by the syndicate under the chairmanship of the watch-leaders, who act as chairmen in rotation. In the discussions, the trainees other than the watch-leaders present their individual opinions in the form of reports. The final report is prepared by the watch-leaders and finalized by the syndicate. The reports of all the syndicates on a given subject are then presented to and discussed by all the participants in the course. The syndicate studies promote better comprehension of the substance of lectures through discussions and exercises. They also develop co-operative thinking and powers of expression, judgment, and decision.

The syndicate method is also used in the advanced course given at the Australian Administrative Staff College for preparing senior administrators. Syndicates undertake series of assignments and case studies, one member acting as chairman and another as secretary for a particular topic. The chairman, with the guidance of the staff member attached to his syndicate, plans the work, conducts the discussion, and paves the way for the syndicate to prepare a report on the results of its work on that topic. The chairman then presents the report to the college. This method calls for sustained effort from every member and gives him every opportunity to build up personal skills of leadership. In parts of the course, the composition of the syndicates is changed, sometimes to bring together those who have specialist knowledge and experience and sometimes to give members the stimulus of working with a different group of colleagues.

In the Philippines, a modified form of the syndicate method, namely, small-group executive panel discussion, supplemented by a seminar in plenary session, is used in the senior training programmes of the Executive Academy.

A variant of the syndicate method, known as research syndicates, is used in the advanced management courses organized by the National Institute of Pakistan. The emphasis in these syndicates is on acquainting the participants with research methodology and group collaboration techniques. The participants have to do a great deal of library study as well as field research.

The syndicate method has been used with great advantage by the Administrative Staff College in India. The college provides a three-month programme for the executives, both from business and government, in the age group of thirty-five to forty-five and having ten to fifteen years' experience in some special area of management or administration, who are moving from middle to top management. The total 1,408 participants, in the thirty-one courses held so far, were divided as follows: central and state governments, 308; public sector, 261; private sector, 831; and miscellaneous, 8. The bulk of the work in the college is conducted through syndicates. The membership of the syndicates is carefully selected so that each one of them represents a fair cross section of the executive life of the country, i.e., men from industry, civil service, public-sector undertakings, defense forces, banking, insurance, and so forth. A syndicate must also provide for a well-balanced mixture of functional specializations, such as production management, marketing, finance, and personnel. Each member of the syndicate, in turn, is appointed as the leader of the group (chairman) for the performance of one or more of the tasks so assigned. Each member also takes his turn at acting as secretary to his group for at least one subdivision of the course.

Each syndicate is given an assignment by means of a detailed brief; it indicates the nature and scope of the subject under study, its place and importance in the build-up of the whole course, and provides a list of prescribed readings and specially prepared background materials in the form of papers, exercises, and cases. A written report is required on most of the subjects. It is initially drafted by the secretary (who keeps notes of discussions on the subject) and is approved by the syndicate. It is a joint effort and represents the highest level of thinking in the syndicate and the maximum degree of agreement. The report is then circulated to other members of the college. The chairman of the subject formally presents his report to the principal in the conference room when the whole college is in session in a speech of about eight minutes. After the different chairmen have presented their reports, the subject is thrown open for discussion by all members. When no report is required on a subject, the syndicates are asked to frame issues for a general discussion at the open conference.

In the syndicate method, although lectures form an important part of the course, they are limited to topics of general interest or to the exposition of new concepts and techniques, and the specialist's guidance is more often made available to the group through "visits" to the syndicates. The college also uses cases dealing with problems of management which have arisen in actual life.

On the face of it, syndicate work looks as if it consists only of discussion, but there is much more to it than that. It is in fact a form of organization for the performance of a specific task—a task of management with the help of a team, much as in real life.

This method of work is based on the system followed at the Administrative Staff College at Henley-on-Thames. This system helps each participant to get a proper perspective of himself and his job in relation to the activities in areas other than the one in which he has specialized. In an environment far removed from his daily working situation, he begins to understand and appreciate the value of specialists in other areas and develops a sense of composite responsibility for the enterprise as a whole. As chairman he learns to take responsibility for, and secures the support of, the whole group. The syndicate method gives the participant concentrated practice in handling techniques and procedures which an executive has to use in his day-to-day work. The member improves his skill in communicating with and understanding his colleagues and in group thinking and decision making. He develops a better understanding of people around him and acquires greater ability to utilize other people's ideas and efforts.

The syndicate method has two additional advantages in the oriental settings. It helps explode blind faith in the wisdom of authority and promotes emotional integration among responsible persons drawn from the various parts of the country.

The syndicate method is also used in the short-term courses in executive development conducted by the Indian Institute of Public Administration, but it is supplementary to the discussion group method. The members of these syndicates come from the same area of specialization and the usefulness of the method lies mainly in promoting group thinking, sensitivity to different points of view, and problem solving.

The experience with the syndicate method of the National Academy of Administration of India, however, has not been at all encouraging. The syndicate method was introduced on an experimental basis at the National Academy soon after it was set up. The probationers were divided into groups of about fifteen to twenty. Each group took up a topic for intensive study under the guidance of a staff member. These topics covered various subareas of administration, economics, law, history, and so forth. The probationers met the staff member once a week over a period of about four months. During this time draft reports were prepared on the various subdivisions of each topic and were discussed. The final draft report was formally presented by the syndicate to the entire group of probationers, numbering approximately 300, in a conference.

After its use for about five years, the syndicate method was given up in 1965 by the National Academy of Administration because it had not been found to be particularly useful. Since the topic could be subdivided into only four or five sections, most of the work was done by the four or five probationers who were assigned the responsibility for drafting the report on these sections. The other probationers did very little work and participated only slightly in the group discussions. The discussion on the final report was perfunctory, as the entire body of probationers was too large for any fruitful deliberations. It was found that most of the criticism made was motivated by the desire to be witty rather than the desire to make any serious contribution. In 1964 a slight change was made. The report was formally presented to a smaller section of the batch of probationers, consisting of about only eighty of them. This system, however, was also found unsatisfactory. The number was still too large to enable a proper discussion of the report.

There was one other important drawback. None of the probationers had any practical experience in the subject of their syndicate. The reports, therefore, consisted mostly of a compilation of material from different books. Syndicates are effective as a training method only where the participants are able to contribute to the discussion something from their personal experience.

The syndicate method is also used in Rajasthan Officers' Training School, Jaipur.

Case Method

The use of the case method in training for middle and higher administrative responsibilities in East and South Asia is only a recent development. Its potential, however, is very great.

Public administration is essentially culture-bound. "Proverbs" and "principles" of public administration evolved in a particular setting do not have much appeal to those exposed to the hard realities of a completely different setting. Hence there is a need for indigenous teaching/training material. Even in countries where the "proverbs" and "principles" of public administration evolved, they sounded like platitudinous clichés when the opportunities to test them against specific administrative practices arose. Hence there is a need for indigenous *diagnostic* training material.

A noteworthy feature of the situation in developing countries is the almost virgin field of exploration into the realities of public administration arising from (a) superimposition of modern forms of government over primitive/traditional societies and (b) evolution of newer forms of government in response to the specifics of a particular situation in a particular country, e.g., the Panchayati Raj in India and basic democracy in Pakistan. How the processes of public administration emerge in this unparalleled interaction between the modern and the traditional; what the norms of administrative behavior in such situations are; how one knows the "right" answer when faced with a "real" problem situation are among the many questions which assail the minds of those responsible for bearing the burden of administration in these countries. And these do not come easily out of any textbooks—much less from textbooks written elsewhere. Indigenous case studies would provide "chunks of realities" which would help promote meaningful debate based on what is rather than on what should be; for who really knows what *should be?*

Let us consider the story of Panchayati Raj presented in a case study: *The Distribution of Subsidy to the Adviasis,* produced latterly by the Indian Institute of Public Administration (IIPA) Case Programme. The rationale of Panchayati Raj is to decentralize decision-making—mostly in the developmental field—and put it nearer the scene of action: to make it more responsive and adaptive to the specific needs of the local people, to develop local administrative/political leadership, to cause people's involvement in processes of change affecting them, and so forth. But what does the story of the "subsidy to the Adviasis" tell us? The Taluka Panchayat president, a domineering and politically powerful person, got the panchayat to adopt criteria for the grant of subsidies for agricultural development projects different from those prescribed by the state government; he said he was motivated by egalitarian considerations and "the socialistic pattern" advocated by the government; the Agricultural Extension Officer thought he was motivated by political considerations: the revised criteria would, therefore, exclude from the benefits of the subsidy scheme the president's local political rivals. The aggrieved parties appealed to the district panchayat president, who was a political force in his own right. He belonged to the party "ruling" in the state government, while the Taluka Panchayat president was a "dissident" who had won the election to the post of Taluka Panchayat president against the official candidate put up by the District Panchayat president, when he was the president of the district party organization. The Zilla Panchayat president instructed the District Development Officer to have the Taluka Panchayat resolution on the subject "quashed" as empowered by the Panchayat Act. The District Development Officer instead asked the Taluka Development Officer to desist from acting in accordance with the resolution of the Taluka Panchayat but to act in accordance with the existing government orders on the subject. Both these bureaucrats—the Taluka Development Officer and the District Development Officer—faced difficult choices. The Taluka Development Officer had orders of his elected "chief," but these were contrary to existing government orders; the District Development Officer had orders of his elected "chief" to countermand the orders of the Taluka Panchayat president; the buck passed between the two bureaucrats, each wishing the other to take a decision. The Taluka Development Officer was reluctant to carry out orders which were inconsistent with government directions; the District Development Officer was reluctant to quash the resolution of the Taluka District Panchayat and cause annoyance to the Taluka president, who was very influential at the state level; also there were standing instructions of government to all District Development Officers that they should avoid quashing resolutions of elected bodies as far as possible. Meanwhile, the work relating to grant of subsidies for agricultural production was held in abeyance, and developmental work suffered. Ultimately the matter was lodged at the state headquarters where directions for the quashing of the Taluka Panchayat resolution were given. The resolution was quashed. The Taluka Development Officer, for whose transfer the Taluka Panchayat president had been agitating, was transferred. But the quashing of his resolution did not interest the Taluka Panchayat president. Fresh national elections were in the offing. He had been won back into the ruling party and given a party ticket to contest an Assembly seat. His interest shifted from the Taluka level to the state level.

What were the "bureaucrats" to do in a situation of this type? Nobody can provide "capsule" answers. But it is hoped that diagnostic narratives of this type may help participants focus attention on the hard realities of administrative situations and possibly develop capabilities of how to handle such situations. Such narratives also offer the unique opportunity of role-playing as a means to acquiring as much flavor of real-life situations as is possible in the classroom.

Lastly, the technique of instruction by the case method, while it imposes a certain discipline on the instructor, also involves the adoption of certain roles by the participants. While the instructor sheds his "authority" role, the participants have to learn to think for themselves, to meet the challenge of views from fellow participants, to listen and modify their own approach, and above all to learn group co-operation. The technique forces participants to stop expecting an "answer"—much less the "right" answer—from the instruction. It forces them to ask questions instead and to learn to seek the "right questions." Initial attempts to respond to the new situation presented by the case method of teaching can be agonizing indeed. But they can, if successful, enable participants to shed the "authority-subject" relationship so characteristic of the traditional societies in developing countries and to develop the independent attitude of inquiry in which the asking of the right questions is often more important than the urge to find the right answer. Usually this difficulty of adaptation to the case method of instruction is cited as a handicap in its use in mixed groups of participants from developing and developed countries. But if skillfully employed in indigenous executive development programmes in developing countries where the participant groups would be more homogeneous, the case technique of training could help promote change in traditional attitude which may have advantages far greater than the immediate purpose at hand: participation in a training programme.

The recent intensification of the IIPA Case Study Programme lends support to the view that, given the will and a certain modicum of resources, it should not be difficult to attempt the production of a sufficiently large number of case studies to provide a basis for indigenous executive development training programmes. The main burden of producing diagnostic studies of this type will inevitably fall on bureaucrats in such countries. And this, by itself, will do much to involve bureaucracy in a meaningful study of public administration processes in their own countries and promote a mutually rewarding relationship between the academic scholars and the practitioners of public administration.

The Administrative Staff College of India follows the case method along with other teaching methods. In its three-month course for senior executives, generally about fifteen cases are used; in addition, a comprehensive live case on a business problem is used. The number of cases in short courses varies from programme to programme, the average being about five cases per course.

The college has undertaken, since 1961, a special programme for preparation and development of case studies. The college convenes, from time to time, "case workshops" consisting of ten to fifteen teachers and executives who bring with them case materials and, after detailed discussions, write cases. The college has so far produced about 150 cases, most of which are published under the titles: (a) *ASCI Case Collection—First Series,* and (b) *Problems in Management, ASCI Case Collection—Second Series.*

These cases describe real situations and problems faced by managers in the private and the public sectors.

The college has also established a central library of cases written in India and has undertaken to publish a national bibliography of cases in business administration. The first volume of this bibliography has already been published, and the second one is on the press.

The Indian Institute of Management in Ahmedabad uses cases for 80 per cent of its courses. The faculty members are expected to collect cases for their own courses. The way in which cases are used in the classroom is left to the individual faculty member. Each will have his own style. The main emphasis, however, is on the active participation of the students in the application of conceptualized knowledge to the actual situation of the case. The important aspects stressed are: problem determination and formulation, relevance and validity of information, analysis, and working out alternatives. Every faculty member is given an annual budget for case collection. The case collection effort has been very successful, and there are over 700 cases registered and in progress.

The National Academy of Administration does not use case studies, as the participants are fresh graduates from universities and do not possess knowledge and practical experience adequate to be able to perceive and analyze the various problems posed in a case. A few practical problems have, however, been used in discussion groups and these have been found to be useful. The academy has found that, in courses for fresh entrants, case studies can introduce, enliven, or wrap up a subject lecture but cannot be substituted for it.

The Indian Institute of Public Administration has made a beginning with the use of case studies in its executive development courses. The Institute launched in 1964 a programme of preparation of cases in Indian administration, which has recently been reactivated. About sixty case studies have been produced. The revised case programme focuses mainly on planning and programming of development proj-

ects, administrative reforms, the leadership role of senior administrators, and the interaction among political, administrative, and
technological factors in development.

The Administrative Staff College in Pakistan has also made progress in the preparation of cases and their use in the training of senior
civil servants.

In the administrative training courses in Japan, the trainees are
divided into groups of fifteen or sixteen each, and each group studies
three to four cases. During discussions the chair is taken by a trainee
who is briefed in advance by a member of the staff of the Institute.

The Executive Academy of the Institute of Public Administration
in the Philippines and the National Institute of Development Administration in Thailand also use case studies in their training programmes for higher administration.

Sensitivity Training

T-group or sensitivity training is new to the countries of East and
South Asia. A start has been made in India during the last three or
four years in T-group courses, for example, at the Small Industries
Extension Training Institute (SIET) at Hyderabad (on a regular
basis) and at the Institute of Management at Ahmedabad and Cal-
cutta. These courses run from one to two weeks. At the SIET Institute, T-group training is supplemented by skill and concept sessions.
The skill sessions aim at development of the participant's skills to
perceive the reactions of his colleagues, to speak and listen more
effectively, to observe group behavior and temporary informal systems, and to diagnose organizational problems in microcosm. The
concept sessions are complementary to the experimental learning
and deal mostly with perception, sensitivity, leadership styles, management processes, dynamics of change, problem-solving behavior,
needs and motivation, and the like.

In T-group sessions, a skilled social scientist with special training
works with a group of fifteen to twenty-five persons. The participants
in a T-group learn, often for the first time, the causes of their ineffectiveness in groups and in leading others. They learn how to communicate more effectively with others, what needs to be done, and
how to interpret the attitudes of individuals and groups toward the
work situation. They experiment with different ways of solving problems to find out which are the most effective. For example, a group

may experiment with permissive leadership, autocratic leadership, and democratic leadership and consider carefully the advantages and disadvantages of each of them. The social scientist, who is the leader, introduces in the programme, from time to time, information about principles and techniques of social science research which will help the participants understand individual, group, and organizational behavior. The participants often discuss how the principles can be applied to their personal lives as well as to their official relationships. It has been found that a group led by an Indian social scientist and made up of nationals only learns more than a mixed group of nationals and foreigners. (Participants from Libya, Mauritius, Afghanistan, and some other countries have attended some courses given at SIET.) In short, the leaders of the laboratory and the persons attending it work together better when they have a common culture and a common language. Although some good progress has been made in T-group training in India, there is still a great lack of knowledge about the techniques. Indian experience confirms that laboratory training should be given only by a person who is fully trained in it.

The techniques of sensitivity training were used in the training of federal employees during 1960–65. This method of training, when handled by skilled practitioners, can assist maladjusted administrators in arriving at a more accurate perception of their personality shortcomings. However, according to one school of thought, in many instances a maladjusted administrator could still be doing an effective job if his own acceptance of his personality permitted him to function adequately. He was at peace with this perception and his maladjustments in no way disturbed his management effectiveness. It was feared that short-term sensitivity training courses might disrupt this personality equilibrium and make him a less effective official. The risk of disrupting an individual's present, responsible, acceptable behavior patterns may be too high to permit the use of this technique on a wholesale basis. Sensitivity training, it was pointed out, could, therefore, only be really effective and useful in specific, well-selected cases. The experience at the SIET, Hyderabad (India), does not confirm these apprehensions found in the U.S.A. It has been found that, depending upon the nature of the group and their willingness to cooperate, the emphasis can be shifted from intrapersonal aspects to interpersonal aspects and vice versa, in other words, from the very personal aspect to the aspects of group life and organizational behavior.

B. INDIVIDUAL-ORIENTED TRAINING METHODS AND TECHNIQUES

Field Visits, Practical and Project Work

Field visits, practical work, and work on selected projects are useful tools of training for senior administrative positions. Though they are often used as a part of institutional training, each of these tools can be profitably adapted to meet the needs of individual training. At the French National School of Administration practical work covers the whole of the first year and two months toward the end of the second year of the training of civil servants. The new recruits to the Indian Administrative Service are trained on the job in the states for a period varying between twelve and eighteen months after they have completed their institutional training at the National Academy of Administration. During the latter training they go on a six-week tour, "Discovery of India," which includes attachment to villages (three weeks) and to a public enterprise (one week). There is a growing awareness that the utility of the institutional training at the academy will increase considerably if the probationers, after a short time at the academy, spend nine months or a year on practical work and then return to the academy.

At the Administrative Staff College in Pakistan the trainees are required to take up a field project covering a firsthand study of a rural problem. The intention is to broaden their knowledge and insight about the rural problems, the rural people, and the officials' dealings with the citizens. Involvement in projects and field work form a part of many of the programmes given in other countries of East and South Asia (such as Japan and the Philippines) for preparation for higher administrative positions, but more so for the junior levels.

Programmes of Self-development

Planned programmes of self-study have a great potentiality for widening the knowledge and outlook of senior administrators. These programmes can be pursued on study leave or on special fellowships awarded by professional institutions, universities, or educational foundations. Attachment to an institution has the advantages of access to a library, interaction with scholars, and facilities for desk study as well as for field work.

A fruitful individual-oriented method of preparing middle-level administrators for senior responsibilities would be to evolve a well-organized programme of career development on the job. Plans of career development may take into account not only aptitudes and interests of the individual administrator but also the need for giving him some well-rounded experience in a broad area of administrative activity. The individual administrator can do much by himself in terms of self-development by being mentally alert to all that happens to him in his job and to his department, by questioning all proposals which come to him, and by trying to make some original contribution. In fact, any organized programme of training for senior management must, in the first instance, try to arouse and whet the individual's desire for self-development.

C. STUDY AND TRAINING ABROAD

Advantage has been taken during the last two decades of the various international or bilateral programmes for foreign technical assistance for study and training abroad by a large number of senior civil servants of the countries of East and South Asia. Similar opportunities offered by the fellowship programmes of certain foundations, like the Ford, Rockefeller, Nuffield, and Asia, have also been utilized.

The Harvard Graduate School of Public Administration also provides facilities for advanced research and training for a small number of matured and talented students from abroad, including administrators.

Foreign study and training usually take one of the following forms: (a) attachment to a foreign university to attend regular courses or special programmes, (b) tours of study and observation in a specified field, and (c) research on a specified problem.

In terms of the experience of the countries of East and South Asia, advanced study at a foreign university with a specific study assignment has been more helpful than seminars and conferences in broadening the outlook, in increasing the knowledge of one or more areas of administration, and in deepening the perception of the interrelationship between the administration and its external environment. Advanced study has also been useful in sharpening and enhancing the conceptual abilities. However, its usefulness in the matter of development of specialized skills or problem-solving capabilities has been very limited. Nor is the content of the courses given abroad, in large measure, relevant to the conditions prevailing at home.

Tours of study and observation abroad have been found to be less useful than advanced study at a foreign university. The trainee is seldom able to spend sufficient time in one place, such as an individual government agency, to observe or learn a significant amount. He makes some good contacts but gains only a superficial familiarity with the advanced technique used abroad in various agencies. Several of these deficiencies arise from the lack of proper and detailed planning of the study programme. There is no detailed guidance or information available about the agencies and the persons who would be able to contribute most in terms of the trainee's needs. The effectiveness of foreign training programmes is further circumscribed by the deficient methods of selection of the trainees and the lack of any policy as to their proper placement in their fields of study on their return to the home country. In several cases the selection is not made on the basis of merit. In most of the cases the trainee is, on return to his country, given a job in a field different from the one in which he has specialized. To some extent this is not material, as the purpose of foreign training is to advance the intellectual and social horizons of the trainees. But in the context of the development needs of the countries of East and South Asia, training of senior administrators without some broad specialization has obvious drawbacks.

D. TRAINING AIDS

It is necessary to adapt the training aids for preparation at the senior levels of administration to the training needs of the administrators. For the most part, the main training aids required are: (a) guides to selected readings on concepts and theories of organizational and administrative behavior, tool subjects, and economic aspects of administration; (b) case studies and research reports, particularly on national and local administrative problems, and (c) facilities for quiet study, for interaction with scholars and experienced senior administrators, and for firsthand study and observation of administrative procedures. Audio-visual aids, charts, automatic data processing equipment, and the like are needed in a limited measure, according to the requirements of the course.

It is necessary to emphasize here that any training programme for higher administration in the countries of East and South Asia cannot be really effective unless a large number of appropriate case studies relating to local conditions are available. The paucity of indigenous cases is at present a great handicap in deriving full advantage of discussions in syndicates, round tables, seminars, and conferences. The use of cases helps lend realism and concreteness to such discussions. The topmost priority in the matter of training aids should, therefore, be given to preparation of clusters of cases on various aspects of administration.

E. CONCLUSION

The preceding analysis of the techniques and methods used for preparing administrators for senior responsibilities shows that the syndicate and case methods have an advantage over other methods. Conferences and seminars are useful only to the extent that they are well planned and properly steered. Attachment to a foreign university with a specific work assignment has been very useful in many cases, but it has not been so with foreign tours of study and observation or attendance of courses at a foreign university. However, these are tentative findings, as detailed information about the contents of courses and tools of instruction given in various countries of the region is not available.

Some of the conclusions which emerge from the present survey briefly are:

(a) The usefulness of the training methods and techniques cannot be assessed in isolation from the effectiveness of the training course as a whole. Sophisticated techniques for evaluating the usefulness of a training programme have still to be developed.

(b) The utility of a particular training method or technique will depend upon the objectives and contents of training to be imparted, and upon the national and local conditions of a country or region.

(c) Preparation of suitable case studies, in large numbers and on different aspects of administration, needs to be given a high priority if training for higher administration is to be really effective.

CHAPTER FIFTEEN
Management Training in Developing Countries*

INTRODUCTION

Most of the developing nations are now embarked on a program of rapid economic development with the help of developed nations—especially the United States of America. The process of industrial development requires both technical knowledge and the administrative and managerial capacity to utilize such knowledge effectively. Whereas technology (and capital) can be imported easily from highly developed nations, administrative skills cannot be directly transplanted from one culture to another. This is because management techniques and philosophies are affected by societal norms, cultural values, and socio-emotional issues which enter into the transfer process. At the United Nations Conference on the Application of Science and Technology for the Benefit of Less Developed Areas (1963), it was suggested by a number of speakers that the cultural milieu in which management has to operate exerted a strong influence, both on managerial practices and on its supply of competent managers. Management techniques must, therefore, be adapted to the milieu in which they have to operate. It is necessary to develop the indigenous administrative talent or high-level manpower.

It is in the area of the development of adequate high-level manpower that most of the developing nations are lagging behind.

For example Professor Abramson reports about Pakistan: "Pakistan does want to move ahead rapidly but yet many observers agree that the human relations problems of administration constitute some

* This chapter was prepared by R. Nath and R. K. Ready.

of the main road blocks impeding accelerated social and economic development" (Abramson, 1967, p. 24).

Thus there is a great unfulfilled need to develop appropriate and adequate indigenous administrative and managerial manpower in developing countries. And, since World War II, there have been some serious attempts to fulfill this need. These attempts can be broadly classified in two broad categories: inventing new training techniques in the developing countries and adopting new training techniques from the developed countries. In this chapter we will first describe and analyze the experience in each of these two areas. We will then discuss some important issues in adapting and institutionalizing these new training techniques.

INVENTING NEW TRAINING TECHNIQUES IN DEVELOPING COUNTRIES

To date, the developing countries have not been much of a source for inventing new training techniques. The first difficulty is that they apparently do not have enough economic and political development to generate educational innovations of much importance. When a new training technique does appear indigenously in a developing country, there are rarely the supportive energies to nurture and advance it; so often training inventions fail before much trial, or are in some cases snuffed out by hostile political or economic forces.

We briefly review three training inventions, one that occurred in Brazil, one in Ecuador, and one in Ceylon and India, that at least survived and influenced other training events enough to be reported, although the forces of opposition were considerable in each instance. We select the particular three because we have been able to learn more about them than some others, and because they illustrate important difficulties in getting new training techniques invented in developing countries. The general picture we have, however, is that information about training inventions in developing countries is very scarce and not organized. We hope that this chapter will stimulate wider documentation in the future.

Readers should be forewarned that the three training inventions we review were all aimed for people in or representing the non-elite mass of the population, not directly for the managers. We shall hold until the end of this chapter speculations about the significance of this for training, development, and management training generally.

The Paulo Freire Method

The Paulo Freire method has perhaps the most profound implications for training and development of any of the training techniques
we shall review in this chapter. Ostensibly the method is an innovative way of literacy training; but that is like saying that an iceberg is the
part out of water. The key concept of the method is *conscientizacao*
in the Portuguese of Freire's original use (or *conscientización* in
Spanish-speaking countries, where it is common usage). *Conscientizacao* adds the philosophical position that literacy training (or *al-
fabetizacao*) is not "acquiring a mere technical skill" but is "a process
implying values, forming mentalities, and leading to social and political consequences."

> The Paulo Freire method makes of literacy training a critical,
> active process through which habits of resignation are overcome.
> The critical capacity of the pupils grows out of dialogue about
> meaningful situations in their life, on which they have insights
> to contribute. Both teacher and pupils join sympathetically in
> a common purpose, seeking truth about relevant problems while
> respecting each other's opinion. The teacher serves as the co-
> ordinator of a discussion, while the pupils become participants in
> a group trying to understand existence in a changing society.
> . . . Properly understood and applied, *conscientización* has no
> predictable directions. Although it does not prescribe politiciza-
> tion, its content of dignity, criticism, and transformation almost
> inevitably leads to a quest for channels of effective action.[1]

Our focus in this chapter is on how the invention occurred and
what happened to it. Paulo Freire was professor of the history and
philosophy of education at the University of Recife until 1964. There
he put together the method in reflecting on and absorbing ideas from
three principal sources:

—the language, culture, and problems of illiterates themselves;
—philosophies of knowledge, human nature, culture, and history;
—analyses of underdevelopment in Latin America after World
War II.

In 1963 the Brazilian Ministry of Education committed itself to a
literacy campaign using Freire's new method, and a massive goal was
set to train and "conscientisize" two million people in a three months'
course in 1964. But the method also frightened many people, who
worried that too many of the masses would be stirred up in the train-

ing. In the military coup of 1964, Freire was jailed for seventy days and then was allowed to move to Chile. He is now studying and teaching at Harvard University.

Some general observations: The Paulo Freire method was the invention of one brilliant man working in isolation for many years in Northeast Brazil. The method was a true and remarkable invention, and it is being and will continue to be studied and applied in many training-for-development situations around the world. Its widest use is in Chile. But the method did not survive in the developing country of its origin.

> Since 1964, literacy training has continued in Brazil on a modest scale, but notably without conscientizacao. . . . Certainly, if the Paulo Freire method has political implications, the same can be said about the present system of literacy training: it is carefully planned to check expectations and to restrict the formation of a critical perspective.[2]

Base Level Training in Ecuador

A training innovation of considerable interest sprouted in Ecuador in 1967–68. Several people were involved, but two of the earliest "workers" who went out and actually tried the training were Raul Arturo and Edgar Jacome, Roman Catholic priests with strong sensitivities for people at the "base level" of Ecuadorian society. They were supported by a few Peace Corps volunteers and a growing number of "local hire" Ecuadorians in the USAID Mission in Quito, with encouragement from several Americans in the mission.

The method at the beginning in Ecuador was to have meetings with small groups of people at the base level of the society—people not connected with the institutions of modernization, such as schools, factories, or co-operatives—and also meetings with other people trying to make contacts at the base level—priests, nuns, extension workers, teachers. These meetings were led non-directively, except that the focus tended to be primarily on feelings, motivations, and what the individuals and groups might do to better themselves even a little. In mid-1969 the approach was described in a USAID document as follows:

> (a) to inject . . . educational methods which will tend to assure fuller participation . . . and more democratic attitudes . . .

(b) to work directly with communities with group methods . . . encouraging communal efforts at self-help . . .

(c) to sensitize . . . to discard traditional paternalism and to adopt methods which will increase the capacity of the underprivileged to participate in decision-making and problem solving. . . .[3]

These words sound more sophisticated than anything written in 1967–68 about the experiment in training, and by 1969 the training group and supporters had an acronym for their technique: GEM, for Group Experience in Motivation. They also "discovered" in 1969 that GEM had several similarities with "group dynamics, T-groups, or sensitivity training." What had happened was that early in 1969 some members of the Ecuadorian and USAID groups decided that what they were doing was interesting, exciting, and puzzling enough to see what people outside the country would think of what they were doing. They made some contacts, rather randomly, and they definitely got response. (R. K. Ready was contacted and responded with strong and continuing interest.) Since early 1969 it has been harder than before to point to the inventiveness of their training technique. The Ecuadorians have rapidly expanded their contacts with kindred trainers in other countries, especially the U.S.A. and Puerto Rico, and they think strongly of themselves in the traditions of group dynamics, sensitivity training, and organization development. They have moved rapidly to institutionalize their efforts.

They have expanded their number and continued to seek and get further training for themselves.

Some general observations: There seems to be little doubt that GEM was a true training invention. Whether GEM was a reinvention of sensitivity training is harder to conclude. There was some "contamination" from Americans in the Peace Corps and USAID Mission, although none of these people were professionals in training. After mid-1969 there was ample contamination from outside, so that what the training they do in 1970 "looks like" is very much like sensitivity training. They have also abandoned much of the emphasis on base level training, and express much more interest in reaching the leaders and organizations where power for social change seems to reside. And they definitely seem to be responding to pressures from Americans in AID, which is the principal source of funds for continuing the training in Ecuador.

The Aloka Experience

The Aloka experience reaches into the 1950s, but we select it for this chapter because it shows another contrast in how training innovations sometime occur in developing countries. The Aloka invention happened in Ceylon and then moved to India, but the prime mover was not Ceylonese or Indian. He was Rolf Lynton, who is not easily identified with a single country, but is West European and North American by background. Aloka was established, institutionally, by resolution of the World Assembly of Youth, but in developing the training program Lynton and his wife started as essentially lone agents in Ceylon. The Aloka experience differed from the innovation in Ecuador in the absence of the strong bureaucratic presence of the U. S. Peace Corps and Agency for International Development.

The Aloka program was an intensive three months in nascent community living plus case studies, diaries, and other written studies of the participants' own experiences. As Lynton[4] has described it:

> The project was put together as a practical immediate contribution to the development of more leaders, and more skilled leaders; its scale was determined above all by the scarcest and most essential resource: the faculty. . . . The group living and manual work were the parts of the training programme which involved all members most directly and unmistakably. One-half of the programme was devoted to the manual work and discussion of it by the group. . . . The other major part of the regular programme was discussion of teaching cases. . . .
> In terms of hours of work per week, the division was approximately as follows:

> | | |
> |---|---|
> | manual work at Aloka | 6 |
> | discussion of manual work and incidents in the course of living together | 4½ |
> | case discussions (4 sessions of 2½ hours each) | 10 |
> | review of the week and discussion of programme for next week | 2½ |
> | village demonstration | 2½ |
> | field visit | 6 |

> . . . In terms of daily division of the week, it was often as follows:

> | | |
> |---|---|
> | manual work and discussion (3 half days) | 1½ |

case discussion (4 half days)   2
village work   ½
field visit   1
review of the week and programme   ½

The selection of participants was also a matter of hard attention in the Aloka project. Alokans were young doers who were intensely feeling the strains of breaking the traditions and building new forms of organized activity in education, farming, social work, trade unions, and other occupations. They were already experiencing success and feeling pressures.

> The people who came to Aloka and became participants in this study were among those whom experience and position had already brought hard up against the need for greater freedom, personally for themselves and generally in their organizations and communities. . . . Many . . . were dissatisfied with the state of affairs at home or with their methods of dealing with it.[5]

Like the Paulo Freire method, the Aloka experience was innovative in its comprehensiveness. It was an attempt to address and stick with the total experience of living and learning. It was a very early use of many ideas now more familiarly recognized in concepts of learning communities. In the uses of the case method, Aloka was adaptive; but in selecting people for and building a total learning community—from doing the work, setting the schedules, harvesting the food, studying cases and doing other written assignments, and regularly discussing and reflecting on the experiences, with back-home application increasingly in mind through the three months of each program—Aloka was another powerful training invention.

Some further observations: Aloka was heavily the product of the creative and sustaining energies of Lynton and his wife, but the training designs and contents increasingly showed strong influences from the Asian and African participants. Aloka was probably the least doctrinaire of the three training innovations reviewed in this chapter. Aloka depended on the benign and non-interfering umbrella of outside financial support, from the Foundation for Youth and Student Affairs, and when that support ended so formally did Aloka. The training inventions have not died.

Summary

The three training innovations just described have some uniformities and suggest at least some tentative generalizations for thinking more widely about training inventions in developing countries.

One uniformity is that each instance was an effort to take training where it had not been taken before—literacy training to illiterates, participation training to non-participants, leadership training to new young doers.

A second uniformity is that each instance represented a mix of training techniques and ideas, and each evolved a theory to account for itself. Also, the stronger and more systematic the theory, the more likely the invention was to retain its uniqueness. Of the three, the Paulo Freire method had the most rigorous theory and is the only one of the three that still has a clear and unique identity today; the Ecuador invention was least developed theoretically and lost much of its uniqueness rapidly as it came into contact with the general market place of ideas.

Third, too rapid exposure and expansion was almost a sure kiss of death. The plans for massive application of the Paulo Freire method in Brazil were too much too fast for many politically defensive people to take. The Ecuador experiment became labeled sensitivity training so early that whatever was truly unique about the invention, or reinvention, got largely lost in the effort to understand sensitivity training.

Finally, each invention was largely the creation of one or two highly energetic, relatively highly educated, and non-traditional people.

ADOPTING NEW TRAINING TECHNIQUES

In the absence of a good indigenous training invention, the task often falls on adopting something already available somewhere else. This experience in the developing countries, as with training inventions, is not well documented, so we have to be selective and more tentative than we would like in pointing to instances and drawing conclusions.

In this section of the chapter, we will briefly review the experience of developing countries with the case method, the syndicate method, instrumented programs, sensitivity training, and an experiential program based on systems approach.

The Case Method

This method is a prodigy of the Harvard Business School and has generally worked well in management education in North America. But it is not being swallowed easily in Latin America, or in many other developing countries. One indication is the paucity of indigenous cases that have been developed in countries where this method has been seriously tried. A quick check of the bibliography of cases compiled by Harvard shows that only a minimal number of cases come from the developing countries. Thus, teachers in developing countries have to use cases developed in the United States. And these cases are usually not appropriate for the situation prevailing in the developing countries. This reduces considerably the effectiveness of this method of training. Secondly, the case method requires one to see oneself, from a written description, in someone else's situation. This includes visualizing the situation, having empathy for the central characters, being critical of particular actions and knowing intuitively the rough goals, i.e., profit, harmonious relations, expansion, etc. The assumption that students in management education in most of the developing regions of the world have these capacities, even in studying written cases from their own countries, cannot be made as a general proposition. Divisions in the social structure, the recency of development, the sudden complexity of the problems, the small number of educated people, and educational traditions all contribute to this difference of many parts of the world from North America.

Before leaving this topic we must point out that the case method does have an advantage over the lecture method because it does allow greater trainee participation. Also, we are aware of a few isolated cases in the developing part of the world where the case method has met with some success. In particular, we must mention the situation at the Indian Institute of Management at Ahmedabad in India. This Institute was developed with direct assistance from the Harvard Business School. In the first two years the Institute staff (American as well as Indian) made a major effort to collect case material from Indian enterprises. And this case material has been successfully integrated into the teaching at the Institute. But it may be a special case since the first few batches of students were drawn from a highly educated portion of the Indian community. In fact many of the students had masters' degrees in science or engineering from leading universities and institutes of the country. The real test will come when these cases are used at other schools which don't draw its student body from an elite group.

The Syndicate Method

The syndicate method allows even greater trainee participation than the case method. This method has been primarily used in the training of relatively senior administrators with a number of years of experience.

When trainees are appropriately selected so that they have useful experiences to share with each other, this method seems to have worked fairly well. At worst, it becomes a social gathering and a pleasant vacation since these programs are usually run at exclusive places in the developing countries.[6]

The main drawback of this approach is that it underutilizes the faculty and staff talent, since the staff is expected to play the rather passive role of a moderator. Also the learning is limited by the past experience of the trainees. Thus it helps to perpetuate the status quo. But development process involves change and the administrator in the developing countries has to understand the complexities of the change processes (and not status quo) as well as develop leadership qualities necessary to bring about the desired changes.

Though the syndicate method might have been a useful technique in training military officers and civil servants in the old days[7] when these bureaucratic systems were relatively stable (hence the usefulness of learning about maintaining the status quo through enforcement of rules and regulations), it is questionable that it is a suitable method for training in developing countries which are experiencing and aspire to bring about rapid change.

Secondly, this method, even at its best, is only applicable to senior people with long years of experience. And developing countries need to train young people with no experience as well as junior administrators.

And thirdly, there have emerged, since World War II, several newer techniques of training which seem to be superior to the syndicate method.

NEWER TECHNIQUES OF TRAINING

Foremost among these newer techniques are those based on the laboratory method, namely sensitivity training or the T-group method, and the instrumented laboratory method.[8] The main difference between these two methods is that the T-group is completely unstructured and has a trainer while the instrumented laboratory is completely structured and has no trainer.

Some Experience with Newer Training Techniques in the Developing World

Though these newer techniques have been around for more than two decades[9] it is only recently that they have gained a wide acceptance in the United States.[10] At this time they have not been adopted widely in the developing countries. Secondly, literature regarding evaluation of these techniques in developing countries has been rather limited. However, the authors visited several countries in Asia, the Middle East, and Latin America. In each country we had a chance to talk to a number of scholars, management consultants, management association representatives, directors of training institutes, representatives from Chambers of Commerce and other similar organizations, and senior administrators from industry and government. What follows then is primarily based on impressions gained during these interviews.[11]

First of all, we found only limited use of package (instrumented) programmes. A number of reasons were given as to why this is so. There were three reasons about which we found the most agreement among respondents. First of these is the fact that these programmes use material which is based on U.S. experience and the manager in developing countries finds it interesting but not something he can tune with and take seriously. Thus he develops an attitude of playing games and having fun and this hampers the educational value of the programme. Secondly, those who market these package deals have failed to develop an intellectual rapport with the collaborating institutes (scholars) in many developing countries.[12] This arises from a lack of sensitivity and appreciation of local culture on the part of U.S. representatives and too much emphasis on profits to the exclusion of other considerations. And thirdly, these programmes are tightly controlled by proprietary interests in the U.S. This inhibits development of local talents and requires large fees to be paid to U.S. representatives on a continuing basis. And most of the institutes in the developing countries do not have such dollar reserves for payments over a prolonged period.

Sensitivity Training

In view of the reasons outlined above, it is hardly conceivable that the package programmes will gain any wider acceptance in developing countries than they already have.[13]

What about the sensitivity training or T-group method? Here the record is slightly better than in the case of package programmes. However, the reasons for rather limited use of this technique are different than for package programmes. First of all, T-group is a flexible method due to complete lack of structure in such a group. No instruments or tasks are needed. Also a T-group can be conducted in the local language, thus eliminating almost completely the problem of adapting material to local conditions. Secondly, there is no limitation on the development of local talent since NTL is a non-profit organization and does not get in the way of development of local trainers.[14] And finally, the Ford Foundation has helped for almost a decade in financing several U.S. trainers in developing countries—Nylen in Africa, Ready in Egypt and Colombia, King in Egypt, Lynton and others in India, etc.

In view of all of this, one may very well ask why sensitivity training has not had a wider acceptance and use in developing countries. What are the resisting forces? Our interviews in developing countries identified a few of these. The leading one is a clash between the meta-goals of sensitivity training and the societal norms and cultural values in the developing world.

The T-group method propagates a philosophy which is based on the values of democracy. This is what has been variously referred to as Theory Y or participative management. Yet most of the nations in the developing world believe in a hierarchical structure. According to Haire et al. (1963), this is like selling democracy to people who believe in the divine right of kings. When presented with the argument that if you want to develop economically like the United States you should be prepared to adopt their values, our interviewees almost unanimously referred to the case of Japan, which has achieved a remarkable industrial growth during the last two decades without sacrificing their culture.

Secondly, the T-group method has an individual rather than an organizational orientation. By and large, the research conducted so far in the United States has indicated that sensitivity training does change individual behavior. But, as Mangham and Cooper[15] point out, in this latest review of the research on sensitivity training, simply because a man changes, this is no guarantee that he is more effective on the job. And the *Wall Street Journal* in its issue of July 14, 1969, has even gone further, pointing out that companies which have made use of sensitivity training are having second thoughts about its value. And some, like TRW Systems, Inc., are developing newer kinds of training designs which have an organizational orientation. A well-meaning leading businessman in Latin America summed up the views of most of our interviewees in the following words:

"The United States is an affluent society. So they can afford to spend money on developing individual managers without regard to how much this will contribute to the company performance. We are not blessed, in Latin America, with such abundance of resources. Our resources are limited. So we cannot afford the luxury of trying training techniques which offer questionable benefits to our organizations."

Thirdly, there has been no systematic effort on the part of NTL to undertake the development of local trainers in developing countries.[16] The Ford Foundation, not so much through design but happy coincidence,[17] has been the only agency to support the limited development which has happened so far. And a few individual trainers have dedicated their own time and effort to help in the development of indigenous trainers in some of the developing countries.[18] At the time of writing of this chapter there is no indication that NTL is planning to develop a systematic programme in this direction. It may be because NTL has, so far, found it difficult to meet the challenge of a rapidly growing demand for its services in the United States. And secondly, its International Institute in these days of funding squeeze has found it difficult to find funds needed for this purpose.

In view of the formidable obstacles to the acceptance of the T-group method in the developing countries, it is not very likely that this technique will gain a wide use in the developing world in the foreseeable future.

In this section, we briefly reviewed the experience with newer techniques in the developing country. To sum up, these techniques have not made any considerable dent in the developing countries.[19] Thus, in most of the developing world, management and administrative training is still carried on using classical techniques. On the other hand, our interviews convinced us beyond any doubt that there is a great unfulfilled need for a better approach than the classical approaches to administrative training. We sensed a great desire on the part of our interviewees for experiential programmes which can help managers and administrators acquire skills to manage organizations which function in a rapidly changing environment. What does seem to catch on for management education in developing countries is real experience and discussion of real experience. Thus the demands and the opportunities for designing experience-based management education programmes in the developing part of the world seem overwhelming.

We will now briefly review an *experiential* programme based on the systems approach.[20]

An Experiential Programme Based on the Systems Approach

This programme developed as a result of an action research project in the area of managerial problem solving.[21] Based on this research, a one-week training programme for executives was designed. Since 1964, this programme has been primarily organized in the United States for executives, administrators, and graduate students of business administration. During the summer of 1965 it was organized for a selected group of Africans visiting the United States.[22] Outside the United States, this programme has been organized during 1967 for the chairmen of the boards of corporations in Middle East. Similar programmes have also been conducted for executives in India during 1966, and in Brazil during June 1968.

The most distinguishing feature of this programme is that it is based on the concepts of the open system theory and recognizes the organizations as they really are, rather complex problem-solving entities. It views the organization as a complex open system with rather loose boundary and constantly interacting with its environment. As shown in Figure 1, this complex system has at least four *overlapping* subsystems: functional (economic), social, informational, and political.[23] The subsystems are always interacting with each other. Thus the organization is an ever evolving dynamic and problem-solving entity. In such a concept of organization, the managerial role is far more complex than assumed by the classical or laboratory theorists. It was sufficient for the manager to look after only the economic aspects according to classical theorists and human (social) aspects according to laboratory people. According to this approach, the manager has to perform both of these functions (economic and social) and many more. He has to know and understand how the information is structured within the organization. Thus he must be up to date in the recent developments in this area, particularly the computer technology. Also, he must be skilled in the political processes of bargaining, power tactics, conflict resolution, resource allocation, and objective setting. Above all, he must have a keen sense of the dynamics of complex open systems, and skills to manage these dynamics and/or changes. The manager is thus a problem solver constantly alert to the changes in the environment that may ultimately challenge the current organizational structure and policies. He has to be innovative and creative to devise organizational solutions to these challenges, adventurous and risk-taking to experiment with new structures and policies, bold to make decisions under uncertainty, and skillful enough to manage the changes involved in introducing new structures and policies.

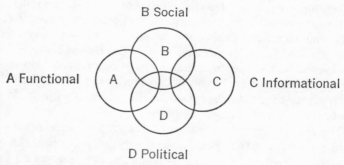

Figure 1   Organizational systems

This programme attempts to expose the participant to a systems approach to problem solving using such concepts as free-field analysis.[24] Participant manifestations occur in all the four subsystems of the organization as well as in interactions with the environment. Also the manager is helped to think of emotional as well as rational forces and to recognize the impact of emotional issues on organizational roles. Of course, only those emotional issues are considered which are relevant to organizational work. Emotional issues that are not relevant, but are important from an individual standpoint only, are left out.[25]

Some Experience with the Programme in Developing Countries

In general, the programme has been favorably evaluated by participants in developing countries. A few typical excerpts from participant evaluation follow:

"This programme was the best learning experience I have ever had in my life."

"Each one in my organization should attend a similar seminar."

"I learned importance of the free dialogue in problem-solving and decision-making process."

"I feel I have gained a greater capacity for analyzing problem situations and dealing with subordinates."

"I gained new ideas on personnel management and how to delegate authority."

"I realized the importance of becoming an agent of change within my organization."

"I developed better communication skills. I learned the importance of good listening."

"I realized the importance of giving and receiving feedback in every case."

"I learned who I am, where I stand, and what I want to become in my organization."

However, many difficulties were experienced in trying the programme overseas. These relate to the problem of adapting ideas developed in the United States to developing countries. What follows is a brief discussion of these problems.

PROBLEMS OF ADAPTATION

In addition to the costs involved in developing effective collaboration with local scholars and going through several often agonizing translation-retranslation phases, several major problems were encountered during the running of the actual programme, subsequent followup phase, and development of local professionals.

First it was found that participants in developing countries, compared to U.S. managers, require more time to understand instructions, like verbal instructions better than (and often in addition to) written instructions, have greater need for more conceptual discussion sessions, like much more personal contact with the foreign scholar (who is usually the programme co-ordinator), and part of this contact has to be in a social setting rather than a work situation. All these requirements force a reduction in the number of activities scheduled for a given time, but each activity is often explored in greater depth than with the U.S. population. These differences may be due to the difference between the Anglo-Saxon culture and the cultural traditions of developing countries. Many U.S. (and British) scholars have mistaken these symptoms to be a sign of laziness or incompetence on the part of managers of developing countries. And this shows up in their attitude of impatience, which is easily detected by the natives and interpreted as a sign of a "superiority" complex. Thus, the relationship of basic trust which is essential between the trainer and the trainee is non-existent from the start. This usually results in an aborted effort. It is, therefore, vital that programmes be modified to meet the needs (emotional and rational) of the participants and their culture.

Adapting Materials Developed in the U.S. to Local Context

First of all the material must be understandable in terms of local context. For example, it makes no sense to use material developed from U.S. companies in a socialistic country with no private enterprise. Similarly, labor laws vary widely from country to country. A labor-management negotiation simulation developed in the United States is of little use in a country which has compulsory arbitration or, worse still, where labor has no right to strike. Materials developed in the context of a highly competitive industry in the United States have little meaning for countries where most of the big industry is a virtual monopoly. And finally, all psychological types of instruments involving attitudes and values have to be modified so that the value dimensions they contain are relevant in the local culture. To do all this often requires years of cross-cultural research. And rigorous cross-cultural research has been almost non-existent till recently.[26] A massive funding by foundations and/or international companies and/or international agencies will be needed before this situation is corrected.

Development of Local Staff

Fully trained local staff is almost a must if any training effort is to succeed. But this requires enormous initial investment. In any programme it is absolutely necessary to develop local professionals. Yet the record so far has been far from satisfactory. This problem is intimately tied in with the issue of institutionalization, which will be discussed now.

Institutionalizing New Training Techniques

Getting new training techniques invented or adapted or just transferred is only the beginning if training is to be for development. The techniques must be indigenously rooted, and this requires some form of institutionalization.

The problems are (a) finding an indigenous institution in which a new technique can find a home and grow, or (b) getting a new indigenous institution established to spawn the new technique, and this could include the propagation of the new technique or (c) importing an extension of some outside institution. It is not the purpose of this chapter to go into the complex and tough issues of institution building, except as they can be touched on briefly in terms specifically of institutionalizing new training techniques. Some examples of the options that have been tried and the hazards run are germane to the thesis of this chapter.

Locating the practice of a new training technique in an existing indigenous institution has not been easy, and the odds on success are low. Universities especially tend the world over to be ultraconservative in teaching methods, and they are still more supportive of the traditional lecture than of any other method. There are exceptions. The Universidad del Valle in Cali, Colombia, is an exception in several respects, where innovative techniques have characterized several efforts of the Facultad de Administración, and where some adaptations of sensitivity training have even been used for improved development of teaching and administration within the university—a very rare instance of a university using the insights of some of its faculty members for practice in the university and in terms of its own mission. We guess that the world-wide crisis in universities stemming from the challenges students are making to traditional university practices will soon change the resistances of many of those institutions to innovations, and several will become favorable spawning and extension grounds for new training techniques. This is on the horizon, however, and nothing we can report as having occurred more than rarely in the 1960s.

In our view, part of the disaster that fell on the Paulo Freire method in Brazil stemmed from the attempt to propagate the method through the Ministry of Education. This is not to say that there was much choice at the time. Ministries of Education are no more known, however, for their boldness in introducing innovative training techniques than are universities. There are exceptions again, and we hope that signs of change toward more receptiveness to new methods by Ministries of Education hold strong.

Experiences with establishing new indigenous institutes or associations to propagate a particular new training technique have been largely negative. The notable efforts with which we are familiar have been attempts to found human relations or sensitivity training or group dynamics organizations. Rarely have the efforts gotten off the ground, and where they have, even in the more industrially advanced countries—they have stayed weak and ineffective for accomplishing much if anything more than some professional colleagueship for their members. They have been seen as sufficiently high-risk ventures that they have failed to attract more than tokens of outside financing, professional management, or even full-time members.

In Ecuador, the exception that may prove the rule is currently being attempted. There a new, autonomous, indigenous institute has been established to carry on the training work described earlier in this chapter. Trainers in Ecuador have the advantage of considerable knowledge and counsel based on most other attempts to date, and they are trying to evolve a successful model.

Perhaps the most successful institutional form for assisting new training techniques in developing countries has been the broad-gauge, independent management development institute. This is especially true where the institute focused more on industrial than other areas of management, but included in fact as well as rhetoric strong emphasis on managers from all organizational sectors (government national and local, education, military, service, commerce, etc.). These institutes have tended to be relatively strong and stable financially, free of undue government pressure but mindful of their development mission, and open to new ideas and techniques. Two examples with which we are most familiar are INCOLDA in Colombia and NIMD in Egypt. Both have experimented with and been receptive to a number of training innovations.

Mixed have been the experiences with management development institutes and degree programmes that have been institutional extension efforts of universities and other educational organizations outside the developing countries. Included here are administrative staff colleges (such as the one at Hyderabad, India) as offshoots of the Administrative Staff College, Henley-on-Thames, England; management institutes and degree programmes spawned by Harvard University (such as the Indian Institute of Management, Ahmedabad, India, and the Institute Centroamericano de Administración de Empresas, Managua, Nicaragua), Stanford University (such as the Escuela de Administración de Negocios para Graduados, Lima, Peru), and many others. These efforts have usually involved large costs in money and time, dependency and identity problems that have several times gone badly, and sometimes a commitment to a particular educational method (i.e., case method, syndicate method) that has hampered experimentation with other techniques.

SUMMARY AND CONCLUSIONS

There are three areas that demand immediate attention, namely that of cross-cultural research, training professionals from the developing countries, and establishing institutions which will encourage innovation and adaptation of newer techniques. We will now discuss what is needed and a design to accomplish it.

What Is Needed?

The first and most important need is to develop indigenous staff resources in areas related to training and research in these newer techniques. And these resources have to be developed in large numbers in each developing nation. For relatively large countries like India, Brazil, Egypt, etc., it would involve development of a network of the size of the National Training Laboratories in the United States.[27] In case of smaller countries, several countries may have to combine resources on a regional basis to develop such a network.

There are several issues in developing such a large pool of indigenous resources. First is the identification of relevant scholarly areas. Based on our experience both in the United States and the developing countries, these areas are: applied behavioral sciences, especially industrial, social, and organizational psychology; organization theory and practice; organization development; organization change; comparative administration; and systems theory. We have included comparative administration rather than business administration because our experiences in the developing countries have convinced us beyond any shadow of a doubt that the division of management between private and public organizations is not viable in the case of developing countries.[28]

The second issue relates to the availability and selection of trainers. In the area of selection critera, we are faced with an unfortunate situation since little research has been done in this field. As a result, even NTL has failed to enforce any rigorous and professionally viable criteria.[29] It is essential that this mistake should not be repeated in the developing countries. We need to establish academically viable criteria. And it is here that scholars from developed and developing countries have to work together in a team.[30]

And finally there is the issue of availability of local scholars. Here again the picture is rather gloomy. In our trips to Latin America, Asia, and the Middle East we found a paucity of such people in the universities and institutes of higher learning. For the most part, the educational systems have been completely geared to classical approaches, and little structural change has occurred since colonial days.[31] As a result, there is a paucity of people with the interdisciplinary background which is needed for these new training programmes. Thus there is a crying need for additional educational systems. With the help primarily of the Ford Foundation, some countries like India and Egypt have met this need by creating special institutions like NIMD in Egypt and IIMs in India. But this is only a partial solution to the problem. What we are recommending here is a nationwide change in the educational system. Of course, such a change will require major resource commitment from the developing nations but developed countries can provide invaluable assistance here.[32]

The Challenge for the United Nations

We have discussed some issues relating to the twin need for research and development of local talents. What is needed to fulfill these needs?

There are many areas in which the developing nations have to provide the leadership and resources. The foremost among these is the overhaul of their educational systems.

There are other areas in which regional collaboration may be needed, particularly in the case of small countries. A recent example of this kind of effort is the consortium called CLADEA (Comite Latino-Americano de Decanos de Escuelas de Administración). This consortium developed as a result of a meeting of several deans of the graduate schools of business management in Latin America, in early 1966, to develop collaborative projects among their schools.[33]

And finally, there is a need for setting up an International University or Institute for the Development of Human Resources. Ideally, such a university should be located centrally to provide easy access to the developing countries of Latin America, Asia, Africa, and the Middle East. Its primary function should be to train trainers and to conduct cross-cultural and comparative research in areas relevant to training. It should also have a central data bank to store data from cross-cultural and comparative research conducted by its own faculty as well as other faculties. And it should issue a journal of cross-cultural and comparative research to keep its graduates and other scholars in this rapidly developing area up to date.

It might offer a one-year postgraduate programme in comparative administration with applied focus. This programme should be primarily to develop trainers. In addition, it should offer, at a later date, special short-term continuing education programmes.

This university should have a minimum core faculty drawn from all parts of the world—developed and developing. These scholars should be recruited on the basis of demonstrated competence rather than their nationality.[34] In addition special faculty should be invited for short-term assignments.[35]

In the area of research, there will be a need to assemble inter-disciplinary and multinational teams around specific projects.[36] These teams should be organized like RAND Corporation project teams.

This university would require multinational sources of funding, including developed countries of the East and the West, developing countries, and private foundations.

It is in bringing together all these sources of funding as well as scholars from all nations of the world that the United Nations is uniquely equipped to play a leadership role.

CHAPTER FIFTEEN—FOOTNOTES

1. The quotes and much of the information in this section are from "The Paulo Freire Method" by Thomas G. Sanders, American Universities Field Staff Reports Service, West Coast South American Series, Vol. XV, No. 1 (Chile), June 1968.

2. Ibid.

3. From Noncapital Project Paper, Ecuador, Project No. 518–15–810–092, sent July 28, 1969 (unclassified).

4. R. P. Lynton, *The Tide of Learning: The Aloka Experience*, London, Routledge & Kegan Paul, 1960, pp. 4, 28, 31.

5. Ibid., p. 5.

6. For example, in India this method is used in training programmes organized by the Administration Staff College, which is located in one of the most exotic marble palaces (Bella Vista) in Hyderabad.

7. In modern times, even these bureaucratic organizations have experienced rapid change.

8. The instrumented laboratory method was first developed by Blake and Mouton, using the Managerial Grid. Bass has recently developed a similar programme based on self-administering exercises. Another package-type programme in the area of decision making has been developed by Kepner and Tregoe.

9. The T-group method was discovered, more by accident than by design, in 1946 by a group of psychologists at the Research Center for Group Dynamics at the Massachusetts Institute of Technology.

10. For example, the National Training Laboratory Institute for Behavioral Science scheduled more than thirty laboratories in 1969 and reported that attendance at their 1968 laboratories had been double the number involved in the programmes five years earlier (*Wall Street Journal,* July 14, 1969).

11. In addition, we have tried to make use of the limited literature

available in this area, particularly reports by Don Nylen about experience in Africa and by Abramson about experience in Pakistan.

12. We found some exceptions, where a good rapport and understanding were developed, but by and large they had failed to materialize.

13. It is a different type of ball game as far as developed countries of Europe are concerned. For example, Bass has been able to organize several ongoing programmes in Europe but only two one-shot programmes (one in Mexico and the other in India) in the developing world.

14. In principle, NTL encourages such a development.

15. For other reviews, see Robert J. House (1967), and Campbell and Dunnette (1968). These reviewers have also come to essentially the same conclusion as Mangham and Cooper (1969).

16. It was only in September 1969 that NTL hired its first full-time director of its International Institute.

17. The Ford Foundation has helped primarily in the development of local institutes of management like ESLAN in Peru, NIMD in Egypt, IIMs in India, etc. It so happened that some of the American faculty assigned to these institutes has helped to develop local trainers.

18. Most notable among these are Rolf Lynton of the University of North Carolina and Fred Massarik of UCLA.

19. We must, however, again emphasize that there has been a lot of good work done by some people like Ready in Egypt and Colombia, Don Nylen in Africa, Lynton and Bennis in India, Massarik in India and Japan, etc. But this has made a rather limited impact in view of the need and potential in the developing part of the world.

20. For a more detailed account, refer to Nath (1968a).

21. This research was carried on during 1961–64 in a large multinational company and the results are reported in Nath (1968b).

22. This programme was sponsored jointly by the Regional Council for International Education at Pittsburgh, Pennsylvania, and the Agency for International Development.

23. For a detailed description of these subsystems, see Nath (1967).

24. Lewin developed this concept. For further details as to how this is applied to managerial problem solving, see Nath (1968a).

25. This organizational orientation is one aspect that differentiates this approach from sensitivity training where the primary focus is on the individual and his emotional issues.

26. For a detailed methodological review of cross-cultural research, see Nath (1969).

27. There is already an attempt to develop this kind of network in some countries. For example, Udai Pareekh is organizing such an effort in India. Fred Massarik and Raghu Nath will be involved in the later part of the effort to organize a training programme for these local trainers.

28. In fact, it is highly questionable that such a situation is viable in the U.S. of today and tomorrow. It is our view that this has been a historical development which just lingers on due to the inertia of our educational system in the U.S. It may have been useful when business dominated the national priorities in the early part of this century. It has no place today when public and social issues have become as important as the profit motive.

29. In fact this is one of the major objections leveled against sensitivity training and NTL by such people as George Odiorne. For its internship programme, NTL requires a doctoral degree in behavioral science. Not having the stature of the American Medical Association or a university, NTL has failed to enforce this criterion. As a result there are many quacks running rampant in the field. Lately this issue has received increasing attention from NTL and other professional organizations.

30. It will be the first of several cross-cultural research projects needed in this area. The experience of the Tavistock Institute in London, EIT in Vienna, the Trainer group in Holland, the National Institute of Management Development in Cairo, Japanese and Indian groups may be usefully pulled together along with U.S. experience.

31. There has been considerable increase in capacity as far as quantity is concerned. When we talk of structural change, we are concerned with the type of education, i.e., the quality.

32. Again this is another area in which massive assistance is needed from the developed world, preferably on a multinational basis like the consortium idea. The United Nations is uniquely equipped to provide leadership in this area. Most of the aid has been in the industrial area and very little in the educational area. What we are suggesting is massive aid in developing human resources, for it can be argued that investment in education is as important as industrial investment.

33. For further information regarding CLADEA, see Ready (1968, pp. 78–79). For another collaborative effort, see *Training in Africa* by Don Nylen and Anthony Stoul.

34. Much of the UN effort has suffered because of the quota representation requirements. It is absolutely necessary to avoid such procedures in this new university.

35. These assignments would be for a semester or an academic year.

36. For example, one such area is that of trainer selection criteria identified earlier.

CHAPTER SIXTEEN
New Techniques in Management Training: A Future Perspective*

I. PRELIMINARY SYNTHESIS

This book has described the use of newer training techniques for helping managers of complex organizations acquire improved management capabilities. It has included in the analysis both developed and developing countries and countries with different economic and political systems. Within the broad general framework of analyzing newer techniques, the essays were individually conceived. The chapters are not directed toward the support of an all-encompassing theory relating to the usefulness of specific techniques or to the diffusion of training techniques across national boundaries and between different cultures. Outstanding theorists and practitioners from a number of countries, with well-established programmes, were asked to present their views concerning training approaches and techniques in which they are expert. Many of the essayists have had extensive experience conceiving and conducting management programmes for developing nations and for international organizations. Consequently, the experiences of these nations and international organizations have not been overlooked. For the most part, the views are those of the academic and consulting worlds in the most developed nations. The uniformly high level of competence of the persons who have given us the benefits of their observations and experiences permits us to draw tentative generalizations with a high degree of confidence in the reliability of the anecdotal and research data.

* This chapter was prepared by Sidney Mailick and Solomon Hoberman.

One obvious conclusion is that there is no agreement on the usefulness of any technique, or even of any single set of techniques. Some of this lack of agreement stems from differences in goals for management development.

However, all of the contributors are agreed that, while management development is a risky investment and one which means different things to different people and different organizations, it is an investment that organizations must make if they wish to successfully continue to operate.

Examples of the types of conflicting goals which have effects on the choice of a specific training technique and its usefulness are: (a) to help the manager to operate effectively within a given system and (b) to help him obtain the will and ability to change the system in which he will manage.

Formal training, particularly training using the newer techniques, usually has the second of these as its goal. The manager is trained to look for something to change and to create the opportunity for change, rather than to wait passively for the opportunity to arise. A major objective is almost always change in the active role of the manager upon re-entry to his job. Consequently, these programmes, generally, seek to do more than to impart knowledge of how to solve technical problems, they extend to including knowledge, skill, and practice in inducing changed behavior. Many programmes emphasize how to go about getting acceptance for desired change—whatever it may be.

There is general recognition that there is a wide gap between the knowledge of a management principle or technique and the ability to use it effectively as a manager in a specific organization. The newer techniques make the assumption that there is a relationship between the manner in which the principle or technique is learned and the will and/or the ability of the person to make the behavioral changes which are the training objectives.

Although there is a wider range of opinion among the essayists with respect to the effectiveness of different training approaches and techniques as instruments for producing organizational change, we will identify only four which consider the problem of training managers to act as change agents.

One suggests that all that formal training can do is to provide the manager with the necessary knowledge and, if possible, insight. From this point of view, the problem of effecting change is too complex and dependent upon too many unpredictable and uncontrollable factors. Only the manager, upon re-entry, can determine how to effectuate the change, after he studies and analyzes the actual situation. This approach tends to use few of the newer techniques directed at changing behavioral relationships. A second approach hypothesizes that there is no necessary relationship between knowledge and insight and action, that in order to be a change agent the manager must know himself, know how he affects others, and practice trying to change his own behavior and that of others. Some techniques, to provide this practice, which have been used with varying degrees of success primarily in private management in the North American and Western European nations, are role-playing and sensitivity training. A third approach hypothesizes that one can learn how to be a change agent only by acting as a change agent in a real-life situation. The project and task force relate to this approach. They both provide experience in a real but controlled situation. The fourth approach hypothesizes that people can learn how to effect change in a specific organization only by actually working to effect change in that organization. This approach assumes that, in an operational sense, all organizations are unique and that the number of factors which affect the nature and degree of change and the complexity of the interrelationships among these are so great that the ability to accomplish change is not a personal but only a team potentiality. The focus in this approach is on vertical training and organizational development. We seem to have completed the circle: the first and last approaches apparently start from the same hypothesis—programmes for training individuals cannot focus on organizational change. The last approach tries to cope with the situation by training all the major possible change agents at the same time, the first by leaving the adjustment up to the manager and his organization.

Another conclusion which can be reached is that there are two schools relative to the answers to the question: Should training be normative or should training focus on process and make no claim as to superiority of one answer over another? Using the first approach, trainers tend to use techniques which help managers to learn "the answers" and when to use them. Using the second approach, trainers tend to use techniques which help managers to learn how to develop answers which might be useful. The second of these two approaches seems to have more general cross-cultural applicability as it may permit the introduction of local factors without affecting the basic process.

It seems clear from an analysis of the chapters that we have had much less experience and far less success in training managers to solve their interpersonal problems than to solve their technical problems. Some of the reasons which are advanced for this are: (1) we rarely have as much information about interpersonal relations as we have with respect to other problems; (2) many of the factors are not only unknown but even if they were known could not be influenced to any significant degree by a relatively short training program; (3) the certainty level of an "answer" or even an approach being generally acceptable is very much lower than the answer to a technical problem, e.g., an accounting problem or one in electronic data processing; (4) the manner in which the answer or approach is received is crucial; while only the manager can tell if the changed approach is new openness or more skilled manipulation, he cannot do much about convincing the receiver that it is indeed "new openness" unless the receiver wants to see it that way; (5) people cannot learn to change their organizational behavior in any decisive way as organizational behavior is a form of stable equilibrium over which the individual has only limited influence.

There are few techniques which are useful for the analysis of the total training process. The best we can do at present is to use a crude form of input/output analysis. Even in this crude model we do not know all the elements of the "input" or their values, are not able to measure, either quantitatively or qualitatively, the output, and do not understand very well the "transformation process." A simple model for participants in a formal, away-from-home training programme is given in Chart 16.1. This model consists of INPUT, TRANSFORMATION PROCESS, a three-stage OUTPUT, and a NATURAL CHANGE effect.

The INPUT is *n* participants, each the nucleus of his own space, subjected to the forces of his organization and his society (both as they are and as he perceives them), and the interrelations among these. The TRANSFORMATION PROCESS is the total experience during training, including training process, training techniques, the interrelations among participants and with staff, the content, etc. The OUTPUT is broken down into three stages. STAGE 1 is immediately upon completion of the programme at the point of leaving training and returning home. STAGE 2 is a short time (one week, one month) after re-entry

Chart 16.1

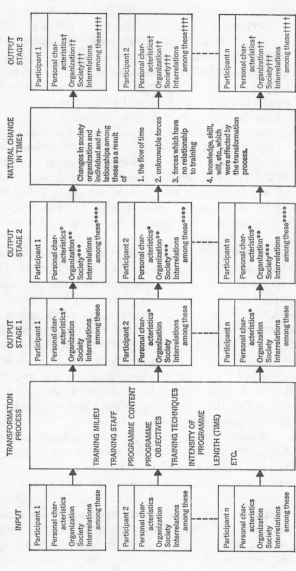

| INPUT | TRANSFORMATION PROCESS | OUTPUT STAGE 1 | OUTPUT STAGE 2 | NATURAL CHANGE IN TIME‡ | OUTPUT STAGE 3 |

INPUT

Participant 1
Personal characteristics
Organization
Society
Interrelations among these

Participant 2
Personal characteristics
Organization
Society
Interrelations among these

Participant n
Personal characteristics
Organization
Society
Interrelations among these

TRANSFORMATION PROCESS

TRAINING MILIEU
TRAINING STAFF
PROGRAMME CONTENT
PROGRAMME OBJECTIVES
TRAINING TECHNIQUES
INTENSITY OF PROGRAMME
LENGTH (TIME)
ETC.

OUTPUT STAGE 1

Participant 1
Personal characteristics*
Organization
Society
Interrelations among these

Participant 2
Personal characteristics*
Organization
Society
Interrelations among these

Participant n
Personal characteristics*
Organization
Society
Interrelations among these

OUTPUT STAGE 2

Participant 1
Personal characteristics*
Organization**
Society***
Interrelations among these****

Participant 2
Personal characteristics*
Organization**
Society***
Interrelations among these****

Participant n
Personal characteristics*
Organization**
Society***
Interrelations among these****

NATURAL CHANGE IN TIME‡

Changes in society organization and individual and relationships among these as a result of

1. the flow of time
2. unknowable forces
3. forces which have no relationship to training
4. knowledge, skill, will, etc., which were affected by the transformation process.

OUTPUT STAGE 3

Participant 1
Personal characteristics†
Organization†‡
Society†††
Interrelations among these†††

Participant 2
Personal characteristics†
Organization†‡
Society†††
Interrelations among these†††

Participant n
Personal characteristics†
Organization†‡
Society†††
Interrelations among these†††‡

* Changed participant characteristics resulting from TRANSFORMATION PROCESS.

** Changed organization resulting from absence of participant and passage of time.

*** Changed society (if any change at all) resulting from passage of time.

**** Interrelations at time of re-entry which must be different from those which existed at time of leaving.

†, ††, †††, ††††. Changed characteristics of individual, organization and society and the interrelationship among these resulting from NATURAL CHANGE IN TIME and the efforts of the individual which were influenced by the training program.

‡ The changes are, of course, unique for each participant.

into the organization. STAGE 3 is some time (at least one year) after re-entry. Between INPUT and OUTPUT and between STAGES 2 and 3, we recognize that unknown, and in fact unknowable, forces act with unknown strength to support or to undermine any will and ability to effect change that the participant brings to STAGE 2.

The asterisks beside the PERSONAL CHARACTERISTICS in the OUTPUT indicate that the participant (hopefully) was somehow changed as a result of the transformation process and that the nature of this change is, probably, different at each of the three stages.

The only thing that this crude, yet complex, model tells us is to put training efforts into perspective with the "real" world. It indicates that techniques may play some role in producing change. It indicates that the success of the TRANSFORMATION PROCESS may depend upon choice and use of training techniques. It does not present any hypothesis of the role played by training techniques in the TRANSFORMATION PROCESS. It does not give any specific help in determining the techniques to use.

The model does not explain any cause-effect relationships. It simply diagrams some of the activities or stages as they occur in the linear passage of time. However, it does point up some (occasionally conflicting) training assumptions. Some of these are: (1) By control of the TRANSFORMATION PROCESS, we can significantly affect STAGE 3 OUTPUT. (2) Control of the TRANSFORMATION PROCESS can be obtained by conscious use of specific training techniques. (3) STAGE 3 OUTPUT can only be affected by controlling to a significant degree INPUT and STAGES 1 and 2 of OUTPUT. No one has asked, yet, for control over society, but some approaches call for exercising influence over the individual and organizational INPUTS and relationships in the interval between STAGE 1 and STAGE 2 OUTPUTS.

The model also indicates the importance of feedback for gaining better understanding of the TRANSFORMATION PROCESS and for efforts to increase efficiency and effectiveness of the process.

While each of the elements of the diagram is shown as a monolith, obviously none is. Each is a complex process in time. Consequently, it is possible to obtain feedback from within the TRANSFORMATION PROCESS to affect later stages of the TRANSFORMATION PROCESS itself. Most feedback used to influence the training process, in particular the use of training techniques, is of this type. The methods in use include: the traditional instructor evaluation of participant learning by both informal and formal testing; participant, individual and group, analysis and evaluation; providing opportunities for participants, usually through return to their home organizations, to use their new abilities and to report on the results; and incorporating working in the actual organization and analysis of results into the TRANSFORMATION PROCESS as integral elements of the training technique.

Further, some training approaches attempt to combine elements. Organizational development brings STAGE 2 of OUTPUT into the TRANSFORMATION PROCESS.

Some other general points made and issues raised in the individual chapters are:

The newer techniques attempt to go beyond learning and the acquisition of technical competence to help the participant acquire "sensitivity" to problems, people, organizations. The degree to which people acquire and use this "sensitivity" is not as easily measurable as the acquisition of knowledge.

The new techniques as contrasted with the older ones, such as the lecture and assigned reading, have a slower average rate of dissemination of information. Their proponents claim they increase the ability of the learner to use the knowledge gained.

Training is often too superficial, too fragmented, and too general to yield a significant return. Not infrequently, a trainer attempts to do too much with too few resources because these are the conditions for establishing any programme. This tends to be particularly the case with organizations and countries with very limited resources for long-range investment. Consequently, these tend to receive far less return on their investments than do organizations which make adequate investments.

Development on the job under the direction of a willing and competent manager is probably the most effective way of training managers if the goal is system stability and training on how to function within the system. Experienced managers are the only ones who can teach a neophyte how to get along within the system. In systems which depend wholly on this type of training, systemic changes, if they occur, occur primarily as the opportunity and the need for change develop as the results of failure within the system or of outside pressures. One argument for expending valuable resources for training managers to gain skill in effecting change is that the expense for implementing decisions where there are many views to consider is high. As this is an important difference between the older and newer techniques, we have charted the analysis (Chart 16.2).

Chart 16.2

COSTS OF MAKING AND IMPLEMENTING
A MANAGEMENT DECISION

	One view to consider	Several views to consider	Many views to consider‡
Reaching decision	low*	low/medium	high†
Implementing decision	low	high/medium	high

* May pay to train one good decision maker if cost of implementation does not go too high.

† If implementation without participation is very high, it may pay to train how to get near unanimity.

‡ If feelings of persons involved are really of little effect, then there is no benefit in training to affect these.

Training and development, to be successful, must become an internalized, endless process in which the manager subjects his performance and that of his organization to critical self-analysis, evaluation, and change. The training experience has a significant effect on this process.

Some trainers have suggested that the usefulness of specific training techniques and approaches depend upon national cultural, social, and economic characteristics. For example, we have included consideration of these in our INPUT-OUTPUT model. Some trainers go on from this observation to recommending specific techniques as appropriate for nations falling into arbitrary categories such as "traditional," "pre-industrial" and "least developed," and leadership patterns. Although we agree with observers who see these as crucial factors in determining cultural change, we believe that to jump from these general necessary conditions to very specific sufficient conditions is a dangerous oversimplification of the actual situation. Use of this type of categorization is only of marginal value for predicting the usefulness of a training programme or a training technique. The actual situation is so much more complex that, as indicated, little formal analysis is of value. The only approach that seems to be of value is to organize what seem to be the relevant factors into categories and to consider all of these at one time, depending upon our experience and insight to help us.

Some of the innumerable factors which can affect the usefulness of a technique, organized in terms of the elements and factors which we considered in the INPUT-OUTPUT model, are:

A. *Society:* Ideology, forces for stability and change, economic and technological development, nationalistic forces, value systems, international relations, educational system, ethical norms, culture, leadership pattern, labor-management relations, expectations, managerial and management science resources, bureaucratic structure, accepted means for selecting and promoting managers, class structure, power structure, acceptable means for accomplishing change, closed or open national and subnational systems, cohesiveness, role of family, elite, maturity of institutions, accepted means for dealing with conflict, history, etc.

B. *Organization:* Goals, role and expectations from management, managerial resources and needs, bureaucratic structure, accepted manner of selecting and promoting managers, power structure, history, accepted methods for dealing with conflict, consequence system, forces for or against specific changes, labor-management relations, accepted behavior patterns, desired managerial style (management science or politico-administrative, rational objective or negotiate compromise, competitive or co-operative, trust or manipulate, take risk-play safe), expectations from training programmes, relationships with other organizations and the society, etc.

C. *Participants:* Life story, experience, education, natural management style (analytic-intuitive, dictate-negotiate, avoid or seek conflict, manipulate or trust, take or avoid risk, competitive or co-operative, accept or avoid uncertainty, etc.), work and life goals (mobility or stability, incremental or radical, etc.), family and class structure, ethical norms and value system, forces affecting behavior other than work forces, etc.

D. *Training Programme Objectives:* (1) *Organization:* change agent or stabilizer, generalist or specialist, increased knowledge and ability, improve capabilities for present job or for promotion, remove participant temporarily from organization, etc. (2) *Participant:* improve knowledge and managerial capabilities, improve promotional opportunities, change system, vacation from job, etc. (3) *Trainers:* help sending organization, help participant, strengthen training organization, use specific technique, diffuse management philosophy, seek material and financial rewards, etc.

E. *Training Programme Boundary Conditions:* Time and space; trainee abilities, expectations, and relationships; instructional staff ability and will; expectations of organizations from which participants come; consequences of success or failure of programme to training organization, etc.

F. *Training Content:* Problem solving and decision making, planning, controlling, handling and resolving conflict, leadership, negotiating, gaining acceptance for change, encouraging innovation, dealing with uncertainty, EDP, PPBS, PERT, organizational theories, community structure and relations, accounting, personnel management, budgeting, how to get people to accept leadership, power redistribution, working effectively with superiors, peers, subordinates, participative management, etc.

II. THE DIFFUSION OF THE NEWER TRAINING TECHNIQUES

In the light of the many points of view which have been expressed, it might be useful to summarize and review the nature, direction, and diffusion of training techniques.

For the most part, the development and earliest use of the newer techniques was the use, by the university business schools in the United States during the 1920s and '30s, of the case method, the role-play, and the business game. In the 1940s the National Training Laboratories developed and conducted sensitivity training programmes which were later extended to management development. These approaches, coupled with the increased interest in the instrumental role of decision making, have led to virtually all of the American techniques.

Underlying many of the newer techniques and approaches are a number of hypotheses relating to the ways adults learn, the ability to use learning and to change behavior on the job, and the forces which motivate workers and managers in a democracy to work together co-operatively and productively. They also assume the existence or desirability of a work-place value system which is a combination of the values of scientific management and political democracy. While the various hypotheses and values are not entirely consistent with each other, are not universally accepted, and are not needed to explain the usefulness of the techniques, it is important to be aware of them. The derivation of the values has been indicated. The hypotheses are derived from models used in the behavioral sciences and from findings relating to social processes generally and to systems and processes in large complex organizations. Some of the major concepts are the superior effectiveness of learning through active participation over passive intellectualization, the use of non-coercive, participatory management based on trust and free two-way communication; and the ability to internalize, through proper training, approaches which strengthen self-motivation and self-control.

There is little conclusive evidence to support the validity of this body of theory and practice even within its country of origin. There is even less evidence that the techniques will produce the same results in all countries and cultures. Obviously, there are some nations in which the hypotheses are not valid and many with different value systems.

Despite these factors, the influence of the various U.S. approaches has been widespread—British, Western, and Eastern management trainers have been intrigued by the new methods. They have successively resisted them, experimented with them, used them, and have been in the last few years modifying them to meet their own needs.

The U.S. influence on British management development, as described by Professor Morris in Chapter Four, is not atypical of its influence on management development in general. During the past twenty years a number of university-based business schools have come into being in Britain, each strongly influenced by the approaches and techniques of one or more U.S. schools. During this period the Tavistock Institute adapted and modified U.S. approaches to make them more usable for training British managers. In the last few years there has been considerable use and modification of sensitivity training and use of proprietary programmes such as Kepner-Tregoe and Blake's Managerial Grid. While these U.S. influences have been strong, the programmes never supplanted two strong British approaches—the syndicate and project methods.

The greatest diffusion of United States methodology has taken place with respect to the case method, role-playing, business games, and sensitivity training. While the disadvantages of using U.S. materials as well as techniques is obvious, there is still great reliance on U.S. materials. In some Western European nations, in which English is widely spoken, cases are frequently not even translated. Further, there has been a tendency to assume that, as for centuries university professors did not have to be taught how to lecture, there is no great need to train instructors in the use of these methods. Sadly, this is not the case. The need to prepare effective local material and to train people in the effective use of the techniques is even greater in the developing countries than in the developed countries.

The experiences with business games has been similar. Sensitivity training, however, working on the affective level, could not be used unchanged. Here, there has been an integration of U.S. and European values and approaches.

The use of the case method and management games has spread to Eastern European countries. Here again rapid absorption of these techniques is limited by the shortage of appropriate materials and trained teachers. Some Eastern European attempts to use sensitivity training have been made with, at times, counterproductive results. However, it may be that there will be a productive integration between U.S. "sensitivity training" and Eastern European "self-criticism" approaches.

There has been borrowing from country to country in many different directions. The widespread use of the syndicate method is only one example. The developing countries have experimented with several of the newer techniques with mixed results. Several contributors point to the exciting possibility that new approaches introduced by the developing countries will result in a reverse diffusion of technology from the less-developed to the well-developed world.

Thus it would seem that, while management conditions, problems, approaches, value systems, and acceptable solutions differ for even organizations within the same nation, there are sufficient common elements in management development to permit some useful cross-national and cross-cultural borrowing of learning theory and technology. The major hindrance to even more rapid diffusion seems to be the inability to adapt imports rapidly and effectively to local needs and circumstances. Let us examine this problem in a little more detail.

III. CROSS-CULTURAL AND TRANSNATIONAL APPLICATIONS

How effectively can management development and training programmes, courses, approaches, and techniques which have been used successfully in one nation be used successfully by another? To what extent can techniques which have been useful for developing managers in the most developed nations be useful for developing managers for the least developed nations? To what extent can approaches which have been used for groups of managers, all of whom come from the same society, be used with groups of managers who come from different societies? These are some of the questions which are of interest to persons from the developing nations and international organizations.

Not only are we concerned with the cost-benefit relationship for such borrowing, and whether or not this relationship can be made more beneficial, but we are concerned with possible unexpected "spillovers." One spillover effect, which is little considered by trainers but which is of crucial importance to administrators, is the effect on hardworking administrators in developing countries of persons coming back from expensive, prolonged programmes no more able to accomplish anything than when they left but with a superficial air of superiority and a new vocabulary. Sending promising young managers from developing countries to the most developed to learn management is a hazardous enterprise which may be harmful to the young manager and his nation. Some of the problems which must be explored include the effect of absence, the shock of re-entry, the possibility of returning with unacceptable proposals, and the nature of the manager's job upon leaving and re-entry.

The problems related to developing adequate managerial competence in the developing nations are quite different from those in the developed nations and in international organizations.

The pool of managerial skills in the developed nations grew in an evolutionary fashion over a relatively long period of time during which the growth of industry could not far exceed the growth in managerial talents. The basic approach in these countries until recently was for the would-be manager to learn on the job, for the best of the would-be managers to be selected to become managers on the basis of performance, and for most of those who turned out badly to be dropped back or be placed in non-managerial positions. This approach does not have many of the built-in re-entry problems of formal outside training programmes. Only in a handful of instances have countries built managerial classes more rapidly. In these cases there were the will and ability to control industrial growth, to use outside consultants and managers profitably, without totally incapacitating xenophobia intruding, to invest in training far more people than would be needed so that a sufficient number of able managers would be available, and to plan to continue the process over a period of time.

Neither of these two approaches is usable for either the developing countries or international organizations. Neither have the pre-existing conditions, or the time, or the resources that both of these approaches require.

Chart 16.3 describes some of the ways in which the problems of management and the objectives of management development programmes differ in developed and developing nations and in international organizations. While the chart is relatively a superficial comparison, it does indicate by inference some of the reasons why the effectiveness of specific training programmes and techniques can be expected to differ in these three cases and the type of analysis each trainer must make.

Chart 16.3

SOME WAYS IN WHICH MANAGEMENT AND MANAGEMENT DEVELOPMENT OBJECTIVES DIFFER IN DEVELOPED AND DEVELOPING NATIONS AND INTERNATIONAL ORGANIZATIONS

1. Developed Countries

a. SOME TECHNICAL MANAGERIAL PROBLEMS: To gather, organize, and use data efficiently and effectively. To develop, use, and improve techniques to reduce operating uncertainties, e.g., PPBS, PERT and Critical Path. To learn to identify and take profitable risks (resources are great enough to permit repeated small losses for overall gains).

b. SOME WORK FORCE MANAGERIAL PROBLEMS: To reduce management-worker conflict. To gain co-operation and production from a militant, organized work force. To motivate a large, diversified, capable bureaucracy to accept and participate in change, accountability, etc. To provide challenge to all levels of work force. To develop skilled managers.

c. MANAGEMENT DEVELOPMENT OBJECTIVES: To maintain and improve a competent managerial corps. To despecialize competent specialists to handle general management. To build a sense of confidence in own ability independent of organization. To develop people who can trust and co-operate and obtain trust and co-operation within a competitive system. To increase ability in managerial techniques and acceptance of greater responsibility and accountability.

2. Developing Countries

a. SOME TECHNICAL MANAGERIAL PROBLEMS: To operate effectively in the absence of usable data and under conditions of continuing uncertainty. To avoid unprofitable risks but to accept profitable risk (resources are not great enough to withstand a number of failures). Screen and adapt foreign methodologies and technology for effective national use. Know the technical aspects of the organization's work. To cope with a general lack of standardization of equipment and unpredictable time delays resulting from mixed, foreign supply sources.

b. SOME WORK FORCE MANAGERIAL PROBLEMS: To meet the expectations of all members of work force. To employ as many people as possible. To develop a skilled work force and an adequately large and capable technician corps. To gain acceptance for those elements of cultural change which are necessary conditions for technological change.

c. MANAGEMENT DEVELOPMENT OBJECTIVES: To build a managerial corps which can handle present industry and help industry grow. To develop enough specialists to handle technical aspects of production of goods and services. To build organizational stability and continuity. To be able to build a skilled, willing work force. To increase ability to pull operations together to improve control without decreasing speed of response and flexibility. To learn to manage well under conditions of uncertainty.

3. International Organizations

a. SOME TECHNICAL MANAGERIAL PROBLEMS: To operate effectively under conditions of great uncertainty without undue increase in response time. To develop and maintain flexible response systems. To develop and maintain effective long-range planning. To maintain controls over widely separated areas with greatly varying purposes and schedules. To get products used.

b. SOME WORK FORCE MANAGERIAL PROBLEMS: To meld professionals and technicians from many different nations and cultures into an integrated effective work force. To develop loyalty to the international organization without reducing national loyalty or subjecting the person to deculturization. To use the skills of people rather than to plan on long-range development. To work with people with different work habits. To emphasize client satisfaction without eliminating concerns for efficiency.

c. MANAGEMENT DEVELOPMENT OBJECTIVES: To utilize the managerial skills of managers to the fullest. To improve understanding of problems and hazards of managing international organizations without becoming unable to take necessary action. To develop ability to co-ordinate and lead a multinational, multicultural work group. To learn to manage with fewer of the variables under control than in national operations.

There is an unexpressed assumption that almost anything that a developed nation does to improve its management can be used profitably by a developing nation. As our analysis of the factors which affect the usefulness of training shows, this is not true with respect to management development.

Chart 16.3 should neither be taken to indicate that all developing nations (or all international organizations) are similar in all characteristics nor to imply that a technique which has been used successfully in one developing country will necessarily be useful in another. We cannot assume that causal relationships between training technique and state of development are invariant with respect to changes in the many other variables involved.

Developing countries, in the course of trying to develop in a very short time the managerial talents which were developed in the most developed countries over centuries, may, because of their limited resources and restricted time, seek to use techniques which emphasize speed and quantity, for example the lecture, rather than techniques which seek to insure the capability to apply, for example the project. This is understandable. However, programmes which emphasize speed and quantity, to be successful, must train many more persons than are needed for managerial positions, and relentlessly cull the less capable from the group and assign them to non-managerial positions.

A variable which we did not discuss in our earlier analysis is timing and speed of national change. Consideration of these variables is of greater importance in meeting the needs of the developing countries.

Speed of change is important as it affects the continued usefulness of information on which programmes are based. If data are outmoded before they are analyzed and fed back into the training programme, we are in a very real sense in the position of training persons to manage organizations which do not exist. If we cannot predict what values key variables will have because of the erratic, discontinuous behavior of the total system, even the best training may be useless. These conditions tend to indicate the need for training programmes of general applicability and of short duration. Unfortunately programmes with these characteristics are, so far as we can tell, the kind of training programmes which have least effect on performance. If the values of specific techniques depend, in some manner, upon characteristics of a nation, and these are in a state of flux so that we have no sure knowledge of them, the techniques we use may be completely inappropriate. In the developing nations, the number of forces to consider are as great as in the developed, but the opposition of forces within the national systems seems to be greater.

The absence of information makes it easy to assume that developing nations are more alike with respect to many factors than they may be.

There are a number of regional training efforts. These are based upon the hypotheses that countries in the same geographical area are not too dissimilar in national characteristics to prevent using the same training approaches; developing and conducting programmes for a region is more efficient and effective than developing and conducting programmes for individual small nations; acceptance and utilization of a technique introduced in a regional center will produce less national resistance than a technique from a developed nation; and the proximity of the nations will encourage them to exchange information and to complement and supplement each other's studies. With isolated national systems, there is little need for co-ordination and co-operation among systems, but in regional systems, these become overriding considerations. Among the differences which need resolution are differences in language, understanding of methodology, objectives, and methods for arriving at agreements.

IV. THE UTILITY AND LIMITATIONS OF SPECIFIC TRAINING TECHNIQUES

While the extent to which a specific technique may be useful depends, as we have said, upon many variables and cannot, in general, be predicted, it is possible to note some characteristics of the techniques which may help increase the trainers' ability to predict the degree of a technique's usefulness with somewhat less uncertainty.

In the following, the major approaches discussed in the text are categorized in terms of general characteristics, and characteristics which indicate usefulness and limitations on use for developing nations and international organizations. We have tended not to repeat comments under different headings where we felt that common applicability is obvious.

The Lecture

Characteristics: No risk to participant; little feedback to instructor; most useful for rapid communication of complex information; assumes participants have the capacity intellectually and emotionally to absorb the instruction, very useful for introducing new material and summarizing; few provisions for individual differences, participation, or feedback; emphasizes cognitive only; is not effective for changing affective characteristics; effectiveness can be increased by screening instructors and students; is the most widely used teaching technique, enrichment possible by using audio-visual and other teaching aids.

Usefulness for Developing Countries: Easiest kind of programme to develop; particularly useful for learning specialist skills, as an introduction for new managers, and for giving practicing managers information about new techniques; among least expensive in terms of instructor and student; management and language concepts only barriers to surmount.

Limitations on Usefulness for Developing Countries: Encourages passive reception rather than doing (this is supported by the absence of feedback on quality of reception); calls for qualified instructors who are capable teachers and knowledgeable and experienced in management; tends to be too narrowly focused to help in learning how to solve complex management problems.

Usefulness for International Organizations: Can be conducted in many languages at the same time; easy to develop and conduct using lecturers from many nations; a written document can be developed for future use and reference; inexpensive in terms of manpower; effective for briefing, orientation, etc.

Limitations on Usefulness for International Organizations: Is not flexible; assumes common base of knowledge, points of view, receptiveness which, at times, may not be the case with members of a multinational staff selected on the basis of political as well as personal criteria; does not focus on use; tends to reinforce separation among staff members of various nationalities; uncertainty of translation by non-management people.

Programmed Instruction

Characteristics: Is completely structured and inflexible; cognitive only, no affective role; individual, not group, use; no risk to participant; no competition; emphasizes, however, active response and feedback for learning purposes; is most useful for communicating non-managerial information; permits the participant to set his own pace and select his own time for learning; has greater appeal to some national value systems such as the British than to others; has been successfully used as an introduction to experiential programmes; high initial cost with low cost for repeated use; several forms available, the most important of these being the linear and branch types.

Usefulness for Developing Countries: Reduces the need for trained teachers and for trainees to assemble in one place, thus overcoming problems relating to geographic separation, combines the characteristics of a book and a trained classroom teacher, both of which are familiar to most participants; the individual adaptations possible help to meet conditions of uneven development; not necessary to assume learning by reading as it is possible to develop equivalent audio tapes; permits planned sequential learning and can be used profitably to bring all prospective participants in a live programme up to a common knowledge level before attending the programme.

Limitations on Usefulness for Developing Countries: Expensive to prepare and use, unless the material can be profitably used by many managers and continue to be used for a considerable period; tends to be very closely linked to the background, experience, and problems of the country for which it was developed; there are difficulties in use across national and cultural lines; high motivation is required for participants to complete any extensive programme, particularly if the material is foreign; while it can accommodate a range of participant knowledge and sophistication, the range is relatively narrow; is not useful for helping managers in acquiring skills in interpersonal relations.

Usefulness for International Organizations: Eliminates the need for assembling all participants in one place, thus overcomes problems of geographic separation; can be translated into different languages without difficulty if the concepts and goals of the instruction are the same; is particularly useful where the number of participants at any one time is small but where there is a continuing turnover; avoids problems stemming from shyness and uneven prior training and experience; tends to overcome fluency in language of instruction by permitting participant to set his own pace.

Limitations on Usefulness for International Organizations: Cost of preparation and the skill required are great; unless common concepts and goals can be assumed, cross-cultural use may not be assumed; does little to help resolve problems relating to interpersonal or intercultural relations.

Conferences and Workshops

Characteristics: Great flexibility; almost any area of management can be included; primarily cognitive although some affective results are possible; calls for groups which are relatively homogeneous in interests, status, and ability; requires a skilled, knowledgeable leader; is usually used as an integral part of a programme employing other techniques; is essential for group cognitive exercises; there is little personal risk.

Usefulness for Developing Countries: Permits the use of borrowed material without pre-adapting for a specific nation and organization; can be used as the vehicle for making such changes for other programme elements; useful as an approach to get participants to discuss common local problems and approaches; can get participation without the interference of foreign concepts and approaches.

Limitations on Usefulness for Developing Countries: Difficult to give participants freedom and move toward desired training goals efficiently and effectively; can easily degenerate into superficial, unfocused conversation; most vocal participants can easily dominate; this is particularly the case where participants are from different social classes and different levels in the official hierarchy; is a very inefficient means for transmitting information.

Usefulness for International Organizations: Helps develop cohesion by the discussion of common problems; does not require extensive preparation of material in advance; its flexibility allows simultaneous use for several purposes, for example, the introduction of people to each other, the dissemination of information which should be shared by all, and the exchange of experience for the purpose of both helping and becoming more friendly.

Limitations on Usefulness for International Organizations: May be difficult to conduct in a multilingual fashion; forcing the use of a single language may destroy free and easy exchange and the ability to reach other goals; limitations described under the developing countries tend to apply here as well.

Case Study

Characteristics: Can be used either as an individual or group learning technique; cognitive, not affective; rational use of learning and experience focused on problems; non-directive instruction; instructor is catalyst rather than teacher; focus on process of solution rather than content of solution; can be used for reinforcement and feedback; unless carefully prepared and guided may degenerate into unfocused discussions and yield superficial solutions; little risk to participants; calls for high level of instructor skill to get forward movement with little direct intervention and to guide analysis of the process to reinforce experience; usefulness drops sharply as material is more general and less germane; many variations: living case, incident technique, and sequential cases; preparation of case material can be used as a learning technique.

Usefulness for Developing Countries: Local case materials can be developed; real problems increase interest; participant preparation of case material can be used to develop sensitivity to existing problems; group analysis and discussion can be used as consultation; feedback on "live cases" increases use and interest.

Limitations on Usefulness for Developing Countries: Good, carefully prepared case material, such as the Harvard cases, is costly to prepare (skilled people and sufficient time are necessary), poor case material is useless; little local material available; assumes participants have knowledge and/or experience; foreign cases not generally usable; requires acceptance of technique and agreement to move in a relatively straight line forward to a set of conclusions; if national or cultural style is conducive to "wandering" in discussion, may have less value; calls for capable local instructors.

Usefulness for International Organizations: Acceptability of many points of view and different solutions emphasized; adaptable to the international context; the low level of affective content permits use with little risk; however, there is some interplay among participants; encourages co-operative group efforts in problem activities; provides exercise in listening to peers, discussing with peers, and receiving peer evaluation in low-risk exercise.

Limitations on Usefulness for International Organizations: There is very little good international managerial case material; special material as carefully prepared as the Harvard cases would be extremely costly; the assumption that participants are at approximately the same level with respect to knowledge and experience may not be valid; the great variety of national and cultural styles may produce very diffused discussions which, possibly, will be of more hindrance than help; it would seem to be important that the case study leader have had some international experience.

The In-Basket Technique

Characteristics: Very structured by content; almost entirely cognitive; little or no affective influence; some degree of competition but little participant risk except self-evaluation; requires great skill in preparation; must be tried out in advance and requires trained discussion leader; emphasizes the use of feedback for learning; provides practice in problem sensitivity definition, analysis, and solving; forces some degree of commitment by requiring that actions to be taken be written rather than "told"; in some cases goes beyond describing action but not quite to the point of taking action; is most useful for programmes at lower and middle management levels and in conjunction with other training techniques.

Usefulness for Developing Countries: Provides an opportunity to evaluate performance for participants and to compare their performance with others in a structured, quasi-realistic setting; provides direct feedback by discussion of "answers"; exercises focusing on specific local needs and problems can be developed with periodic content changes to meet changing needs; a sequence of in-baskets can be used to expose participants to more and more difficult situations; a wide range of problems and situations and technical skills can be included; helps participants to integrate knowledge in a number of fields; has been used in some developing countries successfully.

Limitations on Usefulness for Developing Countries: The material must be real and relevant; must challenge the participant without overwhelming him; as there tends to be little interchangeability from nation to nation and even from organization to organization, it may be necessary for each organization to prepare entirely new materials; preparation is costly; assumes that all participants are at approximately the same level with respect to knowledge, experience, and technical abilities; single sessions are less effective than a series developed from the same basic material or covering the same area; unless there is good discussion after participant reports, the entire exercise may be of little value.

Usefulness for International Organizations: Demonstrates the possibility of more than one solution to a management problem; may help to break down insularity; elements common to management in international organizations may be combined with elements unique for specific organizations; keeps interpersonal relations at a low conflict level while bringing differences in approach out into the open; a wide range of problems and situations can be included; the development of a common bank of "in-baskets" for use in different international organizations is possible; gives practice in determining management priorities.

Limitations on Usefulness for International Organizations: Does not help, except on a cognitive level, to improve interpersonal relations; tends to assume relative equality and similarity in background (experience, education, value systems, etc.); must be relevant to the operations of all participants; is costly to prepare and use unless used repeatedly; requires a skilled conference leader to obtain benefits and reduce possible harmful effects.

Role-playing

Characteristics: Very flexible; varies from little structure to much structure; attempts to simulate reality; some participant risk; provides practice in stress situations; usually seeks affective rather than cognitive learning; calls for a skilled leader for the purpose of setting up and leading the analysis of the role-playing; may not have any direct carry-over to actual operations unless it is used repeatedly in practice sessions; feedback and learning from experience are strong points; there is a great variety of approaches including formal, spontaneous, individual, group, and multiple role-plays.

Usefulness for Developing Countries: An extremely flexible technique which can be used in any context and modified to meet local conditions; permits experimentation, demonstration, and practice of different approaches; relatively low participant risk level.

Limitations on Usefulness for Developing Countries: Participants must be able to identify with roles appropriately; these should flow out of their work or training experience; in some cultures, role-playing may be strongly resisted either by failure to respond spontaneously or by undue levity; there must be acceptance and understanding of the approach by the participants; spontaneous role-playing, in particular, calls for very skilled leadership; may not result in significant learning when used alone, in isolation from other techniques; time-consuming; there is a tendency for superficial resolution of situations; formal role-plays are inflexible and costly to develop; spontaneous role-plays, as indicated, may be useless.

Usefulness for International Organizations: Can be used to bring intercultural misunderstandings into the open for analysis; can help participants gain competence in dealing with ambiguous and unfamiliar interpersonal situations; can be adapted for use with multinational groups; the feedback element can be especially useful for developing understanding of different approaches.

Limitations on Usefulness for International Organizations: Most effective where all participants use the same language with the same ease and understanding; there are different degrees of acceptability for the approach from different cultures; may be used as a means to ventilate feelings dysfunctionally; unless there is skilled leadership and a willingness by participants to learn and change, the approach is extremely time-consuming and inefficient; differences in nation and culture tend to inhibit useful feedback.

Management Games

Characteristics: Very flexible; can be used for the complete range of management situations and problems; the degree of structure varies from completely structured to moderately structured; there usually is a high degree of team competition combined with low personal risk; is experiential and may have as objectives affective as well as cognitive experiences and learning; requires extremely careful preparation and tryout; some games do not require skilled leaders; others mandate a high degree of leader skill; nature of carry-over to the job is in doubt; focus on a limited number of factors while purporting to be realistic may reduce effective carry-over; adequate time must be allowed for analysis and discussion; failure to do this is a very common shortcoming; the tendency, in the past, to focus on quantitative aspects of management (scientific management) is changing; some newer games direct attention to value systems and behavioral patterns; there is considerable STAGE 1 feedback information but almost no STAGE 2 or STAGE 3 feedback; emphasis is on working with others to solve a common problem rather than on understanding, communicating, changing attitudes, etc.; most useful for middle level and senior managers.

Usefulness for Developing Countries: A very flexible approach which can be based on simulation of almost any managerial process or situation or any managerial decision-making circumstance; has been used in almost all developed nations and many developing nations; levels of interpersonal conflict can be controlled; appeals to the "gaming instinct" and consequently great interest can be aroused.

Limitations on Usefulness for Developing Countries: Few games can be imported without considerable change as they tend to assume national value systems and specific sociocultural norms; very expensive to develop and try out to eliminate counterproductive effects; where the "gaming instinct" is extremely high, the focus may be on the game rather than the learning; where gaming is not accepted culturally, participants may become too concerned with competitive aspects.

Usefulness for International Organizations: Some international games have been developed and used; there is a fair number of general and simple games which can be used with multinational, multicultural groups; may develop some team cohesiveness which may persist.

Limitations on Usefulness for International Organizations: Most complex games assume that all players are at the same level of knowledge and ability; if they are not the more positive, knowledgeable participants may take "command" while the other participants may neither participate nor learn; may provoke antagonisms which may persist.

The Syndicate Method

Characteristics: Very structured in terms of the entire programme with participant freedom of action within elements; focuses on experience in behavioral situations appropriate for higher management; however, is primarily concerned with cognitive learning; assumes high and equivalent levels of participant knowledge and experience; a comprehensive programme with a number of different experiences and techniques including: self-evaluation, use of consultants, analysis of data, working under severe time limitations, use of imprecise data, and report writing; permits interpersonal and intergroup comparisons; assumes close correspondence between management in industrial and politico-administrative organizations.

Usefulness for Developing Countries: Completeness of programme may make it feasible for use in its entirety by simply changing the nature of the substantive content to meet local conditions; encourages experimentation with new ideas and concepts; close collaboration is developed among trainers, organizations, and participants; has been used by developing nations.

Limitations on Usefulness for Developing Countries: Costly in time and effort; wasteful if skilled trainer talents are used on standby basis only; requires very careful planning, scheduling, and execution as well as participant completion of assignments prior to residence; large skilled staff necessary; close collaboration which is required may be difficult to achieve; most effectively used on a continuing basis with permanent staff.

Usefulness for International Organizations: Living and working together may provide lasting bond useful for interorganizational efforts; provides framework for a complete programme which can be modified to fit exact conditions found in international organizations; lack of outside imposed risk makes it possible to use with individuals from different cultures.

Limitations on Usefulness for International Organizations: Assumes acceptance of "consultants" by participants, meaningful overlap in management goals, behavior, and problems and process in all organizations participating; close collaboration which is necessary may be difficult to achieve; costly to set up; should be used on a continuing basis with permanent staff to be most useful; may result in little learning as it is possible to get by with minimum participation.

The Project Method

Characteristics: A leading technique, based on "learning by doing" principle; uses the concept of educating an individual manager by providing him with the opportunity to change an organization; adds to "real-life situation" by learning in a stranger organization; expensive; calls for considerable participant time, consultant support, evaluation, organization implementation, and feedback; as described by Professor Revans, is a complete system for learning, not a component; others, however, have used projects as components of programmes; has both affective and cognitive elements; essentially uses management consulting for training purposes; includes the risks, interactions, emotional involvement, stress, and intellectual challenge of consulting work; participant selects problem and defines priorities.

Usefulness for Developing Countries: In addition to training the manager, may yield a useful work-product; permits individual training on basis of background and need; useful for training managers who may be selected for top-level positions; feedback during the TRANSFORMATION PROCESS permits redirection and encourages learning; provides a complete, meaningful experience for the participant; does not require local adaptation as primary training is carried out in local organizations.

Limitations on Usefulness for Developing Countries: Local organizations may not be rich enough in managerial talent or well organized enough to permit this type of learning experience; is an expensive approach which calls for very knowledgeable and skilled managers and consultants.

Usefulness for International Organizations: May develop a core of top managers who have strong cross-cultural ties and knowledge; may encourage more rapid diffusion of managerial concepts; permits maximum use of existing managerial strengths.

Limitations on Usefulness for International Organizations: Assumes common problems and adaptability of approaches; decreases the value of specialized skills; may lead to "job seeking"; expensive; assumes availability and usefulness of "outside" consultants; may arouse hostility among organizations as a result of recommendations.

Sensitivity Training (T-groups)

Characteristics: Almost completely unstructured; affective goals; focus on individual behavioral change; considerable emotional risk to participants; assumes that trust and co-operation are preferable to competition; provides experience and practice in working with people in an ambiguous setting; requires a skilled, experienced leader.

Usefulness for Developing Countries: Can be used to produce group cohesiveness if there are unexpressed but strong feelings in that direction; may help managers to understand better their own motivation and behavior and those of others; if "leveling" is accepted as not dangerous and as desirable social behavior, may help in building trust, co-ordination, and co-operation; provides experience for working under ambiguous and uncertain conditions.

Limitations on Usefulness for Developing Countries: Basic assumptions concerning value systems, behavior patterns, and ways in which people learn may not hold in certain contexts; may produce lasting overt antagonisms as a result of in-group conflicts; may induce severe, disabling anxiety in some participants; expensive and may be counterproductive; absence of trained native leaders.

Usefulness for International Organizations: May be used to build identification with international organization through open statements and agreements on national loyalty, discussion and confrontation with respect to interpersonal behavior and problems, gaining insight into value systems and acceptable behavior patterns of people from other cultures.

Limitations on Usefulness for International Organizations: Goes counter to accepted behavior in international organizations; the basic assumptions concerning value systems, behavior patterns, and ways in which people learn may not hold; may produce lasting overt antagonisms as a result of in-group conflicts; may induce severe disabling anxiety in some participants; expensive and may be counterproductive; absence of trained international leaders; a great facility in the language used is almost a necessary condition.

Field Visits

Characteristics: Instruction by observation of ongoing operations, questioning of practicing managers, and group discussion of observed activities; structure imposed by the process and limitations of usable organizations for observation; expensive in terms of overhead costs and participant time; effective for evoking interest in management approaches and processes of others.

Usefulness for Developing Countries: Field visits within the country tend to increase the rate of diffusion of usable procedures and techniques; visits outside of the country tend to encourage the adoption and adaptation of imports; both tend to increase the interest of the manager in other possibilities and to observe his own operations more closely.

Limitations on Usefulness to Developing Countries: The cost may be great and the return, if any, may be in interest rather than knowledge or skill; requires careful planning, knowledgeable selection of organizations to visit, and searching analysis and discussion before and after the visit to relate the problems and approaches of the organization visited and the home organization.

Usefulness for International Organizations: Provides ready-made operating models of another way of doing things and a direct means for getting additional insight and knowledge about the ways in which other organizations and managers operate; tends to sharpen the powers of observation.

Limitations on Usefulness for International Organizations: Problems and general rules of national organizations, in particular industrial organizations, are very different; otherwise limitations are those listed above for developing countries.

Consulting

Characteristics: Structured in terms of situation and problem affective and cognitive; assumes considerable knowledge and/or experience on part of trainee; individual—not group; calls for careful supervision; can be used as apprenticeship, as a full programme, and as means for re-entry; can be tailored to meet capabilities of the individual and the needs of the organization.

Usefulness for Developing Countries: Re-entry, broaden and increase skills of lower and middle managers, and train new managers —all tied to local organizations.

Limitations on Usefulness for Developing Countries: Requires skilled supervision and senior consulting staff; consulting is not management, skills and knowledge acquired are not necessarily transferable to the manager's job; very costly even though there may be useful work-products; getting organizations to co-operate may be difficult.

Usefulness for International Organizations: Provides means for giving lower and middle managers greater experience and providing organizations advice and views of sympathetic, knowledgeable outsiders; increases the size of the pool of international interorganizational managers.

Limitations on Usefulness for International Organizations: Costly; learning both cognitive and affective elements may not be transferable; unless there is skillful senior consultant supervision and counseling, there may be no more learning than if the participant remained on his own job.

Laboratory Training

Characteristics: Sensitivity (T-group) training plus lectures, discussions, and role-plays, primarily affective; some structure with the ability to change as views of needs change; sometimes emphasizes self-administered and group-interpreted rating scales (instrumented laboratory); controlled psychological environment; considerable participant risk; group programmes; can be used as entire programme; makes most of assumptions made in T-group training; focuses on process, not content; when used with family group may be used as a form of organizational development; primarily for middle and top managers.

Usefulness for Developing Countries and International Organizations and Limitations: Similar to those for sensitivity training. The varied input makes this less intense, provides a greater content input and a greater variety of experiences.

Organizational Development

Characteristics: A complete development programme for an entire system; uses almost every one of the newer and older techniques with emphasis on the newer ones derived from the behavioral sciences such as laboratory training, T-group, confrontation, and feedback;

uses identified organizational problems as content to affect convergence between personal and organizational goals, integration of human resource planning and utilization and power redistribution; integrates with other non-training programmes for improving management; both cognitive and affective; variable risk for participants; structured in terms of theoretical underpinning but not specific application; flexible; focused on organizational change with individual as part of organization; most advanced example of vertical training.

Usefulness for Developing Countries: Flexibility in determining goals and approaches and ability to change both during course of programme makes a high degree of tailoring possible; the focus on the organization in terms of where it is physically and operationally may eliminate some effects of unknown and uncontrollable social, cultural, economic, etc., factors, training all the key people in the power structure at once and carrying through from problem to solution to evaluation of implementation can produce usable and dramatic results.

Limitations on Usefulness for Developing Countries: Assumes acceptance of hypotheses and desirability of value system of U.S. "behavioral science" approach; requires a strong core of capable, willing managers and strong top-management support; costly in terms of trainer and participant time; may disrupt or interfere with operations; calls for very skilled knowledgeable native trainers; strong, but not absolute, assumption that a complete system, not a subsystem, is client; this is rarely the case in politico-administrative organizations.

Usefulness for International Organizations: Similar to description for developing countries.

Limitations on Usefulness for International Organizations: In addition to all those described for developing countries, the power structure assumed does not seem to exist in any single international organization and the tensions which this approach may induce may be totally incapacitating in an international organization.

V. THE DEVELOPMENT OF A TRAINING PLAN

Training cannot carry the load of being the only change agent for a large, complex system. If there is a felt need for change in the system, a total plan should be developed for effecting the desired change. The role for managerial training can only be defined within this context.

The analysis of the responses, forces, and techniques available to produce the change, including an evaluation of the cost and probable contribution of each, is an essential precondition for the development of a training plan to support and complement the other efforts. Training and development considered as a systematic change agent can never be effective acting by itself against the inertial or the active resistance of the many other forces which have shaped and maintained the administrative style and the technical and methodological approaches of an organization. At best, training can develop the atmosphere, prepare some people in the organization to accept a new approach, indicate possible directions for change, help some to acquire the skills needed to analyze the existing situation and to develop appropriate plans for change and even to spark a few new approaches. Success or failure depends, in great part, on forces upon which training can exercise no influence. From the viewpoint of the trainer, his starting point is the goals he has worked out with management. Assuming that these are agreed upon, the next step is to develop a training plan.

Unless one is an advocate of a single approach, e.g., sensitivity training, and is committed to helping managers acquire and improve the skills, understanding, insight, and behavior on which this approach is focused, the selection of appropriate training techniques is an integral part of planning the management development programme.

Several different formal approaches are possible. They are useful only if the investigator does not get so caught up in the procedure as to ignore overall consequences or to accept the procedural results as the ultimate in truth.

VI. A SUMMARY OF THE STEPS IN THE MANAGEMENT DEVELOPMENT PROCESS

In summary, the management development process includes a number of clearly identifiable steps. Eight are described below. The more of these the trainer is involved in, the greater certainty there is that he will be able to provide more effective training and development. The major steps which are discussed in the volume as a whole are:

1. Working with appropriate persons in the organization to identify the organization's management needs and the nature of problems

faced by management; to determine the organization's total plan to meet its management needs and the role of training in this plan; and to evaluate the organization's readiness for training, expectations from training, willingness to invest in and risk training, and capability to use trained managers.

2. Developing, on the basis of the data gathered, a theoretical frame of reference for the training effort including: assumptions and hypotheses relating to the organization, effectiveness of alternative training content approaches and techniques, and methodology and criteria for evaluating these alternatives and the components of the actual programme.

3. Identifying, clarifying, and gaining acceptance for the specific programme objectives as subobjectives of those assigned to training in the manpower plan.

4. Developing and planning the programme to achieve the agreed-upon objectives.

5. Selecting the participants who best meet the needs of the organization and the limiting conditions of the training programme.

6. Conducting the planned programme, getting feedback during the programme, and modifying the content and process to keep the programme in course.

7. Obtaining, analyzing, and using feedback and other data during the TRANSFORMATION PROCESS and at OUTPUT STAGES 1, 2, and 3 to help direct follow-up and improve future programmes.

8. Following up on participant's performance on the job and to provide consulting assistance within the conditions of the programme.

VII. DETERMINING TRAINING NEEDS AND OBJECTIVES

In determining training needs and objectives, the trainer must work directly with the managerial corps, including the top organizational executives, the managers who will directly supervise the managers being trained, and the managers to be trained themselves, the managers who will work for them. This costly, time-consuming process cannot be dispensed with unless we can safely assume that we know why a management development programme is wanted, what problems are faced by the organization and the individuals, what skills are needed, what kind of behavior is acceptable, what the problems connected with leaving and re-entry will be, how change has been traditionally accomplished, and the answers to dozens of other questions. If we know little or nothing about the answers to these, we are selling untested patent medicines as cures for all organizational ills.

An important element in this investigation of training needs is the determination of the nature of training programmes desired and acceptable and the training approaches expected and acceptable. If there are differences between management and the trainers on these matters, it is desirable to resolve them as early as possible.

The convictions of the many competent executives in both the developed and the developing countries who believe that formal development programmes are not helpful and cannot help managers acquire any useful capabilities stem not only from the partial truths that training does not help some managers and that learning on the job (which is usually the alternative) is an effective training technique but from their experiences with highly touted training programmes which had no relationship to the needs of their organizations and from experience with advanced, esoteric techniques which they did not understand and mistrusted.

The background training information and hypotheses from which trainers programmes stem are of two different types—descriptive and prescriptive.

The descriptive information is mostly historical. Content and techniques are described along with details relating to objectives, why the content was selected, resources which were expended, the participant group, the conduct and acceptance of the programme and the techniques, observed results, etc. Usually information about the participant group includes information about the nations and the organizations as well as the individuals. Findings are usually not pushed to the point of proposing hypotheses or prescriptions. Where some hypotheses are put forth they are usually not sufficiently generalized or projected for other circumstances. Frequently, the most useful information that a trainer has is of programmes in which he participated as a trainer or participant.

The prescriptive approach develops on a more or less clearly enunciated set of hypotheses relating training with desired objectives. Usually the hypotheses involve both the effectiveness of the approach and the desirability of specific objectives.

The existing base from which training takes off is the key consideration of the evolutionary approach which attempts to build on what exists and to introduce alternatives to strengthen and advance the existing system. The evolutionary trainer plans to meet need in a series of gradual steps and to aim for applicability to the present job. Where possible, he attempts to bring higher-level managers directly into the process—as teachers, not as learners.

Where we want to be is the key consideration of the revolutionary approach, which attempts to propel managers to where they should be by a series of controlled shocks. The revolutionary trainer plans to reach his goal in one comprehensive programme. This is the case even though he realizes that it cannot be accomplished and that follow-up will always be necessary. In this type of programme higher management usually joins all other levels of management as learners.

Whichever approach or combination of approaches is adopted, the key point for the trainer is that training alone can rarely significantly influence the forces which determine whether or not learning will be useful. Consequently, the choice of goals, programmes, and techniques should depend upon the direction of the forces which will affect utilization. This is not to suggest that training can only follow pre-existing forces. This has not been the case historically. However, training's most effective role seems to be to strengthen and hasten organizational forces which are ready to move a given system in a given direction.

Essentially, the national trainer works by analogy. This is both a useful and dangerous approach. The trainer must develop a new training model using the experience and insight gained in other nations only as a jumping-off point. He cannot use the foreign training model.

If he knows his nation and organization well and is sensitive to their needs, aspirations, and conditions, his intuition is far more valuable than are the detailed knowledge and wide experience of a foreign expert. The difficulty with intuitive programmes is that the ability to reach the necessary insights is not transferable and that there is less chance of learning from either success or failure.

The only way that a trainer can improve is through the method we try to get managers to adopt—observation, analysis, and evaluation of training programmes to improve the ability to understand, explain, and forecast. It is necessary to move from intuition alone to intuition plus knowledge and meaningful experience.

Professionals in the field of management development have a responsibility to develop and use feedback systems, both to help them to determine and understand what happened in the course of training and after a given programme and to provide general information about the concepts, variables, and transformation processes which are involved in management development.

While the diffusion of training technology will probably become more rapid from the most developed nations to the least developed nations, as these latter countries seek the alchemist's stone in each new technique, the use of the newer techniques in the least developed nations will undoubtedly be less effective than in the most developed countries. Some of the causes of this lesser effectiveness are: less critical adoption; the presence of stronger native forces resisting importations from abroad; circumstances different from those which called forth the invention and the techniques in the country of origin; and failure to accept the theoretical and philosophical bases from which the technique was derived. Thus, as the links between techniques, methodology, and society become weaker, the borrowers' disappointment will probably become greater. Only when a technique is carefully examined in advance and modified to support native structures and/or to encourage movement in the direction of native forces can it be hoped that it will be useful.

As the developing countries find that borrowed training techniques do not yield the management skills needed, the amount of borrowing will probably decrease. It is to be hoped that these countries do not take this lack of success as a sign that good management cannot be learned by formal means but that instead they will begin to experiment and develop their own training techniques. If they do there may be a reverse flow which should be profitable to the most developed societies.

It is generally easier, but far less useful, to adopt a specific technique or methodology than to examine critically the set of assumptions from which the technique and methodology are derived in the innovating nation, to determine whether or not the assumptions hold in the receiving nation.

The more directly a model of behavior is transferable from one nation to another, the more directly transferable are the techniques used to help managers to learn to employ the skills demanded by the given model. For example, the knowledge and skill needed to manage an electronic data processing installation in one nation are closer to those needed in a second than the capabilities needed to manage a hospital. Consequently, the techniques used to teach the former set of knowledge and skill are more transferable than those needed to teach the latter. We can reasonably well assume that the techniques used to teach such subjects as accounting, PERT, and

PPBS will be more transferable than the techniques used for teaching, labor relations, motivating small work groups, and insight into bureaucratic behavior. With respect to such subjects as organizational theory, planning, and control, the transfer of techniques has the greatest chance of success between countries which make the same managerial assumption and have the same quantity and quality of data available, etc.

Some factors, in addition to those listed earlier, which affect management development in the lesser developed nations to a greater extent than in other nations are:

1. Administrative slippage within the training organization itself. This, of course, is a serious problem for all organizations in developing countries. It results from operating under less than perfect conditions, with less protection from outside forces, less ability to seize opportunities, inappropriate resources, and being subject to more and greater chance factors and irrationalities.

2. Unavailability of timely data, resulting in poorer scheduling, delayed reactions, and poor timing.

3. Uneven staffing and other training resources.

4. Greater uncertainty, few controllable factors, and less continuity in all operations. These tend to be accentuated in training, which is often considered to be a marginal operation.

5. Absence of sufficient numbers of capable local managers to supplement and complement formal training by on-the-job training.

6. Foreign management development patterns are more difficult to use, even after being adapted, as the relative rates of cultural, social, political, economic, and technological change among the developing nations differ from each other and from those experienced by the developed nations to a greater degree than the differences among developed nations.

7. As in management generally, the developed nations can afford to take greater risks in individual training projects even though these may divert management talents from operations to development. The lesser resources of developing countries presents them with two equally unacceptable approaches—to be very cautious and to do nothing or to place all resources into a single effort.

There are many factors which affect management development in international organizations, other than those described in Chart 16.3. International organizations are probably the most difficult to manage effectively or efficiently. Some of the causes for this, which also affect the goals and nature of management development, are:

1. The boundary conditions which determine the limits of the international manager's response are not only subjected to many more constraints than those faced by managers of national organizations, but in many cases are in such a state of unstable equilibrium that displacement of a minor element can result in a basic change in policy. To counteract this, international organizations tend to develop internal stabilization systems which provide for careful review by all interested parties and which tend to prevent effective change.

2. In international organizations, the specific values assumed by the variables which determine policy and programme may have nothing to do with the efficiency or effectiveness of the policy or the programme but may have to do with acceptability of these on other than rational grounds.

3. There are many more competing and conflicting objectives, both for total systems, specific programmes, and individuals, than there are in national organizations.

VIII. FEEDBACK AND RESEARCH

While many training approaches emphasize the importance of feedback for participant learning, few have a similar built-in element for trainer learning. Probably the most important neglected element of the entire TRANSFORMATION PROCESS is reliable, valid feedback. Recognizing all the technical and theoretical problems involved and the very practical problem of how to alter a carefully planned programme once it is under way, it is still the trainer's responsibility to take readings on his programmes and to alter his course when the readings indicate that the programme is not headed in the right direction.

Little operational research has been reported other than some descriptive research and some evaluative research on the effects of complete programmes and of specific techniques. The data are not available on which to base decisions to use or not to use any training technique, new or old. Most of the research is carried on in a sporadic, discontinuous, uneven manner by academics, students seeking advanced degrees, and proponents and opponents of specific techniques. These efforts are supplemented by some inquiries by the organizations which pay for the training to determine, "Was it worth while?"

While much of the research purports to be evaluative, almost all of it is actually descriptive. It consists of information describing which nations and organizations have tried which techniques in what kind of programme, the nature and degree of client (nation or organization or participant) satisfaction and participant rating of the programme or technique on the basis of some kind of criteria at STAGE 1 of the INPUT-OUTPUT model.

Viewing the entire field of management, research has been conducted in the following areas: the nature of the manager's job, measures of managerial effectiveness, the goals of management development and training, the effects of management development and training programmes, and the use and effectiveness of management development and training techniques.

While all of these are of interest to us, we will focus on the last area, recognizing that, unless reliable, valid findings are available in all the other areas of research, not much can be done in this one.

The findings with respect to complete multitechnique and broad-content programmes have been mixed, some indicating accomplishment of planned change; some not. The preponderance—better than 75 per cent—of the studies indicate significant positive change. Only a few (and this is true for most of the research we are reviewing) of the studies seem to be properly planned and executed, e.g., with respect to use of controls and the elimination of contaminating factors. Universally, as could be expected, the findings were somewhat better at STAGE 1 than at STAGES 2 or 3 of our INPUT-OUTPUT model, and here, as in every other case, the positive effects reported are almost entirely at STAGE 1.

The findings relating to the effectiveness of "human relations" training are equally mixed. Here again, however, the great majority of studies indicate positive change at STAGE 1.

Relatively few investigations have been made to measure the effectiveness of the problem-solving and decision-making approach. Such as there are, they tend to be negative.

Studies of the effects of sensitivity and laboratory training, almost entirely of STAGE 1 output, have produced the usual mixed results. In these cases the negative results outweigh the positive. However, it should be noted that there have been positive results, albeit again mostly at STAGE 1.

We have indicated that there are some success stories and some failures. However, the difficulty is that we do not know what most of the reports mean even when labeled "positive" and "negative."

There is a large number of unsolved problems which hinder interpretation. Some of these are, apart from problems of research design: the effects of ability of the trainer, the composition of the group, distinguishing among the effects resulting from different techniques in a multitechnique programme, the relationships among study criteria, programme objectives and organizational objectives, reliability and validity of the measuring instruments, and the relationships between STAGE 1, 2, and 3 effects.

There are almost no data on the value of cross-cultural adoption or adaptation of newer techniques. If such borrowing is to be of value, it is important that an international agency accept the responsibility to identify the areas for study, define the objectives, suggest research designs, work toward developing acceptable criteria, encourage international co-operative efforts, and gather and disseminate the findings.

A partial reason for the absence or failure of attempts to determine the relative usefulness of training techniques is that there are few useful models for the analysis of the total training process.

We are in the position that the constructors of a cyclotron would be in if there were only a few accepted hypotheses concerning subatomic phenomena such as a usable atomic model and electromagnetic fields. Management development, at this point, is in great degree a matter of trust that the costly, complex, not well understood process produces useful although not usually measurable results. The simple INPUT-OUTPUT model which we used for primitive overall analysis is not sufficient.

We have shown that training and development is only one element of an organization's efforts to improve its chances for reaching its goals, that there are many national and organizational systems which cannot be influenced by training and development whose output affects organizational results to a far more significant degree than training and that the techniques at hand, to measure the effects of training, are flawed. While these conditions point to the wastefulness of efforts, except for sales purposes, to produce definitive evaluative research results, they equally point to the need for professional, conducted exploratory research. We propose research undertaken for the purposes of exploring possible relationships among variables in the process, turning up interesting testable hypotheses, gaining deeper insight, comparing effects of different approaches, etc.

Let us give some examples:

While there are studies on the effects of training programmes and on programmes for performance evaluation and advancement, there are no combined studies relating to who is selected for training. Are they persons who are expected to advance, or persons who are advanced because they have completed a training programme, or what? How are training needs determined? Who makes the determination? Why are some programmes conducted and others turned down? What are the relationships between bureaucratic style and the training process? What are the re-entry problems? How are they handled? How do these relate to the training process?

What differences are there in training for managers in a system based upon the scientific-management model and a system based on the politico-administrative model? What are the relationships between participant knowledge about a training technique and his acceptance of it and his satisfaction with a programme using it? What are the secondary and tertiary effects of training in areas other than performance of the individual on the job? What is an efficient and effective methodology for the description and dissemination of information relating to the assumptions, programmes, and results of specific efforts? What are hypotheses and findings in other fields which would provide clues for the conditions under which cross-cultural borrowing is of value to the borrower? To what extent can this value to the borrower be changed by regional screening, pooling of efforts, etc.? What does "continuing education" mean operationally? What alternative avenues are there for "continuing education"? How can the different techniques now at our disposal be used most effectively?

Can the developing nations expect good returns using the training techniques found to be useful today in the developed nations, or must they repeat the history of the developed nations?

How and why does the nature of participant's usual or native language affect his ability and will to use the approaches learned? What are the relationships between language and training technique?

How do training methodology and technique affect ability and will to use learning?

Which techniques, if any, seem to produce the self-analytic, the self-critical, the self-changing manager who is capable of self-sustaining development? Why do they do this?

There is a great need for structured, continuous, reliable feedback both for operational research directed toward improving specific programmes and approaches and for exploratory research for advancing the field as a whole. Until we have at our disposal considerably more hypotheses, data, and analyses than we have now, evaluative research efforts are premature. The best that a trainer can do in the absence of valid evaluation is to know the field and to develop and use the simplest programmes possible which, on the basis of his knowledge and experience, seem to give reasonable promise of achieving management goals and to refuse to undertake programmes which must fail ab initio.

IX. CONCLUSIONS

Our conclusions at this point are that there is a great need to weave together the many different strands in management training and development. This is true not only of management improvement programmes in their entirety but also for individual training and development programmes and for specific training techniques, themselves. The point has been made repeatedly that training must not only be related to doing but must incorporate itself within and be part of doing. Repeatedly it has been said that the return to the job, after training, is crucial, and consideration of re-entry must be integrated into the training effort itself. We expect that there will be increased efforts to integrate more strongly than in the past off-site training of individuals using such means as institutes, formal training programmes, and work for advanced degrees, which focus on increasing the capabilities of the individual manager, with on-site training activities which are programmed to meet the needs of both the individual and the organization through horizontal training with emphasis on common problems and needs of peer groups, and vertical training with emphasis on common problems and needs of a complete organizational unit.

We expect that the training techniques which have been discussed in this volume will improve, evolve, and become much more powerful and flexible training tools as we develop and use more effective models of the training process than the one we presented; learn more about the effects of external conditions and forces on the process, including INPUT, TRANSFORMATION PROCESS, and the different OUTPUT stages; and acquire increased knowledge and experience, through a pooling of efforts, relating to the effectiveness of the techniques we employ.

This volume has been an effort to initiate this process of sharing and exchanging information. Future analyses will undoubtedly extend and enrich the understanding and applicability of the training techniques presented in the volume, explore at deeper levels the validity of the concepts on which the use of these techniques is predicated, and introduce new techniques and new uses for present techniques as they are developed.

INDEX